FROM
REDUCTIONISM
TO
CREATIVITY

MW00340341

FROM REDUCTIONISM TO CREATIVITY

rDZOGS-CHEN
AND THE
NEW SCIENCES OF MIND

HERBERT V. GUENTHER

FOREWORD BY
JEREMY W. HAYWARD

SHAMBHALA
BOSTON & SHAFTESBURY
1989

Shambhala Publications, Inc.
Horticultural Hall
300 Massachusetts Avenue
Boston, Massachusetts 02115
www.shambhala.com

© 1989 by Herbert V. Guenther

All rights reserved. No part of this book may be reproduced in any form or by any means, electronic or mechanical, including photocopying, recording, or by any information storage and retrieval system, without permission in writing from the publisher.

Printed in the United States of America

Distributed in the United States by Random House, Inc.,
and in Canada by Random House of Canada Ltd

LIBRARY OF CONGRESS CATALOGING-IN-PUBLICATION DATA

Guenther, Herbert V.
From reductionism to creativity.
Bibliography: p.
Includes index.
ISBN 1-57062-641-3
1. Buddhism—Doctrines. 2. Spiritual life (Buddhism)—Psychology.
3. Rdzogs-chen (Rñiṅ-ma-pa). I. Title.
BQ4150.G84 1989 88-33017
128′.2
BVG 01

To Ilse with love

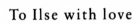

Contents

Foreword

Dr. Herbert V. Guenther, foremost scholar and translator of Buddhism, has long been most forthright in his insistence that, as a living tradition, Buddhism must be communicated in the living language of our time. Rather than entombing Buddhism in concepts appropriate for another era, he has offered us translations and commentaries that, while being strictly faithful to the meaning of the originals, have been framed in contemporary language. Buddhism is the study of mind—its essence, nature, and functioning—and as scientists begin to turn their attention to mind, this most intimate aspect of the human process of being in the world, it is not surprising that we find a wealth of insight in the traditional Buddhist texts that are directly relevant to the scientific study of mind. Sadly, these insights have not been accessible to cognitive scientists and psychologists precisely because of the archaic language in which they have been presented. It is therefore of great value that Dr. Guenther has, in this book, attempted to convey the tremendous depth of understanding of mind in the Buddhist tradition through concepts drawn from the language of the sciences.

A major theme of the work is the evolution of the understanding of mind from being seen as a set of operators "representing" the world to being seen as a self-organizing process in which the totality—mind/experience/world—evolves dynamically according to inherent guiding principles. This change of understanding, from a representational to a process view, is also at the forefront of the study of mind in the modern cognitive sciences.

The attempts to view mind as the output of the brain considered as a computer is currently the majority version of cognitive scientists. This leads to the description of mind as built up of smaller units or "agents" acting autonomously, either independently or in sets. A set of such agents would itself act as agent at another level; thus these agents are arranged in nested heirarchies of sets. At the bottom end of the hierarchy the agents correlate to the nervous system, according to this theory, in some as yet undefined way. At the top end of the hierarchy the highest-level agents represent experience, including "consciousness." While the correlation of the lowest-level mental agents with aspects of the physiological nervous system is one way to begin to overcome the absolute duality of mind/body pervading our culture, the identification of all aspects of mind with the output of the brain is the groundless hope of materialist reductionists. Thus, the representational theory of mind is essential to the computer model, elaborated by many enthusiasts from Douglas Hofstadter[1] to Marvin Minksy.[2] The description of mind as hierarchically organized sets of operators that Dr. Guenther lays out as the basis of the theories of early Buddhism have recognizable parallels with this mainstream version of cognitive science. At the same time, one should always remember that Buddhists never, even in the early days, held a purely reductionist view of mind. These parallels, and the manner in which Buddhism as well as current work in the cognitive sciences goes beyond the reductionist view, are very clearly described by the neuroscientist Francisco Varela and the philosopher Evan Thompson.[3]

There is current work in cognitive science that seeks to go beyond the dualistic idea of a "mind," which represents a "world" preexisting outside of it. Varela and Thompson,[4] for example, seek to find a "middle way" for cognitive science that falls neither into the objectivist/eternalism of assuming a world already existing independently of mind nor into the subjectivist/nihilism of a world that is entirely mind's fabrication. This middle way acknowledges the role of mind as a process in which subject and object are mutually brought forth in experience. Such mutual bringing forth was understood by the Mahayana Buddhist thinkers as they began the transition from representational to process thinking about mind and experience. Their insights, particularly those of the Yogacarins elaborated here by Dr. Guenther, can be very helpful at this juncture.

Buddhist insight reaches its fullest flowering in the writing of the Tibetan Buddhist rDzogs-chen thinkers. Here Dr. Guenther differentiates "experience-as-such," the totality of a person's being in the world not yet separated into mind, body, and environment, from mind or experience alone. The totality, experience-as-such, is treated as self-organizing system, evolving or devolving according to organizing principles inherent to the system.

Much work has been done, by a number of research groups in the past few decades, on the principles of evolution of self-organizing systems and the development of complex stabilities in the dynamics of systems that are not in static equilibrium. The popular belief that, according to the second law of thermodynamics, all systems must eventually decay to a state of maximum chaos (highest entropy) applies only to closed systems. Recent work has shown, in precise mathematical detail, how highly ordered, open systems could arise in nature in accordance with the second law of thermodynamics. An open system—that is, any system that exchanges energy and entropy (a measure of the degree of chaos or "noise" in a system) with its environment—may undergo sudden changes of state from a state of lower energy and less order (high entropy) to a state of higher energy and greater order (lower entropy). Such states are metastable, that is, stable within a limited range of energy input. If the system receives an influx of energy above this limit, then it will either break down to a lower energy state or evolve upward to another metastable state of higher energy, characterized by greater internal ordering. A very simple example of such a system is the flow of water from a faucet in a regular twisting pattern. If we increase the flow a little, the pattern will remain the same with a slightly faster flow. As we increase the flow further, the pattern might suddenly change at some point to a higher vibratory frequency, or it might just break down resulting in a chaotic splash.

Ilya Prigogine derived the mathematics of these phenomena strictly in relation to chemical systems, but the general principles apply equally to all open systems and provide an understanding of how order arises in natural systems—from the building of a termites' nest to the learning curve of an animal to the way an economy might respond to sudden influx of capital or a society to the sudden appearance of a virulent virus. Any such open system may evolve along its own unique pathway to states of increasing energy and order. Because such a system has a degree of internal order, it is a structure. In going from a state of lower to higher order, it dissipates entropy (disorder) into its environment; that is, it is dissipative with regard to disorder. Hence Prigogine coined the term *dissipative structure* to describe such phenomena. Dr. Guenther points out that the concept of dissipative structure applies to the system experience-as-such, as well as to the other natural systems for which it was originally used by Ilya Prigogine.

Although rDzogs-chen thinkers did not, of course, have Prigogine's concept to work with in his precise formulation of it, Dr. Guenther has shown that their work may be seen as treating experience-as-such as a dissipative structure. The translation of the Tibetan term *sangs-rgyas*, meaning "buddha," as "dissipative structure" is both an accurate rendering of the intended meaning of the term as well as a way of making an immediate link with the recent understanding of the evolution of self-organizing systems. The Sanskrit term *buddha* is conventionally translated as "awakened one." Here *one* refers to structure, or dynamic blossoming of all potentialities in an individual, while *awakened* refers to the dispelling of confusion, or the dissipation of disorder, entropy. As so often happens when concepts developed in one field are applied in another, the result is tremendously illuminating. It is also directly applicable to the pioneering work on mind being done in the modern cognitive sciences.

The organizing principles of the system's dynamic unfolding can be expressed in terms of symmetry transformations. The notions of symmetry transformations and approximate and broken symmetries are very simple, yet they have been shown to be extremely powerful concepts in many fields. As is well known, consideration of symmetry transformations, approximate symmetries, and broken symmetries has brought great insight into the structure of the physical universe. The appearance, a minute fraction of a second after the Big Bang originating the known universe, of particles of definite mass localized in space and time is best described in terms of the breaking of the primordial perfect symmetry prior to this first event.[5] Dr. Guenther shows that considerations of symmetry and symmetry transformations, particularly of time and space, were applied to mentality and experience-as-such by the rDzogs-chen thinkers, with very powerful results.

To aid the nonscientific reader, some definition of these terms might be helpful here. According to Joe Rosen,[6] a system is "whatever it is that we wish to examine with regard to its symmetry properties." Anything can be a system and have symmetry: a geometric figure such as a square; a physical entity such as an elementary particle, a plant, an animal, a brain, the earth, or the solar system; a process such as a chemical reaction, biological growth, or the evolution of life on earth; or a system might be abstract, like an idea or a mathematical relation. As long as it can be separated out by us from its background, it is a system. The knowable universe may be considered a system, against the background of fullness/nothingness (vacuum to the physicists), within which it arose and has its existence.

A transformation is any action performed on a system that leaves its integrity intact as that particular system; that is, it does not destroy the system. A transformation is known as a "symmetry transformation" if that transformation leaves some property of the system unchanged. For example, a transformation that rotates a square in its own plane through 90 degrees is a symmetry transformation leaving unchanged the property "orientation in its plane," but a transformation through any rotation that is not a multiple of 90 degrees is not such a symmetry transformation, nor is a transformation that rotates it out of its original plane through any angle other than a multiple of 180 degrees.

A system may have spatial or temporal displacement symmetry if a transformation of the system displacing it in space or time does not alter it. For example, the pattern of an infinitely long railway line would be symmetrical under any transformation that moves it along its length a distance equal to any multiple of the distance between ties. This transformation leaves unchanged the property "location of the pattern of ties relative to a fixed point on the ground." The pattern of a railway line that is very long, so that we may approximately ignore the effects at the ends, would be approximately symmetrical under the same transformation. Therefore we call this an "approximate symmetry transformation." We may be more interested in the fact that it is not infinitely long and that the symmetry is not preserved at the ends. In this case we refer to this situation as a "broken symmetry."

Another example of a system with perfect spatial symmetry would be a supercooled salt solution of infinite extent. If the solution were contained in a very large container, it would have approximate spatial symmetry. If the solution were to crystallize out homogeneously throughout its volume, it would retain its approximate spatial symmetry. However, if the solution were to crystallize in such a way that domains were formed in which the crystal lattice had varying orientations, like the domains in a magnet, then the spatial symmetry would be broken. The entire crystal, as well as each domain, would now be localized in space, bound into a particular location, by the boundaries between domains. Hence a spatial broken symmetry is known as "space-binding." Similar considerations apply to symmetry with regard to time.

The image of a supercooled liquid having space-binding broken symmetry as it crystallizes into domains of local patterning may be helpful to the reader as an aid to understanding the way in which the space- and time-bound individual known as man is a devolution, a broken symmetry transformation, a lowered energy state, of the totality that is experience-as-such. This devolution brings with it the reductionistic attitude to our lived world, and the possibility of man not to "go astray" in this direction but to evolve in the direction of *sang-rgyas* is the creativity referred to in the title of this book.

In part because our mentality is so accustomed to precisely the kind of representational thinking in terms of static "things" that the later Buddhists were so critical of, rather than to thinking in terms of "process," with heart as well as brain, the book may not be easy reading. Nevertheless, Dr. Guenther leads us step by step out of this kind of rigid thinking, taking us through the stages that the Buddhists themselves went through in their historical evolution. Thus the experience of reading the book itself provides a flavor of the kind of change in thinking being pointed out. We hope, in presenting this work, that the reader will be able to appreciate the deep insights of Buddhist thinking about mind deriving from their direct meditative observation, unhindered by the narrow preconceptions imposed on Buddhism by the projections of Western scholarship, and in the fresh light that Dr. Guenther has brought to these studies.

Jeremy W. Hayward

NOTES

1. Douglas Hofstadter, *Metamagical Themas* (New York: Basic Books, 1985).
2. Marvin Minsky, *The Society of Minds* (New York: Simon and Schuster, 1985).

3. Francisco Varela and Evan Thompson, *Worlds without Ground* (forthcoming 1989).
4. Ibid.
5. Heinz Pagels, *Perfect Symmetry* (New York, Simon and Schuster, 1985).
6. Joe Rosen, *Symmetry Discovered* (Cambridge: Cambridge University Press, 1975).

Acknowledgments

I WISH TO THANK the following persons for their constant interest and generous help: Jeremy W. Hayward for his critical and constructive comments leading to the clarification of vague statements and the elimination of unnecessary verbiage; Mariana Neves and Candace Schuler for the drawing of the numerous figures; and, last but not least, my wife Ilse for her untiring and supportive patience.

Introduction

THE HISTORY OF BUDDHIST THOUGHT is a unique example of the interplay between creativity and reductionism, between novelty and confirmation, and it is the purpose of this book to trace the interaction between these complementary movements. Therefore this book is not just another restatement of what is considered to be Buddhist philosophy, even if references are made to the various systems that prevailed at one time or another. Actually, any intellectual system—philosophical, religious, political, or any other kind—is geared to reductionist ways of thinking and is bound to end up in the utter stagnation and rigidity of a tyrannical dogmatism. Buddhist philosophy, in this respect, is no exception. The much vaunted Madhyamaka philosophy, particularly in its Prāsaṅgika version, is the ultimate in reductionism, and its manifestation as dogmatic intolerance in Tibetan history is well known. This system has much in common with the now-defunct Western school of logical positivism and its anemic revival, "analytical" philosophy. For this reason, the Madhyamaka system has attracted the attention of academics who, because of their tacit presuppositions, unwittingly paint a one-sided picture of Buddhist thought.

Despite this reductionist quality, however, system or model building is itself a creative process, one through which we attempt to develop a generalized world view out of observations and valuations. Unfortunately, we then impose this world view on our dealings with the physical, social, and cultural-spiritual aspects of our environment, with the inevitable result that the free play of creative imagination is strangled.

The rejection of the static notion of a self (Skt. *ātman*), which is usually claimed to mark Buddhist thought off from the rest of its Brahmanical environment, is not truly an innovative idea. Rather, it merely clarifies the distinction between that which exists "materially," as for instance the so-called atoms that the early Buddhists accepted uncritically, and that which exists "nominally," as for instance, ideas, notions, meanings. The truly innovative idea aspect of early Buddhist thought was its emphasis on mind—or, more properly, mentation (Skt. *citta,* Tib. *sems*)—and the conception of it as a feedback and "feedforward" mechanism reflecting the then-still-prevailing "thing-likeness" type of thinking as described by Carl Gustav Jung (Jung 1971/1976, 42). Preference of the term "mentation" over the more commonly used term "mind" is due to the consideration that "mentation" does not have the markedly static, entitative connotation of the latter term. Although it took a long time for Buddhist thinkers to free themselves from the idea of the thingness of mentation, the notion of it as a process eventually had far-reaching consequences. In this new idea of mentation as a process, we can detect a shift from the syntactic level of information to a semantic level of information. The syntactic level is geared to the reconfirmation and strengthening of already-existing structures and patterns of life, while the semantic level pertains to the context of particular meanings.

To a certain extent, language with its linear arrangement of words locks us into the trap of thinking of the individual's growth as building up from the bottom. The complications resulting from this starting-point or "initial condition" have to be resolved by critical investigation, which is the path or the actual going; and the end of the process is a crowning superstructure or goal. In a static world view, this goal is intellectual, spiritual, and cultural death camouflaged by evocative linguistic devices. Whichever direction the escape entailed by such a static view may take, be it into the myth of an objective world minus man, or into the myth of subjective idealism—mentation minus world, it reflects man's quite irrational need for security, which is rooted in fear.

This idea of mentation as process has found its expression in the idea of "path" or "way." Essentially, path is a dynamic notion, and its process character became ever more evident in the course of the development of Buddhist thought. The path thus became synonymous with the unfolding of an individual's potential rather than being conceived of as merely a "way out." This latter connotation continued to dominate Buddhist thought only so long as a static world view prevailed, in which creative participation on the part of the individual was seen as minimal and where the only alternative to stagnation was escape into a "state" that remains without consequences. This ideal state was that supposed to be attained by the arhant in early Buddhism.

The emphasis on mind/mentation, not only as a dynamic factor, but as an operational system, is already present in early Buddhist thought, where it initiated a further probing into the dynamics of the system and paved the way for a new vision of reality and the human being's embeddedness in it. This does not mean that the old model was simply discarded; rather the old model was incorporated into the new one and given a new meaning. With mentation at the center of the individual's life, it was clearly seen that the granular constituents of the overall attitude a person displays toward the world and toward himself were more of the nature of distinct modes of a unitary ongoing process than discrete atomic entities. On closer inspection, this process revealed a dual character and movement. The first movement presented a continuous transformation in the direction of what is commonly referred to as "consciousness." It is instrumental in the structuring of one's world experience as it becomes predominantly geared to representational and objectifying thinking. In this manner objects exist for a subject which then "grasps," "manipulates," and "controls" them. In this respect, this renewed emphasis on mentation is not very different from other psychologies of subjective dominance. What is new in this reassessment of the operation of mentation is the recognition that the subject-object structure of thought is an emergent structure that is *far from being normative for all experience.*

The other movement within mentation presents, as it were, a complete reversal of this trend toward dichotomic thought patterns. Not only is the subject-object structure of thought suspended in this reversal, but the experiencer himself is "changed." He no longer apprehends himself as an isolatable entity called "subject" among other entities called "objects," which he has to struggle against and control in a vain attempt to preserve his "splendid isolation." Rather he apprehends himself as a way of being embedded in a life-world of open possibilities. In other words, the change that has come over the experiencer through this reversal of the direction that mentation ordinarily takes is a radical status transformation—the experiencer has become a person fully awake, a "buddha." We might illustrate this reversal by referring to the change from caterpillar to butterfly, in which almost everything alters and only a few significant features remain invariant.

This radical status transformation effected by the reversal of the thematizing and objectifying trend in experience (to which the term "mentation" properly belongs) is not a denotable object. Nor is it, in view of its experiential character, a subjectivistic absolutization of an ego in the manner of subjective and/or objective idealism. Rather what we are terming and describing as a transformation manifests in a gestalt or, more precisely, in a triad of gestalts, of meaning-bestowing intentionalities within Experience or experience-as-such. Here a word of caution may not be out of place. In speaking of Experience (with a capital letter) or experience-as-such, I try to emphasize the dynamic character of what in the Tibetan texts is termed *sems-nyid* and clearly differentiated from *sems,* "mind/mentation." The Sanskrit language uses *citta* for both mind/mentation and experience-as-such, and this has led to endless confusions.

Objectivists, like other reductionists, are unable to understand the dynamic image of the living individual as it is presented by the Yogācāra thinkers through the notion of *yoga,* indicating the process of a person's tuning into the dynamics of life. For the objectivist, nouns, whether they refer to mentation or to a gestalt, as in the example here, stand for things that are supposed to have properties in and of themselves and stand in relationship to one another independently of any individual's understanding them. However, it is not only the Western interpreters of Buddhist thought who started from the objectivist's fallacious premise. Many Buddhists also subscribed to it, as may be inferred from the Sanskrit names applied to the rigidification of what was basically a process, such as *vijñānavāda, cittamātra,* and *vijñaptimātra*. With their insistence on a "nothing but" (*mātra*), they played into the hands of those who were held captive by their structure-oriented, objectifying thinking, and thus were largely responsible for the fact that Buddhist thought stagnated and eventually disappeared from the Indian scene. There was little left to distinguish it from the static, structure-oriented Brahmanical systems.

It was the creative approach initiated by the Yogācāra thinkers that had the greatest impact on those who came into contact with it. They were not so concerned with the building blocks to which a dynamic system such as mind/mentation might be reduced, although they (or at least some of them) could not resist the temptation to add a few building blocks to the existing number. They were mainly concerned with the question of how one could understand oneself in one's psychospiritual development, how one could understand the spiritual way as a process rather than an inert link between two static states. Thus this innovative and creative approach is reflected in the presentation of the texts that go by the name of "tantra." In its technical application, this term sums up all that goes into the "weaving of life's tapestry." As the designation for a holistic process, it takes into account man's multifaceted nature and deals with him as a concrete reality rather than as a mere abstraction that screens off all other possible perspectives. Since the concrete individual, the embodied experiencer, is always sexually differentiated, his or her comprehension of the "world" involves a sexual awareness that expresses itself—as does every form of awareness—in images that cut across the physical and the psychic. These images are both "felt" images and "imaged" feelings; they do not reduce man to the merely sensual, as is claimed by the cultists of the "nothing-but." By such a preposterous claim, these reductionists merely display their distrust of, if not implacable hostility toward, imagination, which alone can open up new visions of reality and stir up resonances in people.

On the other hand, the Yogācāra thinkers' process-oriented view, which emphasizes the human system's process of unfolding, fitted well into the rDzogs-chen view, which emphasizes the system's self-renewal and freedom and expresses a fundamental complementarity in the system's overall dynamics. This truly holistic view, which has found its most profound presentation in the writings of Klong-chen rab-'byams-pa (1308–1363/64) does not derive from any Indian prototype, but must be considered as a distinctly Tibetan contribution, which revitalized Buddhist thinking and redeemed it from the rigidity to which a multiplicity of "schools" of thought had reduced it. There is no Tibetan author who can compare with Klong-chen rab-'byams-pa for depth of insight and vastness of vision.

Nonetheless, there have been attempts by the rDzogs-chen interpreters themselves, and by other lesser spirits, to reduce its scope and fit it into the narrowly circumscribed limits of their particular understanding. Rather than being a specific teaching, rDzogs-chen thought touches in its dynamics upon what in modern terms we would call the "principle of evolution," "seeing" to it that the structures that evolve do so in the manner of a free play that determines its own rules as the play goes on. The play itself may be likened to a giant fluctuation preparing the meaning, a process of tuning in to the dynamics of the whole, to its movement toward its next structure. What in a static world view is the end, in a dynamic, evolutionary world view is always a new beginning.

The presentation of these and other related points, which are the subject matter of the chapters that follow, is based on the original texts, Pali, Sanskrit, or Tibetan, which I have allowed to speak for themselves through ample quotations. In constantly referring back to the original source material I have heeded Husserl's call, *Wir wollen auf die 'Sache selbst' zurückgehen* ("we will go, from our habitual empty talk *about* things, back to the things themselves"). We have also heeded Heidegger's admonition that in dealing with the thought of thinkers of the past we have to adopt a dual attitude: to examine their thoughts critically and to make them into one's own. This is done by first listening and attending not so much to "what is expressed in explicit formulations, but what is laid before our eyes as still unsaid through the formulations that are used" (Heidegger 1962, p. 182). The implication is that one has to gain an original understanding that in itself already contains the possibility of explicating and communicating what is meant. This varies from context to context reflecting back on the situation in which man finds himself. Buddhism with its abiding concern for the human individual has always adopted a phenomenological approach rather than the abstract-theoretical one that has been favored in the Western world until recent times and has inevitably led to the dehumanization of everything human. It is a philosophy without gnosis (knowledge), a psychology without psyche (mind), and a universe without man and life. This extreme reductionism is now being more and more discredited by modern science. Modern science, unlike the humanities, which still pursue their course of dehumanization, has been forced by its own relentless probing of reality, not only to reinstate man as a participant in it and an integral aspect of its unfolding, but also to recognize that the universe is pervasively intelligent, not in the sense that it has a mind (or Mind), but that it is meaning, superthought (a neologism meaning a concept still in the making). Through the ideas of modern science runs an element of paradox that connects them, though not mechanistically, with Eastern (Buddhist, Hinduist, and Taoist) thinking, and the number of scientists who acknowledge their indebtedness to, or affinity with, Eastern thought is growing. Similarly, Buddhist thought, from its side, because of its preeminently nonreductionistic stance, is closer to the ideas of modern science than to the outdated notions of a past age through which Buddhism was originally interpreted in the West. This interpretation was based on Newtonian mechanics applied to language (as if words had an independent existence) and on a sentimental escape into wishful thinking (dubbed rational philosophy). Such ideas were simply forced upon the Buddhist texts without the slightest attempt being made to understand what the texts themselves might have to say.

My use of modern scientific terms in the chapters that follow is not an attempt on my part to show that Buddhism is somehow another form of science, but is meant as a tool to bring to light that which has remained unsaid in what has been said and thereby to show that Buddhism still has "something to say," and that this something is significant. If such scientific concepts as "dissipative structure" (developed by Ilya Prigogine in the context of nonequilibrium systems characterized by a high degree of energy exchange with the environment), "symmetry," "symmetry transformations," "symmetry break" (once restricted to geometry, but now expanded into the idea of cosmic evolution), "homology" (applicable both in biology and mathematics), and many others, have already shown their usefulness in unraveling problems in other areas than in the ones in which they originated, there is no a priori reason why they should not be able to do so also in the field of Buddhism with its, in the broadest sense of the word, evolutionary leanings.

To elaborate, it is the characteristic of a dissipative structure that it dissolves its web of relations before evolving into a new structure. In its narrower sense, reflecting its origin in the domain of nonequilibrium thermodynamics, a dissipative structure maintains continuous entropy production and dissipates the accruing entropy. From a wider perspective, a dissipative structure describes the self-renewal and coherent evolution of a cyclically organized system. From a holistic point of view, a dissipative structure describes the evolution of a new structure in terms of the unfolding and fanning out of the system's (Being's) potential through its endogenous dynamics or creativity. This development, with its phases of emergence as a play and its concomitant display of beauty, culminates, through an act of deeply felt understanding, in the manifest abilities and capabilities of a fully developed system—a mature person.

The term "symmetry transformation" contains two elements. One, symmetry, emphasizes the invariance of a system in the course of an operation; the other, transformation, emphasizes the operation, which, strictly speaking, proceeds by "symmetry breaks." These can be described in terms of their approximation to, or deviation from, the initial state of the system. This means that if the initial state of Being (in more precise philosophical diction, Being-in-its-beingness) as excitatory dynamics is pure potential, then its unfolding would itself be a symmetry break. To the extent that such a symmetry break reflects the initial undivided whole, it is an approximation symmetry transformation, while to the extent that it "narrows" itself down to a more "unexcited" state, it is an approximation-displacement symmetry transformation. What is popularly referred to as "Buddha" would be an approximation symmetry transformation of Being, and what is known as an "ordinary person" would be an approximation-displacement symmetry transformation. In no way is the original symmetry affected by its transformations.

It should not come as a surprise to the reader to learn that in the course of the development of Buddhism, set theoretical considerations played a significant role in dealing with specific features of psychic life. After all, the Indians were always interested in mathematics and geometry and in what we nowadays call topology (sometimes nicknamed "the mathematics of distortions"). For instance, Brahmagupta (ca. 625) was the first mathematician ever to give a general solution to indeterminate equations (so-called Diophantine equations), the Gregory-Leibniz series for $\pi/4$ was already found by Nīlakaṇṭha (ca. 1500), and all aids to meditative visualization are based on geometric principles. Is it therefore too "far out" to speak in the Buddhist context of the geometrization of psychic life or of the evolution of a human being in terms of topology?

One final point. In the new concept of autopoiesis (developed by Humberto R. Maturana and Francisco J. Varela), which states that "the mechanism that makes living beings autonomous systems is autopoiesis" (Maturana and Varela 1987, 48), a convergence of Western and Buddhist ideas is detectable. We will have no difficulty in understanding "autonomous" as (living by one's) own norms. However, "autopoiesis" and its adjectival form "autopoietic," intended to mean that a system is not concerned with the production of any output (technically spoken of as "allopoietic"), but with its own self-renewal within the same process structure, pose problems because of the verbal component (*-poiesis, -poietic*) in them. If these terms are meant to describe "the system as acting," they are synonymous with the Buddhist idea of karma, which is descriptive of a system in action. But if *auto* is conceived of as being of the same level as *allo* (the object of the action), the Mādhyamika logicians would have an opening to make a devastating attack. Why should a system create itself when it is already there? At least, this was the attack they made, rightly or wrongly, on the Yogācāra notion of *svasaṃvitti* ("self-knowledge"). All of which goes to show that language is full of traps.

In conclusion, let me take my cue from Klong-chen rab-'byams-pa, who so often introduced his essays with the words, "Listen to my explication of how I have understood this" (Tib. *ji-ltar bdag-gis rtogs-bzhin bshad-kyis nyon*). What follows is how I have understood the evolution of Buddhist thought.

1 *ABHIDHARMA* *Its Scope and Meaning*

THROUGHOUT THE VARYING PHASES of its historical development, Buddhist thought has unmistakably preserved certain traits that at the outset formed its very life force. These traits still vitally concern us as participants in an evolutionary movement that is an unfolding of its inherent dynamic potential. These traits are: emphasis on immediate experience and rejection of everything that makes us lose sight of what is essential in dealing with the many problems we encounter as we participate in this evolutionary movement. For when we overlook or lose sight of what really matters, we are at once entangled in all sorts of speculations and arguments about matters that may have little meaning for us as living beings. The very fact that no amount of discursive reasoning will ever convey that which must be experienced within ourselves (and which therefore is also known quite independently of logical method) may be gathered from the legendary history of the origin of the Abhidharma, which the Buddha is said to have revealed while residing in the realm of the Tāvatiṃsa gods.

The reference to a realm of gods must be understood as being symbolic of a shift in attention and interest away from the surface of sensuous and mental objects and toward the dynamic background and source of all that is. Ordinarily our senses deliver only specific, limited, and determinate data within an otherwise indeterminate and unlimited field. The notion of the transcendence of the realm of gods reflects the unboundedness of our lived field of experience. This unboundedness is so emotionally moving, so spiritually quickening, precisely because it goes beyond the narrow scope of mere intellectual judgments. A deep sense of reverence for the value of all that exists is instilled in us. This is—as far as our mechanistic linguistic devices allow us to depict it—a heightened sense of reality. And the Abhidharma (Pali, *abhidhamma*) show us the path to this heightened sense of reality by pointing out the possibilities and potentialities for it in our everyday lives.

THE MEANING OF THE TERM *Abhidharma*

In the Pali text *Aṭṭhasālinī*, Buddhaghosa (probably fifth century) understands the preposition *abhi*, which could indicate either direction or superiority, in the latter sense: "Why is *abhidhamma* called *abhidhamma*? Because of its abundance in topics and its specificity of topics. Here the term *abhi* serves to elucidate abundance and specificity."[1] In the Sanskrit

Mahāyānasūtrālaṅkāra, Maitreya-Asanga (also probably fifth century) emphasizes the directedness of a person's development: "Abhidharma is called so because of coming face to face with nirvana (*abhimukha*), because of repeated analytical procedures (*abhīkṣṇa*), because of repudiating detractions by means of logical statements (*abhibhava*), and because of reaching an understanding of the impact of the Buddhist teaching (*[abhi]gati*)."[2]

Vasubandhu, Asanga's younger brother and author of the *Abhidharmakośa,* stresses the complexity of the processes involved in an individual's development, in which his analytical-appreciative acumen (Skt. *prajñā*) is seen as of primary importance:

> Abhidharma means man's analytical-appreciative acumen, flawless in not being contaminated by affective pollutants together with the milieu in which it operates,
> As well as what leads to such flawless analytical-appreciative acumen and what is so laid down in the didactic treatises.[3]

Specifically, this analytical-appreciative acumen is selective and focuses on that aspect of reality that is said to be a higher-order level that has ultimate validity. This ultimately valid level is contrasted with our ordinary world, which is constituted by concepts that we treat as solid building blocks, only to find out that they collapse the moment they are subjected to a critical investigation. In spite of the claim that this acumen operates from a higher level than our ordinary thought processes, which are contaminated by affective processes that distort them, it still remains thematic and structure-oriented, attempting to reduce the whole to its parts.

It was with the notion of a higher-order level of reality that a split in Buddhist thinking occurred. Throughout the Hinayana and most of the Mahayana, the higher-order level of reality, also termed *nirvāṇa*—that which is unconditioned, not made up of parts (Skt. *asaṃskṛta*) and yet comprises three or more entities*—remains static. The Vajrayana or Mantrayana marks a shift of attention from abstractable qualities and objectifiable entities to the immediacy of experience and its internal logic. Here the higher-order level is dynamic in the unfolding of an evolutionary process. In it, that which we tend to term "mind," by becoming increasingly aware of itself, becomes the organizing principle of the universe. Conceived of as a dynamic system with the highest degree of symmetry, if

*"Entities": such as "space" (*ākāśa*), "voluntarily induced suspension of representational thinking" (*pratisaṃkhyānirodha*), "involuntary suspension of representational thinking" (*apratisaṃkhyānirodha*), and what is known in modern psychology (Reber 1985, 773) as the "detection threshold" (*āniñjya*).

not perfect symmetry, this higher-order reality remains invariant through any or all transformations it may undergo. One such transformation is termed *nirvāṇa,* which possesses approximate symmetry with respect to the transformation; another such transformation is termed *saṃsāra,* which presents a broken symmetry with emphasis on the deviation and finiteness of this intriguing "mask."

It is in the nature of the analytical-appreciative acumen that it is active preeminently as representational thinking, regardless of the level in the hierarchical organization of an organism or system (such as a human being) it operates on. That is to say, the intentional character of this acumen involves both an act of reflection and that which is reflected on in such a way that it tends to direct itself onto, and absorb itself in, specific data. These data then lend themselves to quantification, measurement, and control. It is these objectifiable data that are referred to by the Sanskrit term *dharma.*

All texts agree that the term *dharma* is derived from the verbal root *dhṛ* "to hold, to carry, to possess." However, it seems that in the notion of what a *dharma* holds or possesses, there was a wavering between what in Western scholastic usage was referred to as *existentia,* a designation of thatness (*quid est*), on the one hand, and, on the other hand, *essentia,* a designation of whatness (*quod est*) by virtue of which existing entities are marked off from each other. Buddhaghosa defines the term *dharma* (used in the plural) as follows: "They carry their own existence (*sabhāva*); they are supported by conditions; and they support according to their existence."[4] and in his *Visuddhimagga,* he laconically says, "*dhammā ti sabhāvā*" (existents in their own right.)[5] But Vasubandhu in his autocommentary, the *Bhāṣya,* on *Abhidharmakośa* (here I 2b) explains *dharma* as "that which carries its own characteristic (*svalakṣaṇa*)."

Since *svabhāva* and *svalakṣaṇa* came to be used interchangeably, it can be stated unequivocally that Indian Buddhist thinking favored an essentialist and ontic approach. To be precise, the term *dharma* covers a multitude of programs and has never been understood as having a single monolithic meaning. Vasubandhu in his *Vyākhyāyukti* lists ten different usages:

> The knowable as well as the path,
> Nirvana as well as what is the domain of representational thought,
> Meritorious acts, one's life span, the Buddhist canon,
> The physical universe, certainty of deliverance, and life style.

In his commentary on Padmasambhava's *lTa-ba'i phreng-ba* (eighth century), the Tibetan Rong-zom Chos-kyi bzang-po (eleventh century) obviously has this passage in mind when he explains the meaning of the phrase "each and every *dharma*" (Tib. *chos thams-cad*). Here he understands the "knowable" as involving the intentional arc of the act of reflecting and that which is reflected on. He considers all the other topics to be actional properties rather than static objects.[6]

This actional character of what is referred to by the term *dharma* (Tib. *chos*) is clearly brought out by as late an author as mkhan-po Yon-tan rgya-mtsho (nineteenth century):

> The quintessence of what is referred to by the term *chos*, is that any obscurations, be they of an emotional or intellectual nature, have been gotten rid of; or that which has become the means of getting rid of them.
>
> The real meaning of this term is that like medicine given for a disease, it cleanses the polluting matter in one's system.
>
> The different features it refers to are the spiritual message and deep understanding of it or the two truths of the cessation of frustration and the way leading to it.
>
> The meaning of the word itself: since *chos* takes its cue from the Sanskrit word *dharma*, it means to hold back; that is, it does not let us travel the path to samsara and evil existences, but holds us on the proper road to spiritual growth.[7]

Thus in the Tibetan interpretation of Buddhist ideas and terms, emphasis is laid on what is operative in the context of human experience and is, as we might say, as yet preobjectified. As an organizing principle, that which is termed *dharma* (either in the singular or plural) discloses itself in the dynamic development of experience, which as such is the ongoing elucidation of the actual context of a person's life.

It should now be abundantly clear that there is no such thing as "the Dharma," a notion popularized by uninformed writers and orators who may well have had a vested interest in this kind of presentation. The conversion of a set of dynamic programs into a single static something together with the use of the capital letter arouses the suspicion that this something is meant to serve as a deterrent—inquiry must not be carried further or, better still, it should be completely abandoned!

Yet it is through a systematic investigation of the network of factors that constitute a human being's growth in his social embeddedness and intellectual-spiritual dimension that a heightened sense of reality with ever growing emotional satisfaction is achieved. This systematic investigation is based on a system of instructions that in the intellectual-spiritual domain is summed up by the term *abhidharma*. Buddhaghosa quite explicitly states: "Those who systematically study the Abhidharma experience unending joy and serenity of mind."[8]

Still, the study of the Abhidharma is merely a step, albeit a very important one, in the direction of a much needed opening up of new levels of awareness in which what is labeled "lower" or "higher" has lost its meaning and thus also its stranglehold. This is something quite different from the "wisdom" soup of contemporary Buddhists, who either merely continue pursuing Western wishful thinking or have come under the spell of this fallacious objectifying approach.

It is true, most people are content with merely looking at the surface of things, and instead of probing the inherent dynamic of their existentiality in order to widen their horizons, confine themselves to the narrowest plane of meanness (euphemistically termed "morals") and prejudice propagated as "spirituality." Such a reductionistic attitude is willfully ignorant of, and oblivious to, the fact that in every domain of life, restructuring due to influx of information takes place at every moment. It is precisely a person's analytical acumen (Skt. *prajñā*), exercised specifically with reference to the programs contained in the Abhidharma texts, that paves the way for the realization of that intellectual-spiritual acumen (Skt. *jñāna*) that is exercised by the "buddhas."

Indeed, it was by thoroughly understanding the nature of reality, not so much in terms of the blinding glitter of the outer surface, but on the basis of the illumining glow deep within, that the scion of the Śakya clan, Siddhartha Gautama, earned the title of "the one who has become fully awake" (*saṃyaksambuddha*). Thus Buddhaghosa declares: "The fully awakened one was the first to know the Abhidharma. While sitting under the Bodhi Tree he penetrated the Abhidharma. He became the awakened one (*buddha*)."[9] Furthermore, "the Abhidharma is the domain of the omniscient awakened ones, not the domain of others."[10] But for the Hinayana, even this awareness of the Buddha(s) remains analytical-representational.[11]

THE MEANING OF THE TERM *BUDDHA*

The above quotations are intriguing in many respects. There is, first, the attribute "omniscient" (*sarvajñā*), which in view of the general analytical and reductionistic trend of early Buddhist thought, lends itself to a quantitative interpretation. Actually, this attribute describes a nonrepresentational operation, a heightened sensitivity that is unimpeded and unobscured by any limiting thought constructions and ever ready to respond to whatever may enter the sphere of its light and lucency.

It is quite misleading to use the Sanskrit adjective *buddha* as a noun. As a past participle of the verb *budh* "to awake," it describes an experiential state; it does not denote a thing in nature as does the word "rock." However, within the Hinayana, especially among the Theravadins, some made the preposterous claim that there was only one thing (person) that corresponded to the definition "fully awake," and that, by implication, there could be no other such thing. In the wake of this reductionism one came to speak of "the Buddha" as some object. This object then captured the fancy of cultists, who were thus given a unique opportunity to make their sleepiness into a virtue.

Another point to note in this connection is that the emphasis on a state—the state of being awake—introduces a static element to which we cannot relate in terms of life, but only in terms of a rigidly determined cosmos. However, the fact should not be overlooked that a state is shaped by the interplay of various processes. While, for various reasons, the Indian tradition favored a state/structure-oriented view, the Tibetan tradition, especially in what is known as rDzogs-chen, favored a process-oriented view. rDzogs-chen takes as its starting point the description of the awakening process "darkness has gone and light has arisen."[12] The standard Tibetan term for buddha, *sangs-rgyas,* "gone-unfolded," has retained its dynamic connotation and has been interpreted in terms of a self-structuring process or dissipative structure that goes beyond the merely physical domain.[13] But if what we term "buddha" evolves like a dissipative structure, its dynamics as such comprise neither form nor quantity, but the non-unfolded totality of qualities as pure potential. Thus Klong-chen rab-'byams-pa says:

> To the extent that such endowments (*yon-tan*) as the system's gestalt quality (*sku*) and originary awareness (*ye-shes*) are already there as the blueprint for their evolution, we speak of field endowments, because, although already present in the field's excitability, they are not yet manifest. When they have reached their destiny we speak of buddha (dissipative-structure) endowments, because these endowments, already existing in the system, have unfolded (*rgyas*) in the process of their lighting up by virtue of the power of the ongoing dissipation (*sangs*) of the system's low-level excitability. In other words, we accept *sangs-rgyas* endowments as pure potential and as manifest climaxing.[14]

In this process-oriented perspective, structure remains fluid, and *sangs-rgyas* is the system's self-organizational dynamics proper, which pervades all domains and all levels of life. Each level presents a gestalt quality and each gestalt has its own cognitive dynamics.

In the structure-oriented perspective adopted by the Abhidharma and most of Buddhist philosophy, process is subordinated to its structure, and emphasis is on a static universe. In this static universe, either the unrepresented aspect has been considered of little relevance—the Western attitude until recently—or the representational aspect is too shaky to rely on—the Indian Buddhist approach, which ends in an escape into a sterile absolute that is without consequences for actual living.

2 *The Operational System "Mind"*

FROM THE OUTSET it must be noted that the concept "mind," even in its Western context, is not precise, because it reflects two conflicting trends. One trend is to elevate it into a metaphysical entity; the other is to reduce it to a metaphor for neurophysiological processes of the brain. (Thus quotation marks have been used above as a cautionary device.) Because of the inherent vagueness of this term, its use to render the Sanskrit Buddhist term *citta* carries with it not only the risk of oversimplification but also the danger of our becoming oblivious to the rich nuances of meaning of which the Buddhists were well aware when they used the term *citta*. It is true that, from its very beginning, Buddhism has emphasized the primacy and importance of "mind." Hence, if we carelessly and blindly impose our preconceived notions of mind on the Buddhist view, this emphasis may seem to support and subscribe to the dualistic view that mind and matter are separate entities, each having an "objective" reality. This insidious assumption needs to be examined.

What strikes us at once in studying Buddhist texts is that the concepts and terms used are not so much denotative as connotative. They always reflect the experiential situation as the basis from which they derive their particular application and meaning. Furthermore, having originated in India, Buddhism drew from the Indian intellectual context a concern for the question: *how* do we perceive, and how do we organize our world on the basis of our perceptions?

Answering this question demands a deep probing of factors that contribute to the complex result. It seems that four such factors can be ascertained. They are the conative (the individual's disposition to act); the evaluative (positive or negative, healthy or unhealthy); the affective (the emotional tone that pervades the whole process); and the cognitive (rationalistic/reductionistic or visionary/creative). In the total person, these factors act in a coordinated manner, but fluctuate in their relation to each other, so that at any given moment one or the other may be in the ascendant.

The Importance of a Healthy Attitude

Buddhism's insistence on immediate experience emphasizes and evaluates the present moment. The present moment is not regarded as valuable for its own sake, but insofar as it functions as a conduit for that which, in all its inexhaustible and overwhelming richness, can be most intimately felt and known in what is usually termed in Buddhism "enlightenment." Apart from having no relationship to the original Indian term *bodhi,* of which it professes to be a translation, this term is singularly inappropriate as a description for this experience, because it reflects the lingering on of a cult of pure reason that belongs to an earlier period of Western history. Certainly, it will not do, in trying to find this experience, to raise one's eyes to the heavens or idly scan the endlessness of a dubious future; nor will it help to brood with self-recrimination over a beginningless past. Each of these alternatives is as useless and, may we say, as morbid as the others. In order to relate to "enlightenment," we have to deal with problems of life as they arise, and in order to do so we must be alert and efficient. The complexity of these problems is the real meaning of the much vaunted "here and now." It is, therefore, not surprising that the first book of the Pali Abhidhamma, the *Dhammasangaṇi,* begins with the significant and meaningful words: "When a healthy attitude, belonging to the sphere of human activity where desires hold sway, accompanied by and permeated with serenity, and associated and linked up with intellectual-spiritual acumen (*ñāṇa*), has arisen. . . ."[1]

Four points should be noted in particular with regard to this passage:

1. In this passage, a certain attitude has been specified with respect to a certain occasion, and the occasion, in its turn, has been specified in terms of a certain attitude. An attitude is the end product of all factors that influence, and thus produce, certain psychic operations as their consequences. At the same time the attitude patterned by all these factors will either determine an action in this or that definite direction, or will apprehend a stimulus in this or that definite manner. According to Buddhaghosa, the little word "when" (Pali *yasmiṃ samaye*) is full of meaning. From among nine possible connotations of this phrase, five are of special import: (a) this word points to the totality of circumstances and conditions favoring and producing a definite operation (Pali *samavāya*); (b) it denotes a unique opportunity (Pali *khaṇa*); (c) it designates the momentariness of any given moment or situation (Pali *kāla*); (d) it hints at the simultaneous cooperation of many other psychic functions (Pali *samūha*); and (e) it reveals the interdependence and interrelatedness of all factors involved as mutually autocatalytic reinforcements (Pali *hetu*). Each of these factors is considered to be a "building block" (Skt. *dharma*) among other such quantifiable and measurable entities.

2. The attitude or experiential situation is stated to belong to that sphere of human activity in which desires hold sway (Skt. Pali *kāmāvacara*). This technical term points to the sensuous as well as sensual character of concrete experience, which in the context of human existence involves feeling, perceiving, conceiving, wanting, knowing, and much more. Specifically, feelings, through which we confront our world in terms of lived values, are sensual and affective.

This sensuously and sensually felt sphere of activity ranges from the lowest hell, called Avīci, to the highest heaven, the realm of the Paranirmitavaśavartin gods. It may sound strange to our modern "enlightened" ears to hear that the sphere of our activities not only comprises the world of men, plants, and animals, but also the world of gods, ghosts, and demons. However, it should not be forgotten that an abstract idea such as god or demon—at least nowadays we try to conceive of them as abstract ideas—is not something arbitrarily hypostatized and transplanted into a world of the beyond. The labels heaven and hell are primarily attempts to describe the psychic reverberation of experiences so emotionally charged that, when they are represented, are so sensuous and sensual that we actually see and feel them. There is absolutely no reason to ridicule the fact that we may at any time experience for ourselves the tormenting pains of hell and the all-surpassing bliss of heaven. We would commit a grave mistake if we ignored the metaphorical character of such terms as heaven and hell and transferred a linguistic device into the realm of metaphysics. However, this sensuous and sensual realism contains a real danger, because it tends to identify the object with an emotion of the moment and this, of course, destroys or greatly curtails the possibility of accurate cognition. This identification has been clearly recognized and stated by Buddhaghosa in his explication of the Sanskrit Pali term desire (*kāma*): "Desire is twofold: object and affective process. Affective process means passionate desire, and object means the three levels of existing. Affective process is spoken of here, because it passionately desires, and object is spoken of here, because it is passionately desired."[2] The identification of the affective process with the object and vice versa, as indicated by the comprehensive term "desire," implies that any object whatsoever, whether a concrete thing or an abstract idea, can have an effect on an individual to any degree, and that any emotion on the part of an individual immediately violates the object. Such a mentality, which may be called autoerotic, because the individual (subject) loves himself in and through the object, is a serious handicap and certainly cannot be claimed to be a healthy attitude. A healthy attitude is necessary for growth; hence the insistence on it in Abhidharma literature.

3. Although with respect to an attitude, healthiness is a fundamental and outstanding feature, the term used to describe this feature, "healthy" (Pali *kusala*), includes still other connotations that evolve out of the basic healthiness and emphasize the dynamic character of an attitude. These are faultlessness, efficiency, and generation of happy results. Buddhaghosa offers quite a lengthy interpretation of this descriptive term "healthy." He says that factors operating at a particular moment

> are called *kusala*, because they make base factors tremble, shake, be upset, and finally abolish them. Or, the word *kusa* indicates those factors that lie in an individual in a base state, and the term *kusala*

> has the meaning of chopping off, cutting off, those reprehensible factors that are termed "unhealthy" (*akusala*). Or, *kusa* is another term for intellectual-spiritual acumen (*ñāṇa*), because it curtails, reduces, and eradicates that which is reprehensible; and *kusala* is that which should be grasped and activated. Or, just as the *kusa* grass cuts any part of the hand with both edges of its blade, so also this acumen cuts the affective processes in both their actual manifestation and in their latent potentiality; and therefore the term *kusala* is used, because, like the *kusa* grass, an attitude that is healthy cuts off that which is reprehensible.[3]

By distinguishing between manifest and potential ("subthreshold") affective processes, Buddhaghosa has made an important observation. Both types of process, no doubt, present a considerable hindrance to a person's intellectual-spiritual growth and confine him to compulsive behavior. In other words, they prevent the system from functioning optimally. In view of the fact that they clog the avenues of proper operations, the literal meaning of the Pali term *kilesa,* rendered by "affective process(es)," in its manifest aspect or by "pollutant(s)" in a more general descriptive way, gains added significance. For these pollutants, when left unattended, eventually poison the whole system. Hence *kilesa,* pollutant, and Pali *visa,* poison, are used synonymously.

The propensity to become infected, poisoned, and polluted by an affective process makes an individual weak and inefficient. If a person who is physically ailing is unable to attend to his work properly, an individual who is mentally unbalanced and prone to emotional outbursts at the slightest provocation, is even less able to cope with any new situation or problem he encounters. No doubt, mental instability is a serious disease. By way of simile we are told, "Just as a man is called healthy when he is neither sick nor unwell in body, so also we may speak of healthiness in mental-spiritual matters when there is absence of illness, sickness, and disease through and in the form of affective processes."[4]

One other point should be noted in this connection. Even when an affective outburst has worn off and the individual has "regained his senses," as we are accustomed to say, he will, only too often, with the same lack of comprehension, wallow in self-recrimination and feel utterly ill at ease because of the sickening and gloomy feeling of moral guilt. In other words, he has merely slipped from one polluted state into another. For this reason, healthiness with respect to an attitude has been defined as faultlessness or irreproachability by virtue of the absence of affective, that is, pollutant intrusions.[5] And for this reason also, the domestication of an individual's unbridled affective nature has played a very important role in Buddhist practice.

Affective outbursts unleash forces that inevitably carry an individual away with them, coloring any and all of his responses. In responding to a challenge, an individual not only reacts to, but also acts on, the given situation. This reacting-to and acting-on has been given the code name *karma*. There is reciprocity between karma and affective processes. The latter severely restrict an individual's actions and any attempts to restructure his world view. They trap him in *saṃsāra*, a term that very aptly suggests running around in circles. Karma reinforces the affective processes, which then quickly decide which actions they will support and perpetuate. It is this combination of headlong actions and affective processes that makes us live out the program termed "a human existence." It does not, however, leave room for the possibility of individual self-transcendence, which requires a radical change in attitude.

Sthiramati (probably fifth century), commenting on Vasubandhu's *Triṃśikāvijñapti*—a Yogācāra work that marks the transition stage from structure-oriented thinking to process-oriented thinking—dealt with this problem of headlong actions, affective processes and the radical change in attitude leading to self-transcendence in a rather lengthy discussion in the grand scholastic tradition of Indian thinkers.[6] The main purpose of his argument is to provide logical underpinning for the validity of the idea of a supportive cognitive force called in Sanskrit *ālayavijñāna*, a "latently perceptual operation (*vijñāna*) that underlies (*ālaya*) all overt aspects of sentient life." This Mahayana idea is much wider in scope than the corresponding Hinayana idea of a *bhavanga*, a "constituent of becoming," which by virtue of being merely a constituent remains a granular entity. Anyhow, in view of the fact that the various thinkers and authors we have mentioned so far were somehow contemporaries, their common interest in the deeper strata of conscious life (*bhavanga* in Pali and the Hinayana tradition becoming ever more rigidified, and *ālayavijñāna* in Sanskrit and the Mahayana tradition allowing for further elaboration) reflects the collective spirit or *Zeitgeist* of this epoch in Indian Buddhist thought.

Sthiramati begins his discussion with the valid observation that the combination of headlong action (Skt. *karma*) and affective processes (Skt. *kleśa*) is the reason for the continuance of *saṃsāra*, a shorthand term for an individual's passage from one existence to another. In this combination, affective processes are of primary significance, because they prompt the individual to act and thereby, in the manner of a feedback loop, to reinforce the possibility of renewed affective outbursts and headlong actions leading to further unpleasant and disagreeable experiences. Equally valid is his observation that the exhaustion of the effective power of an ongoing affective process is not sufficient for its nonrecurrence. He obviously has in mind the fact that very often impulses to act that are in conflict with the ideas and aims of the ego are blocked and to a greater or lesser extent repressed. But in spite of their repression, they do not submit to defeat and die out. On the contrary, they continue to be active and contribute largely to the "world" coming to be perceived in a warped manner. Our actions then reinforce this distorted image. Of course, many of these impulses will gradually subside and eventually disappear entirely; others, however, will linger with the individual despite attempts to forget them, that is, repress them. While an actual, manifest affective process will inevitably run its course and little can be done about it, something can be done about its not occurring again. We can deprive it of its potential power. This is done by activating its potential antidote, claimed to be already present in the *ālayavijñāna.* In making this concretizing assumption, Sthiramati himself and the Yogācāra followers in general became trapped in a logically indefensible mechanism, as later authors like Rong-zom Chos-kyi bzang-po were quick to point out. Similarly, the idea of the *ālayavijñāna* as a container locked them into a static universe in which such key notions of Buddhism as emancipation and radical reversal of the trend to continue to slip into *saṃsāra* cannot but sound hollow.

4. The term *citta,* which we have rendered by "attitude" in connection with the context in which we have used it, is the most generic term among several other Sanskrit terms—such as *manas, vijñāna, prajñapti*—describing various aspects of mental activity. Having a certain attitude means to be ready for something, and this readiness for something is due to the presence of certain group patterns or sets that may be termed subjective in the sense that it is "I myself" who is ready to receive certain impressions and engage in certain activities. This "I myself" displays an amazing unity and continuity in spite of the fact that from time to time it may cease to perform those operations that we commonly associate with consciousness, that is, sensing, thinking, or experiencing. This readiness may have been brought about by various events. Unconsciously, it may have been brought about by an individual's innate disposition, or, in a subtle, partly unconscious and partly conscious manner, by the influence of our environment. Consciously, it is brought about primarily by our concrete experiences in life (which, nevertheless, account for only some of the numerous and varied forces involved). Moreover, any strongly toned content in consciousness may, either alone or in conjunction with other contents, initiate an attitude that favors certain ways of perceiving. Those qualities and motives are stressed that seem to belong to or fit into the subjective disposition and readiness, while simultaneously everything that is dissimilar is inhibited. Thus an attitude is both the resultant of many factors and the determining factor in our life inasmuch as it molds our actions and even our ideas down to the minutest detail.

However, the importance of attitude should not be overestimated. Any attitude whatsoever has an inbuilt limitation insofar as it operates on a certain level of the hierarchical organization of a human individual. Only one of these levels, as indicated by Buddhaghosa, is the domain where desires, with their concomitant irresistible drives and compulsive behavior, hold sway (Skt. Pali *kāmāvacara*); and it is on this level that the Buddhist notion of *citta* may be understood as organismic mentation. There are two other levels different from this one. One is the realm of aesthetic forms or gestalt perceptions (Skt. Pali *rūpāvacara*), still intimately linked with the domain of desires; and the third level is such that on that level gestalt perceptions are suspended, as are desires (Skt. Pali *arūpāvacara*), yet there is also allowance for their reemergence. All these levels have their own mentation or mind or attitude, so that, due to coordination and cooperation of all three levels, mentation is an integral aspect of a human person. Thus mentation plays the leading role in his development as a dynamic system embedded in a world that is primarily of a perceptual (visual) nature.

A rich array of the connotations of the term *citta* has been presented by Buddhaghosa. His words are:

> *Citta* is so called because it intends its referential terminus; the meaning is that it makes a perceptual judgment. Or, since *citta* is the common denominator for all mental operations, what are termed healthy, unhealthy, or generally inoperative attitudes within a worldly context are so called because they build up their own continuity by way of successive stages in becoming conscious. As the outcome of specific forces, *citta* is so called because it has been built up by action programs and affective processes. Furthermore, each and every *citta* is so called because of its variedness according to its manifest content. Lastly, *citta* is called so, because it generates variety.[7]

He goes on to give examples of how varied *citta* can be, adding that this variedness is due to an inner dynamic. He thus breaks away from a static conception of *citta* and emphasizes its dynamic aspect. He does not hesitate in this connection to speak of *citta* in the plural. The implication, though not stated explicitly, is that the commonly held notion of *citta* (mentation, mind, attitude) as a single entity is an oversimplification and that a human person emerges as a multitude of varied *cittas*. However, the notion of a human being either as a single or as a multitude of entities reflects the fallacy of reductionism inherent in a structure-oriented view.

Vasubandhu explains *citta* as "that which builds up" as well as "that which has been built up by healthy and/or unhealthy building blocks";[8] and Yaśomitra in his *Vyāhkyā* elaborates by stating that *citta* "builds up that which is healthy and/or unhealthy" and that the idea of its being something that has been built up was developed by the Sautrāntikas and Yogācāras, who also conceived of "information" (Skt. *vijñapti*) as a synonym for *citta*. The general consensus seems to have been that *citta* refers to a feedback and feedforward mechanism. As such, it is not just a responding device passively receiving information from the external or internal environment, but also a creative agent giving out information.

As has been pointed out already, the term *citta* derives its meaning from the context in which that which is so termed operates. Hence *citta* itself is not some discrete granular entity in splendid isolation, even if the noun *citta* suggests an entitative character. After all, nouns stand for things and things are separable and separate from other things. Rather, *citta* operates in an environment from which it cannot be isolated and which it needs for its operation. Buddhaghosa quite explicitly states: "An attitude does not arise as something isolated. Therefore, just as in the saying 'the king has arrived,' it is understood that he has not arrived alone and without his retinue, but that he has come together with his attendants, so also it should be understood that an attitude has come with more than fifty healthy operators. An attitude is an action-initiating forerunner."[9]

It is tempting to see in this reference to a king as the supreme authority in a sociocultural system something like the establishment of a controlling hierarchy in which *citta* becomes a kind of dictator and where confirmation of the already existing order is maximized. However, any controlling hierarchy ultimately leads to the rigidification of all life. It is true that as human beings we are biologically normalized, except for a few minor racial differences; but mentally we are innovators and creators, constantly attempting to give form to a vision that is already an act of self-transcendence. When this activity of ours is blocked, mental and cultural stagnation and sterile dogmatism, often pursued with unrelenting fanaticism, are the result. Rather, what is to be understood by this metaphor of the king and his retinue is a contextual hierarchy where there is stratified autonomy.

This hierarchy becomes evident from the discussion in rDzogs-chen literature, where a multilevel sociocultural system, pictured in terms of a king, his minister, and his subjects is used to illustrate the organization of the multilevel process of experiencing.[10] Thus, the king is a metaphor for the total system's excitation, which is felt by us as our own ec-static* cognitive intensity (Tib. *rig-pa*). The minister is the complex set of operations, summarily termed "mind/mentation" (Tib. *sems*), operating on a low level of excitation. And the populace is the five sensory operations of seeing, hearing, smelling, tasting, and feeling (touch). Both mentation and the sensory operations are, as is their nature, the thematizing-representational trend in experience. When this trend gains the upper hand, it leads to a

---

*The unusual hyphenation of the word *ec-static* is intended to emphasize the continuous character of the intensity. It is not some final state.

disruption of the integrity of the system. The increasing fragmentation of experience results in a low-level, deficiency performance, which is felt to be aesthetically, emotionally, and spiritually unsatisfactory. With the "enthronement of the king," the whole system regains its integrity, is renewed and quickened. Furthermore, it is explicitly stated[11] that when these three levels—the king, his minister, and his subjects—combine, there is consultation. This can only mean that there is, in modern terms, long-range planning, in which the role of the king is to remain creative, if not innovative, and to be primarily concerned with the continuation of processes that move in the direction of the total system's optimization and to stop those which are deemed to be counterproductive.[12]

This hierarchical order of a unitary experiential process carries with it a certain evaluation of its levels in the sense that the thematizing-representational trend termed "mentation," which has its own self-organizing dynamics but tends to terminate in rigid structures, is deemed to be of an inferior nature, because it operates in a less "excitatory," and hence a self-limiting, manner. By contrast, the high-level excitatory operation, which involves the whole system, is of superior quality, because meaning, which circumscribes the dimension of the creative process, is allowed to come to the fore. This is a very important point of differentiation. It constitutes the distinction between a reductionistic, self-limiting view and a holistic, open approach to personal growth. Thus this point has been a major concern of rDzogs-chen thinkers. But the strictly Indian view was structure-oriented and tended toward reduction of reality to a model that could not but rigidify what is better left flexible and alive. For even if Buddhaghosa states that "in mundane matters, an attitude (*citta*) is the chief, the leader, the forerunner; but in matters spiritual, analytical-appreciative acumen (*paññā*) is the chief, the leader, the forerunner,"[13] he is nevertheless concerned with the structure of the situation, which is very much what we intend it to be and we relate to it in a healthy or unhealthy manner. Similarly, for Buddhaghosa, a person's intellectual acumen remains analytical. It isolates and objectifies. The only difference he admits is in frame of reference.

A STRUCTURAL MODEL OF "MIND"

The earliest Buddhists prided themselves on having reduced the whole of reality to discrete entities and their transitory relations. This made it impossible for them to account for the unity of the human individual and even more impossible to account for the unity of the multifarious programs of his brain/mind. Clearly, there must be something wrong with the initial premises; when they are pursued to their logical conclusions as was done by the Mādhyamika thinkers, they are found to be self-destructive. A change in perspective not only was called for but actually took place, ushering in, if not part of, a *Zeitgeist* that made Buddhism move in a new direction.

Two points are worth bearing in mind at the outset. The one is the almost irresistible urge to reduce reality, inner or outer, to models that quickly turn into myths. We come to believe firmly in these myths for no other reason than that we have created them ourselves. We are reluctant to change them because they serve as an effective basis for further actions (Jantsch 1975, 1980). The other point is that since *citta,* attitude, refers to a feedback/feedforward mechanism, it presupposes for its operation an environment that, in the human context, is primarily the sociocultural milieu. This milieu presents a set of expectation values; it certainly is not something that is given as fundamental and immutable.

As a feedback/feedforward mechanism, *citta* is an operator among other operators, which together constitute the system "mind." In this schema *citta* is merely the principal operator. Its co-operators are termed in Sanskrit *caitta* (or *caitasa* or *cetasika*), and the connection between the principal operator and the co-operators is so close that one usually speaks of *citta-caitta.* Whether the one or the other is emphasized depends on the context in which they are used. Actually, in order to grasp the full implication of this complexity, one would have to perform the almost impossible feat of fusing the rather static concept of attitude and the more dynamic concept of feedback/feedforward operator into a single dynamic notion. This is precisely what the Buddhist term *citta* is about.

In commenting on the recurring canonical phrase "a person's analytical-appreciative acumen together with its milieu," which includes not only feelings but also morality as a specific structure of one's consciousness, Yaśomitra observes:

> *Citta* is the principal among the *caitta.* Does this mean that the analytical-appreciative acumen must be counted as an attendant to the attitude and not the other way round, because it is of the nature of being an attendant (co-operator)? That is correct. However, when there is discernment as to what is polluting and what is clean, analytical acumen lords it over all other attendants; but sometimes some other problem may be of primary concern, as, for instance, when it is a matter of becoming convinced, in which case belief is the principal operator.[14]

Important to note here is the recognition of fluctuations within the system that contribute to its healthiness and resilience. Also, as the examples indicate, the complex combination of an attitude and its co-operators is active in establishing the validity of that which we attempt to convince ourselves of. This operation is a function of our interaction with the environment and involves internal fluctuations that force the system to cope with a new problem or situation. Consequently, the make-up of an attitude varies continuously.

In this emergent new perspective the relationship of *citta* and *caitta* is not one of ownership but one of *primus inter pares*. This intricate patterning can be made very clear by resorting to modern set theory and its symbols. We can say that all feedback/feedforward mechanisms form a set, which we can write

{all feedback/feedforward mechanisms}

Letting x stand for feedback/feedforward mechanism, we can rewrite the same set as

$\{x | x$ is a feedback/feedforward mechanism$\}$

which reads "the set of all x is such that x is a feedback/feedforward mechanism." We can further specify a set by some property such that there is only one item (entity or object) with that property. Hence it is possible to allow sets with just one member and write $\{x\}$.

It is imperative not to confuse sets with one member with the member itself. It is simply not true that x and $\{x\}$ are equal. The set $\{x\}$ has just one member, namely x, but x may have any number of members depending on whether or not it forms a set, or if it does, which set. To bring out this difference the Buddhist texts use the term *citta* to indicate a set with only one member, namely *citta*, and the term *caitta* to indicate sets with several members.

Indeed, set-theoretical considerations seem to have been at work in the discussion of the various co-operators (this rendering of the term *caitta* has been chosen to differentiate them from the principal operator *citta*) that are listed and explicated by the Vaibhāṣika school in five different sets and by the Yogācāras, apparently reviewing the Vaibhāṣika listings, in six different sets (to mention only the two major opinions on this point within the Buddhist tradition). The Theravada tradition has remained more or less silent on this subject, although its followers seem to have been well aware of the usefulness of sets.

In the list given by Buddhaghosa, writing in Pali, the term *citta* occurs in the following five member set:[15]

{*phassa, vedanā, saññā, cetanā, citta*}

Vasubandhu , writing in Sanskrit, presents this set:[16]

{*sparśa, manaskāra, vit* (= *vedanā*), *saṃjñā, cetanā*}

The five operators found in all sets are explicated rather consistently by all authors as follows.

Sparśa (Pali *phassa*). This technical term is essentially a process-product word that covers the whole range of that which we have divided into the physical and the mental. We can "touch" a solid object, whether it is something in our immediate environment or on the surface of our own bodies. As embodied beings, we are tactilely programmed and coordinated. But we may also speak metaphorically of "being in touch with" something that may not be a physical thing. As an operator/co-operator, *sparśa* establishes some contact and/or rapport and also is the complexity of a contact and/or rapport so established. How important this operator is within the totality of the system, the living human being, may be learned from the descriptions of it by Buddhaghosa. In explaining the reason why it has been placed foremost among the operators, he likens *sparśa* to the main pillar in an architectural structure in which each structural element is different, yet contributes to a harmoniously interrelated whole. His words are:

> This *phassa* is like a pillar in a palace, providing a firm support to the rest of the structure; and just as beams, crossbeams, wing supports, roof rafters, transverse rafters, and neck pieces are fastened to the pillar and are fixed on the pillar, so also does *phassa* provide a firm support to the simultaneous and associated operations. It is like the pillar; the rest of the operations are like the other building materials in forming the structure.[17]

Although the image of a pillar may lead us into the assumption that *sparśa* is something static, Buddhaghosa is careful to point out its dynamic character: "*Phassa* is a so called, because it touches. Its essential feature is touching; its specific property or flavor is a colliding; its occasion is the gathering of three components; and it provides a basis or foothold for any object to enter its orbit."[18] He is also aware of the fact that the very idea of touching carries with it a strong connotation of concreteness—things do collide, but what about the encountering of an idea? The objection that one should speak of collision only with reference to sensory-specific operations, not with reference to what occurs in the realm of thought, he dismisses[19] partly by quoting from texts using analogies that he takes literally, but also by tacitly recognizing the fact that all language is metaphorical.[20]

But not only does *sparśa* provide an occasion for our being in touch with an external and internal environment, it also is the very state of "being in touch with," which for all practical purposes may be said to be a conscious situation that prompts us to act in one way or another.

This feature of *sparśa* is of particular importance. As human beings, we are tactilely programmed; but this does not mean that only endless repetition of the same processes is possible. On the contrary, our being tactilely programmed is a constant source of novelty, and only to a certain extent is there predictable regularity. If there were only repetition and absolute predictability, life would not be worth living. We value life and our world because of the novelty it offers. As a dynamic operator, *sparśa* is therefore more than a mere mechanistic collision of three factors (the sensory organ, the sensory object, and the sensory consciousness).[21]

Vedanā. If it were not for the fact that we are tactilely programmed and that the receptor system is spread all over our bodies, we would not be able to feel anything. The tactile program already provides information that invites further exploration. It is with that sense of further exploration that feeling begins to operate and impart value to the world we encounter through our activities. We always experience our world in a "subjective" way, as a felt and appreciated world (Vickers 1968, 1970). The reductionist-objectivist's opposition to anything subjective that he is unable to understand and therefore dismisses as "merely subjective" is rooted in his alienation from himself as an experiencer and his reluctance to come to grips with what counts most in actual living. The close relationship between *sparśa* (the tactile program of our being-in-touch-with) and *vedanā* (feeling) has been noted by all Buddhist writers. Buddhaghosa, for instance, says, "It (*phassa*) occasions feeling, gives rise to it."[22] And Sthiramati declares, "It (*sparśa*) operates by providing a basis for feeling."[23]

The evaluative character of feeling expresses itself in what we shall call judgments of feeling. These are prompted not so much by logic, which is the method of rational (and often not quite so rational) thought, as through resonance and dissonance in relation to our environment, natural and spiritual. We accept (like), reject (dislike), or remain indifferent (for even indifference is a value judgment).[24]

Feeling is very much a total experience to which the other operators in this set remain subordinate, although they contribute and, indirectly, share in the world that is appreciated as part of our existence. The role feeling plays in the psychic household—if we may use this metaphor for the structure of "mind"—is like that of a king who, in the words of Buddhaghosa, by virtue of his authority and understanding as master of the palace, relishes and enjoys whatever he desires and whatever has been prepared for him by the other operators. Specifically he enjoys the tactile program, which is compared with a cook preparing and serving food. In addition, feeling in enjoying what is desirable is also anticipatively selective in enjoying and relishing what promises to be desirable. In this way, feeling opens up new perspectives for vital communication with life.

It will have been noted that in the discussion of feeling all that which we in the West tend to list as feelings or forms of feeling, such as love, trust, confidence, anger, aversion and so on, are not listed at all. In Buddhist thought, this assortment belongs to different sets of operators that either promote a healthy development of the individual or, quite literally, foul up the working of the system. These "feelings" will be discussed in the section on sociocultural operators and in the chapter dealing with pollutants and quasi pollutants.

Saṃjñā. While feeling (*vedanā*) provides the "climate" of the situation, with the effect that the world we live in is felt to be a valuable one, *saṃjñā* is a sign-creating operator as well as the user of the signs that it creates and that become symbols through this use. These sign-symbols somehow correspond to features of the environment that communicate information to individuals concerning how to go about their business. To be precise, signs are like tags put on something for future identification, or as Buddhaghosa states: "When a king's treasurer and guardian of the state jewels puts a name tag on the jewels, he will, when he is told to bring this or that jewel, light a lamp and with it enter the vault and read the name tag and bring the jewel to the king."[25]

Although signs are connected with certain physical correlates, as the above example shows, they clearly transcend the framework of mere physical correspondence and exchange. In so doing, they become symbols that carry with them some indication of meaning and significance. An essential feature is their emerging gestalt quality, through which the outer world becomes manipulable and is recreated, first in thoughts and ideas, later in creative action. The complexity of the symbolic representation process intimated by the sign/symbol-creating operator *saṃjñā* is well brought out by Buddhaghosa in a lengthy discussion in which he makes the following points:

First, from an overall point of view, the essential feature of *saṃjñā* is its cognitive activity of conceiving in such a way that the sign or symbol so conceived becomes a guiding force for cognitive judgments. Second, the specific feature of *saṃjñā* is the generation of "images," which, as ideas or visions, urge the individual to create form, like a sculptor working on his material. Third, the occasioning operation of *saṃjñā* is actual involvement with an idea, as when blind men "see," and make statements about, an elephant. But such an involvement, lacking concrete correlation, may be a fleeting sensation, like a flash of lightning. Lastly, *saṃjñā* sets the scene for acting on what the symbol representation may indicate is important for survival, as when a young deer, seeing a scarecrow and "thinking" it to be a human person, a hunter, takes flight.[26]

Ideas, to be sure, are nothing immutable; their texture depends on the context in which they occur. As Buddhaghosa noted long ago, when the context is one in which man's analytical-appreciative acumen is operative, any idea that arises will emulate the trend set by this acumen.[27]

Cetanā. This operator is closely related to the previous one. We can conceive of *saṃjñā* as planning, which as a kind of anticipatory action may even involve an "alarm level" and which by its very nature aims at fixation and stability. In relation to that, *cetanā* can then be said to be actual project execution, in which all the resources of the human system are employed. Vasubandhu laconically states that "*cetanā* is a performance by and within the framework of an attitude; it is the activity of consciousness."[28] Actually, this definition does not say very much; neither do Yaśomitra's and Sthiramati's elaborations.[29] A better understanding is provided by Buddhaghosa. Following an older tradition, he distinguishes between furthering the execution of a program or project moving in a healthy or unhealthy direction and organizing and coordinating the activities that go into the execution of the project. In either case, the role of *cetanā* is less that of an administrator, who relies upon dependable operators within a well-established system, than that of a manager, who by his initiative acts like a catalyst. Referring to a statement by the "Ancients" (the authors of the lost *Aṭṭhakathā*) who compared *cetanā* with a landowner, elaborates:

> This *cetanā* has the nature of a landowner, who having gathered fifty-five strong men, went down to the field in order to harvest. He is exceedingly energetic, exceedingly strenuous, he doubles his efforts, doubles his exertions and, with the words "take your sickles" and other orders, he points out the portion to be harvested. He knows what the laborers need of drink, food, perfumes, garlands and so on, and he takes an equal part in the work. This is the way this simile is to be understood: the *cetanā* is like the landowner; the fifty-five strong men are operators whose work produces healthy results and who themselves are members of the attitude as a whole; the doubling of efforts, the doubling of exertion by this *cetanā*, which, in furthering the enterprise, leads to healthy or unhealthy results, is like the time when the landowner doubles his efforts, doubles his exertion. Furthering of the enterprise by the *cetanā* should be understood thus.[30]

Manaskāra. This term does not occur in Buddhaghosa's five-member set, but does in Vasubandhu's set, which presents a logical redistribution of the ten members of the set propounded by the Vaibhāṣikas.[31] Buddhaghosa uses *citta* instead of *manaskāra* (Pali *manasikāra*). In so doing, he is well aware of the fact that his presentation involves a circular argument. For him, *citta* operates in having a thematic focus—reflecting on what is found in the experiential situation or in the experiencer's attitude and fitting it into an already existing cognitive domain. It seems that for him this is the only possible way of structuring of the experience of a "world," which, for this reason, remains a rather narrowly circumscribed world. To have a thematic focus is to make perceptual judgments. Thus, *citta* makes the perceptual judgment that something is, say, a colored patch, which is "seen" by the eye (which, in turn, can do so because of its affinity with light) and presented to *citta* for judgment. This is done routinely and with immediacy; and it is this to which we give the name consciousness. He describes this operation in the following words: "Just as the police superintendent holding office in the center of the city where the four main traffic routes converge stops and identifies the people who come by noting, this is a resident and this is a visitor."[32]

In preferring *citta* to *manaskāra*, Buddhaghosa seems to have been influenced by the idealistic trend that is so marked in Indian Brahmanical thinking. Here he was also falling in with the new *Zeitgeist*. However, Buddhaghosa refrains from hypostatizing *citta* into something immutable and eternal. It retains its event character, remaining a sender and receiver of information at the same time. In this operation, it changes the situation and is changed by it. This was indicated already in the opening phrase of the *Dhammasangaṇi*, which we quoted at the beginning of this chapter.

The operator *manaskāra* listed in Vasubandhu's set is specified by Yaśomitra as "a tilting of the cognitive system" (*cetasa ābhoga*). "This tilting of the cognitive system is to make it lean in the direction of its objective reference and to restrict it to a certain instance (provided by the latter). It is an act by the *manas* or, in other words, the *manas* acts in making (itself) lean towards."[33] This definition presents some difficulties because the Sanskrit terms *manas* and *cetas* are apparently used as synonyms, thus adding a further dimension to the contention that *citta, manas,* and *vijñāna* are synonymous or mean one and the same "thing"[34] with the modification that *citta* sets the scene, *manas* thinks its thoughts, and *vijñāna* makes perceptual and cognitive judgments. It is because of this complexity that I here introduce the term "cognitive system" for *cetas* so as to cover every aspect. It is obvious that the general trend has remained the same: what we call "world" is presented as an external ("objective") totality of entities with clearly definable contours, somehow presented to an internal ("subjective") mind. This is precisely what in Western phenomenological studies is called "representational thinking" and described as a movement in one particular direction (Schrag 1969). Long before phenomenology drew attention to the objectifying character of representational thinking, Sthiramati had already exposed this feature:

> Tilting refers to that act by which the mind (*citta*) is brought to face its objective reference. This is an act to keep the mind restricted to its objective reference and this, in turn, means to tilt the mind over and over again in this direction. But this activity is specific to the objective reference belonging to the ongoing process termed "mind"; it is not an instant-by-instant tilting, because this would not ensure the continuity (of the process).[35]

There is also what appears at first glance as an additional set of five operators which Vasubandhu presents in Sanskrit as follows:[36]

{*chanda, adhimokṣa, smṛti, samādhi, dhī*}

The first set we have discussed can easily be understood as an emphasis on the act phase in thinking and a gradual build-up of what may be said to emerge as the "subject," which by virtue of being one pole in the intentional structure of all thought is always engaged with an "object" as the other pole. This second set exhibits a graduation in picking out those features that make objectification and control possible. The meaning of these features lies in their function as termini of "objective" significance. Therefore, on the basis of the inseparability and complementarity of the act phase and object phase in thought, Vasubandhu's splitting the Vaibhāṣikas' ten-member set into two five-member sets must be understood as mutual set-theoretical exploration and clarification.

Chanda. *Chanda* indicates predilection, implying both a strong liking and a predisposed preference for certain kinds of things. As such, it reflects the individual's embeddedness in his world of desires.

Adhimokṣa. *Adhimokṣa* strengthens this selectiveness and adds to it the dimension of restriction—that which has been intended becomes the focus to the exclusion of everything else.[37]

Restriction to whatever has been intended can work in two different directions. It can aid in developing and deepening one's understanding of a chosen topic or it can make one intolerant and dogmatic; which direction it takes depends very much on the overall positive or negative character of one's attitude. Dogmatism is the tacit admission that one is intellectually and spiritually dead, because one has come to the end of one's questioning (and is satisfied with the answer that has turned up), and because any further questioning is discouraged and disallowed.

Since one accepts much on trust, the problem of who can be said to be an absolutely trustworthy person looms large. Only too often we learn the hard way that the person whose words we took on trust was well-meaning but stupid and hence unable to guide us through the maze of problems we encountered in growing up. Or we discover that that person had a vested interest, like a politician on an election campaign. This is an example of the negative development of *adhimokṣa*.

Smṛti. This operator performs two different operations. The one is commonly referred to as "memory" or "recollection." The other is more in line with what the computer scientist understands by memory—an instrument initiating action programs. Thus *smṛti* operates as an action system that is effective in the individual's growth to the extent that it is modified to suit this process. We shall use the term "inspection" for this operation of *smṛti*. Memory and inspection are different in the sense that memory, as commonly understood, refers to that which is past, even if the act of recollection takes place in the present, while inspection is concerned with the present objective constituent in a cognitive situation, which it attempts to keep as constant as possible in order to learn more about it. The intimate relationship between these two operations is made evident by the fact that the inspected objective constituent in a cognitive situation is very often also the objective constituent in a coexistent memory situation (Broad 1951). In the context of Buddhist psychological considerations, *smṛti* is not the futile running after fleeting memories through which one might lose sight of the present exigency, but rather the operator that aids in focusing on the problem at hand. The complexity of its connotations is amply brought out by the various explications provided by various authors. Thus Sthiramati, elaborating Yaśomitra's terse definition,[38] states:

> *Smṛti* is not losing a familiar object; it is the mind's addressing it. A familiar object is one that has been previously experienced. Not letting go is ascribed to it, because the object grasped is prevented from slipping. The repeated inspection of the objective features of the object previously grasped is the addressing it. It operates as nondistraction. For when an object is addressed, there is no distraction for the mind by or toward another object or feature; hence *smṛti* acts as nondistraction.[39]

Because of its overall importance in concentrative processes, Buddhaghosa deals with *smṛti* in terms of its being part of a controlling system (*indriya*): "By it people recollect, or it itself recollects, or it is just recollection. It is a control in the sense of sovereignty, because it overcomes forgetfulness, or it takes the lead in being in attendance."[40] He goes on to explicate its role in furthering whatever is healthy and useful in an individual's development while at the same time inhibiting all that which might impede this development.

Samādhi. Similar to the relationship between *cetanā* and *saṃjñā* in the previous set is the close relationship between *samādhi* and *smṛti*. *Smṛti* is the operator that holds whatever has been selected for inspection as steady as possible before the mind's eye. *Samādhi* is the operator that ensures successful concentration, which has the character of fine focusing. As to this fine focusing, all texts agree that it is both a process and a state. Here, Sthiramati's explication may be cited: "*Samādhi* is the mind's being focused on a topic to be investigated further. This further investigation is concerned with its qualities or defects; and to be focused means that there is no other objective reference to the investigated. It provides a basis for a deeper appreciative understanding (of reality), because if the mind is focused, (things) are understood as they (really) are."[41]

It is worth bearing in mind that concentration as here defined is not an end state as suggested by the popular (and often also scientific) use of the term *samādhi,* for which the usual translation of the term is "meditation." This usage basically serves only an evocative purpose, as is so evident from its propagation by cultist groups. Thus it has little bearing on the key problem, the individual's growth and possible self-transcendence.

Since this operator is also mentioned in connection with other concentration ("meditation") exercises, technically known as *dhyāna,* Yaśomitra makes the interesting statement that inasmuch as *samādhi* is a normal feature of the mind's operation, the *dhyāna* practices merely serve to strengthen concentration. This shows that *samādhi* is not a term for some altered state of consciousness or any other possible object of sensationalism.

Dhī. This term itself is an archaism dating back to the oldest literature of India, the *Ṛgveda,* where it is frequently used. In this set, it is used synonymously with *mati* "intellect" or "judiciousness" by Vasubandhu, and synonymously with *prajñā,* "analytical-appreciative acumen," by Sthiramati. (Both *mati* and *prajñā* are neologisms in the sense that they do not occur in the *Ṛgveda.*)

As an operator, *dhī* remains strictly confined to the domain of representational thinking. According to Sthiramati, its main operational features are that it is involved with

> the examination and investigation of any topic to be scrutinized further; this investigation proceeds in a proper, improper, or nondescript manner. Investigation means screening. It is a discerning judgment, properly or improperly done, with respect to any topic that is a mixture of specificities and generalities. Proper procedure means proper use in that it makes use of statements by trustworthy persons, inference, and immediacy of perception. Its proper procedure is based on this triple operational mode. It further operates within the context of listening, thinking, and creative imagining. A discerning judgment based on statements by trustworthy persons, inference, or immediacy of perception is critical-appreciative acumen operating within the domain of listening; a discerning judgment based on the application of the logical method is critical-appreciative acumen operating within the domain of thinking; and a discerning judgment based on concentration is critical-appreciative acumen operating within the domain of creative imagination.
>
> Its improper procedure is based on the acceptance of statements by persons who are not trustworthy, fallacies of inference, and misdirected concentration.
>
> Its nondescript procedure is based on taking things for granted and on judgments made on the empirical level of reality by the common people.[42]

Sthiramati's insight that this operator can also operate in an improper manner, as it often does, should be ample evidence that the rendering of the Sanskrit term *prajñā* by "wisdom" is contrary to textual evidence and reveals wishful thinking on the part of those who use this rendering. Moreover, such usage also contradicts the accepted connotations of the word "wisdom" in the English language. Such a translation, speaking in the context of the contemporary scene, would make wisdom a characteristic of such notorious destroyers of man and his environment as the military (government-sponsored) and the terrorists (free-lance or agency-sponsored). Both have an uncanny ability to use whatever critical acumen they have to select and act on that which is sinister, degrading, and pernicious.

"Mind" as a Self-Structuring Process

Within the framework of representational thinking so prominent in what is generally referred to as Buddhist philosophy and psychology, we have noticed that set-theoretical considerations were instrumental in the attempt to rediscover the unity of the mind that had been lost in the welter of entitatively conceived operators. We also noticed that there are sets with a plurality of members and sets with only one member. It is a matter of choice whether attention is focused on sets with many members or on a set with only one member. The Yogācāra thinkers, who continued the quest for unity within the framework of representational thought, focused their attention on a set with only one member and referred to it by the term *cittamātra*. In this technical term *citta* was understood to refer to a complex experiential (cognitive) field or situation, and *mātra* to the exclusion of everything else. In other words, *citta* was used to convey the unity of insight and action, knowledge and valuation, thinking and feeling, and much more. This is in contrast to an earlier conception of it as a granular entity among others that in one way or another were connected or associated with it.

Another term used by the Yogācāra thinkers was *vijñapti*. This term indicates information, not in the sense of a transfer of knowledge from one system to another, but in the sense of an announcing of how matters stand with regard to the system's self-organization and self-generation, through which the system renews itself in a prognostic manner specific to its niche—say, the human world—which is experienced as the sum total of all its constituents. These the experiencer describes connotatively on the communicative level and enacts, or acts upon, denotatively. In strictly philosophical terms, the followers of this new trend said unequivocally that the phenomenal world exists only as the apprehended meaning of a system of concepts externalized by language into what is believed to be a physical (and not quite so physical) reality. Since self-organization may be conceived of as an aspect of an overall organizational dynamics that is physical and psychic at the same time, the assumption of any kind of dualism is superfluous and unwarranted. The Yogācāra thinkers who emphasized self-organization must be credited with having been the first to present a unified evolutionary (dynamic) perspective. Consequently they also understood yoga not in the sense of a particular practice but rather as an overall tuning-in to this evolutionary dynamics.

Lastly, the use of the term *vijñāna* (*vijñānamātra*) is ample proof of the fact that in spite of having glimpsed the dynamic character of all life, they were unable to break away from the limitations set by representational thinking.

The process character of the one-member set on which they focused attention was referred to by the term *ālayavijñāna*. In this technical term, *ālaya* was understood as a qualifying attribute of *vijñāna*, but since it is, grammatically speaking, a noun indicating a repository, a site, a place (with the implication of status), the static notion of "container" crept into this term. It had the dynamic character of a large-scale feedback/feed-forward operation that actively "stored" initiated potentialities of experience (Skt. *vāsanā*). Statically, passively, it was these "stored" potentialities.

The decisive and truly innovative point was that the *ālayavijñāna* was seen as involving a triune transformation that ensured its own continuity in an evolutionary manner. No matter what view and interpretation the various thinkers of Yogācāra movement subscribed to, they agreed that the *ālayavijñāna* could be subsumed under three headings: *vipāka*, *manana*, and *vijñapti*, as indicated by Vasubandhu in his fundamental treatment of this movement, a writing called the *Triṃsikā*.

The first concurrent transformation: Vipāka. In its literal meaning this term corresponds to the static notion of "result," but it can be and is used as a process term meaning "maturation." It was this latter connotation that led to the understanding of *vipāka* as a transformation that is both a dynamic process and the outcome of the process. In its former aspect, this transformation corresponds to what in the older mechanistic terminology of structure-oriented thinking was called "cause," but which in this new perspective is better understood as the "momentum" imparted to the evolutionary process emerging from the experientially initiated potentialities of experience (Skt. *vāsanā*), which as microstructures are termed "seeds" (Skt. *bīja*).

These microstructures are of two kinds, pure potentiality (Skt. *niṣyandavāsanā*) and potentiality-in-the-process-of-becoming-actualized (Skt. *karmavāsanā*). As pure potentiality, they are the sediments of operations that reflect the nature of their origin—whether they occurred within a valuative (moral) context that could be described as healthy, unhealthy, or neutral and as having operational consequences or not. But they are themselves amoral, because as pure potentialities, no valuation applies to them. As potentialities-in-the-process-of-becoming-actualized, they mature into healthy or unhealthy operations, which are, generally speaking, such as to have operational consequences. On the purely potential level, they merely foreshadow the "niche" in which the actual operation takes place.

The outcome of these two microstructural operations is the actual psychophysical cognitive process, the macrostructure with the two poles of the intentional experiential act, the act phase reaching toward a meaningful content, and the object phase (Casey 1976). In sum we can say that the code name *vipāka* describes the simultaneity of macro- and microevolution in the universe called experience. Macroscopic structures become the environment for microscopic structures and influence their development in a decisive manner, while the development of microscopic structures becomes an equally decisive factor in the evolution of macroscopic structures.

The term *vipāka,* which dates back to a mechanistic assessment of lived reality as a linear progression, has its shortcomings when it is used in a new context that is attempting to give a dynamic account. Thus it happened that, on the one hand, the overt (conscious) experiential operation and its macroscopic structure were understood to be the result of the maturation of the experientially initiated potentialities of experience that constitute its microstructure; on the other hand, these very microstructures and potentialities were understood as the result of the maturation of the overt operation or macrostructure. One could then choose either perspective to satisfy one's linear thinking. It seems, however, that in the dynamic interpretation of the term *vipāka* by the Yogācāra thinkers, the mechanistic notion of causality, which is valid within certain narrow limits, has been replaced by the overall evolutionary notion of homeorhesis which describes a flow-process. Or, as Vasubandhu picturesquely put it, "It (the *ālayavijñāna*) moves on like a river in spate."[43]

Metaphors are imaginative devices to assist the experiencer in his emancipation from the tyranny of the concrete. Their wide use in Buddhist thought is testimony to the intention of making people think and of making difficult problems easier to understand. Sthiramati's commentary on Vasubandhu's statement is a fine example of how this can work:

> "River" is (a metaphorical description of) a flow in which cause and effect go on without interval (or interruption). "In spate" is said with reference to the volume of water in which no separation into an earlier and later section can be introduced. Just as a river in spate sweeps along with it grass, wood, cow dung and other such stuff, so also the *ālayavijñāna* with its potentialities-in-the-process-of-becoming-actualized as meritorious, unmeritorious, or neutral operations,

> sweeps along (the five operators of) the tactile program (*sparśa*), the system-tilting (*manaskāra*), and the other programs, and moves on unceasingly as long as *saṃsāra* lasts, in the manner of a river.[44]

Apart from the dynamic character of this transformative process, which precedes, as it were, all other transformations, though no actual sequence is involved, another idea emerges clearly: the idea of *vipāka* as a dynamic field. It is only recently in the West that the notion of a field has attracted attention. The notion has come to the fore especially in quantum field theory and in works by phenomenology-oriented thinkers. In the Buddhist notion of the *ālayavijñāna,* we can also detect the modern idea of time- and space-binding. The spatial symmetry of the field is maintained at first; but then it is broken by a kind of time-binding whereby experiences of the past may be become effective in the present. These considerations will help us to understand Vasubandhu's presentation of the transformation termed *vipāka:*

> Here, the *vijñāna* which is termed *ālaya,* is a resultant (*vipāka*) and as such the sum total of microstructures in their phase of germination (*bīja*).
> Furthermore, it is such that the organization into what is to become subject, as well as the intended structure in which it will find itself, is as yet subliminal.
> It is always accompanied by the operators (initiating) the tactile program (*sparśa*), the system-tilting (*manaskāra*), the feeling tone (*vit*), the sign-symbol system (*saṃjñā*), and the project-execution operator (*cetanā*).
> Furthermore, feeling here is of a neutral character (that is, it is a feeling tone, not a judgment of feeling), and this (*vijñāna*) is as yet not confined to a particular niche and is as yet amoral.
> So are the program operators, and as such it moves on like a river in spate.[45]

The second concurrent transformation: Manana. This term is used interchangeably with *manyana* and *manas,* which in conformity with the emphasis on the system's character as *vinjāna,* is also termed *manovijñāna,* in which case *manas* is used as a quasi adjective (as was *ālaya* in the previous instance). Its Indo-European root is *men,* "thinking," and thus it is related to Latin *mens* and its derivatives "mentation" and "mind." Specifically in the Indian context, it marks the emergence of what may be described as the sense of being a subject using conceptual systems to structure what is going to be perceived and determine how to get around in the "world." This emergence as the total system's transformation is determined exclusively by the inner dynamics of the system; it introduces a directedness, a vector that clearly indicates in which direction a new structure may be expected. This is a first step toward distinguishing differences in a universe the boundaries of which are as yet undefined and can virtually be drawn anywhere. The universe cannot be distinguished from how we "think" it and implicitly think about it. This transformation is, therefore, best understood as the system's instability phase, which may be likened to a change of state (such as that from water to ice or steam) where any modeling in terms of representational (mechanistic) thinking breaks down.

This vectorial flow, indicated by the term *manana* and linked to the notion of "subject," immediately brings up the so-called problem of the self, which in the Western world has persistently moved either in the direction of a dualism of body and mind appearing as distinct and separable substances, or in the direction of a reductive monism culminating either in some sort of reductive materialism or in some kind of panpsychism, which is in no way less reductive. Any such supposed entitative status of a self—regardless of whether we speak of a self or the Self (the capital letter added to reinforce an already prevailing obscurantism)—owes its supposed existence to the representational mode of thinking, which by no means exhausts the reach and range of what is so inadequately referred to as "mind." As an emergent vectorial flow, the so-called self cannot be equated with the privileged ego or "I" in egological philosophies, nor can it be equated with a transcendental ego or self in transcendentalist philosophies (represented in India by all those systems that advocate an *ātman* theory). No such entitative and lifeless postulate is able to account for a living system's most outstanding feature: creativity.

Any reductionism, however evocatively it may be disguised, reflects vectorial directedness and carries with it a kind of pollution that affects the whole system. Thus, this vectorial flow termed *manana* (*manas*) is always associated with four "pollutants" (Skt. *kleśa*), which, as it were, reinforce its direction and intensity. These pollutants are first the egological preoccupation with one's concrete existence as the Self (Skt. *ātmadṛṣṭi*), which is prompted by a lack of awareness of what actually is the case. Secondly, this lack of awareness is representative of a person's infatuation with a self or *the* Self (Skt. *ātmamoha*), and as such is a stepped-down version of the cognitive nature of the total system. Thirdly, in this state, the individual has lost his bearings and is quite literally groping in the dark. Hence he is prone to succumb to the lure of an overevaluated idea—the delusion of the "I am" (Skt. *ātmamāna*)—as the last word in the matter. Together, these three pollutants prompt the individual to become thoroughly immersed in the fourth pollutant, his clinging to, and craving for, this alleged Self (Skt. *ātmasneha*).

In purely psychological terms, these pollutants can be said to be emotions, but unfortunately the term "emotion" has been much abused by contrasting it with reason and rationality, overlooking the fact that emotions, too, give us knowledge, knowledge that may even be very vital. As the Buddhist account shows, thought and emotion are not separable entities, and in the transformation under consideration they merely specify the vectorial flow. Although vector-specific, these pollutants are still operative in an amoral manner. Implied also is the fact that this vectorial flow prefigures the existential niche in which the individual will eventually find himself and act upon its presentation. It is obvious that this transformation contributes significantly to the formation of a personal identity, but it also entrenches the individual in his niche and prevents him from reaching beyond the limited horizon set by it. The above considerations, which attempt to clarify the global character of this *vijñāna* transformation, may assist in understanding Vasubandhu's concise statement:

> Lodged in it (the *ālayavijñāna*) and taking it as its frame of reference, this *vijñāna* called *manas* is of the nature of "thinking."
> It is always accompanied by four pollutants that are vector-specific but (otherwise as yet) amoral.
> They are known as the preoccupation with one's existence as the Self (*ātmadṛṣṭi*), the infatuation with a Self (*ātmamoha*), the megalomania of a Self (*ātmamāna*), and the attachment to a Self (*ātmasneha*).
> On whichever level or in whichever niche this (*manas*) finds itself, its associated pollutants and the other operators will share in the niche's character.[46]

The third concurrent transformation: vijñapti. This term, as has been pointed out in a previous section, refers to information in the sense of announcing the self-organization of the system as brought into a specific form. Specifically, it covers the six operations that go by the name of perception and are sense-specific. It is through the senses, which have a dual nature, a physical and a psychic one, that we encounter the world around us. But this encounter does not merely consist in passively receiving stimuli. The senses themselves are most active in determining what and how we are going to perceive and thus, according to Alexander Gosztonyi (1972, 68),[47] play a decisive role in structuring the "world" in terms of a reality value, indicating the degree to which a sense transmits material resistance; a formal evidence value, indicating the degree of insight into formal relations; and an existential-evidence value, indicating the intensity of the experience of what a sense mediates. The world we encounter is, therefore, always an informed one in the true sense of the word. In addition to the five classical senses (sight, hearing, smell, taste, and touch), the Buddhists recognize a sixth sense the domain of which is ideas or meanings. Long before Kant in the Western world, they and other Indian thinkers had already realized that no amount of association of sense data and impressions can give us the idea of, say, an elephant. Rather this idea is brought to the contingent data of the five senses by the sixth sense, called *manas*. As a matter of fact, the Buddhists revolutionized the whole of Indian thought in that they did not speak of "things" in terms of substance, whether physical or mental, but of "meanings."

It is with this third transformation of the total system that experiential ethics as information comes into play. This is not something static or, as theistic religions claim, something "revealed," but as a dynamic principle, it is the manifestation of what is referred to as "mind." Hence this transformation is said to be involved in moral operations that may be described as healthy (positive), unhealthy (negative), or neither; and it engages the total system with its innate operators, which were already given as wide-ranging in nature (*sarvatraga*) on the level of the first transformation. It also does so with those operators which the Vaibhāṣikas had listed as also being of a wide-ranging nature, but which the Yogācāra thinkers had realized as bearing on specific, determinate aspects of the multifaceted reality that is our human world. The emphasis on the system's healthy operation, which continues the overall Buddhist concern with a human being's role in the contextuality that is his/her "world," reveals a basic attitude toward life that takes into account the system's creative processes as they unfold in what becomes a life fully lived.

Vasubandhu sums up the complexity of this transformation in the following words:

> The third (transformation) is the perceptions in a sixfold cognitive domain. They are healthy, unhealthy, or neither.
>
> This (transformation) is associated with the wide-ranging operators and with the topic-specific operators, as well as with those that pertain to a healthy attitude.
>
> It is also (associated with) the set of pollutants and the set of quasi pollutants, and it has a triple feeling quality.[48]

3 *The Contextualized System "Mind" Sociocultural Operators*

In the previous chapter the discussion centered on those operations that make up what we describe as consciousness. However, in spite of its primary role in the multidimensional texture of a person's life-world, perception/consciousness is so intertwined with conceptual and volitional acts, all of them fed from deeper layers in the hierarchical organization, that we would be ill-advised to set it over and above any one of the operators contributing to the complex nature of what the Buddhists carefully analyzed and termed an attitude (Skt. *citta*)—a shorthand expression for an intricate network of mutually determining forces. The analysis also revealed the Buddhists' positive outlook on life. They began their investigation with what was called a healthy attitude in a world that is already an appreciated world offering much that is desirable. Of course, not everything desirable is conducive to physical and mental well-being, hence a person has to exercise his or her critical acumen. This implies that perception is not for itself, but is praxis-oriented. Within an individual's cultural boundaries, set up by shared values, interests, and standards, each and every individual is always with *others* with whom he inter*acts*. This being-with has a dual character in that it can be the source for love, kindness, acceptance, and joyfulness, but also for hatred, malice, rejection, and gloom. It is an observable fact, with no prior hypothesis such as a transcendental ego or an extramundane dictator needed, that a healthy attitude makes for better relationships in the human context than its opposite, which unless we are prepared to lock ourselves up in an airtight box, quite literally pollutes and poisons the whole atmosphere.

One should constantly bear in mind that a person's world is not merely a world of objects and utensils, but much more a sociocultural world with many different life styles. The operators (*caitta*) specifically active in a person's relating to his or her world have been assiduously investigated by Buddhist thinkers, and their importance in dealing with various situations has repeatedly been stressed. There is considerable consensus with respect to the "number" of these operators, grouped in specific sets. The earlier Buddhists (Sthaviravāda followers) stand alone in their approach to dealing with these operators as related to the social context. They arranged them according to their relative strength or control capabilities within the perspective of an overall movement away from the world of desires and toward contemplative withdrawal. The Vaibhāṣika thinkers, however, reassessed the rich array of these operators and summarized them in five sets[1] of which the one comprising ten "wide-ranging" operations, as split into two sets of five members each by the Yogācāra thinkers,[2] has already been discussed in the previous chapter. The Vaibhāṣikas' second set of operators generate and regulate behavioral processes and are not rigid norms into which live processes may easily slip. This set is specified as comprised of "wide-ranging operators within the context of a healthy attitude." This set was accepted by the Yogācāras, too. They, however, increased the number of the members of this set to eleven by reinstating the counteragent to delusion (Skt. *amoha*). Buddhaghosa had listed this operator among the three basic nonpollutant operators, and Vasubandhu had equated it with a person's appreciative and critical acumen (Skt. *prajñā*), emphasizing intellectual and intuitive cognition and conceptualization.[3] The Yogācāra thinkers may have been prompted to include *amoha* because they realized that in the interpersonal domain, in addition to what we perceive, what and how we feel and think about others play an important role. The Yogācāra thinkers, who were outstanding logicians, arranged the sociocultural operators according to their internal logic, although there is no particular order to the members within a set. Another point deserving notice is that the Yogācāra thinkers, with their insistence on mind/mentality only (Skt. *cittamātra*), were faced with the problem of accounting for this set without contradicting their initial premise of mind/mentality only. Enter set theory. Often one set is part of some other set. A set S is said to be a subset of a set M provided that every member of S is a member of M. Every member of the set S of sociocultural operators is a sociocultural operator, hence a mentalistic operator (Skt. *caitta*), hence a member of the set M of all mentality (Skt. *citta*). But since the phrase "part of" has unfortunate connotations, (because it suggests a multitude of discrete entities), to avoid this dilemma we can resort to the mathematical notation of

$$S \subseteq M$$

which then reads "S is a subset of M." Taking into account the container metaphor (Skt. *ālaya*) that had crept into Yogācāra thought we can say S is *contained in M*.

The set of ten sociocultural operators is, according to the *Abhidharmakośa*, as follows:

{*śraddhā, apramāda, praśrabdhi, upekṣā, hrī, apatrapa, alobha, adveṣa, ahiṃsa, vīrya*}

According to the Yogācāra followers, the set of eleven sociocultural operators, which will be the basis of our discussion, is:

{śraddhā, hrī, apatrapa, alobha, adveṣa, amoha, vīrya, praśrabdhi, apramāda, upekṣā, avihiṃsā}

Śraddhā. This term cannot be easily rendered by a single word in the English language, because it comprises all that we refer to as trust, confidence, certitude, and fidelity as well as all the nuances and gradations of these. It connotes less what is commonly understood by faith, which has too narrow an application in the Western context due to its religious association. This association suggests that *faith* is no more than a belief about something metaphysical and often implies that it functions in a way that is independent of, or even hostile to, knowledge. But faith is far more pervasive than this. Even in our everyday working life we have to take much on faith! Therefore, and also in view of what the original texts have to say, it seems more appropriate to use the term *belief* with its wide range of connotations for some of the uses of *śraddhā*. Indeed, belief serves a vital function in assisting an individual to cope with the wide range of eventualities and vicissitudes he encounters in all phases of life. As such, it is complementary to man's critical acumen, which emphasizes the "rational" aspect of reality and is thus not always the best means of relating to the profoundly nonrational quality of one's life-world. It simply will not do to repress this nonrational aspect; rather one must learn to broaden one's view and remove obscurations in it so that ultimately knowledge may prevail. It is for these reasons that *śraddhā* is given a prominent position among the sociocultural operators.

One of *śraddhā*'s outstanding characteristics, on which all authors agree, is that of clarity, not so much as a static quality, but as a dynamic process effecting clearness, brightness, and pellucidity. Vasubandhu concisely states: "It is the (clearing) clarity of the mental-(spiritual) capacity."[4] Yaśomitra elaborates: "The mental-(spiritual) capacity, which has been made turbid by pollutant and quasi pollutant agents, becomes clear through the application of this trusting capacity, like water that has been brought into contact with the water-purifying gem." Buddhaghosa uses the same simile in discussing the nature of this trust in terms of dominance (Skt. *indriya*), which, following the interpretation of this term by the grammarians, he understands as both the capacity to overcome one's adversaries and as self-reliance.[5]

The clearest account of the various functions of *śraddhā* has been given by Sthiramati:

> *Śraddhā* is (1) belief in the validity of the relationship between one's actions and the consequences of them that one has to bear; (2) clarity of the mental-spiritual capacity; and (3) aspiration. It operates in these three ways such that with respect to something having qualities or not having them, it is belief; with respect to something having

> qualities, it is clarity; and with respect to having qualities, given the capability to acquire or to generate it, it is aspiration. These three operational features constitute what is meant by clarity of the mental-spiritual capacity. Furthermore, it is said that *śraddhā* counters turbidness of the complex of mind's factors, that is, by coming into contact with it, the squalidness and turbidness generated by pollutants and quasi pollutant agents cease to exist, and the mind, having come within the range of trust, becomes clear. This is what is meant by clarity of the mental-spiritual capacity. It furthermore provides the basis for aspiration.[6]

Trust allows us to get a glimpse of the depth of our life and enables us to achieve those aims in life that add to its richness and value. Trust serves a therapeutic function in the sense that it revitalizes the individual's inner potential, which then expresses itself in optimally performed actions enhancing interpersonal relationships. Some of these actions include ritual and worship, which are part of an individual's development that cannot be severed from the individual's responsibility to others in society. Trust not only relates the whole world comprising man's societal systems, as well as the ecological order, to the individual, it also relates the individual to this whole world. Perhaps the profoundest understanding of what trust can achieve is provided by the Tibetan thinker Klong-chen rab-'byams-pa in this aphoristic statement:

> There are six ways in which trust can revitalize an individual's inner potential:
> Trust that expresses itself as reverence makes a person supplicate and imaginatively address the inner guiding principle (*bla-ma*);
> Trust that expresses itself as enthusiasm makes a person eager to worship the precious ultimates (*dkon-mchog*);
> Trust that expresses itself as loyalty makes a person imaginatively identify himself with his ideal (*yi-dam*) and live up to it;
> Trust that expresses itself as clarity makes a person actualize Being's possibilizing dynamics in his very being;
> Trust that manifests as unflinchingness turns adverse conditions into favorable ones; and
> Trust that manifests as the conviction that there is an ultimate goal makes a person fuse his finite being with what ultimately matters.
> Therefore, it is of utmost importance to actualize within oneself the path that leads to freedom.[7]

Lest there be any misconceptions concerning the Tibetan terms *bla-ma* and *yi-dam,* with which many people have become familiar, it must be pointed out that they do not stand for concrete entities. They present formulated energies, and if personalistic elements enter, the familiar father figure is absent. Within the perspective of lived-through experience, Buddhist thought enunciates the principle of complementarity, which, when imaged in personalistic forms as male and female in intimate embrace, serves as an ideal picture of a harmonious universe worth striving for. This image also can offer much-needed assurances for our endeavors to overcome our dividedness against ourselves. As formulated energies the mainspring of which is the dynamics of the universe, these images make the experiencer aware of his existentiality. Specifically, the image of the "precious ultimates" (usually referred to as the Three Jewels) sums up the experiencer's spirituality, communicativeness, and social relatedness.

Śraddhā ranges from belief in the intelligibility of the universe, and in the narrower sense, of the social order, to trust in our capacity and ability to transcend ourselves and open up new levels of the "mind" as the system's self-organizational dynamics initiates and involves us in developing interpersonal relationships.

Hrī, self-respect, and *apatrapa*, decorum. These are two further operators that are instrumental in shaping an individual's socially acceptable actions. All authors agree on the close relationship between these two operators and their experiential characteristics: self-respect manifests as shame and decorum manifests as fear. Buddhaghosa, however, seems to have anticipated the modern idea of a multilevel ethics involving different optimization criteria for a system's evolution. He discusses each of these operators in terms of four aspects: basis, autonomy, intrinsic nature, and essential feature. According to this schema, self-respect is grounded in one's self as the center of all the intentional vectors of experiencing. It thus starts from the "I who . . ." that is inseparable from the immediate milieu or social context (Skt. *jāti*, "caste" in the Indian context), as well as from age, character strength, and learnedness. Here the "I who . . ." has been made the arbiter of one's actions and is considered to be of decisive importance. Its intrinsic nature is the feeling of shame and disgust, "just as one is loath to touch an iron ball besmeared all over with excrement."[8] Its essential feature is careful evaluation of the worth of one's milieu, training, heritage, and conduct in relation to one's fellow beings. Thus it implies a show of deference, the measure of recognition that is due to oneself and to others.

Decorum is grounded in the opinion of the world; and what the world at large says and thinks about a thing or an action is of decisive importance. Its intrinsic nature is fear, fear of deviating from accepted standards, and its essential feature is to see what is evil and formidable immediately, "just as one does not touch a red-hot iron ball out of fear of getting burned." Here it is the "me who . . ." that is at the center of the stage.[9]

The analysis of moral conduct as depending on either an "objective" or a "subjective" standard deserves special attention, because it is liable to create considerable confusion if it is taken out of context. Certainly, the behavior of a person who takes the opinion of the world as the decisive criterion coincides with the views and demands of society. His morality is in accord with the moral viewpoint of his time. What he tries to do and to be is exactly what society expects of him. However, it is by no means to be presumed that the outlook that bases itself on so-called objectively given facts remains the same for all times and under all circumstances. Any such claim merely exhibits the objectivistic fallacy. It is, moreover, a well known fact that objective conditions and objective values vary; only too often they deteriorate and turn into their very opposites, sometimes even acquiring a decidedly morbid character. An individual whose orientation is based on an outer, objective standard, because it is from there that he expects the decisive value to come, must inevitably participate in the downfall resulting from the deterioration of outer standards. As a matter of fact, the moral thinking of a person whose orientation is based on outer standards in no way hinders evil and destructive elements from creeping into his way of life. Indeed, it facilitates this, because his self-assurance, self-righteousness, his unquestioned sense of being right ("this is what I have been told") makes him overlook what is new and valuable and fail to see that what once was good does not remain so eternally. Although decorum is meant to restrain a person from doing evil, if it is not balanced or checked by self-respect, it is hardly able to achieve this end. Buddaghosa compares decorum aptly with a prostitute. "By having made another person's standard one's own norm, one gives up evil by decorum, just like a harlot."[10] Indeed, a person who always conforms to the judgment of others and is always anxious to live up to others' expectations acts like a prostitute who must always be up to what her customers expect. Any holding back on her part would entail loss of business, which would have undesirable economic consequences.

On the other hand, those who rely on inner, "subjective" norms, which evolve in course of the individual's experience of his innate creativity, very often create the impression of ego-centeredness. But just as "objective" conditions do not remain unaltered, so also that which is labeled "subjective" is bound to change. We have already noted that the ego is but an emergent center in a process in which all the residua of the experiences man has had in the course of evolution are active. Only because it is the orientational center in the organization of the world as the product of our own thoughts and actions, it tends to be overevaluated and to give rise to the subjectivistic fallacy, "If I did not exist, the world would not go on." If, however, "ego-centeredness" is applied as a term of reproach, it may be nothing more than lack of understanding on the part of a person who derives his morality from some outer standard, for such a person simply cannot understand that morality as a living experience may well be the expression of a specific structure of our consciousness. To the extent that we design our life-world by means of our mental constructs, we include in it moral standards that reflect this creative process. Such an awareness not only insists on our own dignity but also makes us respect the dignity of others.

Self-respect and decorum are certainly not metaphysical categories that are assumed to be valid in an absolute sense and to be imposed on us from somewhere in a way that we are supposedly not fitted to understand, thus making it impossible for us to have a say in matters that concern us vitally; rather they are manifestations and expressions of a healthy attitude and an optimizing regulatory device. Their sociocultural importance was already well recognized by the historical Buddha when he declared that, "If these two operators did not guard the world, there would be no recognition of one's mother, of one's mother's sister, of one's mother's brother's wife, of a teacher's wife, or of the wife of one's spiritual preceptors. The world would fall into promiscuity and act like goats and sheep, fowl and swine, cattle and wild beasts."[11]

Alobha, adveṣa, amoha. Although negative in diction, the three sociocultural operators *alobha, adveṣa,* and *amoha* are thoroughly positive in character and hence powerful agents. For reasons discussed earlier, Vasubandhu in his *Abhidharmakośa* only lists the first two operators, but in his *Triṃśikā* lists all three. However, in either case he says little about them. Only Buddhaghosa discusses them in detail under the heading of "healthy roots," because in whatever context they operate, through their triune dynamics, they add to the individual's healthy outlook on life "just as trees that have firm roots are strong and well grounded."[12]

The essential feature of *alobha* (noncupidity) is absence of desire and attachment in relation to any object whatsoever. As an effective antidote to avarice, it makes us give freely and generously. It also makes us modest, so that we do not take more of anything than necessary. Above all, it makes us see flaws where there are flaws. This contrasts with cupidity, which is always eager to conceal any flaws so as to increase our greed.

Through noncupidity, even ordinary people can live happily. Should they still be subject to the duress of having to move from one birth to another, from one existential situation to another, they will no longer be reborn in the world of spirits, symbols of deprivation; for it is through craving, excessive desire to accumulate more than we have already accumulated, that we are made miserable and feel the pangs of hunger or thirst, of never being satisfied.

Noncupidity also causes us to avoid a life directed toward sensual pleasures as the sole aim of our existence. By cutting all the fetters covetousness is eager to put on us, it becomes a condition for health in the widest sense of the word and for the rare quality of feeling content.

Finally, since there is nothing to which we might become attached, noncupidity opens our eyes to the transitoriness of all that is determinate, differentiated, and allegedly unique. Only a greedy and egocentric person, in his futile hope for lasting enjoyments, fails to see the utter falsity of belief in permanence.[13]

Adveṣa (nonantipathy) essentially means being cooperative "like a friend." In removing ill will and worries, it is "soothing like sandalwood paste," and in promoting gentleness and pleasantness, it is likened to the splendor of the full moon. As a potent remedy against bad manners and unethical behavior, it is the solid foundation of ethics and manners.

In the context of modesty, nonantipathy is the correlate of noncupidity. Within a given social gathering, cupidity makes us take more than is appropriate; antipathy may make us offend our host by not accepting what he offers. Unlike antipathy, which causes a person to be obsessed with demeaning virtues and belittling merits, nonantipathy makes us joyfully acknowledge merits wherever they are found and, most important for practical living, it makes us take the vicissitudes of life (such as aging) in our stride.

Another positive feature of nonantipathy is that it instills in us a deep feeling of the boundlessness of lovingkindness, protective compassion, participatory joy, and benign equilibrium. Furthermore, nonantipathy prevents us from indulging in self-mortification, an obsession with evil that is no more than an aggrandizement of self-importance by inverted means. Nonantipathy brings youth, for a person who is not ruled by antipathy nor consumed by its fire and hatred, which causes wrinkles and makes the hair go gray, remains young for a long time. Nonantipathy also helps us in winning friends, because friends are won by lovingkindness and not lost through it.

Lastly, nonantipathy not only enables us to abandon enmity toward those who show us enmity, but also makes us realize that whatever is transitory is frustrating, because it cannot serve as a solid basis for building one's life and hence is the source of continuing misery. This realization reinforces nonantipathy, for "who would like to aggravate the existing misery he knows through further violent outbursts of anger!"[14]

Both Buddhaghosa and Vasubandhu agree that *amoha* (nondelusion) is essentially identical with appreciative and critical acumen, which is inherent in any healthy attitude. For this reason, Vasubandhu does not list this operator again among the sociocultural ones. Buddhaghosa, who discusses this operator in connection with the two previous "root operators," makes several pertinent remarks concerning its importance. It is a preeminent and powerful factor in the development of all that is healthy. Therefore, it is indispensable for the actual practice of that which leads to the goal of being able to stand on one's own feet, free from any artificial props. If noncupidity prevents us from taking too much and nonantipathy from taking too little, whether on a literal or metaphorical level, nondelusion prevents us from making the wrong choice. In addition, it makes us realize what is possible and what is not, so that we do not feel miserable when we do not get all that our desires demand. Through nondelusion, we are restrained from indulging in futile hopes. Thus there is no fear of death for a person who is not suffering from delusion, because it is a delusion that the local, here-now, determinate data in our everyday working life will not be subject to the ravages of time and death. Most important, nondelusion makes for self-improvement. Only a person who is not deluded by opinions about himself, but sees himself as he truly is—as an ongoing task—acts in a manner helpful for attaining his "goal." The goal in this sense remains a process of continual optimization rather than an end state in the manner of a "self" as an entity that stands within itself or is a hermetically sealed "subject" dressed in the garb of a transcendental ego.[15]

Vīrya (diligence). In order to reach one's goal one needs *vīrya*. The two outstanding modes of this operator are attentiveness and perseverance. Specifically, diligence describes the action of a person who is courageous. The Indian (Sanskrit) term for such a person is *vīra*, "hero," and the Buddhist understood him to be one who attempts to outgrow his drives, impulses, and compulsive behavior and to replace these with moral responsibility. He is not just a bully or some uniformed, decorated ruffian. Diligence also refers to the manner in which we go about our pursuits, both physically and mentally. It plays the dominant role in overcoming indolence and is in charge of the manner in which we tackle a problem.[16]

Buddhaghosa's psychological insight here deserves mention. According to him, diligence may simply be getting rid of a temporary mood of idleness or turning one's back upon mere pleasure-seeking. With its intensity increased, it may severe the ties that bind us to our commonplace world or assist us in crossing the flood of desires. At its highest intensity, it may be a strong effort toward, or the actual act of, crossing to the other shore (i.e., transcending *saṃsāra*). As perseverance, *vīrya* may be that which precedes the solution of whatever is difficult, and continually gaining in strength, it may uproot the pillar of ignorance. It may manifest itself as steadfastness both in strengthening one's healthy attitude and the operators constituting it and generally in maintaining the flow of whatever is healthy. Thereby it effects firmness and resolve in going the way one has decided upon as best for one's spiritual welfare. After all, it was through this firm and unflagging resolve that the historical Buddha uttered the proud words, "May my skin, my sinews, and my bones wither away. Not until I have attained my goal shall I rise from this seat." Since diligence does not dismiss the earnest desire to act positively, it also prevents the individual from shirking his obligations.[17]

This emphasis on acceptance of one's responsibilities contrasts sharply with the contemporary clamor and insistence on rights, which on closer inspection often turn out to be uninformed meddling in the affairs of others. There are no rights without obligations.

Praśrabdhi (relaxation of tension). This operator is one that occurs in the older tradition in a set of six "pairs." This presentation seems to suggest a dualism of body and mind. We say "seems," because on the one hand, there is no evidence for any such dualism, and because on the other hand, the Buddhist terms connote much more than what we ordinarily understand by "body" and "mind." These, in the context of our Western thinking, are postulated concepts, not as in Buddhism, intuitive concepts that address themselves to one's feelings and elicit an immediate response. For Buddhaghosa, "body" is the triad of feeling, sign- and symbol-creating operations, and program executions;[18] for Sthiramati it is a specific joy-enhanced tactile (physical) experience.[19]

The variations of this relaxation of tension, listed separately and discussed with reference to both "body" and "mind," are all what is best described as a feeling-awareness of lightness (Pali *lahutā*) that actively overcomes lassitude, particularly stupor and torpor. In the absence of lassitude, there is flexibility (Pali *mudutā*), which does away with the rigidity that makes it difficult to cope with the unexpected in the midst of life's uncertainties. By contrast, in the presence of lightness and flexibility, the total system can function optimally (Pali *kammaññatā*) in the sense that the individual can apply himself diligently to his work and retain his calmness, just as pure gold remains pure gold regardless of the shapes it is molded into as ornaments. As the system's readiness to operate optimally, this relaxation manifests itself as vigor (Pali *paguṇatā*), which overcomes weakness and the dangers that lie in weakness, of which the worst kind is lack of confidence or trust. Acting with this vigor, the system follows a straightforward course (Pali *ujukatā*). The sociocultural significance of such vigor is that it overcomes all kinds of crookedness and specifically opposes deceit and fraud.[20]

Apramāda (concern). This operator disposes an individual to cultivate all that is healthy and positive and is therefore also figuratively spoken of as cultivation of the healthy and positive. In addition, it protects a healthy attitude from succumbing to polluting forces.[21]

Upekṣā (dynamic balance). The rendering of the Buddhist term *upekṣā* by "equanimity" is correct from a static point of view inasmuch as it suggests a settled attitude of mind unassailable by disturbing influences. However, it misses the dynamic character of this operator, which itself constitutes a process passing through several phases, as already noted by Sthiramati: "*Upekṣā* is the mind going through the phases of balancing itself, becoming poised, and maintaining balance. By these three qualifications, *upekṣā* is shown to be a process having a beginning, a middle, and an end."[22]

By way of illustrating dynamic balance in more concrete terms, we may refer to a person learning to ride a bicycle. Balance can only be maintained by looking into the far distance, the moment one focuses on what is nearby, balance is lost. Thus, dynamic balance introduces a sense of direction in the sense of a "tuning-in" to the overall dynamics of life. This tuning-in has been elucidated in detail on the basis of Sthiramati's analysis by Rong-zom Chos-kyi bzang-po (eleventh century), who, writing in Tibetan, distinguishes between *btang-snyoms* (Skt. *upekṣā*) and *btang-snyoms chen-po* (Skt. *mahā-upekṣā*), by which latter term he understands man having become or being the overall dynamics of life. His words are:

> What is *btang-snyoms chen-po?* If one understands (and feels) that all that is is but like a magic show, and is deeply aware of the fact that the undesirable and that which counteracts it are complementary to each other, one will not strive to get rid of the undesirable, nor will one strive to adhere to that which counteracts it, nor will one strive to bring forth life's meaning (as if it were some thing). One will just abide in Being's uncontrived dynamics.[23]

Avihimsā (noninjury). Concern—which is said to operate in close conjunction with the process of tuning in to the dynamics of Being or one's life stream through the process of dynamic balance—gives a human being compassionate fellow-feeling for all that is alive. This must not be confused with sentimentality, which merely pretends to feel for another person. Compassion, because it deeply feels for the other, is averse to any kind of violence or injury.[24]

Meticulous analysis of the mentality-infused sociocultural operators and of their role in actual living prevented the Buddhists from ever falling into the trap of one of the most reductionistic sciences ever developed—behaviorism, in which mind became the first casualty and what remained was and still is a caricature of a human being. It is not surprising that modern physicists like Jeremy Hayward[25] are drawn to Buddhism, for the new physics restores mind/mentality to its central and legitimate position in nature. Also, the Buddhist contention that a human being like any other living being is meaning-sensitive and is in coevolution with the rest of the universe could well assist the cognitive sciences. These, as George Lakoff has shown,[26] are in a transitional stage, breaking away from thinking in terms of categories that cut us off from lived experience.

4 *Pollutants and Quasi Pollutants*

Pollutants

Emphasis on cognition as an intricate network of operators together with insistence on a healthy attitude, on the one hand, and reference to forces that tend to pollute and frustrate the healthy process moving in the direction of self-transcendence on the other, can easily, though wrongly, be construed as implying and vindicating the traditional Western rigid dualism between cognition and emotion. To this dualism is added the further distortion of regarding cognition to be rational (which is quite irrationally considered to be good) and regarding emotion to be passionate (rationalized for no apparent reason as being evil). But cognition (an unspecifiably broad term) and emotion (equally refractory to definitional precision) are never wholly apart, except in wholly mechanistic models that do not allow for any structural change, and in the manner of the notorious Skinner-box—the ultimate caricature of a human being's dynamic and creative nature—determine the behavior of their prisoners for all times.

It is more than doubtful that such a separation between cognition and emotion is practicable or even, from a holistic point of view, wise to try. Emotions enter the picture whenever interpersonal relationships prevail, whenever something happens that affects the individual in his encounter with the environing world. Emotions not only "move" the individual "out" to a multifaceted world of concerns, but also establish a feedback link by which a very personal relationship even with the material world is established. Cognition, wrongly reduced to, and subsequently identified with, rationality, is predominantly geared to a static universe that, it is believed, can be adequately described or "known" in quantitative terms. But emotion with its fluid affective nuances is geared to a qualitative world that is appreciated either positively or negatively in a way that deeply involves the individual. Maybe the very attempt to separate the "rational" from the "emotional," to reduce a living person to a set of unrelated and isolatable compartments, each of which could then be dealt with in terms of quantity and measurement, was literally felt by Buddhist thinkers to foul up and pollute the working of the total system. So, if only for the sake of ensuring life's continuity, something had to be done about this pollution—but without falling into the trap of reductionism.

Here we reach a critical point where utmost caution is necessary. We have to question ourselves how far it is possible to translate the language of the more subtle processes that we associated with feelings—covering the whole spectrum from love to hatred—into the more precise language of reason with its organizing principle of logic, which is needed for scientific inquiry and for a clear presentation of what is investigated. Certainly the two languages, the language of reason and the language of feeling and emotion, intertwine; each language assists the individual to enter into a dialogue with other individuals. But even on the level of intelligent discourse, the inner and outer world appear symbolically represented and language remains metaphorical (Lakoff and Johnson 1980). It is merely a matter of preference whether emphasis is on denotative restrictiveness and exclusion or on connotative comprehensiveness and inclusion. But preference is a highly "inexact" descriptive term, because the prior question of "why" has not been answered.

In order to point to and to describe affective/pollutant processes, the Indian languages (as well as the Indo-Germanic languages) use nouns that suggest thingness and separate existence. Thus language assists and tends to reinforce the analytic and representational operations of the mind, but also adds to confusion by making us speak of "pollution" in a general manner and of "pollutants" in a more specific manner. Our preference of the terms "pollution" and "pollutants" to "emotion" and "emotions" in the present context is based on the consideration that such "emotions" as loving kindness, protective compassion, participatory joy, and benign equilibrium are not considered to be emotions in our sense, but powerful catalysts in an individual's healthy development. (For details, see Guenther 1975–76, 1:106ff.)

The earliest Buddhist (Pali) texts list or speak of several pollutants, primarily cupidity-greed (*lobha*), aversion-hatred (*dosa*) and delusion–opaqueness-of-mind (*moha*). These three are somehow subservient to craving (*taṇhā*), which takes the forms of craving for the satisfaction of one's desires, of craving for one's life to continue (preferably in what is imagined to be the world of the gods, who differ from human beings only in their being more powerful and living longer, but on the whole are less intelligent and even morally inferior), and of craving for life simply to end. Apart from describing them in metaphorical terms, the texts say little about these forms of craving, except that they have to be "given up." To this effect, specific techniques were developed, which, however, on closer inspection, pose more problems than they are able to solve.

The problem of pollution and pollutants (Skt. *kleśa*)—the indigenous term is relatively late—assumed a new dimension when the transition of structure-oriented thinking with its static terms to process-oriented thinking with its dynamic concepts took place and when the new "existential" question, "How do I become autopoietically installed in a/the world?" began to replace the epistemological outlook.[1]

In Indian Buddhist thinking, which remained largely structure-oriented, the original set of three pollutants was soon enlarged to six, but the various schools of Buddhist thought presented various sets. This development may be seen as evidence that the emotions do not readily submit to rational reductionism.

In his *Abhidharmakośa,* Vasubandhu offers the following set of pollutants, which he terms "wide-ranging" and "ever-present," which may be found in an attitude described as polluted, but which are not unhealthy.[2]

{*moha, pramāda, kausīdya, āśraddhya, styāna, uddhava*}

For these, he gives only the following short characterizations. Delusion–opaqueness-of-mind (Skt. *moha*) is the inoperativeness of everything cognitive, whether of an intellectual or experiential nature; it is the dullness and obtuseness that characterizes a person's inability to distinguish between that which merely seems to be and that which actually is the case. Unconcern (Skt. *pramāda*) is the very opposite of concern; it is disinterestedness in cultivating what is healthy in one's outlook on life. Laziness (Skt. *kausīdya*) is unwillingness to make any efforts and the very opposite of diligence and perseverance. Disbelief (Skt. *āśraddhya*) is the very opposite of clarity of the mental-spiritual capacity. Lethargy (Skt. *styāna*) is listlessness and spiritlessness affecting the whole person mentally and physically. Frivolity (Skt. *uddhava*) is the mental-spiritual capacity's unsettledness that prevents it from becoming calm and tranquil.[3]

In his *Triṃśikā* Vasubandhu offers the following set:[4]

{*rāga, pratigha, moha, māna, dṛṣṭi, vicikitsā*}

This set cuts across two levels or operational modes of what is referred to summarily as "mind." One level is made up of what we usually consider to be feelings and emotions; the other is made up of biased cognitive operations active in the formation of the images we have of ourselves and of the outer world. Their bias may well be a spillover of the "emotional" into the "intellectual"—both aspects are cognitive in the sense that they are operations of the mind. Because of their bias they are characterized as system pollutants. It is important, if not imperative, to remind ourselves over and over again of the fact that the terms for these pollutants are descriptive of operations, not representations of entities that can be manipulated at will. Therefore, they also cannot be considered as behavioral acts. Rather, they are moral acts, albeit on a low level. Morality (Skt. *śīla*) is an integral aspect of a healthy attitude, as previously noted. Under certain circumstances this attitude may become polluted, but this is not the same as being unhealthy. Because of its insistence on morality as the cornerstone of human activity, Buddhism stands apart from the Western preoccupation with behavior seen not only as predictable, but also as amoral.

The first three pollutants in the above set belong to what Erich Jantsch has termed "organismic mind" and/or "organismic mentation." This is the level where metabolic and neural processes (mentations) meet as "an integral aspect of the organism in its holistic self-expression and its environmental relations" (Jantsch 1980, 169).

Rāga (passion). The rendering of the Sanskrit term by "passion" seems to be most appropriate and adequate in the present context, because it describes an intense and preoccupying emotion that gives the mind a peculiar bent. In the words of Sthiramati:

> It is (an operator that brings the individual into) a state of being absorbed in a (particular) world-perspective with the pleasures, sensuous and sensual, it offers, as well as of being intent on having such experiences over and over again. It ties (the individual) to frustration, which in this context means the organization of what is physical and mental into (such and such) an individual, initiated by the craving for (any one of the) world-perspectives (described in terms of) desires, aesthetic forms, and formlessness. Hence, this linkage to frustration by passion is alluded to as (moral, karmic) activity.[5]

Pratigha (hostility). This term is synonymous with the more frequently used Sanskrit term *dveṣa* (irritation-aversion-hatred). Its wide range of asocial and immoral implications is well described by Sthiramati:

> It is a vicious sentiment towards living beings, a cruel bent of mind, and a person possessed by it thinks of plans of how to do things to them that are of no benefit to them, such as killing and shackling them. It provides the basis for an inimical disposition and for despicable conduct. (By contrast) amicableness means pleasantness, and a disposition; such is not the case with an inimical disposition, which is suffused with offensiveness. Because of its giving rise to gloominess, the whole mind-set of an individual who is afflicted with such a vicious sentiment is in torment; and following suit the physical component (of his personality) also is in torment, and this inimical disposition with all its wretchedness and destructiveness manifests in each and every movement of the person. No expression whatsoever of despicable behavior remains alien to a person suffused with hostility; hence hostility is said to provide the basis for an inimical disposition and for despicable behavior.[6]

Moha (delusion). This pollutant is essentially the inability to distinguish between that which merely seems to be and that which really is the case. It is most active in preventing any change in the status quo. It does not allow for any mental-spiritual development. It therefore also leads to or supports the fossilization of social systems and the stagnation of culture. Sthiramati says about this pollutant:

> It is the incomprehension of anything that relates to (what are described as) adverse forms of existence, to the appreciable form of (human) existence, and to nirvana as well as to the reasons that logically establish the validity (of all this), and also to the incontestable relationship that holds between one's actions and the effects (one has to endure). This incomprehension provides the basis for the emergence of a globally polluted state of affairs, which is made up of the triad of (specific) pollutant (operators), actions (which have certain consequences), and (the social status that comes by) birth. The emergence of this globally polluted state of affairs is the concretization of a previously experienced globally polluted state of affairs from its subliminal presence into a concrete, subsequent, and overt globally polluted state of affairs. This (triad of) pollutant operators—such as misapprehension, hesitancy, and impetuosity, actions (which have the consequence termed "rebirth"), and (the social status that comes by) birth—operates only in the case of a deluded person, not in one who is not deluded.[7]

The last three pollutants in Vasubandhu's set belong to the level of "reflexive mind" and/or "reflexive mentation," which as an operational pattern of the limbic system or the palaeomammalian brain "contributes significantly to the formation of personal identity" but still has strong ties with the reptilian brain that "manages the processes of the organismic mind" (Jansch 1980, 166–167) described by the first three pollutants. The three pollutants that present this level of greater complexity are *māna, dṛṣṭi,* and *vicikitsā.*

Māna (conceit). *Māna* describes the whole gamut of self-glorification, arrogance, vainglory, and boastfulness, but also the inverted conceit that manifests as belittling oneself (which, of course, has nothing to do with modesty or humility). Because of its emphasis on a self (hypostatized into the Self), conceit overlaps with other ego-centered views already foreshadowed by delusion. Sthiramati discusses the various manifestations of conceit as follows:

> It operates in conjunction with reductionism. Its essential feature is the mind's uptrend. By conferring on (any one of) the psychophysical constituents[8] as they have become organized into an individual, the status of a self, (which then claims the remainders as its property or) "my" (body, my thoughts, and so on). By virtue of this or by virtue of this or that specificity, the individual gives a boost to (his) mind and considers himself to be superior to others. This provides a basis for disrespect and unpleasantness. Disrespect is insensitivity to spiritually minded persons or to (other) worthy persons; it is incontinences in deportment and speech. Its giving rise to unpleasantness means that, over and over again, it leads to rebirth.[9]

While delusion can be said to be halfway between the impulsive (organismic) and (reflexively) cognitive polluting forces operative in a living person, conceit, as is evident from the growing egocentricity associated with it, by adding a further dimension to a person's deepening dividedness against himself, reinforces this sense of self-importance and overevaluation of the ego. This ego, under the pretext of objectivity—a magical and powerful soporific—is turned into an entity called the Self and contrasted with other "objective" entities such as one's body (and maybe even one's mind). These entities are then said to interact; or resorting to the old stereotype of ownership, one declares that the Self (or mind, supposed to be vibrant with life) possesses or has a body, as if this were some lifeless tool to be used. This assumption goes against all evidence. In the modern Western context, Gabriel Marcel pointed out the inherent fallacy of this notion and insisted on the locution of "I am my body." By this statement he indicated that a person's body is a way of becoming and being embodied, and as such is one of the many possible concretions of an ongoing process. The persistence of the mechanistic notion of "Self" and "mine," against which the Buddhists never grow tired of speaking out, has its root in the mind-induced split and symmetry break between the inner and outer world. From this split follows symbolic re-creation and representation of both worlds in such a way that the emissions from the external ("objective") environment are met with an inner ("subjective") model that is active in ordering them. This itself becomes an urge to reduce reality to models that we believe to be meaningful only because we have made them ourselves, but that fail miserably in accounting for the dynamics of living systems as exemplified by a human being's act of self-transcendence, autopoietic existence, and self-organization.

Model building is a continuously ongoing activity. It becomes a dangerous trap if we take the stilts it offers to be reality itself and allow ourselves to be caught in the inevitably static mode, which turns in no time into a stronghold of resistance against change. We need models for an orientation that ultimately coincides with evolution, but any model that blocks life's flow acts as a pollutant. In other words, we need a vision through which we can reach beyond our own limitations as individuals, not pseudovisions, which because of their autistic nature are merely variations of a single *idée fixe*. Such an *idée fixe* is the reduction of reality to a disjunctive aggregate of atomic sensa and their contingent associations, with specific reference to the concrete human individual as a self who owns these sensa.

Dṛṣṭi (vision). Sthiramati's account of the ambiguity of the term "vision," which may be vision proper but also an *idée fixe*, is most lucid. He says:

> Although this term can be used in a general way, here in the context of the system pollutants, it is used with reference to five viewpoints that are of a pollutant nature and that have to do with reductionistic tendencies. This pollutant character, however, does not apply to a proper (world) perspective belonging to the worldly order, which is untainted. While the five viewpoints are alike in their polluted assessment of reality, they differ from each other in their objectives.[10]

The above mentioned varieties of what amounts to a pseudovision of reality tend to confirm an individual in his predetermined opinions and prevent him from acquiring and assimilating whatever new information may come from various sources. All of them, on closer inspection, display an inordinate sense of self that is best described by the slang term "ego trip." This may take the route of a sterile rationalism that attempts to reduce all phenomena to one level of explanation and is irrationally motivated by hostility toward, and contempt for, anything that challenges its "objective" approach. Or it may take the route of any of the aberrations and excesses of the so-called search for spiritual satisfaction, which is equally hostile towards anything that might involve a modicum of critical acumen.

Vicikitsā (dissent). No less an obstacle is provided by another pollutant termed dissent (*vicikitsā*), but which also connotes hesitancy and indecision. Sthiramati has this to say. "Dissent is a disclaimer of the validity of the relationship between one's actions and their consequences, of the four truths, and of the three jewels. Dissent is (the presentation of) different opinions: something might be the case, something might not be the case. It is rightly said to belong to a different category than critical acumen."[11]

It need hardly be pointed out again that all these pollutants have sociocultural implications, too.

The Quasi Pollutants

The distinction which is drawn between pollutants and quasi pollutants reveals a remarkable insight on the part of the Buddhist thinkers into the working of an organism that at each moment presents a different behavioral aspect. There are differences between differences. Some may go deeper and persist longer than others, which may be of only a passing nature. The process of differentiation and the resultant difference indicate a break in the primordial unity. This unity itself may be a mixture of symmetry and complementarity. In terms of mind, mind as a broken symmetry is still symmetrical in view of the pervasive impact of the "wide-ranging" pollutants, while its complementarity is reflected in its subject-object division. There can be no subject without an object and vice versa, in spite of ideological ("metaphysical") claims to the contrary. Within this overall polluted operational state termed "mind" or "attitude," other pollutants with a limited range of effectiveness are also at work, and it is these that are termed "quasi pollutants." They are state-specific in an individual's overt behavior as expressed in bodily gestures, vocal intonations, and ego-centered thought patterns. Being derivative, as it were, of the wide-ranging pollutants, in spite of their limited range, they reinforce the wide-ranging ones in such a way that between them there exists a feedback loop that remains mostly "negative."

It may not be easy to draw a clear line between pollutants and quasi pollutants. This difficulty is reflected in the Buddhist texts. Already in the discussion of the pollutants in the *Abhidharmakośa,* Vasubandhu expressed his reservations concerning what other followers of the Abhidharma tradition considered pollutants. He went so far as to ridicule them as mere literalists with no comprehension of the fact that the use of language is intentional and connotative, not denotative. Anyhow, from the accounts by the various thinkers and authors who played an important role in the shaping of Buddhist thought, we cannot but come to the conclusion that in their attempt to come clearly to grips with this darker side of human nature, they constantly had to review the problem of what should be considered pollutants and what quasi pollutants.[12]

Remarkable insight into the working of the human mind, always concerned with practical living and the acceptance of interpersonal social responsibilities, is once again revealed in the discussion of two pairs of facets in the psychic household that may or may not act as quasi pollutants.

The first pair is regret and drowsiness. Regret (Skt. *kaukṛtya*) is the feeling of deep disappointment at having or not having done something. It is a quasi pollutant when the scar left by something done or not done continues to give rise to the feeling of disappointment at not having done something negative (unhealthy, despicable) and having done something positive instead. By contrast, regret is not a quasi pollutant (nor is it a pollutant in the strict sense of the word) when it makes one sad about not having done something positive when one had the chance of doing so.[13]

Drowsiness (Skt. *middha*) is understood as a soporific power that makes the mind withdraw from what usually attracts its attention and involvement. As an aspect of *moha* (delusion–opaqueness-of-mind), its functioning as a quasi pollutant derives from an attitude that is dominated by the pollutants proper in which it presents a kind of somnambulistic state on the part of the person afflicted by it. In a healthy person, it refers to the normal rhythm of sleeping and waking.[14]

The second pair is *vitarka* and *vicāra,* which are difficult to render in English except by paraphrasing what they convey. Both notions have a long history, but lost much of their significance as process-oriented thinking became more and more prevalent. The high esteem in which these functions were once held was due to the fact that they were part of a concentration exercise, which, however, remained within the domain of the representational. This is evident from Buddhaghosa's definition of *vitakka* (Pali for *vitarka*) as

> a probing, a conjecturing. Its essential feature is to make the mind move up to (its) object; (in other words), it hoists the mind onto (its) object. Just as someone goes up to (and into) the royal palace with the help of a person who is the king's favorite or relative or friend, so the mind climbs onto (its) object with the help of *vitakka;* therefore it is said that its essential feature is to make the mind move up to (its) object.[15]

A more detailed discussion, which also unifies the different notions held about this function by various schools of Buddhism—as, for instance, the Sautrāntikas (much favored by Vasubandhu)—is presented by Sthiramati, who has this to say:

> *Vitarka* is a searching mental addressing (of an objective presence), a special operation by critical acumen (*prajñā*) and project execution (*cetanā*). "Searching" means to ask the question "What is this?" and it proceeds by trying to pinpoint (the meaning of the presence). "Mental addressing" is a metaphorical expression for voicing (the meaning of the presence by naming it). The special operation by project execution and critical acumen is such that project execution directs the mind to its object (task), while critical acumen distinguishes between (the object's) positive and negative aspects.[16]

He goes on to say that *vitarka* is a polluted operation when it focuses on hedonism, destruction, and cruelty. It is a nonpolluted operation when it focuses on renunciation.[17]

The same holds for *vicāra,* which according to Sthiramati, following an old tradition, is "a scanning mental addressing (of the objective presence). It makes the judgment, "This is it," because that which has previously come into the focus of its purview is now circumscribed and defined. Both *vitarka* and *vicāra,* serving as a basis for an amicable or inimical disposition, are differentiated from each other in that the former is coarse and the latter subtle."[18] Sthiramati goes on to say that *vicāra* constitutes a polluted operation when it is directed toward ruining another person, but it is a nonpolluted operation when it is directed toward helping others.[19]

Buddhaghosa merely stresses the discursive character of *vicāra,* but illustrates the inseparableness of *vitarka* and *vicāra,* the one coarse and the other subtle, by a number of similes, such as the striking of a bell and the reverberations of its sound.[20] But nowhere does he say that these two functions are also of a quasi pollutant nature.

SUMMARY

It is an incontestable fact that any living person, whether a man or a woman, always finds him- or herself in a situation the quality of which points back to that person's attitude. This attitude may be positive or negative, healthy or unhealthy, and it colors each and every engagement with the world. Such an attitude is already an expression of a multifaceted pervasive force that for brevity's sake is called "mind." Thus the unwary are at once trapped into the naive assumption—the objectivist-reductionist's fallacy—that it is some "thing" among other things. The complexity of mind, which we encounter in the welter of its manifestations, poses the problem of how to account for the unity that was so vaguely referred to as "mind." Buddhist thinkers attempted to come to grips with this problem by pointing to what we nowadays call the hierarchical organization of levels in a system, which could be the universe or the mind, and by resorting to set-theoretical considerations. These reflected the general Indian and specifically Buddhist inclination toward logic that kept Buddhist thinkers, at least a large majority of them, within the confines of representational thinking and its attendant reductionism.

Considering the fruitful notion of attitude makes the experiencer aware of himself as being installed in a world in which he interacts with others. In this interaction a wide range of forces (operators from a static point of view) come into play. Because of Buddhism's positive outlook on life, all of them are discussed and elucidated in such a way as to enhance the quality of all life and the human situation in particular.

But there are also darker forces at work, which tend to undermine a person's self-growth. These are the pollutants and quasi pollutants, which are often, though incorrectly, referred to as the emotions. Recognition of their presence in the system "mind" is testimony to the fact that the Buddhist thinkers developed their model of mind with a view to understanding the concrete reality of a human being.

In the development of this "model," two approaches are discernible. One remains structure-oriented, the other is, and continues to be, process-oriented.

5 *Concentration, Contemplation, Meditation* *Preliminaries On The Way Of Growing Up*

THE IDEA OF MIND as either a complex network of concrete (psychic) operators grouped in a number of sets or as a unitary dynamic "entity,"[1] as sketched in the previous chapters, was acknowledged by all Buddhists, and this is what gave Buddhism its distinct mentalistic flavor. Being praxis-oriented, the Buddhists paid special attention to what is variously referred to by such terms as concentration, contemplation, and meditation. These are aspects of that activity which we generally call thinking, a term having many and muddled uses. The original meaning seems to have been "to make something (seem to) appear to oneself"; this has a strong visual connotation. It is most active in the symbolic representation and re-creation of reality that constitutes both an inner and outer world. Here we encounter the first difficulty in the human dilemma: how to express the relation between our thoughts and our environment (world). Not only is thinking organized partly around signals from the objects that we encounter in our world, but partly also around signals that arise from the residua of past experiences. Thus, the world that surrounds us and stimulates us sensuously and sensually and to which we respond with our impulses and apprehensions, our expectations and evaluations, already presupposes an attitude, which is an emotional and intellectual tapestry that in a certain sense "defines" the thinking individual in his relationship to his world:

> By one's attitude the world is given guidance;
> By one's attitude the world is exposed to distress.
> Everything follows the dictates of this singular feature (termed) attitude.[2]

The implication, already clearly stated by the Buddhists, is that we find ourselves installed in a world with a certain disposition toward it, which is characterized either by a prevalence of pollutants to the detriment of one's critical-appreciative acumen or by a prevalence of one's critical-appreciative acumen. In the first case, the general outlook is said to be unhealthy; in the second case, the general outlook is considered to be healthy and conducive to further spiritual development. Neither outlook, however, gives us a "true" picture of reality. Rather, at every moment we are engaged in the construction and reconstruction of what we grandiloquently call reality. There is no denying the fact that in either case, experience, which is the core of human life, projects and translates itself into a variety of related aspects. Through these aspects, the process itself tends to congeal into static entities and to lose more and more of its symbolic expressiveness. In our mundane attitudes, we are concerned with the result of the symbolic activity of the mind rather than with the symbol-forming process itself.

Particularly in those attitudes considered to be unhealthy, loss of appreciation and disregard of meaning intended to continue to take on new dimensions as the process unfolds is most conspicuous. Utilitarian considerations are the predominant feature of such unhealthy attitudes. To give only a few examples taken at random from what is constantly before our eyes: We love things and covet them because they are a source of income, and in considering them in this way, we turn them into counters for computing the course of prices in the marketplace. Or, we enter into an armaments race, and at the same time, quite hypocritically, we convene disarmament or arms control conferences. When we project our delusion of persecution on others (which in the language of politics means to think in terms of national security), we want to be ready to be the first to strike the fatal blow. And we are not ashamed of indulging in hostile and subversive activities, the foundation of which in hatred is only too obvious. Under the power of delusion, we make such behavior socially acceptable by calling it a duty to ourselves or to our country. This is just another way of socializing the delusion of grandeur and of spreading the disease of self-righteousness. There is a close connection between delusion and hatred and delusion and cupidity. But there is still another kind of an unhealthy attitude in which delusion alone holds undisputed sway. This is the attitude of the slogan-coiner who believes in all earnestness that any slogan—the sillier, the better—is the cure for all the evils of the world.

Another characteristic of unhealthy attitudes is their inability to develop beyond themselves. They move in a vicious circle in such a way that passion, with its variations of cupidity and attachment, breeds further passion; hostility, with its tendency to manifest as hatred, rouses and intensifies hostility; and delusion unleashes a host of manias of the sort that has become so conspicuous in various contemporary "spiritual" cults. These pollutants and pollutant-dominated attitudes are summed up by the term "worldliness," which in terms of mentation presents, and is part of, the complex organism's environmental relations, including the individual's symbolic and holistic self-expression. But precisely because of the individual's complexity, the unhealthy attitudes and the resulting self-restriction to worldliness have a fluctuating quality. No attitude is ever rigid and permanent. It might persist for some time, but then the transition from one attitude to another is not continuous but marked by an abrupt switch-over. Generally speaking, unhealthy attitudes are concerned with quantitative matters (more possessions, more power, more delusions of grandeur), while healthy attitudes let us feel the quality of the world in which we live and let us participate in its richness by various degrees of understanding.

Against the multiplicity of unhealthy attitudes, healthy attitudes constitute a minority. The interplay between unhealthy and healthy attitudes may be viewed as constituting a tension field that is not resolved by choosing one or the other side, but only by growing beyond what seem to be opposites. From such a perspective, the larger number of unhealthy attitudes listed in the earliest Buddhist texts may be understood as an indication that most individuals are in an "acute" phase of their development.

The idea of healthy and unhealthy attitudes constituting a tension field rather than a granular juxtaposition was hinted at by Buddhaghosa, who in speaking of them in terms of sociobehavioral patterns, offers the following schema of complementarity:[3]

passion (possessiveness)	:	trust
hostility	:	critical (intellectual) acumen
delusion	:	volatility

It is true that, in elaborating on this complementarity specified in terms of affinity and similarity, Buddhaghosa puts an undue restriction on the idea of "passion" (Pali *rāga*) by understanding it as meaning merely possessiveness and an inordinate clinging to whatever one encounters in the world around one. As a monk, he had a profound distrust of passion as intense erotic love; thus he failed to be aware of the other aspect of passion—as a subtle and creative force. Certainly, a person without passion is unable to express or achieve anything, as later Buddhists realized.[4] It will be readily admitted that it is extremely difficult to decide where passion—say, an all-consuming love—ends, and possessiveness and gross cupidity begin. This difficulty is connected with two errors that go hand in hand: first, confusing love with possessiveness; and second, rejecting everything that has the slightest resemblance to love and ardor and adopting an almost incurably negative outlook on life, then persisting in this mental-spiritual sterility.

In a similar way, critical-appreciative acumen may very often appear "cool," because its application lays bare any flaw that may be found in the knowable. Thus it destroys uncritical and merely sentimental attachment, which might be considered to be "warm" by contrast. But to point out defects or flaws is in itself nothing negative. On the contrary, it is something highly positive, for the pursuit of meaning begins with critical-appreciative acumen. Only if we start from the premise that there is nothing but defects and that the world exists to annoy us do we allow our intellectual capacity to overstep itself and to succumb to hostility. Actually there is no evidence that the world is concerned with either pleasing or displeasing us. Denunciation of critical-appreciative acumen is based on a misconception of its function and on a deep fear of it. An example is provided by the anti-intellectualism of the fundamentalists and cultists, who, by adopting this approach, lose their humanness.

It is easy to understand why Buddhaghosa related volatility to delusion. Neither a deluded nor a volatile person ever gets to the bottom of a problem. Such persons soon stop short in their inquiries, because they are content to accept things at their face value. The difference between these two approaches can be stated in this way: the deluded person does not even start questioning; the volatile person quickly turns to other things, since nothing holds his interest for long.

Buddhaghosa's profound psychological insight can be restated in modern terms as indicating that human individuals live on two levels or in two cognitive domains. One level is the domain of the almost irresistible drives and impulses that express themselves in territoriality (possessiveness), intimidation (hostility), and limited capacity for learning (delusion). Persisting on this level for too long is considered "unhealthy." In view of the fact that a human individual as a living system is programmed to grow up, such persistence is, to say the least, a deviation and is ultimately self-destructive. The other level is that of dissociation from the concrete. This level is arrived at by bringing emotional-intellectual preferences and sociocultural operators into play that superimpose themselves on the existing ("lower") material and initiate a symbolic transformation and re-creation of the life-world. Since this level is closer to the life stream than the other, it is felt and judged to be "healthy." Nevertheless, these two levels remain within the domain of the thematic-representational and the limits set by it. True self-transcendence is not found in either.

Concentration, contemplation, and meditation are related terms and are often all subsumed, especially in the Western world, under the evocative term "meditation." This term, however, is used in such a broad sense (ranging from private hallucinations to experiences marketed in connection with the crassest commercialism) that it has become quite meaningless. Buddhists texts distinguish these three as widely differing activities that reflect changing perspectives. These three are:

1. Objectivistic-reductionistic concentration
2. Mentalistic-creative contemplation
3. A holistic imparting of meaning

Because of their importance for picking and pursuing one's way through life, they will be discussed in detail.

Objectivistic-Reductionistic Concentration

Any experiencing of environmental information is related to the whole organism as the existential center of its life-world. Such experiencing may be likened to a structure with limit-cycle behavior that is capable of preventing mental-(spiritual) development over long periods. This organismic mind[5] is primarily concerned with coordination of the functions that characterize the organism as a whole and the relationships it has to its environment. These relationships are tendential, dispositional, and occasion the concretion of experience in a vectorlike manner. As previously noted, they are described as being of the nature of desires (Skt., Pali *kāma*), having an intentional structure and displaying an intentional mode of behavior.

Being a kind of mentation, organismic mind imperceptibly merges with another aspect of mentation that has the capability of devising alternative models of reality or the life-world in which colors and forms, organized into distinct gestalts (Skt., Pali *rūpa*), play a significant role. The most important point to be noted in connection with color is that it is never something dead and mechanistic. It is an all-pervasive light, a form of energy that enriches our perceptions and, in so doing, also deepens our pleasure in what we consider everyday occurrences. Without light and color, the world would be a rather drab and dark place. Because color is a kind of electromagnetic radiation, there is something mobile, fleeting and transient about it. The hues shift and shimmer, vanish and reappear, and each color can be bright or pale, light or dark, saturated or unsaturated. There also is something vital and dynamic about color, as every artist or anyone with a gift for visual imagination knows. In addition, colors have a profound effect on people, who, consciously or unconsciously, orchestrate them into significant forms, patterns, gestalts. A sunbathed landscape evokes different feelings in us than does a rain-soaked one.

It is on the level of reflexive mind[6] that thinking, as we commonly understand this term, begins to come into its own and to become ever more active in projecting new vistas. In concert with this projective activity, the rift between the within (the subject) and the without (the object) becomes ever wider, and the projective activity becomes ever more fascinated by its own projections. In terms of cognition, this activity is a reflecting awareness of a reflected content that constitutes its thematic focus. It can unfold only when it becomes emancipated to some extent from organismic mentation, which narrows down the evolving flexibility of thinking by supporting only those features of it that are likely to ensure the continuity of its fixed limitations. To the extent that anything that aids the perpetuation of existing limitations goes counter to the evolutionary life stream, the mode of the reflexive mind that still aids and reinforces the restrictiveness of organismic mentation is said to be unhealthy. In view of the fact that reflexive mentation can operate both ways (healthy and/or unhealthy), a further emancipation from its unhealthy operations becomes necessary. In the Buddhist texts this emancipatory dynamics has been termed "path" or "way" (Skt. *mārga*), and insistence on its importance is the first intimation of the kind of process-oriented thinking that leads to a dynamic and evolutionary world view. The term "path" itself is used to include expertise (Skt. *upāya*) and project execution (Skt. *cetanā*).[7]

This level of reflexive mentation to a certain extent marks a breakaway from organismic mentation with its emphasis on, and bond with, the collective. It is on this level that there emerges the conscious "I who." This "I who" emerges not as an immutable entity but as an index of the incipient process of individuation, which is variable as to the context in which it appears. Furthermore, reflexive mentation establishes its own operational (cognitive) domain in which the subjective aspect in perception plays as important a role as the objective one. This "new" domain, to the extent that it appears to be a projection into a seemingly external dimension, is termed in Sanskrit *rūpāvacara* (also *rūpadhātu* or *rūpaloka* with subtle nuances of distinction). On this level, the passivity of merely receiving information from the environment is superseded by an active modeling that makes us see information in a new light. That which presents itself ("lights up," Tib. *snang-ba*) on this level and which we "see" cannot be grasped in the manner in which we take hold of a solid object; rather it is appreciated in its aesthetic immediacy. And through this act, not only is our whole attitude toward our life-world changed, but also this world itself reveals new dimensions of an almost unfathomable profundity.

Reflexive mentation initiates creative experimentation. This is what is meant by the technical Sanskrit term *bhāvanā,* which is used in connection with *samādhi* to point to an in-depth experience and appraisal of what is felt to be a singular presence (Skt. *ekāgratā*).[8]

Creative experimentation may be said to be that which occasions the irruption of novelty (the aesthetic, qualitative as against the collective, quantitative), which in this process also becomes increasingly stabilized. The various stabilization phases are referred to by the term *dhyāna.*[9] Traditionally, four such stabilization phases have been listed, each adding a new dimension of contentment and lucidity.

The above considerations may assist in bringing out the deeper implications of the recurring canonical passage:

> (An individual) cultivates the way (leading) toward the emergence of (and encounter with a domain of) aesthetically experienceable forms. Having reached the first stabilization phase, which is characterized by the joyfulness and pleasurableness that come from emancipation

> from the sensuously and sensually concrete and those unhealthy operators (that reinforce the bondage to the concrete), but is still probing and scanning, he patterns his behavior accordingly.[10]

The second stabilization phase is marked by the absence of the relative restlessness that goes with the probing and scanning operations (Skt. *vitarka-vicāra*[11]), which have now been superseded by quiet enjoyment and dispassionateness, respectively. This results in dynamic balance, allowing the latent positive forces to come into play.

The third stabilization phase is characterized by greater clarity and deeper understanding of the experienced content, accompanied by pleasant sensations spreading through the body, making it seem to come alive. This is a kind of balancing process.

The fourth stabilization phase is a state of "lucid awareness," which has been prepared by the preceding phase. In view of the fact that in each stage the individual patterns his behavior in accordance with the current process, the whole procedure has nothing to do with escapism or a steady-state conception of the individual. The emancipation of a mental reality, which in a certain sense is our inner world, from its bondage to a supposedly independent external reality, enables the individual to intensify his life creatively in the present by including experiences of the past and having visions of the future. Thus, what we have been discussing is a time-binding operation.

The thematizing character of the operations of reflexive mind is unmistakable, even if there is a marked emancipation from "re-presentation" and a growing emphasis on the immediacy of a presentment. Representation always presupposes something other that is somehow made to reappear under the guise of something else. However, by contrast "presentment," specifically in lived experience, is not even a presentation of something but a mere presence—a presence that is, paradoxically, both an image felt and feeling imaged. But this very presence evidences a certain restriction of the openness of life, which cannot be analyzed into parts independent of its unbroken wholeness and which also cannot be localized as "out there" or "in here." This nonlocality and nonlocalizability was termed *ārūpyadhātu* in Sanskrit, and it was recognized for what it is by Vasubandhu, who made the significant statement. "The Ārūpyadhātu has no location, but it is fourfold according to the emergence of (and encounter with specific features)."[12]

It is natural that the structure-oriented way of thinking that dominated early Buddhist thought had considerable difficulties in understanding nonlocality. Accessing it as if it were somewhere, analysis proceeded by way of deconstruction and a process of devolution. Thus the thematic nature of the stabilization phases grew less and less marked. Actually, the last stabilization phase could follow two paths. The one, described as a heightened awareness or wider perspective (Skt. *vipaśyana*), led to the creation of a mythological world of immaculate life forms. The other, described as calmness (Skt. *śamatha*) led deeper and deeper into a kind of nondescript contentment and general inactivity and involved psychic processes having physiological ramifications that are still not well understood. The "realm" into which calmness slipped was precisely this nonlocality (Skt. *ārūpyadhātu*), which was interpreted in a thematic way. Thus *dhātu* was said to be a carrier of what amounts philosophically to an essence, yet has a distinct field character. And *ārūpya* was interpreted as nonexistence, as naively understood by the Buddhists as by the Nyāya-Vaiśeṣikas (whose atomistic world view the early Buddhists shared). The early Buddhist logic runs as follows: We have a noun "nonexistence"; nouns stand for things, hence nonexistence is a "thing." On the basis of this peculiar logic, *ārūpyadhātu* came to be understood as "the carrier of the 'thing' nonexistence of *rūpa*." Opposing this rather naive and reductionistic notion, others were of the opinion that there was still some trace of *rūpa* (Skt. *īśadrūpa*) available. But this notion is no less reductionistic and untenable. Accessing of nonlocality is marked by a growing interiorization passing from the "endlessness of space" through the "endlessness of the perceptive capacity" and through the "endlessness of where it is no longer possible to make judgments as to existence or nonexistence" to the "endlessness of a nothing-whatsoever." Finally it climaxes in a state that in modern psychology is known as the "detection threshold." At this level, worldliness has reached its ultimate limits and cannot but fall back on itself—*saṃsāra* begins all over again.

The stabilization phases have a distinct time-binding character and involve the creative projection of "new" realms, codified and concretized into mythic spheres. But the endlessness phases are of a space-binding nature and have the whole universe concentrated in the individual. This adds a further dimension to the notions of locality ("out there") and nonlocality ("in here"). Locality tends to imply objectivity; nonlocality becomes synonymous with subjectivity. This leads to solipsism. Objectivity and locality are fictions of reflexive mentation that are solipsistically viewed as the subject's mind, which is then taken as the only reality. This "spiritual" reductionism remains reductionism despite the evocative terms that are heaped upon it to make it more palatable.

In modern terms, reflexive mentation is capable of suspending historical time and physical space, but not of emancipation from what may be called the (closed) matter/energy configuration. In view of the fact that in this suspension of historical time and physical space, all the fallacies of objectivism and subjectivism remain intact, though in a less conspicuous manner, this kind of "meditation" has a special appeal to many people. It allows them to go about their daily business as usual and "feel good."

Another reason is that it reflects a familiar control mentality, the urge to power by domination, which is inextricably intertwined with a process of externalization and objectification that reaches such an extent that even nonlocality is treated as if it were something objectifiable. When this kind of thinking is applied to the open dynamics (Skt. *śūnyatā*) of Being (universe), this openness is turned into a dead nothingness or *the* Void. Any thematization with its inherent reductionism leads to a rigidification of life; it is not conducive to an understanding of life as a creative process. It therefore comes as no surprise that with the transition from structure-oriented thinking to process-oriented thinking, this restrictive way of looking at reality was abandoned and exposed for what it is, an attempt to control the mind. If one condescended to call this structure-oriented approach "meditation" in view of the stabilization phases involved, it was declared to be an exercise of those who just did not know better. The inability of the structure-oriented approach to display life's grand design and meaningfulness is succinctly stated in a Tibetan text, the *Rig-pa rang-shar*:

> This mind control (as practiced) by the gods (of popular belief) and by (ordinary) men
> (Is such that) after the containment of breathing
> Mentation is (no longer) stirring and no thematic disruption occurs. (This constitutes)
> The state of the cognitive capacity being focused (on its objective reference).
> (This state) is said to be such that no fortuitous thematization obtains in it.
> It is unable to disclose life's meaningfulness.[13]

However, as a dynamic principle, mind cannot be confined to a rigidly determined structure but always reaches beyond itself. Meaning-bestowing creativity supersedes the passivity of expecting or hoping for a static end state. In the words of dGa'-rab rdo-rje (probably beginning of the present era):

> How polluted (and polluting) is that vision that holds to subjectivistic reasoning;
> How depressing is that "meditation" that bases itself on the data so provided;
> How exhausting is that life style that attempts to model itself on the above;
> How deceptive are the expectations of a static goal![14]

This outspoken criticism of concentration (Skt. *dhyāna,* Tib. *bsam-gtan*) and what it entails exposes its internal restrictiveness beyond a shadow of doubt. This is not to say that concentration is of little value.

What is required is an awareness of its scope and applicability. As an aspect of thought, concentration is *objectifying* thinking that, in a narrower sense, "picks out those features of world experience which are objectifiable and in some manner lend themselves to quantification and measurement" (Schrag 1969, 112). Indeed, objectification is necessary if ever one wants to achieve a goal and to control the means to this end. Hence, in a wider sense, concentration is teleologically oriented. This is to say that it aims straight at a recognized goal that is such that its value, sometime in the future, is stipulated now in the present. In this sense, it can be said to be prescriptive rather than open and determinative of its own dynamics and meaning. This teleological perspective is already evident from the Tibetan name given to the procedure of achieving the aim—*thar-pa'i lam,* which may be rendered as the "way (leading) to (a state of) liberatedness (from the bondage that is *saṃsāra*)." What this static end state specifically connotes depends on the level of a person's intellectual development or lack of it. An illustration is the current American obsession with "definitive" formulations, so characteristic of a culture geared to static modes of relating to the world. Even spirituality is a quantifiable and marketable commodity.

To my knowledge, the best account of what is involved in securing one's aim with the help of concentration is given by Rong-zom Chos-kyi bzang-po. He lists five procedures and assesses them critically and, in so doing, evinces psychological insights rarely met with in other authors or even contemporary professionals. He divides his presentation into two sections, one concerned with emphasis on stasis, the other with emphasis on process.

Emphasis on Stasis

The first approach. The procedure mentioned first in the attempt to find the preconceived and predetermined static goal of feeling liberated from the tribulations of *saṃsāra* involves a stabilization process (Tib. *bsam-gtan*). By this process, the six defects that mar the achievement of stability are eliminated and the ten obscurations that hide the desired goal from sight are dispelled. The first three of the six defects that vitiate the stabilization process are:

1. Being swayed by quickly changing or sluggishly moving moods and sentiments
2. Being overcome by drowsiness through the inner glow of the system's optimal excitation having become unavailable and through not being sustained by the lucency in the actual operation
3. Being hardened by the dogmatism concerning some permanent and unchanging "stuff" [15]

These three defects prevent inner calm from becoming effectual. The first two refer to what we would call the physical-physiological side of man, on the one hand, and the mental-psychic setting of the person, on the other hand. Each can be seen externally (as something "objective") and internally (as something experienceable, not necessarily "subjective"—a term which in the prevalent reductionistic climate has derogatory connotations). Thus, the first defect relating to the physical-physiological side of man is likened to a flame that cannot shine brightly when made to flutter by the wind. With respect to a living person the implication is that if he were to suppress his breathing (conceived of as the cosmic force termed "wind" integrated into the system of the living person) in order to achieve stability, he would die or come close to death.

The second defect relating to the mental-psychic setting of the person has to do with the influx of novelty, which can be very upsetting. Therefore, the attempt to restrict or prevent new ideas from entering the established "set" seems to be a legitimate procedure and is even encouraged in social and political contexts. However, if one were to prevent the emergence of novelty as it comes from within the self-organizing dynamics of a system, the very system might be destroyed or be brought close to destruction. Hence extrinsic forces that may be upsetting the process of self-organization should perhaps be prevented from exerting their influence, but not the forces that are intrinsic to the self-organization of the system, such as its thrust toward optimization and its sheer lucency.

The third defect is the ceaseless reiteration of one and the same topic, such a the Ātman-Brahman idea in the Indian context or the God-idea in theistic societies. It is like drops of water falling one after the other in the same spot. This may be alright for a single topic, but quite ineffectual and even obstructing with respect to the many topics found in life. We might paraphrase Rong-zom Chos-kyi bzang-po's insight by saying that a man's life is like a full orchestra, not just a single instrument.

A further set of three defects, the nature of which is to obscure a wider perspective rather than directly inhibiting the achievement of inner calm, are:

4. A blockage through compulsive attachment to any given content in the stabilization process
5. Loss (of cognitive freshness) through adopting a one-sided rationalistic viewpoint oscillating between judgments of existence and nonexistence
6. "Running around in circles" due to the intellectual horizon having become narrowed down[16]

The first defect means that the achievement of the goal of feeling liberated is blocked and even hidden from sight, because one cannot get rid of the compulsive attachment to whatever comes up as a topic of and in the stabilization process. This results from a lack of the critical acumen that understands that ideas have no ontic status in themselves.

The second defect means that the system's originary awareness (Tib. *yes-shes*) [17] declines and becomes obscured through the individual's incomprehension of the dynamic connectedness of all the processes that constitute reality. This prompts him to adopt extremist views of existence or nonexistence with respect to the way he thinks about his reality.

The third defect means that an individual, because of the limited range of his critical acumen as developed by listening and, hopefully, learning from and thinking about what he has heard, does not know what to concentrate on. Just like a bird kept in a dark place, his mind runs around in circles and succumbs to defeat.

Although these three defects are basically obscurations of critical acumen, in effect they are obstacles preventing or delaying the occurrence of inner calm and wider perspective. Therefore, because of the great damage they do, they are included in what is termed the six defects of the stabilization process.

In connection with the defect of being swayed by quickly changing or sluggishly moving moods and sentiments, which themselves are modes of that which marks the first step toward a division of the original unity of the life process, Rong-zom Chos-kyi bzang-po continues discussing these modes as they take on five different nuances. Each of these may be seen as a symmetry break setting the space-time stage for richly diversified thematizing operations in the field termed "mind" (Tib. *sems*).[18] Thus, (1) bifurcation (Tib. *rtog-pa*) is the division (in the original unity) introduced by the search for the concrete entity or substance (supposed to be) one's very being (Tib. *don-gyi dngos-po*); (2) the qualifying attributes (Tib. *mtshan-ma*) of this supposed substance constitute the division introduced by one's craving for such attributes and locking onto them; (3) movement (Tib. *rgyu-ba*) is the division introduced by flux; (4) feeling (Tib. *tshor-ba*) is the division introduced by sensing; and (5) moods and sentiments (Tib. *byung-tshor*) comprise the division introduced by the concentration of the constitutive forces of the organism.

Most important, however, is the distinction Rong-zom Chos-kyi bzang-po draws between the actual onset of this bifurcation with its symmetry breaks, and the concomitant locking onto that which becomes differentiated in this manner. Both aspects operate in a pronounced or a weak manner. Thus with an astute person (Tib. *mkhas-pa*) the onset is very pronounced, while the locking on is rather weak. This means that an astute person engages and attends to everything that can be thematized, but does not become addicted to the differentiations into substance and quality. By contrast, with a stupid person (Tib. *blun-po*), the onset is very weak, but the locking on is very pronounced. This means that he is unable to engage and attend to anything thematic but cannot divest himself of his addiction to his belief in the concreteness (substance) of any ideas he may have. Therefore, when it comes to cultivating that point at which the mind is poised before it sets out on a course of bifurcation, a mind which is marked by a weak onset of symmetry breaks but by a pronounced locking on to the differentiated content, does not constitute the way toward ever feeling liberated from the tribulations of *saṃsāra*. Such a condition of mind is actually an obscuration of the path to liberation because of its similarity to passing into an indistinct phase or state of mind that is such that it cannot be said to have or not to have any ideas. To connect with this path, one has to accustom oneself to attending to a mind that is marked by a pronounced onset of bifurcation but is weak in locking on to the differentiated contents. In this manner, by virtue of this weak locking on, even the pronounced onset eventually becomes weaker and weaker. When finally the mind has been divested of the above-mentioned five nuances of the bifurcation process, it becomes its own cognitive excitation, and when this unbifurcated cognitive excitation operates ceaselessly, what is meant by the formulation "seeing reality in its true nature" emerges.

With this "seeing reality in its true nature," the well-known Buddhist Eightfold Path begins, and it is for this reason that Rong-zom Chos-kyi bzang-po discusses the ten obscurations that have to be dispelled in the attempt to remedy the stagnation into which one has fallen. Actually, there are only nine obscurations, which in sets of three are distributed over the three most decisive phases of the path toward a definite teleologically conceived goal. The first decisive phase is the endeavor it is suitable for a man to make; but this is only too often impeded and obscured by

1. A fixation on some notion or other that in its rigidity prevents a person from giving up old ways and trying to find new ones, so that a person just sits there like a mouse in its hole
2. The path itself disappearing from sight, which leaves a person like an archer who tries to shoot an arrow at a target hidden from his view
3. An experience of a specific content in such brilliance that the sensory awareness is just captivated by it[19]

The second decisive phase is the in-depth appraisal of what ultimately constitutes the value of world and life, which is impeded and obscured by

4. A desire to have many cognitive experiences occurring in one's mental framework of conceptualizing operations

5. A desire to gain supernatural insights
6. A desire to display miraculous feats[20]

In these obscurations we can easily recognize an egocentricity geared for control. But as Rong-zom Chos-kyi bzang-po points out, it is through these obscurations that one misses out on what one would like, like a householder, who in his desire for butter milks many cows, but gets preoccupied with his enjoyment of their milk and curds and loses sight of the butter he intended to get.

Lastly, proper attention to what is at stake is impeded and obscured by

7. The notion of already having reached the highest level of understanding
8. Pride in one's opinionatedness
9. The demolition of others' viewpoints[21]

Regarding "proper attention to what is at stake," the original term means keeping one's goal as steady as possible before one's mind's eye. This means that one does not allow the message of the texts that deal with what is actually meant (as opposed to what is merely presented in a suggestive manner) and the advice of trustworthy and helpful persons to slip from one's mind. If one were to allow obscurations that can be dispelled to continue, one would go through life like kings or the sons of ministers, who swollen with their notions of power, simply do not heed the advice of trustworthy persons.

The tenth obscuration is of a more general nature and consists of the ten ways of devotion to the Buddhist texts: to copy them, look after the places where they are kept, preach or give them to others, listen to their exposition, read them, maintain them, discourse on them, intone them, ponder over them, and observe their lessons. Of course, there is nothing wrong with such activities, but they are not enough.

The second approach. The second approach to an already preconceived goal, too, does not go beyond the structure-oriented view that characterized the search by means of a process of stabilization that we have just described. But in this second approach, attention shifts from the "objective" defects of the process to recognizable behavioral features that are "subjectively" felt and described in terms having moral implications. This shift also marks a departure from mere concentration (Tib. *bsam-gtan*) on some particular topic to the in-depth appraisal (Tib. *ting-nge-'dzin*) of one's embeddedness in a world that is both within and outside oneself. This appraisal nevertheless remains normative-prescriptive, inasmuch as it continues the notion of a fixed goal to be reached through adaptive, controllable variables. An overview is given in the discussion of five "evils" counteracted by eight "activities" felt as aids in the attempt to combat the evils.[22]

The five evils are: (1) laziness (Tib. *le-lo*) in the specific sense of neglecting the counsel of trustworthy persons (a trustworthy person being one who has experienced for himself what he is talking about); (2) forgetfulness (Tib. *dmigs-pa brjed-pa*), connoting primarily a lack of orderly thinking, characterized, among other features, by inability to keep attention on anything that may have been heard; (3) depression and elation (Tib. *zhum-rgod*), which prevent a person from attending to and familiarizing himself with what is life's true value and meaning. These "evils" are closely related to (4) lack of motivation (Tib. *mngon-par 'du mi byed-pa*) in the sense of lack of directedness toward constructive action; and (5) overmotivation (Tib. *mngon-par 'du-byed-pa*) in the sense of overabundance of activity (which may not necessarily be constructive). Both these "evils" are obstacles to the achievement of a synthesis of inner calm and wider perspective.

It seems that laziness was diagnosed as the most conspicuous and also most deeply ingrained behavioral trait, because it alone needs four counteragents to bring it under control. These are: (1) confidence (Tib. *dad-pa*), (2) willingness to do something (Tib. *'dun-pa*), (3) diligence (Tib. *brtson-'grus*), and (4) sustained refinement (Tib. *shin-tu sbyangs-pa*). Forgetfulness is countered by (5) inspection (Tib. *dran-pa*), which means keeping the topic of one's interest as steadily as possible before the mind's eye. It is more than mere memory and its cultivation, because in the search for the goal one also wants to *learn more* about its qualities and its value in one's life. Depression and elation are countered by (6) cognitive alertness (Tib. *shes-bzhin*), which involves both the capacity to keep the object of concern as steadily as possible before the mind's eye and the application of one's critical acumen. Cognitive alertness as the counteragent means that it is inappropriate to go to extremes in trying to motivate a person to snap out of his depression or in calming someone down when in his exuberance he is "like a drunk elephant trampling down trees and houses and destroying many living creatures." Lack of motivation is countered by (7) resolution. This can be brought about by interesting a person in something by encouraging him to make use of his capacity for orderly thought involving analysis and logical reasoning (Tib. *bsam-pa*). Lastly, overmotivation is countered and dampened by (8) continual balancing (Tib. *btang-snyoms*), which in its initial phase is marked by depression and elation losing strength equally, with the result that the mind gradually moves in the direction of regaining its autonomy. This phase is felt as a parity of inner calm and wider perspective as a consequence of which no further efforts have to be made. The relationship between the evils that obstruct the attainment of the desired state of an in-depth experience or appraisal and their counteragents can be diagramed as in Figure 1.

FIGURE 1

OBSTACLES TO IN-DEPTH EXPERIENCES/APPRAISALS AND THEIR REMEDIAL COUNTERAGENTS

	the five "evils"	the eight counteragents
obstacles in trying for an in-depth experience	laziness	← confidence, willingness, diligence, sustained refinement
	forgetfulness	← inspection
obstacles to an in-depth experience →	depression and elation	← cognitive alertness
obstacles to an intensification of the in-depth experience	lack of motivation (to do anything when depression or elation have set in)	← resolution
	overmotivation (when depression or elation have subsided)	← balancing

In summing up this approach it may be pointed out that it reflects a control and dominance psychology in which emphasis is on keeping the object of inspection (Tib. *dran-pa*) as steady as possible, like keeping "a bird in a cage" or "a pot full of water so that it does not spill over," and also on cognitive alertness (Tib. *shes-bzhin*), which is like "a mahout who controls an elephant with his iron hook or knows how to chain him to a pole."[23]

Emphasis on Process

The third approach. Unlike the two previous approaches, which remained strictly confined within a structure-oriented and structure-dominated view and framework, this third one reflects the transition that took place from the strictly structure-oriented view to a more dynamic process-oriented view.[24] This approach is vividly described by the metaphors of catching a restless monkey, tying up a thievish cat, blocking all passages in an empty house, and then opening the treasure box. However, as we have noted before, this approach, in spite of the insights it provides into the working of the mind, also suffers from oversimplification and remains essentially thematic.

The fourth approach. This approach, too, is dominated by the idea of control, which is put to the test in six ways. The starting point for these control techniques is the following statement.

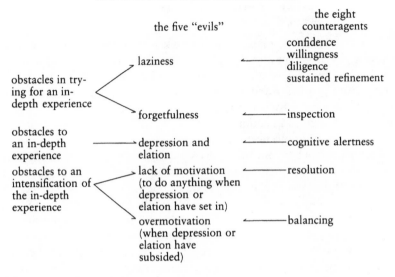

> Mind is similar to a flash of lightning, the wind, and a monkey.
> It is like the waves of the ocean.
> It is a swindler, and forever it delights in external objects.
> This mind, which is unstable and roaming about, must be disciplined.[25]

This verse is self-explanatory. The task is to come to grips with this protean phenomenon and discipline it by means of addressing and stabilizing it. There are, of course, many ways of doing this; but according to Rong-zom Chos-kyi bzang-po, they can all be subsumed under two methods: taking control by conforming to the prevalent character or characteristics of the mind in action; or taking control by restraining it or even reducing its activity to nothing.

Taking control by conforming to its prevalent character, or to any of its prevalent characteristics, means that, just as a flash of lightning is brilliant only for a fraction of a second, so one holds the mind in utmost clarity on its object of concentration only briefly and does not try to hang on longer. Similarly, one may allow the mind to proceed according to various styles, just as the wind blows from any direction: One may allow it to follow its whims like a monkey, taking up one thing and then discarding it for another; or let it move with its various thought constructions, like the ocean surging in its waves; or let it rest with the object of its desire, like a person who delights in any object he fancies.

Taking control by restraining the mind and reducing its activity to some near-nothing (the detection threshold in psychology) involves opposite procedures. None, however, can be said to actually overcome the prevailing dualism that bases itself on the claim that something is "good" while something else is "evil." Certainly, any repressive activity can only lead to stagnation, not to a recovery of creativity.

As to the above two methods of controlling mind by either conforming to any of its prevalent or manifest characteristics or by reducing its activity to some near-nothing, Rong-zom Chos-kyi bẓang-po makes the pertinent remark that no preference of one over the other is in order. To provide a suitable topic of concentration in conformity with the activity present, the manner in which the intending activity of mind proceeds in its construction of reality, the direction it goes in, and the intricacy of its patterns of involvement must all be taken into account. Eventually, the thematizing activity itself will lose its momentum, and in passing beyond the object of its concentration, will find no place where it may go further. This method specifically applies to those who, in general, are concerned with living their life on the basis of an inner calm.

The fifth approach. This method constitutes an in-depth appraisal of the dynamics of the living organism as summed up in the code terms "body" (Tib. *lus*), "mind" (Tib. *sems*), and "deity" (Tib. *lha*).[26] Actually this concentration technique is a transformatory vision presented in the so-called "lower" tantras.[27]

Here "body" is understood as a breathing organism, where the radiation of the organism's constitutive energies is understood as the "breathing." These constitutive energies are named after their "effects": earth (Tib. *sa,* solidification/solidity), water (Tib. *chu,* cohesion), fire (Tib. *me,* temperature), wind/air (Tib. *rlung,* motility), and space (Tib. *nam-mkha'*). The Buddhist always knew space to be an opening-up and simultaneously a force that constrains. Only now, after the advent of non-Euclidean geometry, have we in the West come to understand space other than as a passive nothingness or an empty container.

It seems that the Buddhists had an inkling of the fact that what once was pure radiation then emerges as matter-dominated field factors that are the organism's energetic potential (Tib. *khams*). With various degrees of gravity, they affect the primary "purity" (Tib. *dvangs-ma*) through some "pollution" (Tib. *snyigs-ma*). Moreover, each such field factor "incorporates" the others so that they present a network of interpenetrating forces that shape each other in their operation and are arranged in a combinational hierarchy (Guenther 1988, 42f.).[28] Since their dynamics was felt as that to which we refer as "breathing," breathing itself reflects the quality of the respective field factors. These we also then describe using such metaphors as labored breathing, gentle breathing, hot breathing, and so on. To this domain of felt dynamics also belong their imaged qualities, described in terms of color and range. All this reemphasizes the fact that the body is not an inert tool but a process in which the physical and the psychic are integrated and integral aspects.

Attention to the body in its breathing operation(s) is not meant, as some enthusiasts of breath control claim, to interfere with these operations, but to help the practitioner enter into a state that is not marked by mental and physical stress. Out of this "calm" throbbing with life, he may gain a wider perspective. Breathing rhythmically has its effects on a person's thought processes. Only inner calm and a wider perspective can make a person invulnerable to such reductionistic and concretistic views as solipsism, substantialism, and hedonism/puritanism.

Let us now consider "mind." Breathing as a process of a living body is said to be the carrier of the mind. It is tempting to speak of the body as the "hardware" and of the mind with its multiple organizational dynamics as the "software"; but this analogy, in spite of a certain accuracy, should not be carried too far. The more important point to note is that mind is immanent in the system by virtue of being spread out over and carried about and around in the interconnected and interactional field components of the system. As such it presents the organizing principle in its complementarity to the conservative principle, which is exemplified by the body.

It is further stated concerning this organizing principle mind, which is "carried" by the system's motility (Tib. *rlung*) and emerges from space (Tib. *nam-mkha'*) as a field factor, that this mind itself (1) operates as a lighting up that is a felt presence (Tib. *snang-ba*), that it manifests (2) as an inflationary dilation (Tib. *rlom-sems*), and (3) as a thematically oriented cognition in terms of particular existents (Tib. *dngos-po so-sor rnam-par rig-pa*). It is such that (1) its lighting up in a way that is a felt presence has as its objective and cognitive domain the totality of ideas and meanings, (2) its inflationary dilation turns (the unobjectifiability of) pure experience into its objective and cognitive domain, and (3) as a thematically oriented cognition in terms of particular existents, it has as its objective and cognitive domain the organization of the external and internal into a coherent reality made up of the subject-object dichotomy.[29]

Attention to mind and getting hold of it by means of inspection and cognitive alertness reveals it to be a process phenomenon. This awareness enables a person to discard such reductionistic views as presented by egological assumptions, eternalistic claims, and substantialistic dogmas.

The code term "deity" points to an aspect in experience that has not yet been mentioned in this context, yet is found nowhere else than in what has been discussed as body and mind. Specifically, "deity" refers to the unquestionable existentiality of the experiencer, not in a dualistic manner as interpreted by representational, objectifying thinking geared to the human individual's finiteness, but as it is experienced as a meaningful presence. This meaningfulness impresses itself on us through possibly, though not necessarily, objectifiable figures that vitalize feelings and perceptions that thereby tend to reach beyond themselves so as to become open to the very wonder and mystery of Being. Thus while mind (Tib. *sems*) refers to the finite and quantitatively accessible, it is the originary awareness (Tib. *ye-shes*)[30] with all its nuances that becomes appreciative of the qualitative through the symbol called "deity." As both the expression and the expressed of an originary awareness, the felt and imaged presence of "deity" has a gestalt (Tib. *sku*) commensurate with the intellectual/spiritual needs of those to be guided, whose collective self-image it presents. It expresses itself also in originative speech (Tib. *gsung*), which speaks *of* that which is meaningful, not *about* that which may well be merely trivial. And lastly, its cognitive dynamics (Tib. *thugs*) expresses itself in its resonance with the whole of Being, which in our individual finiteness shows up and is felt as compassion.

This concentrative technique to achieve a state of feeling liberated from the oppressiveness of the quantifiable and suffocatingly concrete, summed up in the three "codings" of body, mind, and deity is meant for the beginner in his search for the lost dimension of pure experience. Its "program," in the words of Rong-zom Chos-kyi bzang-po, is: "This body (of ours in its presentational) immediacy (*lus-nyid*) is an aspect of mind; mind as such (*sems-kyi rang-bzhin*) is deity."[31]

Here no dualistic opposition seems any longer to obtain, but this apparently nondualistic state remains a fragile achievement and easily collapses. This is due to the fact that this achievement is merely state-specific, the state of one's mind (Tib. *sems*) as a lowered version of the total system's optimally cognitive intensity (Tib. *rig-pa*). Therefore, all these methods, however appealing they seem to be (particularly the last-mentioned method, in which the human mind falls together with the divine) merely bring about, in true control-oriented fashion, an amelioration of a prevailing situation felt to be intolerable. But they fall short of the creativity that unfolds in open evolution. In the Tibetan text called the *Klong drug-pa* it has been clearly stated:

> What preposterous nonsense (to claim that)
> One's mind as such (*rang-sems*), in which there is no turbidness,
> and
> One's ec-static cognitive intensity in its auto-excitation (*rang-rig*),
> in which no division obtains, are alike![32]

MENTALISTIC-CREATIVE CONTEMPLATION

The Bodhisattva Approach

The above assessment of what is referred to by the Sanskrit technical term *dhyāna*, vaguely rendered and popularly promulgated as "meditation," has shown that it basically describes a process of concentration and stabilization. Its applicability is limited and even limiting, because it remains within the confines of the thematizing and representational operations of the system's (a human being's) total potential. Hence to put it bluntly, such so-called meditation is growth-inhibiting rather than growth-enhancing.

This is even more the case when related attempts to break away from those influences that were felt to be polluting and to be keeping the individual on a low, nonoptimal level in his dealing with his life-world, reflect a mechanistic approach. Such an approach can take two forms. One is applying "emptying" techniques of sensory deprivation and concentration to a, or even the, void. The other is comprised of "filling" techniques of placing one's sensory awareness into specific parts of the body or its postures and movements and then physically living out this dispersed consciousness.

Whatever secondary interpretation one may put on what is described as *dhyāna*, the idea of control that is "geared to stability and to the optimization of specific parameters under a given set of fixed constraints" (Jantsch 1975, 283) is paramount. A corollary to this restrictiveness is the conception of the "way" as a linear progression towards an already preestablished goal where all life processes come to a standstill.

Yet there is another dimension to the way if it is understood as a self-transcending process in the direction of an openness in which the system's potential can unfold. This changing and changed perspective, from a static order (Hinayana) to a dynamic, evolutionary one, is noticeable in the Mahayana. Mahayana is more than just the two major philosophical systems, the Yogācāra and the Madhyamaka, the development of which coincided with the emergence of a new social order. In particular, it was the Yogācāra teachings, with their emphasis on lived experience and their reinterpretation of mind and/or consciousness as a process, that gave rise to the idea of three holonomic modes of experiencing.[33] (The term "holonomic" is derived from the Greek words *holos,* meaning "whole," "entire"; and *nomos,* meaning "law," "norm." Thus holonomic describes a mode in which the whole sets the norm). These holonomic modes of experiencing not only form a coordinated hierarchy but also reflect the complementarity between the visionary and the perceptual on one level, as well as the complementarity between the overall interpretive and the specific interpretive on another level. This is diagramed in Figure 2.

The new social order with its fresh outlook is presented by and centered in the bodhisattva, who is not merely a mythological figure, as nineteenth century positivism (which is still rampant in the academic world) wanted to make us believe. Rather, he or she is an individual actively engaged in giving form to a vision. It is true, the Sanskrit term *bodhisattva* does not reveal anything of the dynamic character and existential import of either *bodhi* or *sattva*. But all this is implied by its Tibetan rendering *byang-chub sems-dpa'*. As we glean from the indigenous Tibetan texts and, in particular, from the writings of Rong-zom Chos-kyi bzang-po (one of the few Tibetans who actually knew Sanskrit and did not merely bandy about Sanskrit terms), *bodhi* (rendered as *byang-chub*) connotes "the ultimate depletion of all impurities and the resultant transparency of Being as well as the irrefutable understanding and comprehension of reality"; and *sattva* (rendered as *sems-dpa'*) means "desire," "courage," "a firm and unbending intention," "a sentient being" (in the sense of someone having a mind for the pellucidity implied by the Tibetan term *byang-chub*).[34]

The emphasis on cleansing (*byang*) as a means to setting free the innate potential so that it can find its own optimal level (*chub*) rather than on controlling and restraining it within artificial limits, necessitated a reinterpretation of the old terms. This is borne out by the reassessment of the

FIGURE 2

The holistic mode (*yongs-su grub-pa*, *parinişpanna*) → The invariance of pure experience (*sems-nyid 'gyur-med*) that in its pure dynamics (*phyin-ci ma-log-pa*) is the gestaltism of its meaningfulness (*chos-sku*).

The relational mode (*gzhan-dbang*, *paratantra*) → The pure relational (*dag-pa*): visionary experiences of "worlds" in transfiguration, the "buddha realms."
→ The impure relational (*ma-dag-pa*): ordinary experiences of things like rocks, stones, etc.

The conceptual mode (*kun-brtags*, *parikalpita*) → The interpretive-conceptual (*rnam-grangs-pa*): ascribes thingness to one's ordinary experiences.
→ The categorizing-conceptual (*mtshan-nyid chad-pa*): ascribes the categories of universals and particulars to "things."

According to Klong-chen rab-'byams-pa, *Sems-nyid ngal-gso*, p. 213.

Sanskrit term *dhyāna* (Tib. *bsam-gtan*), which on the level of early Buddhism implied something static, while on the level of the bodhisattva, it is used in a dynamic context that intimates a hierarchical organization of levels of experience. The transition from the restrictive-control level to the opening-up level where creativity is given a chance, is marked by the dissolution of the boundaries between subject (as controller) and object (as the controlled). It constitutes a release from the imprisonment of being merely the center of feedback relationships. Still, the bodhisattva level is merely a phase or aspect of the total evolutionary process of what we like to call mind. In the text called the *Rig-pa rang-shar*, this phase character of the bodhisattva level (and of bodhisattva-level "meditation") is clearly, though very concisely, stated:

> Bodhisattva meditation is such that
> The mind does not exert subjective control.
> (Rather, this meditation) originates by its own dynamics.
> By habituating (oneself to this creative process, it itself acquires
> new dimensions of its) autonomy and (even)

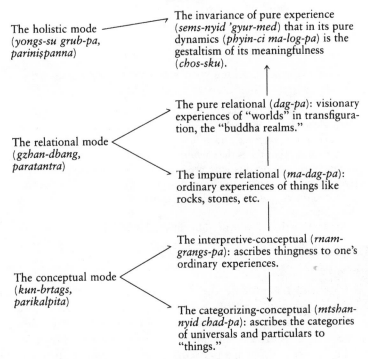

Preoccupation with food is eliminated.[35]
It is the life style of those who live on (higher spiritual) levels.
In a most natural manner, thematic constructions do not interfere;
But even this "meditation" is unable to disclose Being's design
process.[36]

By way of explication Klong-chen rab-'byams-pa's words, which can hardly be surpassed in their clarity, may be adduced:

> Meditation that reflects its own dynamics is such that its state of nondividedness occurs spontaneously and on its own; it is merely (a way of) putting physical and verbal movements to rest.
>
> Meditation that takes the (meditator's) existential concreteness as its reference experiments with a perspective that sees the subtle and gross pollutants as not being something in themselves, and thus is an aid in countering their felt presence; but this is merely suppressing the pollutants.
>
> Meditation that (is practiced by those who find themselves) on the higher spiritual levels is an in-depth appraisal of the scope of that particular level; it is merely a clean-up of the propensities of these levels.[37]

It is now possible to state the difference between enforced stability through imposition of controls on the mind, as attempted by ordinary persons, and the autopoietic regimes as they evolve in the bodhisattva. Autopoietic regimes are globally stable, but never static and resting structures. They are expressive of a particular individuality within an environment comprising its cognitive domain. There is a multitude of such cognitive domains, technically referred to as "spiritual levels," falling into a hierarchical order in such a way that each higher level includes all lower levels. Hence each level brings new gestalt qualities of thought and specific ordering principles into play and thereby establishes a human individual as a creative being.

In this context Klong-chen rab-'byams-pa points to two related phenomena in the process called meditation. The one that is said to occur by itself has as its basis some subliminal movement that is present even if sensory awareness has withdrawn from its involvement with its domain of operation but has not become separated from everyday reality:

> This meditation that comes by itself may originate in all living beings from that subliminal movement that is still present when the cognitive capacity has withdrawn into its own recesses. It is there in the eye of a person straightening an arrow or in the eyes of a hare and a falcon sleeping in its lair or nest. In brief, it is present at all times when the sensory awareness has withdrawn into its own recesses.[38]

The other phenomenon is an imaginative imaging process that has contributed to the tremendous wealth of art forms found in the Mahayana.

Through works of art, the mystery of life is put into a semantic context that invites the contemplator into a relationship that is not fixed but is dynamic and allows new meanings to occur. Hans-Georg Gadamer (1977) compares this relationship to play or conversation and shows how the fluidity of this relationship allows great works of art to speak to us over centuries and let us find new meanings. Of this imaginative process Klong-chen rab-'byams-pa says: "This imaginative meditation covers everything that is referred to by (technical terms of) "developing phase" and "fulfilling phase"—(visualizing and relishing the presence of) a "god" (*lha*), regardless of whether conceptual constructs are made use of or not—and is the in-depth appraisal of a meditative process that experiments with what the subjective mind has intended."[39]

Although we may speak of higher levels reached in the course of the mind's development, the term "higher" should not be taken too literally as merely indicating a linear ascent. Rather it must be understood as also pointing to an expansion into dimensions of openness that are felt to be an enrichment because the system's potential is given a wider scope to unfold. The bodhisattva meditation with its level-specific phases of stability sets up is own norms or programs to ensure the optimization of the ongoing process. The implication is that each level or dimension is at the same time sender and receiver of information. This circularity, which is characteristic of all dynamic systems and, specifically, cognitive processes, occurs in an open and opening manner and is technically known as "emancipation path" (Tib. *grol-lam*).[40] Basically it is a reorientation program and process involving the system in its totality. The information is thoroughly pragmatic in that it generates more pragmatic information and thus sets up new autopoietic levels that have to cope by themselves with their structural problems initiated by an increased influx of information.

To illustrate this circularity of live processes, let us assume that the system sends out a message to the effect that something has to be done about the given situation in its totality. By doing so it makes the receiver of the message change from staying passive (and eventually approaching an equilibrium state in which all life has come to a standstill) into becoming active in doing something about the situation. Since the sending and receiving of the message occurs within the same structural context (the living system), it follows that the sender, too, is changed in the sense that it is forever kept busy in an ever changing semantic and pragmatic context.

Though constituting stability phases, there is little in the bodhisattva meditation that is rigid or solid. It is both autopoietically and autocatalytically operative. Autopoietically it regulates itself in such a way that the integrity of its structure, which nevertheless remains fluid, is maintained; while autocatalytically it reinforces its inherent dynamics so as to force it into a new dimension of openness. This dual character is well expressed by Rong-zom Chos-kyi bzang-po, who speaks of "a stability phase expelling the stability phase's impediments."

Here, the integrity of the structure is coded as "inner calm" and its evolutionary process character as "wider perspective." There are three impediments to each aspect, all of which cast a shadow on the system's move toward the optimization that is inherent in the process itself. Thus:

> To become upset by moods,
> To become dulled by lethargy, and
> To become rigid by immutability
> hamper inner calm;
> Blockage of the emancipation process by addictedness to idiosyncracies,
> Impairment of originary awareness by (the objectivistic fallacies of) existence and nonexistence, and
> A mind being duped and crushed by limited perceptivity
> hamper wider perspective.[41]

It would be quite erroneous to conceive of the inner calm in the bodhisattva context as a state that is merely undisturbed by thematizing operations and unaffected by emotional vagaries, or to conceive of the wider perspective as a mere blankness of the mind. This is what both features seem to present on the level of "ordinary persons who do not know better." Inner calm here is not some static state arrived at by concentrating on a particular object or idea to the exclusion and eventual blockage of the rest of the psychic potential. Rather inner calm is a dynamic force the creativity of which as wider perspective is experienced as providing the possibility of sensing, feeling, and appreciating life's dynamics in its depth and at its origin. Thus inner calm and wider perspective are expressions of the system's self-stabilization and self-organizing.

It is this autopoiesis that differentiates the bodhisattva meditation from the attempts on the part of "those who do not know better" to control by fixation. Hence the difference between these two stabilization procedures can be restated to show that the bodhisattva meditation is the total system's self-finding of optimal stability. It marks the ascendency of pure experience (Tib. *sems-nyid*) over thematizing mind (Tib. *sems*). The code terms for this procedure are "mind evolving into pellucidity and consummation" (Tib. *byang-chub-kyi sems*), "intrinsically valid reality" (Tib. *don-dam-pa'i bden-pa*), "self-existing originary awareness" (Tib. *rang-byung-gi ye-shes*), and "meaning-rich gestalt" (Tib. *chos-kyi sku*). These and other terms were used to highlight the paradox of there being nothing and yet at the same time a lucid presence.[42]

The total system's self-stabilization as a holistic and self-optimizing process is intuitively felt by the contemplator, who is more of a visionary than a mere observer, to be a presence within himself. It is felt to be understandable only by his becoming part of this process through directly experiencing it by tuning in to it. It is for this reason that, instead of the static term *dhyāna*, from now on the dynamic terms *yoga*, "tuning in," and *yogi*, "he who tunes in to life's dynamics," are used. The difference between *dhyāna* and *yoga* highlights an individual's two approaches to his basic predicament. One takes the direction of disengagement from the world, over and against which, in the best possible case, the subject stands bracketed as a poverty-stricken manipulator and controller. The other takes the direction of an understanding and interpretation of "world" as a setting of existential possibilities.

However, it is not enough to have a vision; the vision must be given form in order to be communicable. This means hard work on the part of the visionary (Skt. *yogi*, Tib. *rnal-'byor-pa*). It also means that there is no single "technique" to achieve this end, simply because the creative process develops its own norms as it moves along. The intuition involved is an "originary awareness" (Tib. *ye-shes*), which is not merely stored experience but a capacity to see in a truly holistic manner.

To this creative process Rong-zom Chos-kyi bzang-po refers in a cryptic aphorism the imagery of which is highly suggestive:

> Even after one has caught the good-for-nothing monkey,
> One (still) has to tie up the thievish cat;
> After one has demolished the empty house part by part,
> One (also) has to block the peep-holes and windows.
> When one then opens the king's treasury,
> (One finds that) all the above has for ever been a (process of)
> dissipative unfolding.[43]

He continues, giving a lengthy and highly technical account of each point in this aphorism. He says that "catching the good-for-nothing monkey" summarizes the necessity to constrain one's mind in its representational mode of thought, which picks out any feature in its world experience—which is made up of one's psychophysical complexity and the cognitive-experiential field in which it is installed—and turns it into an entity that is claimed to be something concretely and realistically given. But hardly has the mind done so when it loses interest in what it has picked out and looks for something else. This objectifying thinking is aptly compared with a monkey whose antics may be amusing to watch in a zoo but are a nuisance in an orderly household. Since one cannot get rid of objectifying-representational thinking because it is part of one's being, one can at least contain it as when one locks up a monkey in a cage to prevent it from wreaking havoc with one's belongings. Thus we can find some inner calm.

"Tying up the thievish cat" stresses the necessity to get a hold on all that pollutes one's thinking and perverts it into ideologies. These, as a rule, have a devastating effect on a person's life, perhaps without his noticing it until it is too late. Again the metaphor of a cat is most appropriate in this context. This animal moves about very quietly, stealthily and watchfully. Thus the metaphor of the cat may give us an idea of what "wider perspective" means.

The metaphorical expression "demolishing the empty house part by part" intimates the strategy of going beyond the limitations we impose on ourselves by means of the models of our inner and outer world. The metaphor is a devastating critique of any form of essentialism that constantly encroaches on one's vision. Demolishing the empty house as the last hiding place of a hypothetical ego is an opening and gaining of a wider perspective.

The metaphor of "blocking the peep-holes and windows" alludes to the five kinds of sensory perception and their being restrained from rushing about and lending a helping hand in the construction of a new (restrictive) model of reality. In their being checked, they provide a measure of inner calm.

Inner calm and wider perspective are inextricably interwoven, and to the extent that they have become effective in one's life, they are the key to "opening the king's treasury," the immense wealth that is in us and nowhere else. Ordinarily we may not be aware of this wealth and the possibilities it holds for a life that is worth living, yet this wealth present in us may well provide the impetus for our growing up. This seems to be the intent of a stanza quoted by Rong-zom Chos-kyi bzang-po in this context:

> Even if a precious shining lamp
> Has sunk into the mire of an ugly environment,
> Its lustre will shine (if exposed to the) sky
> By virtue of its property of being autoluminous.
> So also the precious mind as pure experience,
> Even if it has sunk into an ugly body in *saṃsāra,*
> Shines as critical acumen in the sky of meaningfulness
> By virtue of it being (Being's) sheer lucency itself.

Rong-zom Chos-kyi bzang-po's discussion of the bodhisattva's grappling with the problem "Man" is significant in many respects. It combines the old ideas such as inner calm and wider perspective, originally conceived in relation to a structure-oriented way of thinking and meditating (Skt. *dhyāna*), with the changing ideas in the emerging process-oriented way of thought (Skt. *yoga*) that leads to a holistic assessment of man as embedded in a universal dynamics. According to one's level of perceptivity, it allows the searching person to frame his ideas and visions in mythical-religious terms such as "bodhisattva" and "buddha," or in terms reflecting the dynamics of pure process-thinking such as autopoiesis, self-stabilization, self-organization, and dissipative structure.

HOLISTIC IMPARTING OF MEANING

On the bodhisattva level the individual enters into a direct relationship with the life forces in and around him. But this process still does not come up to what ultimately matters—to become and to be the "Mind of the Universe." By this phrase, however evocative it may sound, I attempt to convey the wider connotation of the Tibetan term *dgongs-pa,* which is the equivalent of the Sanskrit terms *abhisandhi,* "insinuation," and *abhiprāya,* "intent." It points to the metaphorical character of most of our activities: how we think, what we say, and what we do. Specifically, it directs attention to that dynamics that subtly regulates, structures, and defines our everyday realities. As Rong-zom Chos-kyi bzang-po noted long ago (eleventh century) persons in different cultural (socio-intellectual) settings (referred to in the Indian context as philosophy-influenced life styles such as Śrāvakas, Yogācāras, and Mādhyamikas), have different conceptions of what is real. Centuries later George Lakoff and Mark Johnson (1980, 146) stated that "different cultures have different conceptual systems" and that "what is real for an individual as a member of a culture is a product both of his social reality and of the way in which that shapes his experience of the physical world." In other words, the world in which we live is not only an appreciated world but also an intended world, whose meaning is the expression of an intelligence far deeper and more encompassing than our limited ("enframed," as Heidegger would say) consciousness or even our "highest" thoughts could ever hope to reduce to their own level. Because of its granting meaningfulness, which is not found outside the granting and which can never be derived from nor reduced to something else, we may (in the attempt to coin a manageable term rather than resorting to lengthy paraphrases, and in line with the many neologisms such as superforce, supergravity, superstring, and supersymmetry) speak of *dgongs-pa* as "superthought."[44] But in using this neologism we must free ourselves from all technical interpretations of thinking that have dominated Western thought since the time of Plato and Aristotle. They took thinking to be a *techne,* a method of observation in the service of doing, and specified it as *theoria.* From this Greek word, our terms "theory" and "theoretical" are derived. This restrictive definition is the basis of the rampant reductionism in Western intellectual life (scientific as well as humanistic). Within the framework of "theory" or representational thinking, whatever is deemed to be meaningful is such that the intended object functions "as the terminus of an objective signification, tested, classified, quantified, or in some sense funded" (Schrag 1969, 113). This, of course, has nothing to do with what is "intended" by *dgongs-pa,* which, to state it bluntly, is neither objectifying nor, for that reason, subjectivistic. It antedates, though not in a strictly temporal and sequential sense, the subject-object dichotomy.

Furthermore, this granting of meaningfulness as the very dynamics in what we have called and shall, for the time being, continue calling "superthought" occurs in utter *Gelassenheit*. This German term expresses a letting be that, however paradoxical it may sound, is the very practice of superthought. It involves a panoramic view (as from the peak of a mountain), an undulating contemplation (as the surging of the ocean), a going about one's affairs with an increased receptivity to stimuli (as in wonderment), all of them rooted in and climaxing in the ec-static intensity of the experience[45] that is visionary through and through.[46] Indeed, a mountain peak, an ocean, and the coming-to-presence of the breathtaking beauty of what we call "world" are moving symbols for the *Gelassenheit* through which the granting of meaningfulness by Being's (the whole's) superthought reaches into our lives. The words of David Michael Levin (1988, 238) concerning *Gelassenheit* are worth quoting:

> The ideal of *Gelassenheit* calls for a gaze which is relaxed, playful, gentle, caring; a gaze which moves freely, and with good feeling; a gaze which is alive with awareness; a gaze at peace with itself, not moved, at the deepest level of its motivation, by anxiety, phobia, defensiveness and aggression; a gaze which resists falling into patterns of seeing that are rigid, dogmatic, prejudiced, and stereotyping; a gaze which moves into the world bringing with it peace and respect, because it is rooted in, and issues from, a place of integrity and deep self-respect.[47]

This granting of meaningfulness in *Gelassenheit*, in brief, "superthought," is referred to by three Tibetan terms that do not denote separate or separable "entities" (the reductionistic fallacy), but describe a multifaceted dynamics. These three terms are:

1. *de-bzhin gshegs-pa'i dgongs-pa*
2. *bde-bar gshegs-pa'i dgongs-pa,* and
3. *sangs-rgyas-kyi dgongs-pa.*

de-bzhin gshegs-pa'i dgongs-pa

The admittedly difficult term *de-bzhin gshegs-pa* has been explicated most lucidly by Rong-zom Chos-kyi bzang-po, who deals with each element in this compound separately. He is forced into such a presentation, because his (like our) language does not admit of a holistic mode of expression due to the sequential arrangement of the words it uses. Thus he says of *de-bzhin-(nyid):*

> As to the term *de-bzhin gshegs-pa,* the term *de-bzhin-nyid* ("Being-in-its-beingness") has the meaning of understanding Being-in-its-beingness. That is to say, one understands, (and has done so) for ever, (Being's) beingness or one comes to an understanding of (Being's)

beingness through an incontrovertible originary awareness. The term (*de-bzhin/de-bzhin-nyid*) thus applies to both Being-in-its-beingness and the originary awareness (pervasive of it).[48]

Readers familiar with the beginnings of Western philosophy will easily recognize the similarity of Rong-zom Chos-kyi bzang-po's interpretation to the famous dictum of Parmenides, "For thinking and Being are the same" (quoted in Heidegger 1975/1984, 79).

Rong-zom Chos-kyi bzang-po continues by discussing the term *gshegs-pa* from the viewpoint of its self-structuring dynamics, ranging over three (hierarchically organized) levels, indicating that, at the danger of being misunderstood, we are what we think. His words are:

> (1) When out of some metal one makes a food plate, one turns it into something to get soiled; (2) when one makes out of the same metal a basin, one turns it into something for cleansing; and (3) when one makes out of the same metal a statue one turns it into something to be worshipped.
>
> In the same manner: (1) Those who in the domain of desires give in to their addictive preoccupation with the dichotomic notion of subject and object turn themselves into (beings caught in) samsaric situatedness. (2) Those who deal with the same dynamics in terms of (the indivisibility of existential) expertise and critical acumen lay the foundation for a world-engagement (as practiced) by those who tune in to (this dynamics) and turn themselves into (beings on) the way toward pellucidity and consummation (their bodhisattvic situatedness). And, (3) where the (indivisibility of existential) expertise and critical acumen comes to the fore (and takes over), this (very dynamics) turns into the realization of the triune character of Being as indestructible as a diamond.[49] Therefore, the way of those in whom (their spiritual darkness) has dissipated (*sangs*) and (the sheer lucency that has been theirs) has unfolded (*rgyas*) is not a matter of emancipation by virtue of the fact that the pollutants have been eliminated, but a matter of (Being's self-organizing) dynamics. This is what is meant by the term *de-bzhin gshegs-pa.*

That *de-bzhin gshegs-pa* is descriptive of a process, not of some static entity, has never been forgotten in the Tibetan tradition. Even so late an author as g.Yung-ston rdo-rje dpal bzang-po (1284–1365) is quite explicit about it.[50]

bde-bar gshegs-pa'i dgongs-pa

The second term, *bde-(bar) gshegs-(pa'i) dgongs-pa,* literally "the superthought that moves into or in the highest intensity of bliss," adds to the first term the idea of optimization, which is contrasted with what was traditionally so highly acclaimed as effecting this desired and desirable end, which is called "imaginative experimenting" (Tib. *sgom-pa*). In the

Nyi-zla kha-sbyor, which seems to be one of the earliest sources for this material, it is stated:

> This optimization superthought is of two kinds:
> Left to itself in its uncontrived (dynamics), moods and sentiments simply fade away;
> Looked at without (resorting to) an imaginative experimenting (that moves within the confines of predetermined objectives), the full measure of warmth is reached.[51]

In what seems to be basically a rephrasing of this statement, Klong-chen rab-'byams-pa adds a new insight that also shows how terms change in meaning when a different perspective is added. His words are: "By letting (this superthought) continue as it likes in its uncontrived (dynamics), moods and sentiments simply fade away without (the necessity of) having to resort to counteragents; and by letting it be what it is, without an imaginative experimenting (that moves within the confines of predetermined objectives), stabilization (*bsam-gtan*) is obtained."[52] Here he reinterprets the Tibetan term *bsam-gtan* (Skt. *dhyāna*), which we have seen to have been traditionally understood as a process of stabilizing the mind through concentration on a specific object or topic, as denoting the mind's most natural "state." This state actually is the mind's very dynamics in the sense that it programs its optimization as presenting an optimal stability that does not turn rigid. By contrast, imaginative experimenting (Tib. *sgom-pa,* Skt. *bhāvanā*) is understood as cutting itself off from this optimization dynamics and eventually channelling it into a dead end. This distinction between imaginative experimenting (*sgom-pa, bhāvanā*), stabilization/stability (*bsam-gtan, dhyāna*), and in-depth experiencing/appraisal (Tib. *ting-nge-'dzin,* Skt. *samādhi*) is based on a passage in the *sGra-thal-'gyur-ba*:

> The end effect of imaginative experimenting (*bsgoms-pa*) is to cut off (all) external and internal movements
> In the mind that has been steadied;
> It is the cessation of the dichotomic movement into subject and object.
> That which has come from (the system's) settledness in itself[53] is to be termed stabilization/stability proper (*bsam-gtan*).
> Imaginative experimentation (*sgom*) (involving the imaging of the organism's) development lines its motility, and the information input (that organizes the whole process)[54]
> As well as the vital centers[55] in the physical body and (attention to alternations between) establishing some objective reference and then turning it into some nothing[56]
> Belongs to the domain of desires.
> (The experience of) the hues and colors of morphemic phonemes as well as

Their progression and retrogression in formative modulations
Are said to be in-depth appraisals (*ting-nge-'dzin*).[57]
Uncontrived self-settledness is the abidingness (of Being) and,
Since there occurs no transformation whatsoever (into something
else),
This is the superthought of those (in whom spiritual darkness has)
dissipated (*sangs*) and (Being's sheer lucency) unfolded
(*rgyas*).[58]

Before discussing the third aspect of the triune superthought (Tib. *dgongs-pa*), intimated in the last line of the above quotation, the dual character of the second aspect, the optimization superthought, needs a few words of explanation. To the extent that it is "left to itself," it is indistinguishable from the Being-in-its-beingness superthought; and to the extent that it is "not interfered with by imaginative experimenting that deals with a predetermined objective," it remains optimization as the dynamic aspect of Being-in-its-beingness.

sangs-rgyas-kyi dgongs-pa

It will be remembered that in the discussion of the meaning of the Sanskrit term *buddha* and its Tibetan rendering *sangs-rgyas* it was pointed out that these terms were descriptions of a process of becoming and being spiritually awake (*buddha*) or of darkness dissipating (*sangs*) and light unfolding (*rgyas*). This is similar to what some physicists nowadays call a dissipative structure. But this process is not so much a coming to an end; rather it remains an ongoing "thinking."

We are now in a position to understand the triune character of the superthought. As (1) Being-in-its-beingness thinking, it "thinks" *its* being in terms of a holistic imparting of meaning. As such, it has ontological implications. As (2) optimization thinking, it "thinks" *its* optimization out of the whole of which it is a part. As such, it has value-perception implications. And as (3) a dissipative-unfolding thinking, it "thinks" *its* linking backward to its source. As such, it has experiential implications.

Not only does this superthought have a triune dynamics, the whole of Buddhist concentration or contemplation or meditation (whichever term one prefers since there is no consensus in Western presentations, which are a motley of Hinduist and Buddhist notions derived from popular writings)[59] presents a triune hierarchic order in which there is an ever widening opening at the top. At the bottom level is what is assessed as "objectivistic-reductionistic concentration," the hobby of those who do not know better—ordinary, mostly gullible, persons and children (the Sanskrit term *bāla* and its Tibetan equivalent *byis-pa,* used with reference to this level, mean both sorts). This level reflects a dominance psychology that focuses (Skt. *dhyāna*) on an impersonal "it." It remains largely ineffectual and not only lets the individual remain stagnant but even removes him from the scene. The next higher level, to which few grow up, is the bodhisattva world-engagement, by which the individual tunes in (Skt. *yoga*) to the forces working in and through him. Here feelings as understood by Suzanne K. Langer[60] as well as imagination play a significant role. The individual becomes alive and is "on the way." Crowning these levels is the third and, as far as we can say from our low-level perspective, the highest one, the level of the holistic meaning-imparting superthought (Tib. *dgongs-pa*). In the total (fully integrated) individual, these levels act in a coordinated manner.

6 THE WAY *The Earlier View I*

INTRODUCTORY REMARKS

WITHIN THE HISTORY of Buddhist thought the idea of a way (Skt. *mārga, pratipad,* Tib. *lam*) has occupied a prominent place, not only as something that leads from one place to another, but also, and even more significantly, as being such that it has to be followed. The difference between structure-oriented thinking and process-oriented thinking is very much in evidence in the interpretation of the notion of the way. One can envisage those who were dominated by structure-oriented thinking spending their time agonizing over the creation of a model of the way and losing sight of its inherent dynamic quality and of the main issue.

Inasmuch as, generally speaking, the way is seen to lead a person out of samsara to nirvana, the assessment of what is meant by samsara and nirvana becomes an immediate problem. Although both terms are nouns that are naively assumed to stand for certain things, they are essentially descriptions of specific experiences. Samsara, in particular, describes mankind's ongoing activity of constructing a rough draft of reality out of the varied elements of experience, which as a generalized system structures his attitudes and valuations. It is therefore aptly called "that which has been constructed" (Skt. *saṃskṛta*). It is, furthermore, the nature of any construction that it is always on the verge of collapse and thus prompts the individual to engage in further constructions to prop up his "original" fragile construction. This has the effect of getting the individual frantically running around in a maze of his own making.

By contrast, nirvana is described as "not being something that has been constructed" (Skt. *asaṃskrta*), as being "calm" (Skt. *śānta*), "unborn" (Skt. *ajāta*), "without origination" (Skt. *anutpāda*), "The cessation (Skt. *nirodha*) and nonexistence (Skt. *abhāva*) of whatever is frustrating and unbalancing," to mention only a few descriptive terms. As has happened so often, a mere linguistic expression has given rise to a "metaphysical" problem. The descriptive phrase, "there exists something that has not been born"[1] contains both an affirmative and a negative element. The Sarvāstivādins-Vaibhāṣikas selected the existentially affirmative part and interpreted nirvana as denoting an entity in which there was nothing of the pollutants and other activities, and which like a dam, blocked their continuation.[2] The Sautrāntikas considered nirvana as a "mere nonexistence (Skt. *abhāvamātra*) of whatever is frustrating and pollutant" and as the "nonemergence" (Skt. *aprādurbhāva*) of further frustrations.[3] They compared nirvana with a flame that has gone out, thus conceiving of it as the end phase of a process rather than as an immutable substance. The aspect of their assessment of nirvana that comes close to process-oriented thinking was, of course, a critique directed against the "thing" and "substance" conception of the Sarvāstivādins-Vaibhāṣikas. Here they made it clear that descriptions of a thing are not the thing itself. This was the case when, in the wake of their critique, the Sautrāntikas developed a solidified conception of nirvana as nonexistence that as a logical construct was on the same level as existence. With respect to the way, this means that it leads from one form of existence (existentially affirmative) to another form of existence (existentially negative). Not only does this reduce the way to an item within the thematic framework, it is even logically inconsistent with the claim that the way steers a middle course (Skt. *madhyama*) between the extremes of existence and nonexistence.

The trend to reduce dynamic forms of experience to static categories of thought and thereby to restrict the very life of man's mental-spiritual dimension gives preference and prominence to that operation of mind that is involved in, and concerned with, logical deductions. These are always linear and partial, because they isolate a single aspect of reality from the rest of it and, by their very nature, are of little help in understanding the context of human existence. Certainly, the existential problem of man is not solved by clinging to one or another interpretation of it or by wavering between one or another, as is, for instance, done by Buddhaghosa, who in his *Aṭṭhāsalinī*,[4] accepted the Sautrāntika interpretation of nirvana, while in his *Visuddhimagga*,[5] he criticizes the Sautrāntikas and opts for the existence theory of the Sarvāstivādins-Vaibhāṣikas.

It is the merit of the logicians, most of them belonging to the Mādhyamika persuasion, to have made it abundantly clear that the logical construct "samsara" is on the same level as the logical construct "nirvana," and that neither can be said to be superior to the other. Thus Nāgārjuna states:

> There is not the slightest difference between (the logical construct)
> samsara and (the logical construct) nirvana;
> Neither is there the slightest difference between (the logical
> construct) nirvana and (the logical construct) samsara.
> The perimeter of nirvana is also the perimeter of samsara,
> In between them not the slightest shade of difference is found.[6]

This very diction makes it clear that Nāgārjuna[7] was primarily thinking in static terms. the impact he had on later Mādhyamika thinkers was such that, because of their commitment to a rational approach to the problems of perception and inquiry with its organizing principle of logic, they failed in gaining a holistic understanding of a human being's living and lived reality. As a matter of fact, the Mādhyamika philosophers in general, and the Prāsangika faction in particular, developed out of the logical climate prevalent in India and ultimately became fossilized in the sterility of their own logical reductionism. That is not to say that they were not aware of the larger issues, but they prevented themselves from dealing with the rich flow of experience by using the blinkers of logical exclusiveness. This awareness that there was more to nirvana than some simplistic reduction is evident, for instance, in the statement by Candrakīrti, a staunch follower of Nāgārjuna, that "the end of indulging in making judgments in terms of existence and nonexistence is said to be nirvana."[8] Candrakīrti was also aware of the fact that the representational operations of the mind move in a circle and never come close to that which really matters: "Any position breeds a counterposition, and neither is valid in itself."[9]

The tacit acknowledgment that there is more to life than what some facile reductionism wants to make of it can be found in the qualification of that which ultimately matters—nirvana, for want of a better term—as nonlocalized (Skt. *apratiṣṭhita*).

While it may be of importance to have an idea of what to expect at the end of one's journey, this very emphasis on the "end" makes for a static conception of the world and tells us little about the way itself. Therefore, the great Indian Mahāsiddha Saraha also dismisses the quibbling about the nature of the end—whether it is a particular existent or a particular nonexistent, or whether the whole can be reduced to either postulate—with the scathing remark:

> Those who postulate particular existents are stupid like cattle,
> But those who postulate particular nonexistents are stupider than these.[10]

One last point. As Rong-com Chos-kyi bzang-po noted long ago, different cultural (socio-intellectual) settings, which in the Indian context comprise philosophy-influenced life styles such as the Śrāvakas, Yogācāras, and Mādhyamikas, have different conceptions of what is real.[11] The implication, hard to swallow for any fundamentalist, neo-Buddhist or otherwise, is that there are *many* ways. This has been bluntly expressed in modern times by Friedrich Nietzsche. "This is *my* way; where is yours?—Thus I answered those who asked me 'the way.' For *the* way—that does not exist."

THE THERAVĀDA CONCEPTION OF THE WAY

The Theravādins (followers of the teachings of the Elders), who started as a splinter group during the intellectual upheaval in the early period after the historical Buddha's demise, which eventually led to the rift between Hinayana and Mahayana, claim to have preserved the "original" teaching. Because of the doctrinal squabbles that took place within this school, this claim cannot be regarded as valid. Nonetheless, it is with the

Theravādins that we already find the basic ideas that were developed in course of the history of Buddhist thought and are the basis of its richness.

Rather than reducing the way to the objectivistic, mechanistic conception of it and seeing it as an inert link between two fixed points, they conceived of it as a process of exploration in which the individual reflects on his own place and movement in his life-world as well as on his responsibility toward it.

The Theravādins conceived of the way as comprising four stages, each of which was called a way.

The stream-enterer. The first stage is described as "entering the stream" (Skt. *srota-āpatti,* Pali *sotāpatti*), the stream that will carry the individual along on its current to distant nirvana. This stage is prompted by a vision that presents a possibility of what the individual might become. Therefore, this stage is tied to the process of seeing (Pali *dassana*), which developed later into a "way of seeing" (Skt. *darśanamārga*). But this seeing is more like a glimpse than an effective seeing. Nonetheless, this glimpse already brings about a change in the perceiver.[12] He is now looking for that which, though within him, is beyond the ordinary and commonplace. He no longer is a specimen of the standardized mass-man (Skt. *bāla, pṛthagjana*), but is of the fold (Skt. *gotra*) of the creators of culture.

However, in order to be effective and to be communicable, a vision must be given form. This constitutes the creative act that combines vision and hard work. It comprises three further stages which in terms of the individual are:

the once-returner (Skt. *sakṛdāgāmin,* Pali *sakadāgāmi*)
the never-returner (Skt. *anāgāmin,* Pali *anāgāmi*)
the arhant (Skt. *arhant,* Pali *araha*)

These three stages are related to and summed up by what has been termed "the way of concentrating on and cultivating the vision" (Skt. *bhāvanāmārga*), of which Buddhaghosa says: "'Concentrated cultivation' is spoken of with reference to these three remaining ways. This triad arises by virtue of paying the closest attention to what has been perceived on the first way. This triad does not see anything new that has not been seen previously, hence it is called 'paying the closest attention to what has been perceived.'"[13] This definition already emphasizes the predominance of thematizing thinking at the expense of a creative experimentation with the new perspective. Nonetheless, Buddhaghosa is aware of two possible directions in which this cultivation can move, hence the enigmatic designation "once-returner."

The once-returner. Being born of, or operating in, a healthy attitude may reconfirm us in a healthy attitude toward, and perspective on, life;

but it also may operate to set up a new level of awareness. Because of these two directions a distinction is made between a "mundane" (Pali *lokiya*) and a "supramundane" (Pali *lokuttara*) cultivation movement, the supramundane differing from the mundane only in virtue of its association with the above mentioned three stages.[14]

According to Buddhaghosa, a person's being on the supramundane way means crossing the world, crossing over it, standing above the triple world (Skt. *triloka*, comprising Kāmaloka, Rūpaloka, Arūpyaloka) after having left it far behind. And in setting up and strengthening the stabilization-concentration process (Skt. *dhyāna*), this cultivation leads a person out of the mundane; or, it is through this cultivation that he gets out of the vicious circle of birth and death. For it is through this operation that a person (1) comes to understand the frustration inherent in, and constitutive of, samsara, as well as (2) the origin of this frustration. Thus he can (3) put an end to it by (4) pursuing the way by which he will "get out of it." These four points are the Four Truths of Buddhism. It is incorporating them in one's life that makes a person rise above the crowd in such a way that, while he continues being biologically normalized as an enworlded human being, he is mentally on a higher plane.

This supramundane perspective and the individual's engagement with it provide the basis for breaking down and overcoming, on the intellectual side, reductionism (Pali *sakkāyadiṭṭhi*), hesitancy-scepticism (Pali *vicikicchā*), and the preoccupation with rites and ritual (Pali *sīlabbataparāmāsa*); and, on the emotional side, passion-attachment (Skt., Pali *rāga*), aversion-hatred (Pali *dosa*), and delusion-opaqueness (Skt. Pali *moha*). Their specific connotations we have already discussed in the section on the pollutants. Breakdown of these powerful agents enables a person to set his foot on "firm ground" (Skt. *bhūmi*) in the pragmatic sense that a person who has attained such firm ground is the embodiment of the positive and healthy in relation to the level of the superworldly. This is also firm ground in the specific sense that a person on it enjoys the advantages of *śrāmaṇya* (Pali *samaññaphala*). This, according to Vasubandhu,[15] is a way rather than a state in that it acts as a catalyst in breaking down the pollutants. It also marks a phase transition from the way of seeing (Skt. *darśanamārga*) to the way of cultivation (Skt. *bhāvanāmārga*), which is the transition from being a person entering the stream to becoming a person who will return only once to his previous state. In this way, it establishes a wider and higher regime that is under the control of experiential knowledge and expressed by the phrase, "I shall come to know that which hitherto has been unknown." The unknown is not something unknowable, but something that has been unobserved because of the limited range and perspective of our ordinary "seeing."[16]

This new regime ushered in by all that is healthy and positive in the superworldly as a way of seeing constitutes a complex situation in which moral action as well as psychic receptivity and psychic activity present an integral aspect.

Moral action expresses itself in language that has something to say rather than in mere talk, and uses kind words that are to the point (Skt. *samyagvāc,* Pali *sammāvācā*); in actions pertaining to the level of our bodily existence in being beyond reproach (Skt. *samyakkarmānta,* Pali *sammākammanta*); and in one's livelihood (Skit. *samyagājīva,* Pali *sammājīva*). It is important to note that none of these represent a prescriptive ethics in the form of a behavioral code geared to a static world view; rather they are manifestations of the healthy and positive on the supramundane level and as such reflect an awareness of responsibility due to a feeling of connectedness with the rest of the universe.

Psychic activity is manifested in the autocatalytic facets of this awakening process (Skt. *bodhyanga,* Pali *bojjhanga*). They are autocatalytic in the sense that they form an integral part of this awakening and induce its unfoldment. There are seven of them (first the Sanskrit then the Pali term being given in parentheses):

1. Inspection (*smṛti, sati*), the attempt to keep the perceptual situation as nearly constant as possible
2. Discrimination among things and ideas as to their intrinsic value for one's growth (*dharmapravicaya, dhammavicaya*), a feature otherwise known as a person's critical acumen (*prajñā, paññā*)
3. Assiduous striving (*vīrya, viriya*)
4. Joy (*prīti, pīti*)
5. Tension release (*praśrabdhi, passaddhi*)
6. Concentrated in-depth appraisal (*samādhi*)
7. Balancedness (*upekṣā, upekkhā*) [17]

The specific active aspect of these autocatalytic facets lies in the fact that they counteract inertia, volatility, mental fixations, strain, indulgence in pleasures, and self-mortification as the aim of life, as well as such wild speculations as the views of eternal existence and nihility. For awakening means "to wake up from the sleep induced by the continual operation of the pollutants, to gain a penetrating insight into the Four Truths, and to come face to face with nirvana." [18]

The transition from the narrowly circumscribed world of representational thinking, which attempts to reduce everything to basic building blocks, to a world of experience with its growing awareness of existential meaning and value marks an opening up. This opening up constitutes a multifaceted release to which this way of seeing provides an access (Skt.

vimokṣamukha). Three such states of release are counted, for which the Sanskrit (and Pali) terms are given below:

> *śūnya(tā)* (*suññata*)
> *apraṇihita* (*appaṇihita*)
> *ānimitta* (*ānimitta*)[19]

The two first give their name to the way itself, because they are contents of representational, objectifying thought, although in a circular way—the "objective reference" or the *telos* (the aim) of the way reflects back on the way toward it and thus is able to serve as a name for the way.

With the Theravādins and in the Hinayana in general, the term *śūnya* (*suñña*) has as yet no such philosophical connotation as it acquired in the later Mahayana. Since it basically describes a cognitive-perceptual process, it is a cover term for the realization that what we as perceiving individuals "see," whether natural things or inspected selves, is impermanent; that what we as feeling individuals feel is frustrating because of its impermanence; and that what we as thinking individuals understand cannot have, or be constituted as, an abiding essence because it includes both being impermanent and frustrating. Moreover, since this supramundane way is pure and immaculate[20] by virtue of being devoid of any pollutants, and since its destination or objective reference, nirvana, also is devoid of any pollutants, as is the actual going toward nirvana, the qualification of this way as "open-(directional," *śūnya*)[21] is appropriate. In passing, it may be pointed out that this triple assessment is the sutra presentation; for the Abhidharma the going is the sole criterion. The traditional rendering of *śūnya* by "empty" or "void" is, in view of its positive character, quite misleading.

This same, dual explication holds for the term *apraṇihita* (*appaṇihita*) "unbiased," "not leaning toward either side." From the perspective of the going, the way is a straightforward march; and from the perspective of the quality of this going, there is no leaning toward passion, aversion, or delusion; and from the perspective of its objective reference, nirvana, which does not know of any leaning toward anything, the way, too, cannot have any leanings. In contrast to this sutra presentation of the way, the Abhidharma is solely concerned with the going itself.[22]

The *ānimitta*, "non-referential," does not give its name to the way, because it lacks whatever might be conceived of as a determinate (or predetermined) aim the direction of which it follows. Rather, the wider perspective operating in this release uproots the representational forms of something as eternal or permanent, hedonistic or egological, and hence busies itself with these terms of reference, but because of its nonrepresentational character, it does not set up an objective reference.[23] There is one other important reason why *ānimitta* cannot give its name to the way. The Abhidharma deals with the real in terms of the (material) building blocks of existence and world, rather than in terms of their ephemeral "appearances," the representational. This objectivistic reductionism is credited with activating a deep trust (Skt. *śraddhā*), which as a sociocultural operator,[24] gives us assurance and clarity and effectively destroys the unwarranted assumption on which we base our ordinary transactions in the world in which we live (namely, that whatever we cherish for the moment, whether an object of perception or our individuality, will persist unchanged). But trust is not a constitutive factor of the Eightfold Path, nor is it an autocatalytic factor in the awakening process (Skt. *bodhyanga*). Hence that which is not a constitutive element of the way cannot extend its name to the way. By contrast, the *śūnyatā(vimokṣa)* which realizes that there is no abiding principle by which something is what it is—in personalistic terms a Self—is equal to a highly developed critical acumen (Skt. *prajñā*), which is a constitutive element of the way. Similarly, the *apraṇihita(vimokṣa),* through which we can pursue our way without ever digressing into the mire of the pollutants, and through which we also can understand the frustration that goes with whatever is impermanent and hence provides no solid ground to walk on, is a highly developed in-depth appraisal of the real (Skt. *samādhi*), which, too, is a constitutive element of the way.[25]

The three specifications of being impermanent (Pali *anicca*), frustrating (Pali *dukkha*), and without self-identity (Pali *anattā*) that the way of seeing with its release phases brings to light are so intimately related that any one of them entails the other two, so that it seems as if all three were present in a single moment of observation.[26]

Since Buddhaghosa presented the Theravāda view in particular and the Hinayana view in general, the upshot of the matter is that this line of thought accepted the prevalent reductionistic approach to the problem of man, according to which the world is made up of objects (particular and granular existents) with certain observable qualities (accompanying characteristics). In thus merely perpetuating the objectivistic myth (and fallacies), the Theravādins were, from a philosophical viewpoint, in no way different from the Brahmanical Nyāya-Vaiśeṣikas, as Rong-zom Chos-kyi bzang-po has pointed out.[27]

This way of seeing, which is expressive of the manner in which a person who has "entered the stream" and looks on life from a wider perspective, cannot but initiate a further probing that is the cultivation (Skt. *bhāvanā*) of the insight gained by this way of seeing. It must be remembered that it is the Four Truths (frustration, its origin, its cessation, and the way toward this goal) that are "seen," and while "seeing" in this sense is certainly a mode of perception that includes visual perception, it yet goes beyond this scope and by virtue of the nature of what is seen becomes a nonsensory experience of reality. This cultivation serves to weaken the forces that block the vision, among which the passionate involvement in the gratification of one's desires (Skt. *kāmarāga*) and ill will (Skt. *vyāpāda*) are paramount. These two forces are closely related to each other in that the more I am engrossed with something and want to be its sole possessor, the more I shall try to hinder another person from sharing in that which I covet and shall not refrain from harming him. After all, in my self-righteousness I can always make excuses—"Look, I am the good guy and he is a nasty fellow."

Inasmuch as the vision of the Four Truths leaves a deep impression on the person who sees and feels them, the vision leads to the cultivation of that which has been seen and the immediate effect is a weakening, though as yet not an elimination, of that which once dominated a person's ordinary attitude. This weakening brings about a further change in the person who is, therefore, aptly called a "once-returner" (Skt. *sakṛdāgāmin*), who is in the second phase of the way as a whole and in the first phase of the way of cultivation.[28]

The never-returner. The next stage is the one of the never-returner (Skt. *anāgāmin*). This stage is cultivated in order completely to get rid of those fetters that already become weak and loose in the stage of the once-returner.[29]

There are five specifically mentioned fetters, known as "fetters that tie a person down" (Skt. *avarabhāgīya*, Pali *orambhāgiya*). These "desires and the eagerness with which one gives in to them" (Pali *kāmacchanda*) as well as ill-will (Pali *vyāpāda*) are such that they prevent a person from getting out of the confines of his ordinary world of desires (Kāmadhātu), while "reductionism" (Pali *sakkāyadiṭṭhi*), "scepticism" (Pali *vicikicchā*), and "observance of rites and rituals" (Pali *sīlabbataparāmāsa*) make him return to his world of desires. Actually, these three last fetters have already been loosened in the entering-the-stream phase of the way of seeing and hence are relatively easily shaken off. But it is the first two fetters that pose a hard task, because their roots go back to the early phase of the appearance of multicellular organisms, when the palaeomammalian brain or limbic system developed out of the reptilian brain. The operations of the limbic system express themselves as feelings and emotions that turn into guiding forces for behavioral patterns already prefigured by the reptilian brain. These feelings and emotions are only too often in direct conflict with the higher forms of consciousness and tend to narrow down the flexibility of thinking and permit only the presentation of a single idea or view, the narrowest one being the reductionist view.

This distinction between what I propose to paraphrase as intellectual fetters and emotional fetters reveals a profound insight on the part of the Buddhists. It is easier to get rid of intellectual fetters like ideologies and other attempts at rationalizing one's behavior than of emotional fetters, which maintain a strong coupling with the person's sociobiological environment and can only be loosened by his sociocultural development, which begins on the way as a breakaway from the herd and a rising above the crowd and is therefore so aptly termed "supramundane."

The arhant. The sociocultural development initiated by the preceding stage is continued on the last stage, the "way of the arhant." On this way, the "fetters tying the individual to the higher levels of his hierarchical organization" (Skt. *ūrdhvabhāgīya*, Pali *uddhaṃbhāgiya*) are eliminated.[30]

There are also five such fetters: a passion for (experiencing) the world of pure forms or gestalts (Pali *rūparāga*), passion for (experiencing) the world of formlessness or no-gestalts (Pali *arūparāga*), conceit (Pali *māna*), volatility (Pali *uddhacca*), and ignorance (Pali *avijjā*), not in the common sense of mere stupidity, but in the sense of lacking the understanding of the nature and truth of frustration and, by implication, the remaining three truths.[31]

Within this set of five fetters, conceit occupies an important place. Whenever a person attempts to break away from the norms and standards of the mass man by questioning and no longer blindly accepting, he becomes dissociated from the herd. At this moment, there is the grave danger that just because of his becoming separate and different from the amorphous mass, he develops a feeling of superiority, puffs himself up in accordance with an overweeningly favorable opinion of himself. In short, he becomes conceited. Conceit is an "emotion" (a pollutant) that poses as a "vision" (Skt. *dṛṣṭi*), which is restricted to the feeling of belonging to an "inner circle" or the "elect." It has nothing of a wider perspective in it. It can only be dealt with by that which has been termed "proper view" (Skt. *samyagdṛṣṭi*), which stands at the beginning of the (eightfold) way. Conceit lingers on and has to be "killed" (Pali *vajjha*) over and over again on each level a person reaches. He who is "in the stream" still harbors a kind of conceit that only the level of the once-returner can overcome, but the once-returner harbors a conceit that only the level of the never-returner can overpower, and the conceit of the never-returner can only be crushed by the level of the arhant. In this way, each facet of the eightfold way in the graded pattern of the Eightfold Path serves a definite purpose.[32]

Since the Four Truths are the sole concern of the Theravāda way—the three accompanying characteristics of each truth (being impermanent, being frustrating, and having no self-identity) aiding a progressively deepening understanding of the truths—it is evident that the whole of reality was conceived of as being reducible to a few basic "facts."

With the attainment of the status of an arhant, the Theravāda way comes to its end in the strict sense of the word.

Buddhaghosa, at heart a Theravādin in spite of occasional leanings toward the Yogācāra teaching, speaks of this end state in glowing words: "Once the sun has risen, its light continues shining, and so once the way of the arhant is traveled, there is no murkiness to conceal the truths."[33]

7 *The Way The Earlier View II*

The Śrāvaka and Pratyekabuddha Ways

The Śrāvaka Conception of the Way

In certain respects the Theravāda tradition, discussed in the previous chapter, stands alone in the history of Buddhist thought. Gradually, it lost all contact with the main stream, whether through accident or intentional isolation. One reason that it remained outside this stream is certainly to be found in the fact that the followers of the Theravāda tradition used Pali as their medium of communication, a vernacular elevated to the lingua franca of a multilingual society, rather than Sanskrit, which was the language of the Brahmanical elite, who in course of time produced the most important thinkers in the Buddhist tradition. Another reason may have been the fact that the followers of the Theravāda tradition addressed themselves to the community of monks rather than to the layman, who was the main supporter of the monk. And yet the monk is only one thread in the rich tapestry of society, not the whole of it (which only too often monks tend to forget). By insisting on the superiority of the monk, whose whole aim in life was to escape from "the world," they also escaped from, or at least shunned, the challenge that other thinkers provided.

As a contrast to this one-sided presentation, it is therefore necessary also to look at the way as interpreted by those who used the Sanskrit language, even if at this early stage of Buddhist thought they were still akin to the followers of the Theravāda tradition in many respects, because they, too, represented the Hinayana way, out of which eventually the Mahayana way with its social awareness grew.

The major representatives of the Sanskrit tradition were the Vaibhāṣikas, whose ideas were summarized by Vasubandhu in his monumental *Abhidharmakośa* and his autocommentary to it. In these works, he assessed these ideas critically, from the viewpoint of the Sautrāntikas (whose impact on Buddhist thought must have been much greater than the few extant references to them suggest). With the Vaibhāṣikas, it is no longer the monk exclusively who can travel the way, even if he is still considered to be far ahead of the others. Now each and every person who could be said to be a śrāvaka was regarded as able to go the way. Not only is a śrāvaka a person who is willing to listen and to learn, but also one who already patterns his life on a certain ethical code. In the Buddhist context, such a code is never a revealed set of rules, but basically a self-discipline (Skt. *saṃvara*) that develops and implements its own norms with respect to the (autopoietic) level on which a person happens to be. This self-discipline ranges over all the hierarchically organized physical-psychic levels of the "engaged" person. To the extent that this self-discipline operates on the level of a person's physical organization, it is termed in Sanskrit *prātimokṣa*. When it operates on the psychic level of the reflexive, concentrative mind and establishes its specific norms for this level, it is known as "concentration-born" (Skt. *dhyānaja*). Lastly when it operates on and as the way, it is termed "flawlessly pure" (Skt. *anāsrava*). It is significant that the self-discipline called *prātimokṣa* is related to, if not restricted to, the domain of man's desires (Skt. *kāmāvacara*). These act as guiding forces for the rich spectrum of behavioral patterns from the domineering influence of which a person has to become emancipated in order to be able to re-create, socioculturally, the world (including himself) in terms of individuation and greater complexity. For this emancipation, this discipline is of paramount importance.

Vasubandhu lists eight types of persons who pattern their life according to the *prātimokṣa*. They are:

1. The *bhikṣu* (roughly corresponding to our idea of a monk)
2. The *bhikṣunī* (nun)
3. The *śikṣamānā* (a studious girl and candidate for becoming a nun)
4. The *śramaṇera* (male novice)
5. The *śramaṇerikā* (female novice)
6. The *upāsaka* (layman)
7. The *upāsikā* (laywoman)
8. The *upavāsastha* (a person who only occasionally concerns himself with the discipline, a "drop-in") [1]

Immediately after having enumerated them, he rearranges them in four individual groups, internally differentiated by sex, but otherwise according to the group's overall moral code.[2] In the course of time, the eighth type of individual was dropped from this list; such a person came to be considered unsuited for the way because of lacking the steadiness needed for doing so.

When Vasubandhu further declares that these disciplines necessary for release from the dominance of the desires, as exemplified in various forms by the above mentioned types of individuals, exist apart from each other, he clearly has in mind the process of individuation and the emergence of the greater complexity of a well-rounded personality. He illustrates this by listing the standard "abstentions." An *upāsaka* or an *upāsikā* abstains from killing, stealing, sexual excesses, telling lies, and consuming intoxicant beverages; an *upavāsastha* abstains, in addition, from using perfumes, garlands, and ointments, as well as from resting on couches and other raised sleeping furniture, and from sleeping at odd times; a *śramaṇera* abstains, in addition, from accepting gold and silver; and a *bhikṣu* abstains from every bodily and verbal activity that is reprehensible.[3]

However crude, because of its numerical listing, this presentation may seem, we can discern in it a multilevel ethics that differs considerably from the Western behavioral code with its vociferous insistence on rights for individuals or groups and its silence about acceptance of responsibility. The Buddhist code derives from self-discipline and in its social framework is a manifestation of man's psychic activity. Thus it is termed "information" (Skt. *vijñapti*),[4] which in this manifest form has a gestalt quality that has emerged from a much higher level of the system's organization and which initiates an information set-up or "information potential" (Skt. *avijñapti*) that is not directly observable but nevertheless operates subliminally. Both "information" and "information potential" constitute man's social activities in his physical environment (which is of course not only physical); it is with this that *prātimokṣa* self-discipline is concerned.

Specifically, the *prātimokṣa* discipline consists of "character, moral conduct, (psychic) activity and restraint."[5] Vasubandhu explains that one speaks of character (Skt. *śīla*), because the individual takes it upon himself or herself to refrain from any unbalanced actions and because "character," according to native etymology, has the meaning of a cooling effect that prevents one's body from burning with passion. Moral conduct (Skt. *sucarita*) is so called because it is praised by knowledgeable persons. In these two facets of the personality, we can easily recognize the activity of the sociocultural operators "self-respect" and "decorum." This underlines the fact that morality is a manifestation of man's psychic activity. This psychic activity (Skt. *karma*)[6] is both information and information potential in the sense that both are active, the one overtly in the contextual structure of a person's sociality, through which the individual, in this instance, is morally engaged in the world; the other, latently active in making such engagement possible. Restraint (Skt. *saṃvara*) is both bodily and verbal restraint.[7]

The essential feature of self-discipline is the readiness of the individual to take it upon himself to refrain from doing anything opprobrious so as not to make someone else feel ashamed. Shame has its root in the information potential,[8] which within a positive setting, restrains the individual from engaging in reprehensible activities. Vasubandhu, in this connection, raises the question of whether non-Buddhists also have self-discipline. He does not deny that they, too, take it upon themselves to refrain from reprehensible activities, but they do not have the *prātimokṣa* discipline. This discipline, while aiming at release (Skt. *mokṣa*), does not aim at the reductionistic establishment of a particular existent, which though termed *mokṣa,* is but one granular particular existent among other particular existents. Vasubandhu's conception of release and moral conduct already reflects process-oriented thinking within a climate that was still rigidly structure-oriented.

The release at which self-discipline aims is a fresh way of seeing the world and oneself. In order to be effective, this has to be cultivated so that henceforward the new vision becomes the guiding principle in one's life. Thus, because of the importance of an individual's undertaking the psychic activity that does away with a pseudo-objective world, cultivation is both experimentation with what is available and creative imagination. And this, in turn, is the going of the way. Vasubandhu succinctly states:

> He who abides with the self-discipline pertinent to his social status
> and is willing to listen and to think
> Can engage thoroughly in creative imagination.[9]

This aphorism sums up a complex program in which creative imagination is the climax of a long process and its fruition. This is the program of the arhant, who through it becomes the living embodiment of the śrāvaka ideal. According to Vasubandhu, presenting the influential view of the Vaibhāṣikas, the śrāvaka way embraces four phases. To each of them the term "way" is applied, and in their totality they are summed up in two distinct major ways as either "mundane" (Skt. *laukika*) or "supramundane" (Skt. *lokottara*). The four phases or ways are termed in Sanskrit *prayogamārga,* "preparatory-engagement way," *ānantaryamārga,* "obstacle-removal way" (also referred to as *prahāṇamārga,* "way of abandoning"), *vimuktimārga,* "way leading to the felt state of release," and *viśeṣamārga* "way leading to a very special state different from everything else." The first two phases/ways are "mundane," the remaining two, though similar in content to the two preceding ones, are "supermundane."[10] This is diagramed in Figure 3:

FIGURE 3

prayogamārga } → *laukika*
ānantaryamārga/prahāṇamarga }
vimuktimārga } → *lokottara*
viśeṣamārga }

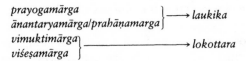

Another concurrent classification of the śrāvaka way deals with its three phases of "seeing" (Skt. *darśanamārga*), "cultivation by experimentation and creative imagination" (Skt. *bhāvanāmārga*), and "no-more-learning" (Skt. *aśaikṣamārga*). Special attention is given to differences in the psychic predispositions of persons pursuing the way, differentiating between believing and thinking. According to the Buddhists, thinking is characteristic of an astute and highly intelligent person, while believing, in the sense of taking things uncritically, is characteristic of the dull witted.

Regarding this differentiation, it must be pointed out that even the most sceptical of us have to take many things "on faith," but some of us will hardly ever outgrow this level and so will continue patterning their life on what they have heard but have not thought through. As this blind trust intensifies, the person taking things on faith (Skt. *śraddhānusārin*), in traveling the path of seeing, becomes a person wholly given over to faith (Skt. *śraddhādhimukta*) and in this style exercises his (predetermined) imagination. But when he embarks on the way of no-more-learning his feeling of release, of embodying the arhant ideal, is only temporary (Skt. *samayavimukta*), because it has not been acquired by experience that is more than just taking things on faith.[11] By contrast, there are those who rely on their capacity to think (which involves more than analytical and discursive operations, to which thought is only too often reduced, particularly when the emphasis is on structure as in the Hinayana phase of Buddhist thought). Thinking is searching for meaning and depends on a person's critical acumen. Accordingly, a person who searches for meaning (Skt. *dharmānusārin*) while going the way of seeing becomes a person who has a fresh vision (Skt. *dṛṣṭiprāpta*) in pursuing the way of creative imagination. When he enters the way of no-more-learning, his feeling of release, of having become the embodiment of the śrāvaka ideal, is lasting (Skt. *asamayavimukta*), because it is the very experience of it.[12]

The cultivation of the way consists primarily in achieving a deeper understanding of the Four Truths, which in a certain sense sum up the human situation and the possibilities it holds for the individual. The First Truth, the truth of frustration and suffering, draws attention to the generally unpleasant and frustrating situation of the living person as an embodied, speaking, and thinking being. This situation is similar to a disease demanding treatment. The Second Truth, the truth of the origin of this frustrating situation, lays bare its cause, which is each individual's activity in constructing and living in a "reality" that cannot withstand any critical investigation and that is maintained by the workings of the pollutants supporting and tainting this activity. The third Truth, the truth of the cessation of frustration and suffering, as its name implies, points to the feeling of bliss and happiness one experiences when one has been cured of a disease or escaped from a prison, the prison in this case being samsara. The Fourth Truth, the truth of the way, is like the medicine one takes in order to get rid of the disease. This conception of the way has been common to all schools of Buddhism, and the idea of health, physical and psychic, corresponding to it, has been predominant since earliest times. Asanga, Vasubandhu's elder brother, expressed this conception of the way as follows:

A disease has to be diagnosed;
Its cause has to be eliminated;
A state of bliss (and health) has to be attained, and for this purpose,
Medicine has to be taken.
Similarly, frustration, its cause, its cessation, and the way
Have to be diagnosed, eliminated, experienced, and cultivated.[13]

These four truths as the quintessence of the way are progressively dealt with in seven sections, which are distributed over four phases or stages of the path as a whole. It is here that the structure-oriented thought of the Hinayana is most evident. In a cryptic manner, Vasubandhu declares:

The seven sections are in this order:
The initial exercises,
The factors that facilitate and effect a breakthrough,
The cultivation (or imaginative variation of the truths) and the actual seeing of them.[14]

The seven sections are distributed over the way as a whole, as it was expressed in the standard terminology of a later time, as follows:

1. The way of preparation (Skt. *sambhāramārga*) is made up of three sections in a hierarchical order.
2. The way of linking up (with seeing the world afresh) (Skt. *prayogamārga*) is made up of two sections indicative of a growing intensification of the process.
3. The way of seeing (Skt. *darśanamārga*) consists of the set of the seven autocatalyic factors of the awakening process.
4. The way of cultivation (Skt. *bhāvanāmārga*) consists of the set termed "the Eightfold Path."

The way begins with the preparatory phase in its, at first, limited scope of breaking the attachment to one's physical existence or the body as lived by a subject as well as any other person's physical existence or lived body (in view of the fact that man is always a social being and as such always with others and always in a physical environment). In order to effect this break one resorts to the technique of inspection (Skt. *smṛtyupasthāna*), which has as its objective reference the body in a state of decay. As Vasubandhu says, "The notion of a skeleton is useful in the case of all who have some passionate attachment."[15] In his commentary to this aphoristic statement, he elaborates on the nature of passionate attachment as it is concerned with a person's complexion, a person's figure, with touching another person, and with paying deference to another person. The first kind of attachment is broken by visualizing the body as a bluish or festering corpse. The second kind is broken by visualizing the body as mangled by animals or as scattered limb by limb. The third kind is broken by visualizing the body as eaten by worms and held together only by sinews. The fourth kind is broken by visualizing the body as an immobile corpse. If one has succeeded in breaking one's attachment to one's physical existence, one may, as Klong-chen rab-'byams-pa adds, engage in a "follow-up inspection" of the body, seeing it as driftwood that has nothing of substance in it.[16]

But a human being is not only a physical being; he is also a feeling being. Thus the next "inspection" in this elementary preparatory stage of the way is the inspection of feelings. Feelings are of three kinds: pleasant, unpleasant, and indifferent. However, they all form part of the individual's generally unpleasant, because frustrating, situation. It is this inspection of feelings that reveals their unsatisfactory nature.

In addition to being a physical and a feeling being, a human person also is a thinking being. His thought processes as they manifest in the thematizing activity of the mind form the topic of the next "inspection." The aim of this inspection is to calm the thematic proliferation of thoughts and to channel this mental activity into a concentrative state of inner calm so as to form the basis for a wider perspective. To this end, breathing techniques are recommended—as everybody knows, taking a deep breath has a calming effect. But as an end in themselves, breathing techniques serve no purpose. They are then only a toy to amuse little children. Specifically, however, inspection of the thought processes reveals that there is nothing in them that could be identified with a self as their owner. Naturally, this kind of inspection involves a person's critical acumen (Skt. *prajñā*), which the Vaibhāṣikas equated with inspection in its various modes (Skt. *smṛtyupasthāna*) on the grounds that inspection plays a decisive role in placing the object under consideration at the disposal of the person's critical assessment of it, "just as a wedge helps to cleave timber." But Vasubandhu criticizes this view and declares that "inspection is used by one's critical acumen in the sense that it is the critical acumen that envisions its object and accordingly addresses it by means of inspection taking hold of it."[17]

Lastly, there is the inspection of what is both the building blocks of our existence and world, as well as what we would call meanings. Meanings according to the Hinayana reifying interpretation, too, are building blocks (Skt. *dharma,* Tib. *chos*) that have an "objective" entitative status. First we find that the first three of the five psychophysical constituents[18]—color-form, feelings, notions—have nothing substantial about them when inspected in terms of our lived body, our feelings, and our thought processes. Then we find that our reality constructions and our judgments of perception, too, have nothing substantial about them. As a consequence, the pollutants that make us hanker after all these building blocks have in many ways been repulsed. Or at least what constitutes the gross features of our existence has been crushed so that one can move on to the higher levels of the way. This analytical and, by implication, reductionistic procedure has been summed up by Vasubandhu as follows:

> Through a thorough analytical investigation, in terms of the two
> defining characteristics (essential and accompanying),
> Of the lived body, the feelings, the thought processes, and the
> building blocks (of reality).[19]

With the severance of attachment to one's physical and not quite so physical existence, the next phase in this preparatory stage of the way, which has a medium scope of effectiveness, sets in. It is constituted of sustained effort and its cultivation. This effort operates through four "proper abnegations" (Skt. *samyakprahāṇa*/*samyakpradhāna*), of which only the first two are abnegations in the strict sense of the word, while the remaining two are an entrenchment of whatever is positive and healthy. It is therefore only with reference to the abnegation of all that tends to move in the direction of the negative and unhealthy that the appellation "proper abnegation" is used, out of the practical consideration that the negative has to be removed first in order to give the positive a chance. These four proper abnegations are described as making efforts (1) to not allow the negative that has not yet arisen to arise, (2) to keep that which has already arisen under control (by not allowing it to grow), (3) to bring about the positive that has not yet been actualized, and (4) to make the positive that has been actualized grow stronger and stronger.

The last phase of the preparatory stage on the way, which has a wide scope of effectiveness, consists of four kinds of in-depth appraisal of how the way is going. They are qualified as (1) a desire or deep interest, (2) a continued effort, (3) a channeling of the mental capacity, and (4) a meticulous probing. Interest serves to focus on that which is positive and healthy in either its commonly accepted form or its ultimately valid form. Effort makes its range extend farther and farther. The channeling of the mental capacity results in its staying focused on the positive. The meticulous probing separates what really matters from the spurious. Since from these procedures, concentrative states of whatever character result, these four appraisals are termed "footholds of success" (Skt. *ṛddhipāda*).

This preparatory phase, with its widening scope of effectiveness proceeding in an ascending order, is followed by the phase or way of linking up with eventually seeing the world "with fresh eyes." In itself, this phase presents a hierarchical order of two major levels. The lower level of these is described as comprising, on the one side, an onset of warmth (Skt. *uṣman*). This increases by three degrees in intensity and then climaxes in a peak value (Skt. *mūrdhan*), which also passes through three degrees in intensity. The two sets of three together constitute six sublevels. These descriptive terms of "warmth" and "peak value" reflect the experiential character of this phase. "Warmth" here is to be understood in the sense that we say that someone "warms up" as he gets into his subject. On the other side, there is a set of five operators, which in their arrangement display a hierarchical order or progression because this set is organized in relation to a purpose. Between the two sides of this level, there exists a feedback loop, which works so that one enhances the other. We may compare this set of operators with a planning committee that lacks executive powers. The members of this set act merely as guiding principles (Skt. *indriya*) as to how to make use of the raw material available to arrive at certain well defined operational targets. This set of five operators consists of (1) trust, (2) effort, (3) inspection, (4) in-depth appraisal, and (5) critical acumen. Trust serves to widen the intellectual horizon with respect to the sixteen modes or properties of the Four Truths, or the raw material. The understanding of the Four Truths is, broadly speaking, the target aimed at by the śrāvaka way. Effort serves to enlarge on them by taking a growing delight and interest in them. Inspection serves the purpose of not letting the understanding of these targets slip from one's attention. In-depth appraisal serves to keep the mind thoroughly focused on any of the targets. Critical acumen serves to distinguish and keep the various targets separate. This process is summed up by Vasubandhu as follows:

> It (warmth) has as its (operational) targets the Four Truths
> Which display sixteen (property) modes.
> Warmth climaxes in its peak value
> Which (in its graded intensity) is similar to the (graded intensity of warmth).[20]

The sixteen properties or modes are distributed over the Four Truths in sets of four. This characterization and assessment reflects the reductionistic approach of reducing the whole of reality to a fixed number of building blocks, which in the present case are already of an interpretative, conceptual nature. His claim is, as noted previously, that the whole world is made up of entities that have an "objective" reality independent of anyone experiencing them. These entities have certain properties and in their relations to each other form a definite structure. Thus, frustration, or the First Truth, is an entity with an objective reality, and it has the inherent properties that it is impermanent (Skt. *anitya*), unpleasant (Skt. *duḥkha*), nothing concrete in the ordinary sense of the word (Skt. *śūnya*), and has nothing about it that could be considered a self (Skt. *anātman*). It is in terms of these properties that we understand frustration. Similarly, the origin of frustration, the Second Truth, is another entity having the following properties: causality, emergence, onset, and situation modification. So also the cessation of frustration, the Third Truth, is an entity and has these properties: cessation, peace, exaltedness, and escape. Lastly, the way leading to cessation, the Fourth Truth, as an entity has these properties: trail, rationality, access, and exiting.

These operational targets are submitted to and accepted by the next higher instance in the phase of linking up with the decisive phase of really seeing. This next higher instance also has two levels. The lower one has a feedback loop between acceptance (Skt. *kṣānti*) and the strategic-planning committee, consisting of the same five operators as those on the operational planning committee, but having executive powers and thus characterized as "powers" (Skt. *bala*). Vasubandhu explains the difference between guiding principles and powers by saying that the former can be rejected or scrapped, the latter not.[21]

Even this lower level of strategic planning involves an internal grading. As Vasubandhu declares:

> From (the peak value) comes acceptance (in three degrees of which)
> The first two are like (the peak values.)[22]

The highest stage in this gradation passes over into the higher of the two levels of this phase of linking up. This may be likened to the top executive of an organization who selects from all that has been submitted and accepted and effects the breakthrough to the way of seeing. That which has been so selected, namely, the recognition and acceptance of the fact that what is called "world" is frustrating, is termed "the supreme mundane material" (Skt. *laukika agradharmāḥ*) with which the five-member executive committee has been dealing. These are, as Vasubandhu explains, still mundane, because the breakthrough to the supramundane path of seeing has not yet been effected. On the other hand, they are "supreme," because they are of the highest quality possible in the mundane context, and unlike other building blocks, which are merely conservative and structure-preserving, are of a dynamic and efficacious nature in attaining the target at which the system aims.[23]

Taking a look at the feedback loops in these two major levels of this phase of linking up with the way of seeing, we find that the upper feedback loop of the lower (operational-planning) level falls together with the lower feedback loop of the higher (strategic-planning) level. This means that this phase itself is already an intricately intermeshed way of going about one's task of growing up.[24]

It is with the completion of the phase of linking up that the breakthrough into the way and phase of seeing takes place. The term "seeing" in this context refers to a mode of perception that goes beyond the scope of merely noticing denotable objects, even if such denotation may still accompany it—one still sees the Four Truths. But the point is that they are seen in a manner as never before; in other words, this seeing is suffused with meaning and reflects a shift in attention in that it bears on the individual's existence in his life-world as experienced, not merely talked about, by him. Meaning is always meaning *for* someone.

Vasubandhu introduces this phase of seeing—a seeing "with fresh eyes"—with the words: "Fifteen moments, because they see that which has not been seen, are the "way of seeing."[25]

There is, however, still a sixteenth moment that is already part of the way of cultivation of that which has been seen "with fresh eyes" and is now present as *meaning* in relation to future possibilities.

Vasubandhu's cryptic reference to "fifteen moments" reveals its significance when, on the one hand, we bear in mind Merleau-Ponty's succinct statement that "Time and thought are mutually entangled" (1964, 15), and, on the other hand, note that these moments continue and deepen what on the linking-up phase was found to be the "supreme mundane material" and so mark a transition from purely representational, objectifying thinking (with its analytical acumen (Skt. *prajñā*) and misplaced concreteness) to an intuitive meaning-awareness mode (Skt. *jñāna*). Thus, these moments as "acceptances" (Skt. *kṣānti*) of the Four Truths as strategic goals constitute the "obstacle-removing way" (Skt. *ānantaryamārga*), and as instances of intuitive meaning-awareness mode(s) (Skt. *jñāna*), constitute the "way leading to the felt state of release" (Skt. *vimuktimārga*).[26] This distinction between representational, objectifying thinking (*prajñā*) and intuitive meaning-awareness (*jñāna*) cannot be emphasized too strongly.

To be sure, objectifiable objects are mentioned—the Four Truths—but they are seen as a *path* that releases thinking from its urge to control, to gain the upper hand in the struggle against the tyranny of the concrete, and moves in the direction of self-understanding. Therefore, Vasubandhu in his commentary on the above aphorism speaks of the individual (Skt. *pudgala*) in whom these ways of understanding arise and how he goes about them.[27]

The breakthrough that makes a person see "with fresh eyes," that is, see the Four Truths and what they *mean* in practical living, results in a curbing of the effectiveness of the pollutants and quasi pollutants in their latent operations. Although the texts speak in this connection of a "discarding by seeing," (Skt. *dṛgheya, darśanaheya*), this discarding is not meant to be taken literally; rather it means "dealing these latent operations a stunning blow" so that they can be "knocked out completely" by the way of cultivation (Skt. *bhāvanāheya*).

In a previous chapter we noted that the Buddhists carefully distinguished between pollutants and catalysts, which Western psychology still continues to lump together under the generic term of emotions. In fact, they went even one step further and also distinguished between "pollutants in their overt operation" (Skt. *kleśa*), and "pollutants in their latent operation" (Skt. *anuśaya*), although this distinction was not always clearly maintained. But all Buddhist thinkers agreed that the pollutants and quasipollutants, whether overtly or latently operative, were the main-spring of a living person's ordinary existence, and by keeping him fettered to a world of his own making (Skt. *karma*), prevented him from breaking free and transcending himself.

The latently operative pollutants that form the substructure of the world as interpreted by a living person—the very notion of "world" is already an interpretation that the objectivist in his subjective blindness is unable to comprehend—are summarized as a set of six by virtue of their factual existence. Thus Vasubandhu declares:

> The mainspring of (a person's) interpreted world are the six latently operative pollutants:
> Attachment in the form of desires, and in its wake, anger-belligerence,
> Arrogance, low-level intelligence, opinionatedness, and
> Indecision.[28]

These latently operative pollutants were reclassified with reference to their target, the Four Truths, as well as with regard to the hierarchical levels of "world" experience over which the Four Truths range, and according to the manner in which they tend to give a distorted view of the world by concretizing that which basically is a process into some sort of particular existent and by inducing dogmatic intolerance. A further subdivision was introduced by distinguishing between those subliminally operative pollutants that could be said to be strictly emotional (in the Western sense of the word) and those that tended to manifest as opinions or ideological perspectives. All this led to a rigid numerical assessment, and it was with reference to the presence of either all or only some of these subliminally operative pollutants that the various schools in Buddhism gave various accounts of what had to be, or was, discarded by "seeing."

Apart from the five emotional latently operative pollutants, there were five ideological latently operative pollutants, as shown in Table 1.

TABLE 1

"IDEOLOGICAL"	"EMOTIONAL"
reductionism	attachment (in the form of desires)
extremism	anger-belligerence
outrageousness	arrogance
dogmatism	low-level intelligence
ritualism	indecision

In passing, it may be pointed out that while the ideological and emotional pollutants operate in close interdependence, they do not mirror each other.

The above ten latently operative pollutants have as their target the First Truth—the unsatisfactoriness of what is called "world"—as it pertains to the domain of ours in which desires hold sway (Kāmadhātu). The Second and Third Truths—the inception of this unsatisfactoriness and the utter cessation of it—are not vulnerable by assaults by reductionism, extremism, and ritualism. The Fourth Truth—the way toward the utter cessation of unsatisfactoriness—is not vulnerable by assaults by reductionism and extremism.[29]

It will be remembered that in the succession of the various acceptance moments (Skt. *kṣānti*) and their intuitive meaning-awareness modes (Skt. *jñāna*) as they evolved in the linking-up phase, the last moment fused with the first moment in the "way of seeing," the last moment of which coincided with the first intensity phase of the way of cultivation. This is not merely the imaginative development of that which has been seen, but even more the application of this intuitive meaning-awareness to the way of life a person is going to follow. This intimate connection between the way of seeing and the way of cultivation is further underscored by the statement that, on the way of seeing, the seven autocatalytic factors of the awakening process are operative, while on the way of cultivation the eight aspects of the way as such—the well-known Eightfold Path—are operative. This is another way of emphasizing man's sociocultural embeddedness in what constitutes his world. This intimate connection between the two ways again shows that man's inner and outer worlds coevolve simultaneously. That which distinguishes the way of cultivation from the way of seeing is the intensity with which it proceeds. This intensity is of nine degrees. The three intensity degrees of low, medium, and high, each have further low, medium, and high gradations. It is on this way also that the idea of "purpose" emerges, in that one practices it in order to attain something one has not yet attained or one refines that which one has already attained.

The way of cultivation, too, discards latently operative pollutants, specifically those that resisted elimination on the way of seeing, because they are grounded in the oldest stratum of mankind's evolution and less amenable to modifications in new situations and contexts. There are four of them. Vasubandhu refers to them in these words:

> Four are to be discarded by cultivation.
> With the exception of anger-belligerence, the other three
> Are also operative in the realms of gestalt and no-gestalt
> experiences.[30]

In terms of lived experience, this growth was felt as the working of an intuitive meaning-awareness (Skt. *jñāna*), which in its liberating effect constituted that which is referred to as the "awakening" (Skt. *bodhi*), itself a process experienced and lived through by the experiencer. Once again it should be emphasized that the term *jñāna* is used in connection with the way (Skt. *mārga*) or the individual's growth process, never with reference to perceptual situations in which the operator's discriminative acumen (Skt. *prajñā*) is active. This shows that the Buddhists clearly distinguished between representational and nonrepresentational operations within the continuum to which we apply the static term "mind."

This nonreductionist intuitive meaning-awareness is, in terms of experience, best understood as the articulation and elucidation of what, figuratively speaking, antedates any concrete experiential act and bears on an individual as subject (though not in the sense of a monadological subject, which with its egological standpoint, conceals what is distinctly human). In being nonreductive, this intuitive awareness is not concerned with the objectifying and essentializing question "What is it?" Or, as its qualification intimates, it is not involved in a "learning" process (Skt. *aśaikṣa*) in the usual sense of this word of importing strange knowledge into a system. Rather, it is an auto-intensification of the experiential process and hence thoroughly dynamic—a feature that our terminology is unable to bring out. Vasubandhu speaks, in this connection, of "mentation" (Skt. *citta*), which he sees as including both representational (Skt. *prajñā*) and nonrepresentational (Skt. *jñāna*) experiencing. Here, in connection with the way, the nonrepresentational is of primary importance. In Vasubandhu's words:

> This mentation, which is not involved in, nor dependent on, the
> learning process, in the very process of its emergence
> Becomes free from the obscurations (that hide its light);
> It is through the way in its process of fading out (into (a
> nonreductive) continuum)
> That its obscurations are thoroughly discarded.[31]

The nonreductive continuum (Skt. *dhātu*) intimated by the above quotation, which Vasubandhu discusses in greater detail in his commentary on this aphorism, is a release (Skt. *vimukti*). As such it is not an entity among other entities that lend themselves to quantification and measurement. The question here is not so much *about* something, but rather about what it *means* to stand free. This, in order to be known, must be experienced without turning it into a construct or denotable object of representational thought, although such denotation may accompany the act of experiencing. As a continuum, this release discloses possible ways for man to be, and it seems that it was understood as a process moving from the severance of attachment (in the form of) desires from the objects in the midst of which the experiencer finds himself, through a discarding of all the other pollutants that keep him imprisoned in his multilevel world, to a complete evanescence of that which constitutes a referential situation with its objective constituents.

The climax of this process is awakening (Skt. *bodhi*), which comprises an awareness of the fact that one is done with whatever had an obscuring and impeding influence (Skt. *kṣayajñāna*) and an awareness of the fact that these obscuring and impeding forces will never rise again (Skt. *anutpādajñāna*). Thus, Vasubandhu states concisely:

> The awareness of being done with (whatever has been obscuring)
> and of the nonrecurrence (of it)
> Is the awakening.[32]

Specifically, in the context of the śrāvaka way, this awakening implies, with respect to the first kind of awareness, the felt knowledge that the truth of frustration has been thoroughly understood, that the origin of frustration has been eliminated, that the cessation of frustration has become a felt reality, and that the way to this cessation has been firmly established in one's self in the sense that one *is* the way. And with respect to the second kind of awareness, it implies the felt knowledge that these truths have no longer to be dealt with in order to prevent the recurrence of frustration.[33]

The person in whom these two kinds of felt knowledge are present is the arhant. Traditionally two broad types of arhant were distinguished. One was a person still continuing in his physical existence (which, of course, is never merely physical) and intent on preserving his detachment with respect to the sensuous and not-quite-so-sensuous objects that make up his environment. Yet his concern remains tied to the pollutants that got him involved with the objects, the independent existence of which he never questioned but naively accepted. The other type was a person who has passed away completely leaving neither physical nor mental trace—"gone out like a flame whose fuel has been consumed."

A further distinction was made on the basis of the manner in which the pollutants are discarded. In this distinction, the first type of arhant attains his release through the application of both his critical acumen (by which he is released from the obscurations operative as the pollutants ranging over the three levels of the universe of experience), and the deeply felt in-depth appraisal of his existentiality (by which he is released from the last barrier to his actually standing free). This barrier is the approximation-evanescence feeling (Skt. *nirodhasamāpatti*) at the "end" of the concentration process. Not understanding this, the aspirant will return from it "to first base," rather than effecting the breakthrough, and give in to moods of depression or ebullience. But not only does this approximation-evanescence feeling impede a breakthrough to the in-depth appraisal of one's existentiality, it also impedes the stabilization of specific mental structures. This follows directly from the śrāvakas' conception of concentration (Skt. *dhyāna*) as a fixation process, as discussed earlier. This conception also gave rise to a confusion between stabilization and stasis. The second type of arhant was released from the obscurations in their operations as pollutants through the application of his critical acumen, but not from the barrier of the approximation-evanescence feeling.[34]

Lastly, a distinction was made on the basis of the mental capacities the failure to develop which would cause a person to fall back from his state of release and the development of which would cause him to persist in his static end state. There were five types, who because of their undeveloped capacities and dull-wittedness, pursued the way on the basis of trust in secondhand reporting (Skt. *śraddhā*) rather than on the basis of critical acumen (Skt. *prajñā*) (which always ranked highest in Buddhist thought). These types were liable to relapse even if they already had reached a near-static end state. Actually, among these five types, two reached a near-static end state from which they did not fall back in the literal sense of the word; one had no chance of refining his capabilities at all, while the others had. Only the person who was highly sensitive and pursued his way with the help of his critical acumen became and remained firmly established in what amounts to a static end state from which he could not be dislodged (Skt. *akopya*). However, only some of the early schools of developing Buddhism accepted the idea that an arhant could fall back. Taken as a whole, the problem of whether an arhant could fall back or not seems to have been largely theoretical.

It was also assumed that an arhant somehow remained within the hierarchically organized universe experienced as a realm of desires, gestalts, and no-gestalts. Thus all six types could be found in the realm of desires. But only the type that reached the static end state of his endeavors and the type that reached a near-static end state could be found in the realms of gestalt and no-gestalt experiences.

The śrāvaka way, as detailed here, is a definite possibility as a model for a man to pattern his life after and has long been so. But, as the Mahayanists were quick to point out, this way is escapist in the sense that the individual shuts himself off from his world, which he does not comprehend as being a projection of his own mental activities, but naively assumes to be "out there," independent of any person who experiences it. The dynamic aspects of this world he perceives as change that can be explained logically and mechanistically.

The Pratyekabuddha Conception of the Way

While there are few references to the pratyekabuddha in the oldest literary tradition, these references increase in the commentaries on the older works and later on become a standard item in the enumerations and gradations of types of highly developed individuals that figure so prominently in later works. Although the pratyekabuddha still belongs to the Hinayana tradition, it is likely that the idea of the pratyekabuddha owes its origin to opposition to Sthaviravāda (Theravāda) dogmatism, which not only claimed that the individual who answered to the description "awakened" (Skt. *buddha*) was unique, but also that there *could* only be one individual answering to the description "awakened." The implications of this contention are tremendous and severely restrict the whole Buddhist program, the development of the human individual. The Theravāda claim bases itself on a substance-attribute categorical scheme. The human individual is first turned into a particular *this*, and then one proceeds to say *what* it is. The explication of the "what is" requires the assignment of different kinds of predicates, "specifically essential predicates, propria, and accidental predicates" (Schrag 1969, 259). The Theravāda claim, therefore, turns out to be a regression to the essentialistic and static view of Man that the historical Buddha had shown to be a mistaken assumption based on the absolutization and fixation resulting from a particular standpoint of inquiry and the concepts used by it.

The pratyekabuddha idea remains an aspect of the Hinayana, but it is broader than the arhant idea, because the process of awakening is no longer restricted to a single person (the historical Buddha). At the same time, however, the awakening process is not given its full scope, but remains, as it were, "locked up." The pratyekabuddha is a person who has had the experience of becoming awake (Skt. *buddha*), but who keeps this experience for himself (Skt. *pratyeka*) throughout his life.

References to the pratyekabuddha are scanty. At a later time, three types of pratyekabuddha were listed. One was a solitary figure, "similar (in his social contacts) to a rhinoceros." The two other types formed larger or smaller crowds "flitting around like parrots." All three kinds were further classified with respect to their intellectual acumen and general sensitivity, the solitary figure ranking highest. Yet, on the whole, they have been unfavorably commented upon, because all three kinds were said to be arrogant, disdainful, and have little compassion. Since compassion, in the Buddhist sense, is one of the four "immeasurably great" catalysts, not an emotion or a pollutant, and unlike a mere sentimentality ranges from friendly interest and deep tenderness to active sharing and helping, the lack of it reflects on the pratyekabuddha's reluctance to exert himself and to practice this basic Buddhist quality.[35] Vasubandhu makes a veiled reference to this reluctance by saying: "It takes one hundred aeons for the solitary person (to get to the point of having the experience of having become awake).[36]

Furthermore, convinced that their present situation and existence offers no chance to attain this experience of having become awake and to live up to its social implications, they make the triple vow: "May I be born in a realm in which there is neither a buddha nor a śrāvaka." "Once I have been born there, may the understanding of the way arise in me by itself in that very existence in which I am reincarnated." "May I teach the educatable by my physical presence but not by spoken words." This latter vow seems to have inspired the translation of the term pratyekabuddha by "silent buddha," evoking the popular conception of a holy man who merely "sits and radiates."

The first two vows seem to be implied by Nāgārjuna's aphorism:

> At (a period when) fully awakened ones have (not yet) appeared
> and when śrāvakas are no longer around,
> The pratyekabuddhas' awareness breaks forth on its own.[37]

The Mādhyamika teacher Candrakīrti explains the term "on its own" as indicating the suspension of the mind's reflective tendencies as they manifest in the intentionality of representational thought and in bodily comprehension, and as also indicating the pratyekabuddhas' nondependence on helpful friends and teachers.[38]

Somehow, the period in which neither fully awakened ones nor śrāvakas are available was given a further dour twist, in that prospective pratyekabuddhas were to linger in cremation grounds. There, so it is said, along with their contemplation of what is revolting to one's aesthetic sensibilities, it was the sight of a skeleton that would make them wonder how life's sordidness had come about, and it was this sight that would lead them to develop the idea of the *pratītyasamutpāda,* whose twelve members describe the principle of the basic connectedness of dynamic phenomena. These twelve members were interpreted in different ways reflecting the structure-oriented thinking of the Hinayana, on the one hand, and the process-oriented thinking of the Mahayana, on the other hand.

The first member in this netlike principle is the system's stepped-down excitation (Skt. *avidyā*), which in view of the fact that Buddhism started from the idea of an "intelligent" universe, prevents the system (Man) from seeing and understanding the universe as it is, and by implication, himself as part of the universe, as he is. This stepped-down excitation (and stepped-down intelligence) is, because of its inherent dynamic, connected with reality-constructing operations (Skt. *saṃskārāḥ*), the second member, which in view of the fact that reality for us as living beings is always an appreciated reality, assume in their actual operation an ethical flavor. They are also connected with perceptual operations (Skt. *vijñāna*), the third member, not so much as actual judgments of perception but as the trend toward such judgments. For this reason, the Yogācāra thinkers equated *vijñāna* with the *ālayavijñāna*, which we discussed in a previous chapter. This trend is connected with the emergence of denotations, which comprise the operations of feelings, ideas, reality-constructing operations and cognitions, as well as with the welter of shapes and colors (Skt. *nāma-rūpa*). *Nāma-rupa* is the fourth member. This complexity of denotations and colors and shapes is connected with sensory-specific fields, of which six were listed in view of the fact that a perceptual situation and a thought situation are alike in having an objective constituent. These six fields are called *ṣaḍ-āyatana* and constitute the fifth member. They are connected with that which is described as Man "being-in-touch-with" (Skt. *sparśa*) his inner and outer environment. Being-in-touch-with, the sixth member, is connected with feelings (Skt. *vedanā*), the seventh member, which judge a situation to be pleasant, unpleasant, or neutral. Feelings are connected with the eighth member, the "thirst" (Skt. *tṛṣṇā*) for having more of the same stuff if it is pleasurable, and less if it is unpleasurable. This thirst is connected with, and instrumental in, the organization of the experiencer as he appropriates the various impressions that impinge on him and make him begin to see clearly the ninth member, the distinction between himself and the rest of the world (Skt. *upādāna*). This organization and appropriation is connected with that which becomes the experiencer's life-world (Skt. *bhava*), the tenth member, with which he identifies himself through being born into it (Skt. *jāti*). Not only is birth, the eleventh member, connected with the individual's life-world, it also is connected with the processes of aging and dying (Skt. *jarā-maraṇa*), the twelfth member.

To the extent that there seems to be a sequential order whereby one member follows from the other, it has been tempting to interpret this web of interconnected dynamic phenomena in terms of a linear causality (Skt. *hetu*), and most authors on Buddhism, both in the East and in the West, still continue talking about Buddhist "causality." However, this mechanistic assessment breaks down if we remind ourselves of the fact that it was the sight of death that led to the formulation of the principle of dynamic connectedness and that this principle can be read in either direction, beginning with the last member and ending with the first or beginning with the first and ending with the last member. If one wants to retain the mechanistic notion of causality within the framework of Buddhist thought, one will have to acknowledge that the Buddhist notion of "causality" is not of a one-way, linear (cause-effect) kind. In terms of the system's internal organization—Man is made of the same stuff as the universe—all the factors that go into this organization (referred to as fundamental forces (Skt. *mahābhūta*),[39] acts, each in its own way, as a "modifier" (Skt. *pratyaya*). Each may, at any moment, be in the ascendent. Hence, that which is usually rendered as "cause" (*hetu*) is itself a "modifier" (*hetu-pratyaya*) within the system as a whole and operates more like the system's sustained and sustaining dynamics.

There can be no doubt that the principle of dynamic connectedness, the formulation of which is attributed to the pratyekabuddhas, breaks with the restriction imposed by the reduction of the Buddhist teaching to the Four Truths, which are geared to the śrāvaka understanding. Apart from this innovation, however, the pratyekabuddha way is in all other aspects and details the same as the śrāvaka way, and both the śrāvaka as an arhant and the pratyekabuddha end up in a final static state characterized as evanescence and quiescence. But for the Mahayanists, as Klong-chen rab-'byams-pa tells us,[40] this allegedly static end state is a dynamic field comprising multiple facets or levels, depending on the effort that has gone into the individual's self-growth or way. These levels each have a field character and are called in Tibetan *bde-ba-can* (Sukhāvatī), *mngon-dga'* (Abhirati, Abhiruci?), *padmo-can* (Padmavatī), and so forth. Each name is suggestive of the field's felt qualities. Here, in these fields, the arhants and pratyekabuddhas reside in the calyxes of lotus flowers, which remain closed until the rays of the sun open them. The sun is "buddha compassion," resonating with and throughout the universe, itself a sheer lucency for which the image of the sun is but a feeble metaphor. Its rays are the "buddha voice," the vibrations of this light, which arouse the arhants and pratyekabuddhas from their slumber and address them in the following words:

> I speak of nirvana in this context, and
> Although you have become emancipated from the tribulations of
> samsara,
> You have not yet passed into the real nirvana.
> You have to continue on with the buddha career.[41]

If ever there was a pratyekabuddha way, apart from the attempt to account for the continuity of Buddhism as it made its transition from the structure-oriented thinking of the Hinayana to the process-oriented thinking of the Mahayana, this way constituted a phase in the opening up of a new level of self-organization as part of an overall evolutionary dynamic.

8 *The Way* *The Later View I*

The Bodhisattva Way I: Prelude

A. The Meaning of the Terms Bodhisattva *and* Bodhicitta

The idea of a bodhisattva, central to the Mahayana form of Buddhism, evinces a social awareness that before the arising of this idea was unknown or largely neglected. Unlike the arhant and the pratyekabuddha, who as has been pointed out, attempt to escape from or remain unaffected by the world, the bodhisattva is a world-engaged experiencer. However, the Sanskrit term *bodhisattva* itself reveals nothing of the dynamic that is inherent here. Linguistically, it refers to a denotatively given particular that fits well into a static world view. It is the Tibetan translation of this Indian term by *byang-chub sems-dpa'* that reveals the fact that this term, connotatively, describes a person's mode of being installed in the world. It should never be forgotten that each and every translation is already an interpretation, even if the objectivist is unable to comprehend or unwilling to concede this fact because of his reductionistic obsession. Any translation-interpretation, therefore, points to a specific standpoint of inquiry. The standpoint in the Mahayana is no longer concerned with picturing the world as a totality of entities, but with the primordiality of experience as it expresses itself in and through an individual's experienced life-world.

Of course, we do not know when the Indian term was interpretatively translated into Tibetan, nor do we know if there was not perhaps already a Tibetan term that was imposed on the Indian one, leading to the many explications of it and the deepening of its meaning. One of the earliest explications is attributed to the great eighth-century Indian teacher Padmasambhava, who succinctly states:

> The pollutants have been completely cleaned up (*byang*);
> An originary awareness[1] has been established (*chub*) deep within us;
> One has in mind (*sems*) the existential value presented by others and one has the fortitude (*dpa'*) to act in this light.[2]

Two other, almost identical, interpretations of this term are given by Rong-zom Chos-kyi bzang-po in his commentary on the *gSang-ba snying-po,* a Tibetan text held in highest esteem by the followers of the Old Tradition (Tib. *rnying-ma*) in Tibet, and in his equally important commentary on the *Man-ngag lta-ba'i phreng-ba,* a work in Tibetan attributed to Padmasambhava. In this latter work he says:

> As to the term *byang-chub sems-dpa'*, *byang-chub* renders *bodhi*. This term has been coined in view of the fact that what it connotes is the ultimate abolishment of all impurities and the resultant transparent purity as well as a correct understanding and comprehension. *sems-dpa'* renders *sattva*. This latter term means "desire," "intelligence stuff,"[3] "a firm and unbending intention," "a sentient (thinking) being" (*sems-can*),[4] "conscious activity," and "summary." In the context here, it is used in the sense of "desiring pellucidity (*byang*) and consummation (*chub*)" or "having a firm and unbending intention to realize this pellucidity and consummation" or "deploying experience in the direction of either pellucidity and consummation or a state in which a person is engaged in representational thought processes."[5]

After quoting from canonical texts, he concludes with the significant statement: "In this context, therefore, the term *sems-can* is to be understood as *byang-chub*. Furthermore, there also is the word *byang-chub sems-can*. Here *sems-can* means an animate being. Any animate being who has this *byang-chub-kyi sems*, is a *byang-chub sems-dpa'*. In brief, this *byang-chub-kyi sems* is the combination of critical acumen (*shes-rab*) and compassion (*snying-rje*)."

In this term *byang-chub sems-can*, Rong-zom Chos-kyi bzang-po implicitly combines the two notions of *byang-chub-(kyi) sems* and *sems-can*. This is easy for him as a Tibetan because of the difference of the Tibetan inquiry-standpoint as compared with the Indian one. It is true, *sems-can* is used to render *sattva*, but this Indian term is denotative in that it refers to something (or someone) existing and is, in philosophical parlance, an ontic and, by implication, static term. The Tibetan term *sems-can*, by contrast, is descriptive of something (or someone) "having a mind (mentation)" and thus is preeminently a dynamic term. However, with respect to the term "having," we have to bear in mind the distinction, first made by Gabriel Marcel and elaborated by Maurice Merleau-Ponty, between "having-as-possession" and "having-as-implication."[6] Where mind or mentation is concerned, "having-as-possession" is ruled out: I do not have (possess) a mind that I can lay aside or dispose of like an old pair of shoes; rather "having a mind or mentation" means that I am implicated, caught up in it by being active in and through it. It is this implication in its most dynamic mode that has been given the code name bodhisattva and invites an investigation into the meaning of its constitutive component *bodhi* (*byang-chub*), a shortened form of *bodhicitta* (*byang-chub-(kyi) sems*).[7]

From Rong-zom Chos-kyi bzang-po's remarks, it becomes evident that the term *bodhicitta*, by its two components of *bodhi* and *citta*, describes two directional movements. These, though not in the manner of a juxtaposition of two discrete elements, are connected with and interwoven with each other in such a manner as to constitute an existential cross section of world experience. Each movement develops its own structural features by way of homologous (related through a common origin) dynamics; each movement, as it were, feeds on the other. Both, therefore, complement each other, so that the experiencer, the bodhisattva, lives both these movements in every occasion of experience. Rong-zom Chos-kyi bzang-po expresses this in the following words: "The root of each and every meaning (of which man's experienced world is constituted) lies in that which is merely mind (*sems*) and this mind's lighting up (*sems-snang*) (as a total phenomenon). But this mind in itself is (the process termed) *byang-chub;* hence the (cover term) *byang-chub-kyi sems*."[8] Here the last trace of an ontic reductionism in which the Hinayana thinkers were caught up, has been wiped out.

As such a "mind," *byang-chub-sems* presents an inner nonequilibrium. As the effectiveness principle in the system's self-organization, it resides "embodied" in the concrete individual who is prompted by it to evolve his innate potential. The evolution of this inner potential moves either in the direction of the total system's optimization, which in this process leads to the most profound experience of Man as a dynamic system with the potential of manifesting itself in a variety of structural levels and cultural settings, or in the direction of an increasing stagnation in a pseudo-objective world that becomes less and less meaningful. In other words, this dynamic principle sums up the tension between a person's existence in its finitude and its transcendence. Embodied it remains finite, but suffused with transcendence it opens itself up to the infinity of the uncreated and unconditioned.

"Embodied" or, as the texts say, "tainted (by finitude)," this principle is referred to by three Tibetan terms: *rigs, khams,* and *de-bzhin gshegs-pa'i snying-po. rigs* and *khams* are as closely related as *byang-chub* and *sems*. In its "untainted" operation, this principle is referred to as *byang-chub* and *de-bzhin gshegs-pa.*[9]

rigs/khams

The term *rigs* sums up a living system's actional programs that ensure that it achieves its target already "encoded" in them. This activity includes the preservation of the system's structural organization and also secures its opening up to new degrees of freedom. The possible combinations and variations of programs, as yet consisting of and being present as the purest of qualities (Tib. *yon-tan*), yield what we nowadays would call genetic programs or genotypes that determine the system's development along its inherent lines and provide the standards by which it (as a phenotype) interacts with its environment. This is expressed by stating that there are different sociocultural "types" (*rigs*), such as śrāvakas, bodhisattvas, and even buddhas; and, as we have noted in a narrower context, such types as monks (Skt. *bhikṣu*), nuns (Skt. *bhikṣuṇī*), the laity (Skt. *upāsaka, upāsikā*), and so on.

The principle of complementarity that so pervades Buddhist thought also applies to the notion of *rigs,* in that, as Asanga states,[10] *rigs* is there as what it is (Skt. *prākṛtya*)—as a program but also as the unfolding (Skt. *paripuṣṭa*) of the program. However, apart from presenting this idea of complementarity, occurring again in his description of *rigs* as the founding stratum (Tib. *āśraya*) and the founded (Tib. *āśrita*), he seems to favor the idea of it as pure potential forever active in its unfolding.

In his *Mahāyānasūtrālaṅkāra,* Asanga presents a survey of the many facets of this organizing principle with its rich set of programs; but in the *Uttaratantra,* once ascribed to him, the salient points of this principle are explicated with special reference to the instances in which it manifests. Rather than being a particular instance of some kind of being that can be contrasted with some other kind of being, this principle as pure potential is what we would call in modern philosophical diction "Being-as-such" or "Being-in-its-beingness." As Martin Heidegger (1962, 1972) has shown in recent years, Being (Ger. *das Sein*) is not a thing that can be located somewhere or even temporalized; but, as Paul Häberlin (1952) has pointed out, it is always present in and as that which is (Ger. *das Seiende*), which can be located and is temporal. Maitreya, the real author of the *Uttaratantra,* is well aware of what thus appears to be a paradox, and speaks of it as "(Being's) authenticity" and elaborates as follows:

> As to this (authenticity), there is nothing in it that has to be removed;
> There also is nothing that has to be installed (as if it were not yet present in it).
> This authenticity sees (itself) as authenticity.
> It is when one (comes to) see authentically that one is set free.[11]

Inasmuch as this authenticity is, in terms of the experiencing individual, the individual's own mind, not as a granular entity but as a sheer lucency and self-organizing dynamics, we can, in the second half of the quotation, recognize the mind's self-reflexivity, through which the whole universe is related to the experiencer and the experiencer to the whole universe. This is also the mind's, and by implication, the individual's, freedom.

It is the first half of the above quotation that has always presented difficulties to the rationalist, who in the Buddhist context is represented by the follower of the Hinayana, the śrāvaka or a pratyekabuddha, because it involves a "both-and," not an "either-or." The situation is even more complex, because two levels of complementarity are involved. The one may be called "existential" in that it is made up of the "tainted" (Tib. *khams*) and the "untainted" (Tib. *byang-chub*). The other may be called "set-operational" in that it is made up of the system's "programs" (Tib. *rigs* = Tib. *yon-tan*) manifest in the individual's abilities and capabilities, and "program executions" (Tib. *mdzad-pa*), expressive of the total system's creativity, first through thoughts and ideas and lastly through their embodiment in man's cultural world.

Maitreya sums up these four points as reasons for the fact that the principle under consideration cannot be encompassed by rational thought. He says:

> Because it has both purity and pollution;
> Because in the absence of pollutants (as an essentialistic feature of it) it is pure;
> Because it is such that (its programs) are indivisibly (omnipresent); and
> Because it just is (operational) without any preconceptions.[12]

The complementarity between the totality of the non-unfolded qualities or actional programs and their unfolding in an interplay of opposites that no dialectical synthesis can resolve, Maitreya has summed up in these words:

> While this principle as system potential (*dhātu*) is devoid of incidental (pollutants) that are such that they can be analytically differentiated and separated,
> It is not devoid of (its) unsurpassable qualities, which are such that they cannot be analytically differentiated and separated.[13]

This passage has given rise to an acrimonious controversy with the literalists (the Prāsangika faction of the Mādhyamikas), who were unable to grasp the metaphorical nature of language and remained tied to objectivistic prejudice. The expression "devoid of incidental (pollutants)" was to indicate that the pollutants, summed up by the collective term "samsara," with which the individual had to cope as constitutive of his finitude, were not constitutive of the system potential in the manner of an essence and hence could be transcended (though not annulled). The expression "not devoid of (its) unsurpassable qualities" was just another way of saying that this principle or system potential was the totality of the non-unfolded qualities, which as the system's power of transcendence, were not constitutive of the system's finitude itself. In the words of Maitreya:

> Because it has its shortcomings, which are incidental, and
> Because it has its actional programs, which are the principle itself—
> As before so hereafter—
> It is (Being's) invariance principle.[14]

In the language of mathematics (which is so often helpful in understanding the complexities of Buddhist thought without having to invoke metaphysical pseudo-answers), invariance is synonymous with symmetry. This means that if a system remains invariant under one or more transformations, it is said to be symmetric. The more different transformations the system is invariant under, the higher is its degree of symmetry. Applied to the Buddhist locution, this is to say that Being (Ger. *das Sein*) has the highest degree of symmetry and remains invariant under any and all transformations (Ger. *das Seiende,* the many "shortcomings").

Admittedly, the idea of *rigs* as a set of actional programs and its overall dynamic character breaks with a static conception of Man and is not easily grasped by someone who is accustomed to a structure-oriented view of Man and his world. It is this structure-oriented perspective that seems to be more pronounced in the notion of *khams* (Skt. *dhātu*), inasmuch as this term is used to indicate the concrete individual's system potential, which is both "physical" and "psychic" at the same time. Its psychic dimension was for the followers of the Yogācāra (Cittamātra) line of thought identical with their idea of an *ālayavijñāna,*[15] describing the trend toward conscious operations that are mainly representational and take the subject-object scheme for granted. Although they were aware of man's urge to transcend himself, they considered this urge to be a special operator within the *ālayavijñāna,* a part of the system's potential (Tib. *khams*) insofar as it presented its "psychic" aspect. Moreover, this operator or, more precisely, germinal program, had been "acquired" at a time when life began or, as the Buddhists would say, "since time without beginning." It was their preoccupation with representational thought, which isolates its figures as denotable objects, that, as Mi-pham 'Jam-dbyangs rnam-rgyal rgya-mtsho (1846–1912) informs us, led them to claim the existence of five "types" (*rigs*) of personalities.[16] Just as there are different kinds of rocks, some containing gold, others iron or copper, and still others no special metals or minerals, so there are also the different types of followers of the path—the decided types represented by the three careers of a śrāvaka, a pratyekabuddha, and a bodhisattva; the undecided type, who could be swayed by contact with a member of any one of the decided types to become a partisan of that particular life style; and, lastly, a "barren" type, whom we might describe as a social "write off." The existence of this last type, though mentioned in the highly esteemed *Mahāyānasūtrālaṅkāra,* which lists the various opinions that were held with respect to these "program sets," and also discussed in the *Uttaratantra,* was rejected by the rest of the Buddhists on both textual and logical grounds. As a consequence, the relevant passages were reinterpreted to mean that this "program set" was only dormant and not yet activated. It is in this sense that Klong-chen rab-'byams-pa interprets *Uttaratantra* I 40, which says:

If there were no potential for (developing into that which is termed)
buddha (*buddhadhātu*),[17]
One would not become disgusted with the frustration (that is
samsara), nor
Would one desire nirvana,
Make efforts (to realize it) or even have any inclination (for it).

Here the text is referring to the dormant state of this program, and Klong-chen rab-'byams-pa adds the gibe that certain despicable persons exemplify it.[18] In support of the activated state of this program he quotes *Uttaratantra* I 41:

Seeing the flaws and merits of frustration and happiness,
respectively,
As they pertain to world and nirvana,
Derives from the existence of (such a) program. Why?
Because this does not happen with those in whom there is no such
program.

de-bzhin/bde-bar gshegs-pa'i snying-po

The rejection of the notion that there was an "unprogrammed" type was based on the statement, found in many texts, that what is descriptively refered to as the "evolutionary thrust" (Tib. *de-bzhin gshegs-pa'i snying-po*) or experientially as the "optimizing thrust" (Tib. *bde-bar gshegs-pa'i snying-po*) pervaded each and every living being. So, how could there be a person in whom it was not present? In the first phrase, the term *de-bzhin* is short for *de-bzhin-nyid,* which corresponds to our idea of Being-as-such or Being-in-its-beingness (Ger. *das Sein*), as well as the felt understanding of it in which the subject-object categorical scheme has been transcended. This transcendence effectuates our move into Being-in-its-beingness rather than continuing in some kind of denotable being. The term *snying-po* indicates the inherent dynamic of this process, which holistically involves the whole person as the experiencer. A word of caution is necessary here. Although the term Being-as-such may suggest a static end state, it is basically that which incites a person; it is a "program" for a person's evolution into his humanity, which is never a foregone conclusion, but an open-ended task. It is in this sense that I use the term "evolutionary."

There is one other important point that marks the tremendous gap between the vision of a person in the *Uttaratantra* and the lingering static conception of him as subscribed to by the followers of the Yogācāra tradition. This is the existentially felt significance of the buddha experience (Tib. *sangs-rgyas*), in which structure and process intertwine and determine each other.

The process of experiencing takes on the character of a gestalt (Tib.

sku) of living intentionalities and lived meanings (Tib. *chos*), which in its very dynamic can be compared with a dissipative structure in the sense that the emerging structure corresponds to the systemic function as the totality of the processes. It follows that the whole process as such is inseparable from the totality of Being-as-such (Tib. *de-bzhin-nyid*) and constitutes its autocatalytic self-organization program (Tib. *rigs*). In philosophical terms, that which is (Ger. *das Seiende*) is, in the narrower sense of the word, an embodied being (Tib. *lus-can*). Thus it can be said, quite literally, to "embody" Being-in-its-beingness (Ger. *das Sein*) and to be inseparable from Being-in-its-beingness and vice versa. Maitreya's statement concerning a person's buddha program reveals a very profound insight. His words are:

> Because of the pulsation of the gestalt as an awakening process
> (evolving like a dissipative structure) in its totality,
> Because of (its) inseparability from Being-in-its-beingness, and
> Because of (its) existence as a program, all embodied beings
> Have within themselves forever this thrust to move in the direction
> of a total spiritual awakening.[19]

This passage is of particular importance as it reflects a living system's autocatalysis and the circularity of the processes of life. These involve a ubiquitous systemic interdependence that cannot be grasped by, or reduced to, a linear causality, although the texts still use the terms "cause" and "effect," simply because language does not keep pace with the development and refinement of ideas. Rong-ston Smra-ba'i seng-ge (1367–1449)[20] approvingly quotes the Hva-shang Mahāyāna, who interpreted the dynamic term "meaning-rich gestalt" (Tib. *chos-sku*), synonymous with Being-in-its-beingness in its being deeply felt and understood (Tib. *de-bzhin gshegs-pa*), as the effect that is nonetheless the "thrust toward it(self)" (Tib. *snying-po*) in all living beings. Its presence ensures its realization. Being-as-such (Tib. *de-bzhin-nyid*) as this very thrust is operative both in a person who deeply feels and understands it and in a person who merely thinks about it (a sentient being, *sems-can*). We might paraphrase this statement by saying that a buddha and a sentient (thinking) being both present Being-in-its-beingness, which does not exhaust itself in the one or the other. And the program climaxing in the understanding of Being-in-its-beingness as its "cause" operates in each and every sentient being.

This system potential (Tib. *khams*), which also is its program (Tib. *rigs*), assumes, as it were, different aspects according to the level on which and as which it manifests itself. In its "finitude" of a concrete individual, it is described as "impure"—synonymous with "tainted"—but this finitude is suffused with transcendence, and as such it is described as "impure-pure." Lastly, as pure dynamics it is described as "very pure." These three aspects are associated with the three levels of sentient (thinking) being, bodhisattva, and buddha.[21] However, this concretistic diction should not incline us toward the objectivistic fallacy. The original texts make it abundantly clear that they are referring to processes, not static entities. Thus "impure" describes the system potential as it is operative in the thinking process of an ordinary person (Tib. *sems-can-gyi khams,* Skt. *sattvadhātu*); "impure-pure" describes the dynamics of this potential as it moves in the direction of pellucidity and consummation (Tib. *byang-chub-sems,* Skt. *bodhicitta;* short for Tib. *byang-chub sems-dpa',* Skt. *bodhisattva*); and "very pure" describes the process of deeply feeling and understanding Being-in-its-beingness (Tib. *de-bzhin gshegs-pa,* Skt. *tathāgata*), which sums up the evolutionary thrust in the emergence of a new dynamic regime in the manner of a dissipative structure (Tib. *sangs-rgyas,* Skt. *buddha*).

It did not escape the notice of the Buddhists that this shift in perspective from presenting the universe and Man in terms of a static collocation of granular entities to seeing it as a dynamic system unfolding in its hierarchical self-organization, and Man in particular as "programed" to evolve into ever widening dimensions, not only brought to light certain ontological—not ontic—features implicitly present in it, but also, because of the novelty of this inquiry-standpoint, presented considerable difficulties to an understanding of it. Furthermore, did not the ontological considerations that came with the introduction of hitherto rejected ideas such as permanence, stability, dynamic poise, and perpetuity (all of which are meaningful in a positive sense only from a dynamic perspective), contradict everything that had been taught so far, namely, that all that is is impermanent and unstable? Certainly, Maitreya is himself fully aware of what to the rationalist must appear as a contradiction, when he says:

> After having stated here and there that
> Everything knowable is absolutely nothing in itself
> But like clouds, dreams, and magic shows,
> Why is it that here the victors say that in sentient (thinking) beings
> there exists this Buddha-thrust?[22]

By way of explication, it may be added that the phrase "everything knowable" in the Buddhist context means that in principle everything can be known, but it also implies that the whole of reality can be reduced to denotable entities *about* which we can talk more or less intelligently or rationally, as was the contention of the Hinayana thinkers. Still, as the Mahayana thinkers noted, there also was an aspect of reality that cannot be reduced to denotable entities, but can and must be experienced. This recognition was tantamount to an opening up of a new level of insight and freedom, and correspondingly, to the awareness that language is metaphorical through and through.

This innovative approach to reality by the Mahayana thinkers, which focused on the living individual as the experiencer of world and himself, not only put him into a fresh perspective but also had practical implications for him. In order to become human, a person has to transcend himself by himself—there is no agency that can do the job he himself has to do—and this he can do only by resorting to the potential lying in him and by bringing it into full play by removing the self-imposed restrictions on it. This is the purpose, as Maitreya states it, of presenting this work to the general public:

> (This work explicating a person's potential) has been made public in order to dispel these five shortcomings in whomsoever they may be:
> Faint-heartedness, contempt for others as inferior to one's self,
> Holding on to that which is not authentic, denouncing that which is authentic, and
> Having an overevaluated idea of oneself.[23]

Against the background of a person's finitude, which yet opens him up to his infinitude, (often compared to the vast expanse of the sky, which may become overcast and seemingly lose its openness—the clouds being the sky and yet only part of it), the theme of the finitude of Man's existence with all its consequences is developed. This open, "authentic" finitude is, figuratively speaking, the level of quietness at which the fluctuations of the mind as mentation set the stage for Man's becoming "en-worlded."

If it were not for the existence of a system potential in each and every living being, nobody would ever be in a position to transcend his finitude and overcome his shortcomings, which on the whole, are socially negative. If this were not pointed out, people would merely be confirmed in their finitude, believing mistakenly that it is something absolute. The result would be the grossest type of egoism.

By contrast, having been made aware of the potential that is in us and that we are, we can develop ideas and values that free us from the suffocating dogmas of a past without trapping ourselves again in some idealizations of a future. Above all, we can develop ideas and values that free us from believing in a stationary self with its "here and now" ideology. Thus the shift from mere negativity to a positive perspective of life and man is expressed by Maitreya as follows:

> By having heard (about the existence of this potential in us)
> Cheerfulness, respect (for others) as if (they were the very embodiment of) the teacher,

(Our) critical acumen, existential awareness, and an unbounded
love come into full play;
And because these five features have come into full play, it is due to
them that
There is no self-depreciation (nor contempt for) others, whom one
sees as being like (ourselves in having this potential);
And (conceiving of) oneself and others as being alike in
Not having any flaws, but rather having capabilities and abilities,
The very status of being a spiritually awakened one (buddha) is
quickly realized.[24]

The Activation of *Bodhicitta*

Careful attention to the use of the innocent looking Sanskrit term *bodhicitta* (Tib. *byang-chub-sems*) in the indigenous texts makes us realize that it sums up a complex program by which mentation (Tib. *sems*)—with its emphasis on thematizing, representational thinking—is made to grow into what is its refinement as pellucidity (Tib. *byang*) as an approximation to Being's sheer lucency, and consummation (Tib. *chub*), by which the original unity with Being is restored. Effecting this growth that is tantamount to a shift in perspective is descriptively indicated by the Sanskrit term *utpāda* (Tib. *bskyed*). Hence the Sanskrit compound *bodhicittotpāda,* usually rendered in the Tibetan texts in the abbreviated form of *sems-bskyed,* can be best rendered in English by paraphrasing this single term in Sanskrit and Tibetan as "effecting a shift from representational thinking to an existential awareness and understanding."[25]

Raising mentation to the level of existential awareness is not only a linking back to the origin in its undivided wholeness but also a restoration of the initial intensity so that the system autocatalytically provides the conditions for a new start that constitutes the core of creativity. Klong-chen rab-'byams-pa expresses this idea in the following words:

Because existential awareness is not in evidence when
During samsara the act and object phases of mentation with its
concomitant operators are in foment,
This activation of the shift from representational thinking to an
existential awareness
Injects power into the very brilliance of existential awareness.[26]

Inasmuch as it can be unequivocably stated that a human person is programmed to grow up and thereby to enhance the complexity of the overall system by setting it free from the limitations imposed by a pseudo-objective world and allowing values to suffuse its whole life, it becomes the task of the individual to give form and content to this program.

To the question, "Who is capable of bringing about this shift in perspective from pseudo-objectivity to existential awareness?" different answers have been given. The followers of the Yogācāra line of thought, who, though generally considered to belong to the Mahayana fold, were still rather conservative in outlook, claimed that any person embodied in any one of the seven ranks of the social nexus (Skt. *prātimokṣa*) as recognized by the Buddhists, and observing the particular obligations that went with his or her rank, was able to effect this shift. The Mādhyamikas, however, claimed in addition that any living being, including mythological personages, provided that they held that which went by the name of Mahayana in high esteem and had a desire to attain the status of an individual who is spiritually awake (buddha), could do so. Emphasis was thus on the psychic readiness to redesign the world in such a way that Man could live in it, rather than on the physical status that was basically representative of a static world view about to give way to a dynamic one.

With the inclusion of mythological figures, a new world view is opened up. It would be a mistake to assume that these mythological figures, among whom a host of bodhisattvas is found, were an invention by individuals either to "explain" (mechanistically, of course) the happenings in life's drama, or to alleviate the dullness and drabness of a world that owes its very existence to Man's rationality leaving out or making light of much that is of vital importance. Rather, the mythological world is a world of qualities and values as well as their interactions, and the individual is a participant in this drama. He addresses these qualities and forces, which as it were, "talk back" to him, so that a dialogue is established. In such a dialogue the "other" assumes an anthropomorphic or semi-anthropomorphic shape, and there is both distance and closeness in this interplay of the experiencer and the experienced forces of life. The most deeply felt and listened-to force addressed in this dialogue is *a* or *the* Buddha. If man's ordinary world with its predictable regularities is the outcome of the reductionistic tendencies of his rationality, then the mythological world and its accompanying world view is the outcome of his creative imagination, which finds its most deeply moving expression in the fine arts. It therefore does not come as a surprise that art was an integral aspect of Mahayana Buddhism, in the sense that at its height it reflected the interplay between novelty and confirmation. In the course of time, this interplay gave way to a gradual increase in confirmation. Creativity stagnated into standardization of form and what once had been of the nature of personal relationships, vibrant with life, became fossilized as rituals.

In the mythological world view, a feedback link is established between the experiencer and the experienced and the focus is on the personal relationship between oneself and the other. From a psychological perspective, it is the "we experience," first pointed out and developed in the framework of Western thought by Max Scheler, that is of primary importance. Practically speaking, here mutual enhancement prevails over self-enhancement and shows up as altruism. In the Buddhist context, mutuality is the guiding principle in bringing about a shift in attitude, because only to the extent that I am sure of myself as presenting an existential value can I see and treat the other as presenting an existential value, too. The implication of mutuality is clearly stated in the following passage:

> Making the shift from representational thought to an existential awareness operative
> Is the desire (to realize) authentic and holistically functional limpid clearness and consummate perspicacity in order to enhance the existential value presented by the other.[27]

Considering the fact that *bodhicitta* is a code term for the complex network of programs to be worked out by an individual, and not a term for some denotable entity, its activation has been discussed in terms of sets listed according to the number of members that belong to a particular set. Although "set" is a static notion, the use of it in the present context has the advantage of helping to highlight the connectedness of certain processes.

Śāntideva describes *bodhicitta,* short for *bodhicittotpāda,* as "the activation of the shift from representational thinking to an existential awareness," as constituting a set having only two members:

> In brief, this *bodhicitta*
> Should be known to be twofold:
> The intent as an inclination toward *bodhi,* and
> The actual engagement in this *bodhi* (realization).[28]

He continues elucidating the difference between these two aspects, which for him form a sequence, by giving the example of a person who merely wants to go and a person who is actually going. He also makes it quite clear that the mere intent, though having some merit, is of little avail, and that a person has to be fully "engaged" if ever he wants to achieve anything in life.

As a set with three members, this activation involves mastering the art of self-discipline (Skt. *śila*), by which one refrains from whatever is unwholesome and unhealthy for one's development, and in so doing, refines one's personality through which one participates in the life of one's community. Inasmuch as community and personality are coextensive (Schrag 1969, 197f.), refinement of one's personality enhances the community in which one lives. This, in turn, may encourage further refinement on the basis of a mutual acceptance of self and other. Secondly, this activation contains mastering the art of making one's outlook on life stay with whatever is wholesome and healthy through concentration and in-depth appraisals (Skt. *samādhi*), which serve as aids in making whatever is positive grow. Thirdly, it contains mastering the art of using one's critical acumen (Skt. *prajñā*), through which one is enabled to differentiate between what is positive and what is negative and to realize one's own as well as the other's existential value—which is not something predetermined by, or identical with, the ideological dictates of any one society, nor is it predetermined by one's personal idiosyncracies. Critical acumen sets a man free and prevents him from being absorbed into any one ideology or any one social mode.

As presenting a set with four members, this activation reveals itself as a process. In a very condensed form, this process is outlined by Maitreya-(Asanga):

> This activation of the shift from representational thinking to existential awareness involves (1) devotion; (2) an out-of-the-ordinary intent that (in addition) is lucid; different from these
> Is (3) the maturation into the upper levels (of one's hierarchical organization); and (4) the elimination of (all) obscurations.[29]

Devotion is already a manifestation of the altruistic principle at work in the activation of the shift from representational thinking to an existential awareness, and its religious overtones are a secondary accretion. Devotion is most distinctly operative in the "build-up phase" (the preparatory way) and the "probability-of-a-breakthrough phase) (the way of linking that which has been prepared and built up to the way of seeing the human situation "with fresh eyes"). It can be either an external or an internal act that is selective in choosing the program (Tib. *rigs*) that contains the "information" for the individual's development within his social environment. It acts on this information as if it were an "objective" reality. Whether an external or an internal act, it plays an active role in reordering experience so that eventually one overcomes the dualistic split into self and other and realizes the identity of the two in the sense that both present an existential value by virtue of their both being part of, and yet the whole of, reality. In addition, it prepares for the felt understanding of the meaningfulness of Being in its immediacy.

The out-of-the-ordinary intent reflects the awareness of the identity of self and other, and since it is divested of the above mentioned dualistic split, it has a certain lucidity not found in the preceding phase of devotion. Hence it is much less opaque than the mere thematic operations of the rational mind. With reference to the various spiritual levels or levels of the individual's development, it is operative on the first seven of the ten levels, each intensifying and broadening its cognitive domain.

Maturation indicates the autonomy of the individual's existential awareness as an undivided whole and in terms of the dynamic application of the various transcending functions that open up new dimensions of being. It is operative on the last three levels of an individual's development. It is on these levels that the "outer" world is being redesigned on the basis of structures of "pure," materially unbound information. For this reason, maturation is said to be different from the two other phases, which were still "object" (matter) bound.

The elimination of all obscurations, intellectual (thematizing-representational) as well as emotional (system-polluting), pertains to the buddha level, which in modern terms, develops like a dissipative structure of unlimited potential. For the literalist imprisoned in a static world view, the inclusion of this phase in the overall program for a bodhisattva was contradictory, because, using mythological language, a bodhisattva is not a buddha. The literalist, of course, fails to grasp the fact that all language is intentional in character and primarily connotative and that, within the present context, the inclusion of that which is described in terms of a level focuses on the process moving in this direction, not on the resulting structure.[30]

Nonetheless, the language of sets carries with it a certain static connotation due to the granular nature of the set members. Therefore, it has appealed to the structure-dominated, and by implication, reductionistic trend of Indian thought. Again, it is Klong-chen rab-'byams-pa, who as a representative of pure process thinking, has clearly understood this process character involving an extraordinary intensification of life and its creativity. Being "in tune with," or resonating with, wholeness, this process allows for different optimization criteria with respect to living beings who represent different organizational levels within the evolutionary movement. It is with respect to this intensification that Klong-chen rab-'byams-pa declares:

> Even if through the efficaciousness engendered by the cessation of mentation when the stream (constituted by the ten spiritual levels) disappears with the level,
> The shift level presenting an approximation to the existential awareness, passes away,
> (The fact remains that) their power is added to this existential awareness, by which
> It expands into the *sangs-rgyas* (Buddha) level and (from there) in resonance (with the universe) aids (the living beings to find their existential) value.
> This is said to be the shift level on which all obscurations have been wiped away.[31]

The process nature of that which is summed up in this "set" with its four members, is also indicated by the statement that it has its root in compassion (Tib. *snying-rje,* Skt. *karuṇā*). Although compassion originates in the individual, by its very dynamic it transcends its initial framework of the interaction of self and other and opens up new levels and dimensions of connectedness. Compassion evolves in such a way that in Being's undivided wholeness it falls together with this wholeness as its ever-active organizing principle, which in our finitude shows up as a system of relations "which become translated into sociocultural macrosystems such as communities, societies and civilizations" (Jantsch 1980, 211). Compassion as the moving force of man's humanity may well be the moving force of the whole universe if we become aware of the paradox of ourselves being the whole and yet only a part of it. Unlike the Sanskrit language, the Tibetan language has a term reserved for this "level" (if "level" is still an appropriate pointer)—*thugs-rje* (*chen-po*) "compassion in resonance with the whole universe."

The activation of the shift from representational thinking to an existential awareness is further conceived of as being constituted by a set with five members. In these, we easily recognize the five stages of the śrāvaka way. This shows that the evolution of Buddhist thought did not occur in quantum jumps but by way of interacting simultaneous processes. The five members in this set are:

1. The way of preparation or the build-up phase. This phase, which specifically pertains to the beginner, comprises listening to and thinking about that which one has heard, that is, been taught, and engaging in activities that enhance the sociocultural setting in which one lives.
2. The way of linking that which one has learned and practiced with the way of seeing, which itself is an existential awareness in which no dividedness by the thematizing operations of the mind intrudes. It is, more precisely, a probability-of-a-breakthrough phase, the breakthrough occurring only when the intensity characterizing this way reaches its highest pitch.
3. The way of seeing "with fresh eyes." In this vision it dawns upon the seer that Being is intrinsically meaningful.
4. The way of cultivating the vision by means of creative, imaginative experimentation.
5. The way of no-more-learning, when from a static point of view, the limits of the system's capabilities have been reached, but from a dynamic point of view, the system has become pure potential.

Another important set with six members, expressive of and reinforcing the activation of the shift from representational thinking to an existential awareness, comprises sociocultural actions that themselves are already expressions of the individual's awareness of his being ethically embedded in a social context, as well as mental activities aimed at breaking the impasse of one's everyday mentation. All of them are in the service of an individual's self-transcendence. They are dynamic features, not static notions as the mistaken rendering of the Sanskrit technical term *pāramitā* (by which they are usually designated) by "perfection" suggests. As a neologism introduced into the Sanskrit language by the Buddhists, this term precisely indicates the individual's self-transcendence through the practice of these six actions. This, it must be stated, the Tibetans recognized in their rendering of this term by *pha-rol-tu phyin-pa,* which literally translated, means "having gone to the other (opposite) shore." These actions are, in general terms:

1. The readiness to give, without being miserly, whatever may be necessary in view of a person's multifaceted reality. It therefore does not restrict itself to mere material gifts, but also takes into account a person's intellectual and spiritual needs.
2. Self-discipline by which the individual restrains himself from engaging in socially unacceptable activities. Here there is special emphasis on his thought processes, because it is these that manifest in forms of ethics and morality.
3. Patience in the sense of accepting the tribulations of the world, though not succumbing to them as in resignation and other fatalistic attitudes, but persevering in fortitude, calmness, and composure.
4. Sustained endeavor in pursuing, and even seeking, whatever is conducive to one's welfare and the common good.
5. Concentration on a single objective, which in Mahayana Buddhism is nothing less than Being's undivided wholeness.
6. Critical acumen by which one questions and probes the uncritical belief in things and ideas as having an ontic status.

A rich array of symbols has been listed in order to explicate the wide scope, as well as the nature, of this activation of the shift from representational thinking to an existential awareness. Symbols are aids in recreating the world, first in imaginative visions and lastly in sociocultural actions, but they are also barriers in that they limit the subject of discourse. These two opposite and apparently contradictory aspects—creativity and reductionism—are simultaneously at work. Thus, when this activation of the shift from representational thinking to an existential awareness with its multiple nuances is, in its onset, spoken of as being a "fertile soil," in this first utterance, creativity is at work by eliciting many associations; but when this shift is declared to be "aspiration," the onset of reductionism is discernable, and a barrier to imaginative variations of the theme "fertile soil" has been set up. The next step is a rigid classification according to the recognized phases of the way as a whole. There are twenty-two "symbols" and their corresponding "resolutions" (reductions) to mental-spiritual dispositions and their active expressions, ex-

TABLE 2

SYMBOLS	DISPOSITIONS	PHASES
fertile soil	aspiration	preparatory phase passing through three intensities
gold	unflagging intent	
moon	out-of-the ordinary intent	
fire	sedulousness	linkage with the phase of "seeing"
treasure	generosity	the ten spiritual levels
jewel mine	self-discipline	
ocean	patience	
diamond	effort	
mountain	concentration	
medicine	critical acumen	
friend	expertise	
wish-fulfilling gem	entreaty	
sun	puissance	
singing	existential awareness (these ten act as aids in self-transcendence)	
king	immediacy in perceptiveness	operative on the last three levels
treasury	merits and awareness	
highway	autocatalytic operators in the realization of pellucidity and consummation	
vehicle	compassion and wider perspective	
hot spring	alertness maintenance	
echo	meaning-saturated feasting	"getting onto" the ten levels, their "core" and their outcome
river	the only way to travel	
cloud	the gestalt experience of Being as "pure" meaning	

tending over the whole of the way as a learning process. Graphically they can be represented as detailed in Table 2.

The above summary goes back to the Indian scholar Haribhadra (tenth century). In the Tibetan tradition, it is the generally accepted one. But this does not mean that there have not been other interpretations and attempts to reduce these many elements to the two aspects Śāntideva had recognized.[32]

The actual activation of this shift from representational thinking to an existential awareness presents itself as the interplay of external and internal factors such that whatever forms part of the process up to the breakthrough owes its effectiveness to environmental factors, such as the advice by friendly persons whose teaching falls on eager ears. However, all that starts with the so-called first spiritual level or "seeing reality with fresh eyes" and then grows in intensity, owes its effectiveness to the system's program dynamics. In the words of Maitreya-(Asanga):

> Through the strength of true friends, through the strength of the system's innate program, through the strength of the system's resource potential, through the strength of one's learning ability, and through one's habituation to whatever is wholesome and healthy (the shift from representational thinking to an existential awareness is activated).
>
> (The first strength assists us in getting rid of our) instability, (the following four strengths ensure) that stability becomes stronger. (All five strengths) are said to (refer to) the activation of the shift from representational thinking to an existential awareness as initiated by information received from elsewhere.[33]

It may seem strange that the iterative feedback loop between an individual's inner and outer world is said to be due to "information received from elsewhere." The point is that the activation of the shift occurs within an individual's social framework and, as a learning process, may well occur in its initial stage as imitation (of others). However, learning is never mere imitation and certainly not mere imitation-without-understanding. Learning is a process of creative experimentation resulting in the felt understanding of our human situation. As such, it constitutes a new autopoietic level, which in terms of the shift from representational thinking to an existential awareness, is termed the "supremely valid and valuable shift (Skt. *paramārtha,* Tib. *don-dam*)." This is because it is from here that we are enabled to grasp the meaning of our life holistically in all its vibrancy.

Seen as an evolutionary thrust, this shift from representational thinking to an existential awareness may, in its incipient phase, be considered in rationalistic terms as the "cause." However, it comprises a triune dynamic program in the sense that it consists of (1) a "purpose" involving a trust in the attainability of the "goal" (which here is nothing less than the whole, termed *sangs-rgyas*—the [system's] unfolding into spiritual wakefulness); (2) a sociocultural program termed "compassion" extending to everything that is alive; and (3) an unrestricted access to the resource material provided by the system's consummatory pellucidity.

Seen as the effect of this thrust, the shift from representational thinking to an existential awareness is felt as a change in one's emotional and intellectual attitude, which influences one's whole environment. When we feel happy, our happiness (which reflects the whole system's optimization initiated by this shift) becomes contagious, and in social terms, we do not shirk our responsibilities to others, including our environment, but even carry others along with us. The emphasis on responsibility, which even in its most rudimentary form implies some kind of altruism, stresses the individual's creative participation in the optimization of the human world. This is not merely "an individualistic ethics in the disguise of a socially committing behavioural code" (Jantsch 1980, 265). Such an immediately felt and simultaneously implemented change is described in Mipham 'Jam-dbyangs rnam-rgyal rgya-mtsho's paraphrase of Maitreya's aphorism as follows:

> Immediately with this climactic shift, a judicious person
> Restrains his mentation from engaging in any crimes against humanity.
> Instead, he will give whatever is positive its widest scope and intensify his (feelings of) compassion and sympathy, whereby he will continuously abide in happiness and display his tenderness and warmheartedness and for this reason he will
> Joyfully accept both the happy and sorrowful moments in life.[34]

In the actual climax of this shift, we not only reach beyond our own limits as individuals, but also beyond the limits of mankind. Śāntideva speaks in this connection of what we have termed an "approximation symmetry transformation" with respect to Being-as-such, which is termed "the Victor" (Skt. *jina*) in the mythological language so frequently used when one attempts to describe the feeling of being embedded in a dynamic whole and one's relationship to it. Śāntideva's words are:

> Firmly grasp this most powerful philosophers' stone
> Named *bodhicitta,* since
> Applied to this impure semblance (that is our finitude as an approximate displacement symmetry)
> It turns it into the priceless likeness of the jewel that is the state of being a Victor (an approximation symmetry transformation of Being-in-its-beingness).[35]

ETHICS AND SOCIOCULTURAL LEVELS

This shift from representational thinking to an existential awareness, from a rational approach to life, set as an absolute, to a world rich in psychic responses bringing quality into focus, takes place within a social context that somehow favors its emergence. Thus it necessarily has sociocultural implications. Among them, participation in collaborative ritual and the development of an ethics furthering the whole of mankind play a significant role. Ritual actions may be understood as forms of symbolic statement about the social order, which itself participates in the evolutionary process. However, ritual actions have the tendency to become fossilized into a set of religio-ideological rules, whereby that which once was a process of mental and social restructuring loses its very life. This rigidifying trend begins already with the attempt to preserve the newly found level in its newly established structure. Thereby it is unwittingly turned into a static entity to which, in the end, it suffices to pay lip service.

According to Asanga and the followers of the Yogācāra tradition that he is said to have initiated, ritual actions with their strong feeling content of awe and reverence are to be kept to a minimum. This was probably because he and his followers, in spite of the insight that mind was a dynamic principle and not a static entity, were still deeply rooted in the rational and structure-oriented approach to an individual's situation. Significantly, ritual derives from sincere and devout mentation (Tib. *sems dang-ba*) and consists merely of folding one's hands as a gesture of respect and of offering a mandala, which in this context, is a gestural/symbolic, rather than a graphic/symbolic, representation of man's universe. These ritual actions may be performed in front of a shrine with the iconic representation of the Three Jewels (The Buddha, The Teaching, and The Community) or in front of a teacher, who then responds by elucidating the benefit that an existential awareness bestows on the student's physical, intellectual, ethical, and spiritual condition. Also, only four transgressions (which, however, rank in severity with the worst setback a person can suffer and have to be remedied as they turn up) are listed. They are:

> To glorify oneself and smear others
> For the sake of gain and honors;
> Not to give spiritual counsel and material sustenance
> Out of avarice to those who are destitute and unprotected;
> Angrily to censure others
> Without listening to their apologies; and
> Forsaking the Mahayana
> To present (and teach) a semblance of (its) noble message.[36]

The Mādhyamikas, who trace their origin back to Nāgārjuna, offer a much wider range of ritual actions. Moreover, for them ritual actions are the outcome of man's "pure systemic condition" (Tib. *rgyud dag-pa*). These actions involve the gesture of respect by folding one's hands before the "object" of one's respect as well as the use of a rich array of ceremonial utensils in the actual performance of worship. There is, by way of catharsis, the admission of having done improper deeds; and by way of an incentive to continue to be engaged in what is wholesome, rejoicing in whatever is wholesome and positive. This is followed by the resolve to keep the teaching of life's meaningfulness alive by spreading the Buddhist message; by the request to qualified persons not to pass into nirvana before mankind has been enabled to set itself free; and, lastly, by the dedication of all that is wholesome and positive to all living beings.

With the change of attitude from mere rationality to an acceptance and inclusion of the rich world of feelings, there emerges a subjective relationship with the forces that act in and through us and appear projected into an outside world as personified actors and witnesses in a hierarchical order of buddhas, vajradharas, and high-level bodhisattvas. It is to their imaged presence that one addresses oneself and asks permission to embark on one's spiritual quest. Three times one repeats the following formula:

> Just as those who in the past traveled the road of optimization,
> Raised their thoughts to the highest level and intensity of pellucidity
> and consummation, and
> Step by step, progressed and established themselves in the
> bodhisattva learning,
> So I shall, for the benefit of those who are alive,
> Effect this change from representational thinking to an existential
> awareness and
> Step by step, make progress in this bodhisattva learning.[37]

In the area of ethics, the Mādhyamikas have also gone beyond a purely individualistic ethics. They seem to have anticipated the modern idea of a multilevel ethics corresponding to the hierarchical organization of society, with each level deploying its own norms, which from the viewpoint of the optimization of the individual are detrimental to the overall evolutionary thrust and hence must not be indulged in. Nineteen or twenty such detrimental norms were listed by the Mādhyamikas. These are distributed over the levels of society as follows:[38]

Five pertain to the royal level: (1) to deprive monastic establishments (The Three Jewels) of their wealth and income; (2) to execute a well-behaved and well-disciplined monk; (3) to force a recluse to abandon his way of life; (4) to commit any one of the five crimes (of matricide, killing a saintly person [arhant], patricide, causing a split or disunion in the clergy, and making a living buddha bleed); and (5) to cling to false views. It might not be too difficult to translate these activities into the modern versions of secularization, power politics, and ideological witch-hunting.

Five pertain to the ministerial level: to exploit (1) hamlets, (2) counties, (3) townships, (4) districts, and (5) provinces. (In passing it may be noted that the administrators of these areas were personally responsible for delivering the exact required amount of taxes to the central government; hence they took the "precaution" of levying higher and additional taxes, which then disappeared in their own pockets).

Eight pertain to the plebeian level: (1) to teach Being's openness (Tib. *stong-pa-nyid,* Skt. *śūnyatā*) to those who are intellectually not yet ready for such teaching; (2) to make those who have entered the Mahayana revert to their former belief systems; (3) to give up the obligations that go with one's social status and to tell others to do the same since flouting conventions means embracing the Mahayana; (4) as a follower of the śrāvakayāna or pratyekabuddhayana, to proselytize others; (5) for the sake of gain and honors to glorify oneself and smear others; (6) to profess (falsely) to possess profound patience; (7) to make donations to monastic establishments and then take them back; (8) to make donations to those who falsely claim to have reached the state of inner calm.

Two are of a general nature and apply to any level: (1) to give up the very intent of changing one's attitude, and (2) to give up the actual engagement in bringing about the change.

With these two "failings," we are brought back to the two basic features in the activation of the shift from representational thinking to an existential awareness: the intent to go in this direction and the actual engagement in effecting this shift. From a practical point of view, it is therefore of utmost importance to keep alive the intent, which thus may imperceptibly fuse into the actual engagement. To this effect, one requires attentiveness (including inspection as a means of learning more about that which is before one's mind, as well as memory in the sense of not allowing what is before one's mind to slip out of view) and alertness (in the sense of using one's mind successfully in coping with the demands made upon it). In the words of Śāntideva as restated by Klong-chen rab-'byams-pa:[39]

> With folded hands I implore
> Those who want to keep this intent alive
> To heed attentiveness and alertness
> Even at the risk of their lives.

In particular, "intent" is kept alive by reminding oneself to avoid four "black" actions and by reminding oneself to bring into being four "white" actions. These have been specified, in the pedantic sutra style, in the *Kāśyapaparivartasūtra*[40] and summed up poetically by Klong-chen rab-'byams-pa as follows:

> In brief, four black things have to be avoided
> And four white things to be effected.
> You will just have to avoid these four black actions:
> Cheating those who are worthy of respect and feeling regret for
> that which is not to be regretted,
> Speaking unpleasant words to worthy people and
> Practising cunning and deceit among people.
> You have to depend on these four white actions:
> Relying on worthy persons and extolling their virtues,
> Exhorting sentient beings to the truly wholesome,
> Seeing in the buddha-sons the teacher,
> And by higher thought ensuring the welfare and happiness of
> beings.[41]

In this distinction between "black" and "white" or "good" and "bad," we easily recognize the familiar ethical injunction to further the "good" and to suppress the "bad," qualities that somehow are already fixed beforehand in a static cosmos. But when it comes to what is described as "engagement" in actually bringing about an existential awareness, the situation changes tremendously, because here the dynamics of the system's self-organization with its creative processes come to the fore. These put the traditional ways of life in question, and a reduction of each and every aspect of them to one semantic level becomes impossible. The emerging process-sustained ethics is well understood by Klong-chen rab-'byams-pa when he speaks of keeping alive this engagement and preventing it from degenerating into mere repeat performances of what is valid only at one specific level of an evolving, multilevel reality. His words are:

> "The welfare of others is more important than personal aims"
> Is the bodhisattva's self-training.
> When it is a matter of changing a situation, the seven unwholesome actions of body and speech
> May be committed and may actually be wholesome.
> The three by mind are never to be committed.
> Wholesomeness insofar as it is the desire for inner peace, and happiness for selfish reasons
> Is a failing in bodhisattvas and buddha-sons.
> That which is otherwise unwholesome and wanton but profitable for others
> Deserves to be studied, so the Buddha has said.[42]

In his auto-commentary to this text,[43] he illustrates the seven unwholesome actions by body and speech—three pertaining to physical acts (killing, stealing, and sexual involvement) and four to verbal acts (telling lies, using abusive language, speaking irrelevantly, and uttering harsh words)—showing in what circumstances they might be wholesome. I will give only one example from each category. If someone sees someone wantonly killing others and out of concern for the rest of the people kills this wanton killer, the act of killing proves to be of immense value for the other members of society. However, the emphasis is on "concern" as "total compassion" (Tib. *snying-rje chen-po*) for others, not on some sort of private sentimentality. Hence it follows that the statement "vengeance is mine" (Rom. 12:19) is an expression of utter immorality, because it elevates viciousness and vindictiveness into metaphysical categories that are claimed to be valid in an absolute sense. In the Buddhist perspective, these together with negativistic views as character traits, fall under unwholesome mental acts that never have beneficial consequences.

Similarly, abusive language directed at both of two parties may be more effective than gentle remonstrations in separating them when it is a matter of holding the one or the other back from being led astray by the other.

There are, of course, no fixed criteria for deciding at what time a generally or specifically disapproved act on one level may become a generally or specifically approved act on another level. In a dynamic perspective, ethics remains experimental and illustrates the principle of "order through fluctuations." With the inclusion of intelligence in this process, the Buddhists were fully aware of the interplay of directness and suggestiveness in the use of language. After all, it is language that plays an important role in the questioning of accepted norms. To carry out such questioning is the prerogative of courageous persons. Since the bodhisattva way is a continuous questioning, it is not for timid people.

9 *The Way* *The Later View II*

The Bodhisattva Way II: The Exact Itinerary

In the previous chapter, we discussed the shift from representational thinking, dominated by rationality, to an existential awareness, including the rich world of psychic receptivity and activity ranging over the individual's inner and outer world. In this discussion, it became evident that this shift increasingly focuses on the role the subject plays (though not as a metaphysical entity or a logical concept of some abstract fixity) in shaping a world in which it can live by opening up new dimensions and levels of understanding.

In connection with the effectuation of this shift, five phases have been recognized. Each phase is termed a "way" and is characterized by a specific feature in the development of this shift. Thus each way or phase progressively merges with the next one, marked by a higher intensity and greater complexity. We shall use the designation "phase" for the first two ways and the designation "way" for the three remaining ones. The total way thus consists of:

1. A build-up phase (Tib. *tshogs-lam,* Skt. *sambhāramārga*)
2. A probability-of-a-breakthrough phase (Tib. *sbyor-lam,* Skt. *prayogamārga*)
3. A way of seeing (Tib. *mthong-lam,* Skt. *darśanamārga*)
4. A way of cultivating what has been seen (Tib. *sgom-lam,* Skt. *bhāvanāmārga*)
5. A way of no more learning (Tib. *mi-slob-lam,* Skt. *aśaikṣamārga*)

This five-phase way is a unitary process that cannot be broken up into isolated bits and pieces with impunity.

The Build-up Phase

This phase is an intricate network of operational modes. It begins with the irruption of novelty, which although taking place within the individual, has its repercussion in society through the resultant exchange of ideas and visions. It may be of interest to point out that Thogs-med bzang-po-dpal explicates the Sanskrit term for this phase, *sambhāra,* as meaning "an iterative feedback loop (*ra*) fed by creative imagination (*bha*) in (the manner of a) stream (*sam*)."[1] This phase continues up to the point where there is the "probability of a breakthrough."

The impact of this irruption of novelty on the individual is that he begins to pattern his life so as to give concrete expression to the vision rooted in his innermost experience. Specifically, here in the Mahayana assessment of the Buddhist way as a whole, the fundamentally dynamic character of the way is brought out and it is clear that there is a purpose in whatever the individual does, a purpose that relies on insight gained by tuning in to the way. Hence, those operations that were already listed as belonging to the various phases of the way in its Hinayana assessment acquire a new meaning at the cultural level. Thus "self-discipline" can no longer be understood as merely operating on a behavioral level; it goes beyond mere negative feedback actions in relation to the environment and incorporates positive feedback actions as well. So also "restraining one's senses," which had been assessed mostly negatively as an attempt to hold them back from following up the sensuous stimuli that come from the environment, acquires a new and "positive" meaning. It is assessed as bringing about a sense of distance and a removal of exigencies and as making possible a more intimate kind of relationship with the environment by paving the way for aesthetic appreciation of it. This purposiveness with its sense of direction, its awareness of a "where-to," is clearly indicated by Klong-chen rab-'byams-pa when he says that

> the joy in staying alert to options, the fact that one does not feel regret over something positive done, enthusiasm and trust, devotion and such other positive features that (from now on) are the sustaining motive power in gaining release, as well as that critical acumen that is developed by listening, thinking, and imaginative (creative) experimentation, serve the purpose of bringing the probability of a breakthrough closer to us.[2]

This build-up phase passes through three degrees of intensity. However, it is stated that at the level of lowest intensity, because of the uncertainty of a breakthrough at this level, it takes "three countless aeons" ("countless" being the name for a number that consists of a one followed by fifty-one zeroes) of sustained effort to attain the desired effect—the state described in Tibetan as *sangs-rgyas* (Skt. *buddha*). On the subsequent level of medium intensity, this probability is in reach in one's next and subsequent lives and will become a certainty in one's present life at the subsequent level of highest intensity. We can readily see and understand how what is fundamentally of an experiential nature involving "subjective," lived time, is reduced to an absurdity by subjecting it to a rational, quantifying approach in terms of "objective" time. No individual will ever be around for such a long time as the time called "countless."

This gradation of the build-up phase in terms of its intensities, as well as its widening scope, presents a stochastic (time-dependent) description of the formation of a fluctuation up to the transition threshold between

FIGURE 4

THE PROCESS STRUCTURE OF THE BUILD-UP PHASE

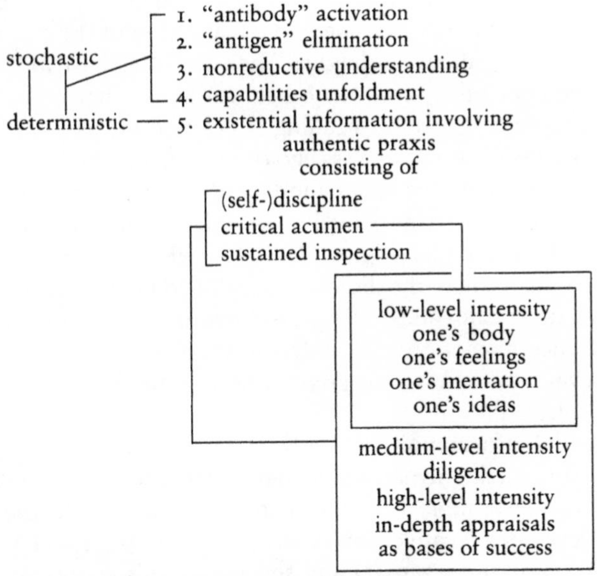

the old and the new phase. In this phase, it was recognized, specific (deterministic) activities enter the scene, introducing intentional vectors indicating in which direction the new phase may be expected. Five such vectorial—meaning-bearing—connectives have been singled out. In order to facilitate an understanding of the intricacies of these vectorial connectives they have been diagramed in Figure 4.

1. There is, first of all, an internal activation and reinforcement of trends (Tib. *gnyen-po*). These weaken the resistance of the system against change and eventually force it to abandon outworn structures or models of reality, all of them bearing the imprint of our deep-rooted emotions and being exposed for what they are by this incipient autoregeneration of the system. This internal reinforcement, which will continue throughout the various phases of the way, may be likened to the emergence of an immune system with its antibodies, improving during the life span of an individual. In this specific case, it aids the emancipation of thinking from its restriction to what which is supposed to be "objectively" given.

2. Secondly, there is the actual abandonment (Tib. *spangs-pa*) of these outworn models, whose limitations and restrictions become ever more patent. With this insight, the compulsive addiction to them is overcome and a rich and varied unfolding of the system's dynamics is facilitated.

3. Thirdly, through this abandonment, a more deeply felt understanding (Tib. *rtogs-pa*) of the person's situation emerges. This takes place in a

more general manner through the exercise of one's critical acumen as it develops with listening and thinking; and in a more specific manner, through the same acumen as it becomes sharpened by creative experimentation. This felt understanding is the realization of the fact that neither that which we call an "individual" nor our ideas have any immutable, ontic status of otheir own. In other words, this felt understanding occasioning the emergence of meaning is not tied to, nor does it carry with it, a doctrine of some timeless ego or intended eternal essences.

4. Fourthly, through this understanding, the system's multifaceted capabilities (Tib. *yon-tan*) are enabled to unfold. Specifically, mind has lost its rigidity and regained its original flexibility, which is indispensable for spearheading the move in the direction of pellucidity and consummation. In this move, inner calm and wider perspective as dynamic features (inner calm as balance in motion and wider perspective, not only as "seeing with fresh eyes," but also as receptivity to existential information) play a significant role.

5. Existential information (Tib. *gdams-ngag*) is obtained through the system's self-organizing dynamics *via* particular forms that are described as buddha manifestations. This information is related to the themes that have to be developed creatively by experimenting with them (Tib. *bsgom-bya*). It is of two kinds, general and specific. In this connection Klong-chen rab-'byams-pa quotes the *Mahāyānasūtrālaṅkāra,* but his quotation is a compilation of various lines from various verses and chapters in this work. This manner of quoting reveals him as an independent thinker, as a person who knew what he was talking about. His "quotation" runs as follows:

> Then, in order to acquire within this stream of existential
> meaningfulness
> That deep inner calm and vast existential awareness
> From the buddhas themselves,
> He travels over (all) the realms of the world and
> Completing all requirements,
> He obtains vast-ranging information.[3]

The general (deterministic) aspects that are tied to existential information and that apply to all three intensity phases of the build-up comprise self-discipline (Tib. *tshul-khrims,* Skt. *śīla*) in one's actions by body and speech; critical acumen (Tib. *shes-rab,* Skt. *prajñā*) as it develops by listening, thinking about that which one has heard, and developing this by imaginatively (creatively) experimenting with it (specifically by distinguishing between the literal sense and the intended meaning of the Buddhist teaching); and by way of a follow-up, the sustained consideration (Tib. *rjes-su dran-pa,* Skt. *anusmṛti*) of certain existential problems from all angles in order that nothing of importance will escape one's notice.

Foremost ranks consideration of the following four axioms, which implicitly reflect the complementarity of objectivity and subjectivity:

1. Everything that is of the nature of a construct is impermanent. This is to say, the span of our life is limited and the task lying ahead of us is enormous and needs immediate attention. Therefore, rather than wasting what little time remains, we should consider the fact that death may overtake us at any moment. If life runs in the direction of self-renewal and self-unfolding in greater complexity and creativity, death is an important ingredient. Although we tend to look at death (from the outside), we actually experience it continuously, be it only in the dying of old notions and the birth of new ones.

2. Samsara, which as the mind's construct is bound to collapse, is frustrating. Not only are we as embodied beings embedded in a physical environment, we are also deeply attached to it. This attachment presents itself as a rich spectrum of behavioral patterns that are governed by the so-called "three poisons" of desire-possessiveness, irritation-aversion, and dullness-obtuseness, which severely curtail any learning process. In particular, it is desire-attachment that blocks the emergence of new models of reality, because it remains tied to the "material" side of human existence, which it attempts to perpetuate. The advice for breaking this deadlock is to entertain nine notions about the foulness of the body-*thing*. These notions are those of a rotting corpse, ravaged by worms, discolored in hues of red, blue, and black, devoured by wild animals, having been simply thrown away, having been burnt, and being putrid.

The remaining two poisons, of course, require a different approach. Thus irritation-aversion can be dispelled by compassion and kindness, and dullness-obtuseness by becoming aware of the dynamic connectedness that holds between the without and within. As a follow-up to these "emotional" and "intellectual" poisons with their state-specific effects, the restlessness and lack of purpose (from an existential point of view) of representational thought, with its breaking up the original unity of experience, is countered by breathing techniques, which, like the other countermeasures, were never meant as ends in themselves. It bears remembering that in Buddhist thinking, even kindness and compassion are cultivated as powerful catalysts. In this respect, the Mahayana does not differ from the Hinayana. All the above measures serving the unfolding of man's sociality are summed up in the following passage:

> When desire-attachment predominates, it is dispelled by looking at
> a filthy and fat (body),
> Its (wrinkled) skin, or at a skeleton.
> Irritation-aversion (is dispelled by) watering it with kindness and
> compassion.
> Dullness-obtuseness (is dispelled by contemplating) the way in
> which dynamic connectedness operates.

(The aimlessness of) divisive thought (is checked by) keeping track of one's breathing.
(The most effective) countermeasure for all (of the above is the contemplation of) Being's openness.[4]

3. The ideas, concepts, and plans that regulate the development of our life have no immutable ontic status of their own. With the release of organismic mentation, caught in the clutches of the three poisons, from its rigidity by the aforementioned countermeasures or "antibodies," the "antigen"-like, "objectivity"-claiming rational approach to the individual's problem situation is transcended, and a much healthier and richer world of imagination is opened up by the mind, which becomes ever more self-reflexive. A first step in this direction is the imaginative development of eight "ideas" that mark a truly "great man." These are expressed in "subjective" language:

1. May I forever be able to banish the suffering of sentient beings.
2. May I forever be able to confer immense wealth on those who are afflicted by poverty.
3. May I forever be able to serve sentient beings by this my body of flesh and blood.
4. May I forever be able to serve sentient beings even if it means that I have to stay in hell for a long time.
5. May I forever be able to fulfill the expectations of sentient beings by the wealth that is of this world and the world beyond.
6. May I forever be able to eradicate the suffering of sentient beings once I have become a buddha.
7. May the case never arise that in generations to come my existence is not of benefit to others; that I spend my time solely in the enjoyment of the flavor of that which is supremely valid; that I ever utter words that are not pleasing to all men; that my life, my body, my intelligence, my wealth, and my might is not of benefit to others; and that I take pleasure in harming others.
8. May the result of the evil done by others come to maturity in me and may the result of the good done by me come to maturity in others.[5]

Our sociocultural world is built out of ideas, even if all ideas cannot be turned into a tangible reality.

4. Passing beyond the distress that goes with both the "construct" and the "constructing" (planning) is calmness and quietude. Imagination freed from limitations in the form of irresistible drives and other expres-

sions of compulsive behavior placed upon it by organismic mentation creates a "different reality," and cultivation of it is an important factor in the cultural life of man. It serves to stimulate the freshness and pellucidity that is ever present, though only too often concealed, in one's engagement in one's sense-specific and thought-specific domains of concern, which themselves represent an exchange process between sensory impressions and tentative models of reality. In this symbolic re-creation of the world in terms of formal and existential evidence values, imagination bridges the gap between the "objective" and the "subjective" in such a way that the creativity issuing from the inner world changes the outer world by infusing it with new meanings.

In this symbolic re-creation of one's life world and its reenactment, language as a means of directing and helping others to envision the actualized possibilities plays a significant role. This means that language itself is a creative act and does not merely refer to that which can be confirmed by sense experience or by logical processes. This creativity of language is what Maitreya seems to have in mind when he says in connection with this symbolic re-creation and re-enactment:

> In whichever way an engaged buddha-son[6]
> Deals with the varied cognitive domains of the senses,
> He makes (his action) clear among sentient beings,
> For their benefit by words appropriate to the occasion.[7]

Returning to the deterministic factors of the build-up phase, the keynote of its low-intensity level is the exercise of one's critical acumen (Skt. *prajñā*) by means of four inspective operations (Skt. *smṛtyupasthāna*). Inspection here indicates the attempt to learn more about the nature of the topic under consideration. The number four is determined by the topics themselves. These are (1) the body-as-lived, (2) the feelings, (3) mentation, and (4) ideas. None of these, however, is subjected to the investigative procedure of quantitative analysis. Rather, inspection is understood as a process both of withdrawal (termed "composure phase," Tib. *mnyam-gzhag*, Skt. *samāhita*) in the sense of a linking backward to the "origin" with its open possibilities, a restoration of the broken symmetry; and a re-arousal (termed "postcomposure phase," Tib. *rjes-thob*, Skt. *pṛṣṭhalabdha*) in the sense of a symmetry break, the emergence of a new autopoietic level by an active outward projection of itself. In terms of perception, this means that in the withdrawal phase, perception melts into pure sensation, the body-as-lived loses its external reference and is perceived as well as felt as an open dimension termed "sky" and/or "space" (Tib. *nam-mkha'*, Skt. *ākāśa*), which is not some sort of amorphous nothingness or passive emptiness, but a dynamic force that affects the shape and, even more, the quality of things. Hence in the re-arousal or postcomposure phase, which reintroduces the division into a subject and object, the body-as-lived is perceived and felt as something foul or as something having some magiclike, phantomlike quality.

The same distinction holds for the topic of our feelings, which in the withdrawal or composure phase are felt as not yet having come into existence (Tib. *ma-skyes-pa,* Skt. *ajāta*), and in the re-arousal or postcomposure phase, as marking a "painful" symmetry break, as unpleasant and having no substance to them, like driftwood.

Similarly, mentation in the withdrawal or composure phase is experienced as "nothing in itself," an utter "openness" (Tib. *rang-bzhin-gyis stong-pa,* Skt. *svabhāvaśūnya*); and in the re-arousal or postcomposure phase, as not localizable in its ceaseless operation.

Lastly, ideas are realized in the withdrawal or composure phase to be examples of Being's identity-with-itself in the sense that, conceived of as a system, Being is symmetric with respect to its actions or symmetry transformations; and since Being is capable of undergoing infinite symmetry transformations, it has the highest degree of symmetry (Tib. *mnyam-pa-nyid,* Skt. *samatā*). In the re-arousal or postcomposure phase, this symmetry lights up in, and as, symmetry transformations (not so much as symmetry breaks in the literal sense of the word), which (in the same manner as Being not being some sort of thing) have no "thingness" about them and can only be described in terms of being "like" an apparition, a phantom, a dream, an echo and so on.

It must not be assumed, however, that inspection with its intent to learn more about the nature of a given topic is merely concerned with the "know-what" or, because of the importance of making use of one's critical acumen, with the "know-how." Rather, as Maitreya in his *Madhyāntavibhāga* points out, inspection serves to provide man with a sense of direction, the "know-whither."

> Inspection is to be cultivated
> (With respect to) getting involved with the Four Truths
> Because (it makes us aware of) our deplorable situation and of the driving force behind it,
> Of the (shaky) ground (of our ego-centered being) and of (how) not to be mistaken about it.[8]

The Four Truths are the objectives of the way of seeing, which is still a long way off. As Klong-chen rab-'byams-pa points out, it is by knowing the frustration that goes with our physical existence (our body-as-lived) that we come to know what frustration means, and this is the first "truth" that is brought home to us in the seeing phase of the way. Similarly, by knowing our feelings to be frustrating when we attempt to use them as criteria for building our world, we realize that they are behind all the frustrations we encounter, and with this realization, we are placed in a position of being able to do something about our predicament. This awareness is the second "truth." Further, by realizing that mentation is a process and not a thing that "lasts for ever," the meaning of cessation, the third "truth," the cessation of eternalistic (reductionistic) beliefs, is directly brought home to us. Finally, by realizing the fact that ideas are not immutable essences, the way as such, the fourth "truth," becomes unobstructed for us to travel, because it has been cleared of the notion of a Self or an ego as an ultimate essence or owner of essences.

Thogs-med bzang-po-dpal gives a slightly different interpretation of the above aphorism from the *Madhyāntavibhāga* by elaborating on Asanga's *Mahāyānasūtrālaṅkāra* commentary, in which Asanga had dealt with the practice of inspection in terms of an organic complex of vectors as outlined by Maitreya. His words are:

> "Deplorable situation" refers to the fact that all the seeds of that which is bound to break lie in the ground (from which conscious life emerges) and are this very ground; and since it is the frustration that goes with one's (reality) constructions, the body-as-lived (in being such a construction) is the result (of the dynamics of the ground from which conscious life emerges) and therefore, by investigating this result through the application of inspection, one understands its cause, the deplorable situation, and this (understanding) is one's involvement with the truth of frustration.
>
> By cultivating one's inspection of feelings, one will understand them to be the cause of one's hankering (after more of the same stuff), and since this (hankering) is the origin of all (one's) frustrations, its (understanding) is (one's) involvement with the truth of the origin of frustration.
>
> By cultivating one's inspection of mentation, one will understand that mentation, which is the ground of one's belief in a (permanent) self, is itself impermanent. Consequently, by having come to know that there is no such thing as a permanent self, one will not be afraid of there being no such thing when the time of release has come; and (this understanding) is one's involvement with the truth of cessation, the very meaning of calmness.
>
> By cultivating one's inspection of ideas, one will not be mistaken about that which is polluting and that which is cleansing, and by immunizing oneself against that which is polluting, one involves oneself with the truth of the way.[9]

The four topics of inspection are part of one's becoming involved with the Four Truths. They are: the body-as-lived as being foul, feelings as frustrating, mentation as impermanent, and ideas as non-ontic. It is in connection with them that Thogs-med bzang-po-dpal points out the enormous difference between Hinayana and Mahayana. In the Hinayana or śrāvakayāna, inspection of the body-as-lived serves to overcome the desire for and attachment to it by seeing it as foul and repugnant in the wake of having observed a corpse in its various stages of decay. Such inspection does not aim at understanding the nature of what is inspected—in other words, the Hinayana attitude remained reductionistic. In the Mahayana or bodhisattvayana, the experiencer not only immunizes himself against the unpleasant experiences coming from desire and attachment, but also against the negativistic (reductionistic) notions about that which he inspects, by understanding that any notion or reality construct has no ontic standing.[10]

The keynote of the medium-intensity level in this build-up is diligence (Skt. *vīrya*), which by processes that engender as well as eliminate (Skt. *samyakpradhāna/samyakprahāṇa*), serves to strengthen that which has been initiated on the low-intensity level. In addition to diligence, it involves imaginative activities, which are meant to develop the non-ontic, magiclike and dreamlike character of the process. In concrete terms, this level of intensity is instrumental in not allowing negative forces to come into existence, or when they have done so, in preventing them from proliferating and in bringing into existence positive forces and then making them grow.

The keynote of the high-intensity level in this build-up is the in-depth appraisal (Skt. *samādhi*) of the situation and the challenge it holds. It marks the emergence of "bases for success" (Skt. *ṛddhipāda*), by which concentration as a dynamic balancing (rather than as a kind of fixation) is assured. This balancing is the unity in action of the inner calm and wider perspective of a mind well focused in the sense that it is looking ahead and never to one side.

Four such appraisals or bases for success stand out: (1) an in-depth appraisal that is suffused with an ongoing interest and acts like an antibody against the antigenlike complacency of just being content with the small and the little in what has been found to be positive; (2) an in-depth appraisal that is permeated with diligence and acts like an antibody against antigenlike distraction and indecision; (3) an in-depth appraisal that involves a firm grip on mind in holding it to inner calm and that acts like an antibody against antigenlike impetuosity; and (4) an in-depth appraisal that is marked by a probing of the situation and is able to keep the mind firmly established in a wider perspective, acting like an antibody against antigenlike faintheartedness.[11]

This hierarchical gradation of the build-up phase in terms of critical acumen, diligence, and in-depth appraisals is a restatement of the laconic assessment of this phase in the *Abhidharmakośa*:

> Critical acumen (characterizes) the exercise of inspection,
> Diligence (characterizes) the proper abandonment, and in-depth
> appraisals (characterize) the bases of success.[12]

THE PROBABILITY OF A BREAKTHROUGH

This probability-of-a-breakthrough phase mediates between the build-up and the actual seeing by establishing a link once it has grown strong enough. It operates on two levels, each marked by two indicators of the degree of intensity reached. On the "lower" level, which does not yet guarantee the desired breakthrough, these indicators are "warmth" and its "peak value," which as metaphors aptly describe that which we express by saying that "someone is warming up to his subject" and that "he is hot on the trail." On the "upper" level these indicators are "acceptance" and "the supreme mundane material" serving as a threshold into the supraworldly. These two we might paraphrase as "someone has caught up with what he has been after" and "he is making the most of it."

Each of the two levels provides us with a set of five operational modes, which are identical on each level except for their intensities. This difference is indicated by qualifying them as "dominant modes" (Tib. *dbang-po,* Skt. *indriya*) and "overpowering modes" (Tib. *stobs,* Skt. *bala*), respectively. Thus the *Madhyāntavibhāga* states:

> Five dominant modes and five overpowering modes—
> Each set in the service of effecting a breakthrough.[13]

These operational modes continue some practices that were initiated in the preceding build-up phase. Here, however, they have acquired a new dimension within the overall design process, due to the intensification of the "know-whither." Specifically, the dominant modes are concerned with refinement of the processes involved and with purification of their thematic adumbrations. In this respect, the sequence in which they are enumerated displays the internal logic in these processes. They are:

1. Confidence-trust, which in this context, according to the *Madhyāntavibhāga,* is identical with aspiration. As we had occasion to notice earlier, aspiration is not satisfied with trivialities or shallowness, but aims for that which is ennobling. This approach was well described by Shakespeare's dictum "that spirit in aspiration lifts him from the earth."
2. Diligence, which makes one eager to persist in the pursuance of one's objective.
3. Inspection, which does not allow one's objective to slip from one's attention.
4. In-depth appraisal, which unlike its myopic Hinayana equivalent, focuses on that which lies ahead.
5. Critical acumen, which in spite of its analytical probing, becomes ever more appreciative of values that defy analytical quantification.[14]

It is by virtue of the dominance of these that whatever is detrimental to the move in the direction of release (as a deeply felt and understood vision of life as intrinsically meaningful) is weakened and eventually overpowered. Thus these dominant modes persist as overpowering modes, as stated in the *Mahāyānasūtrālaṅkāra:*

> Once whatever is detrimental to the move in the direction of release
> has become weakened,
> These very modes are termed overpowering modes.[15]

Whether as dominant or overpowering modes, these five facets of the probability-of-a-breakthrough phase are no longer concerned with the quantitative and granular, the domain of objectifying thought (Tib. *rnam-rtog,* Skt. *vikalpa*). Rather they are concerned with understanding in the double sense of self-understanding and world-comprehension—a way of thinking for which we have used and shall continue using the term "existential awareness" (Tib. *ye-shes,* Skt. *jñāna*). The first terms of reference of this emerging existential awareness are impermanence and the other "meanings" as they are distributed over the Four Truths (which themselves are interpretive meanings, not denotable objects). The second term of reference of *ye-shes* is the distinction between that which is commonly accepted and grounded in the subject-object correlation such that what is to be meaningful "must function as a terminus of an objective signification, tested, classified, quantified, or in some sense funded" (Schrag 1969, 113), on one hand, and that which is intrinsically valid and constitutes a world in which we as humans can live, precisely because it is not amenable to any kind of reductionism, on the other.

In view of the fact that this probability-of-a-breakthrough phase is the continuation and intensification of processes initiated during the build-up phase, it, too, reflects the fluctuation described as withdrawal and re-arousal. Here, in particular, withdrawal marks the transition from thematizing thought, grounded in and perpetuating the subject-object division (Tib. *rnam-rtog,* Skt. *vikalpa*), to an existential awareness (Tib. *ye-shes,* Skt. *jñāna*) in which the subject-object division is progressively transcended. Re-arousal marks the emergence, more precisely, the re-emergence of subjectivity (Tib. *yid*) in such a way that its thinking may be either nonthematizing (Tib. *rtog-med,* Skt. *nirvikalpa*) in the sense that thematization has not yet become explicit and congealed in its constructs, or it may relapse into and reassert its thematizing trends. It was also clearly recognized that this intensification had to pass through at least three intensities in order to become effective.[16]

The intensity indicators were "warmth" for low intensity; "peak value" for medium intensity; and "acceptance" and "the supreme mundane material" for high intensity. But in relating these indicators to time, a confusion between lived (subjective) time and (objective) clock time took place in the same way as it did with the three intensity levels of the build-up phase.

The indicator "warmth" marks the lighting up of a fresh perspective, which becomes less and less shrouded by the objectifications of representational thinking and more and more allows meaning to be felt. In epistemological terms, all that had been naively considered to be an object external to, and hence independent of, the experiencer and observer, loses its external reference and is "understood" as the subject's first or original utterance as a noetic act. The emphasis is on the act, which, as it were, calls up a wealth of meanings, rather than on the product or the spoken word—the relationship between "speaking" and "that which is spoken" being similar to a living person and a corpse. Of this original and originating utterance which does not objectify, Maitreya says:

> A bodhisattva who has developed in such a way that he presents
> (the unity of inner calm and wider perspective as it emerges on the highest-intensity level of the build-up phase),
> In the withdrawal moment (of this probability-of-a-breakthrough phase)
> No longer sees the objects in, and as having, an external reference
> But understands them to be his mind's utterances.[17]

Such utterance, to be sure, neither asserts nor demonstrates anything, but makes everything possible, so that it remains related to the subjectivity that calls it into being without reducing it to a part of a system of essences, either of the commonly accepted world or of any conceptually postulated world. It leads to a deeper understanding of what is meant by inert things and living beings as well as of ideas having no ontic status (Tib. *bdag-med,* Skt. *nairātmya*).

This demolition of any essentialist aim and the opening up that goes along with this demolition is felt as a rising of warmth. Its indicator, peak value, also marks a spreading of light. It is here that diligence is required to obtain the desired effect.[18]

However, the likelihood of relapsing into the former ways of thematizing thought and constructing essentialist world views is still present, and it is only on the high-intensity level termed "acceptance" that the higher regime of a holistic approach to the problem of our being in a world takes over. This new regime as an autopoietic structure, on the one hand, helps the person onward in his quest and, on the other hand, counteracts the tendency to relapse into the belief system of there being an external world independent of the subjectivity that has called it into being. It is, however, still a partial approach, not the final step. This is explicitly stated in the *Mahāyānasūtrālaṅkāra:*

> Once this lighting up of meaning has spread (far and wide)
> The (bodhisattva as experiencer) abides in "mentation only" (*cittamātra*).

All that which (formerly) appeared as (external) objects
Is (understood as) a lighting up in mentation.
At this time the perturbation by (the belief that there exist external) objects
Is in the process of being dispelled and
Only the perturbation by (the notion of there being a) subject remains.[19]

In the history of Buddhist thought, the idea of mentation-only (Skt. *cittamātra*), discussed earlier, has played an important role, but it had, as is intimated here, its shortcomings. These are the same as those of its Western counterpart, subjective idealism, which "subjectivizes experience, interiorizes the phenomenal field, and confers upon the lonely epistemological subject the task of creating the forms of experience" (Schrag 1969, 22). Since mentation-only was also correctly seen to be a "worldly" phenomenon, the pitfalls of a transcendental idealism with its regression to a transcendental consciousness as a subject, which, having an essentialist structure, "grasps" (Ger. *begreifen,* Tib. *'dzin-pa*) the totality of Being within a unity of concepts ("the graspable," Ger. *Begriffe,* Tib. *gzung-ba*), were avoided. It goes without saying that mentation-only also has nothing to do with absolute idealism, beyond which man cannot go. Finally, neither mentation-only nor any forms of idealism can answer the question, "What does grasping (*'dzin-pa*) mean when there is nothing to be grasped (*gzung-ba*)?"

The next step, therefore, as the Buddhists noted, is the phase termed "the supreme mundane material," which follows (if this is still the appropriate term to use) so closely on the acceptance phase that hardly any interval can be noticed. It is such that there is no longer anything whatsoever to prevent the vision that develops in and as the way of seeing. This is expressed in the *Mahāyānasūtrālaṅkāra* in the following words:

At this moment (when only the perturbation by the notion of subjects remains) (the bodhisattva, that is, the experiencer) gets quickly in touch with
That in-depth appraisal in which there are no obstacles whatsoever (to having a full vision).[20]

Inasmuch as this probability-of-a-breakthrough phase is an intensification and modification of the preceding build-up phase, it is only natural that the vectorial connectives reappear "intensified." Thus:

1. The internal reinforcement of trends toward restoring the system's vitality and rescuing it from stagnation, which in the build-up phase consisted in exposing the notions that lead to stagnation for what they are, has grown to such an extent that it "gives them a stunning blow."

2. The abandonment of outworn models of reality, which in the previ-

ous phase amounted basically to rejection of the compulsive addiction to them and the emotional involvement in them, has here become the weakening and downgrading of both the emotional (system-pollutant) and intellectual (thematizing) obscurations in both their subliminal (germinal) and overt presences, as well as the individual's emancipation from the poverty-stricken and deteriorating state of being an ordinary person.

3. The deeply felt understanding of the non-ontic character of things and ideas (as initiated by hearing about and thinking about what this means in the preceding phase) has become here this very understanding by virtue of one's creative imagination concerning these facets.

4. The multifaceted capabilities, which in the previous phase expressed themselves in a renewed flexibility of mentation, spearheading the move in the direction of pellucidity and consummation, have here taken on the character of in-depth appraisals in increasing variety.

5. Although there is a certain similarity between the highest-intensity level of the build-up phase and the operations taking place in this probability-of-a-breakthrough phase, still, because the latter takes over where the former ends, there is a remarkable difference. The build-up phase is still far away from the way of seeing, and the warmth that permeates the existential awareness is still unstable. However, this probability-of-a-breakthrough phase is close to the way of seeing, and the warmth in existential awareness is a steady glow.

THE WAY OF SEEING

This way evolves out of the probability-of-a-breakthrough phase in marking the actual breakthrough. It is the beginning of a process of unfolding (the unfolding itself being the "way of creative experimentation"). As the starting point of both a horizontal and vertical unfolding, this specific phase constitutes, in terms of the emerging hierarchical levels (the vertical unfolding), the first of the ten spiritual levels called "utter joyfulness." The experiencer is filled with immense joy due to his having gained, for the first time in his life, an existential awareness (the horizontal unfolding) that is "out of this world." In the *Mahāyānasūtrālaṅkāra,* this moment is described in the following words:

> In those who see (themselves) close to (what is their) pellucidity and
> consummation and
> (Able effectively to) help living beings,
> An intense joy springs up
> Therefore (this level) is termed "utter joyfulness."[21]

The metaphorical expression "out of this world" that is used in connection with this newly gained awareness does not mean that there is any other world than the one in which we as embodied beings are living. We might also describe what is meant by "out of this world" as the emancipation of a mental reality, of our inner world (which always reaches beyond itself and moves ahead of itself) from the physical, external reality. This emancipation takes place, however, without introducing an unbridgeable gap between the two. "Out of this world" could also be described as the release of interpretive, nonobjectifying, and nonsubjectifying thinking from the stranglehold of its objectifying, representational tendencies. It is not by chance that here, in the discussion of the way of seeing, such descriptive terms as "emancipation," "release," and "freedom" are used. These are not static notions, but dynamic forces that make time- and space-binding possible. This time- and space-binding was already recognized by Maitreya:

> The (Four) Truths beginning with the truth of frustration
> Involve sixteen moments such (that each truth has the four moments of)
> Acceptance-in-knowledge, knowledge-(as-inalienable),
> Follow-up acceptance-in-knowledge, and follow-up knowledge-(as-inalienable).[22]

We will have to remind ourselves of the fact that every cognitive situation displays an intentionality that is "composed" of two distinguishably different phases, which we shall designate, following the phenomenological description of them by Edward S. Casey, as the "act phase" and the "object phase." Through its act phase, the mind directs itself onto and absorbs itself in a specific content, its object phase. What is most remarkable in this self-transcending movement of mind is that what is aimed at in the content, the intentional object, need not be existent. "In fact, such an object is always 'intentionally inexistent': intended and yet not (qua intended) existent" (Casey 1976, 38).

This intentionality is exemplified by the terms "acceptance-in-knowledge" and "knowledge-(as-inalienable)" with reference to the first of the Four Truths, the truth of frustration in its immediate impact on us in our realm of desires, the Kāmadhātu. Acceptance-in-knowledge (Tib. *chos-bzod*) is already the exercise of one's critical acumen in its "flawless" operation. It is flawless in the sense that it is no longer concerned with what was presented to it as the concretization of the intentionally inexistent into an objective existent. Hence it coincides with the "way on which there are no longer any obstacles" (Tib. *bar-chad-med-pa'i lam,* Skt. *ānantaryamārga*), which emerged at the climaxing of the probability-of-a-breakthrough phase. This phase, we have noted, acts as a threshold; hence the emergence of what is termed "acceptance-in-knowledge," though something new in being the first mode of the way of seeing, retains its connection with the past.

Acceptance as a nonobjectifying cognitive act is both acceptance and "admission"—we may accept (more or less unwillingly) the proposition that the world we have created for ourselves, and in which we are so much involved with our desires, is a world of frustration, and we "admit" this proposition after having critically assessed it. In this nonobjectifying operation of acceptance it dawns upon us, that is, we come to "see," as Mi-pham 'Jam-dbangs rnam-rgyal rgya-mtsho tells us, that

> our ideas (*chos*) have been of transparent purity as such since their (beginningless) beginning and are a sheer lucency. From this their nature they have never parted, and even at that time when they seem to be such as to be mistaken notions, they have not parted from their utter transparent purity; so much more so as there is no grounding for and in that which is termed "the opaque" (*ma-dag*). Hence (the awareness that) the forms and shapes (as which the truth of) frustration manifests itself, are neither (something) permanent nor (something) impermanent, is the acceptance of the fact (of what is termed the truth) of frustration.[23]

But this acceptance is shot through with intelligence and it becomes an inalienable knowledge (Tib. *chos-shes*), which on the basis of the nonobjectifying operation of the newly established level of seeing, is such that it understands, "knows," that there is nothing to be taken up or appropriated as some ultimate positivity or ultimate negativity. To this extent, this is the "way of freedom" (Tib. *rnam-grol-lam*) as a self-emancipatory process. The far-reaching implication is that man's existentiality is freedom-in-operation.

However, the domain of desires (Kāmadhātu), which figures so prominently in the individual's experience in constituting his maximum engagement in the physical-material, may be regarded as a sort of "frozen" energy, a hardening of the psychic-mental, which has been able to preserve some "radiant" energy. It is only one domain of perception and inquiry. There are, in addition, the domain of aesthetic forms and pure colors (Rūpadhātu) and the domain of the formless (Ārūpyadhātu), which, far from being something amorphous, is the potential of formative processes. These three domains hang together, and when the whole system becomes activated through searching as a way of learning how to "tune in" to life's creativity, a sense of direction (space) and anticipation (time) is generated. This is indicated by what is described as a "follow-up acceptance-in-knowledge" (Tib. *rjes-bzod*), which realizes that what it is concerned with is such that it is neither devoid of nor not devoid of an ontic principle. As a "follow-up knowledge-(as-inalienable)" (Tib. *rjes-shes*), it understands that the pure fact of being, irreducible to something that can be said to constitute or not constitute a self (or ontic principle), is such that it has never come into existence as something and hence also does not cease being what it is, because only that which has come into existence is going to cease to exist.

All these four cognitive modes constitute the unitary understanding of the fact that reality as summed up by the Truth of frustration is not some entity but a process that becomes intelligible to us through its symbols (which have a transparent, pure character). At the same time we are faced with the paradox that the act of understanding is both a singularity and a plurality and that this act takes in a single reality that is nonetheless "made up" of three levels or domains, which we can only describe in a sequential and ascending order. Since, furthermore, these four cognitive modes also operate with reference to the remaining three Truths—the Truth of the origin of frustration, the Truth of its cessation, and the Truth of the way toward cessation—they were listed, analytically, as forming a set of sixteen (four times four) cognitive modes, while yet remaining a unitary process. Each of these cognitive modes was, as we have noted, qualified as a "moment" (Tib. *skad-cig-ma*). This qualification has remained a stumbling block for those who attempted to come to grips with Buddhist thinking in terms of their reductionistic preconceptions and therefore were unable to notice the dynamic character of this technical term. What the Buddhist term *skad-cig-ma* refers to is precisely what we nowadays describe as "time- and space-binding" in experience. As Klong-chen rab-'byams-pa noted long ago, reality is one dynamic whole, which yet is described in terms of four truths or realities. So also experience is one dynamic whole, accessed in sixteen time- and space-binding experiences.[24]

The transition from representational, fragmentizing thinking to a unifying existential awareness is complete, except for some fine-tuning, with the irruption and start of the way of seeing. This way carries with it a new net of time- and space-binding, which cuts across linear and irreversible time and which makes it possible to "see," that is, to experience the rediscovered unity that had been lost by the symmetry breaks described as the various domains of desires, aesthetic forms, and the as-yet-unformed. The fact that the start of this way of seeing is marked by acceptance reveals an extraordinary insight on the part of the Buddhists, because acceptance implies, on the part of the individual, an opening up to the unfamiliar, and in this very act all the obstacles that the familiar with its stranglehold on the mental life has posed, are swept away. Moreover, since this acceptance is specifically an acceptance-in-knowledge, the individual also realizes that his previous attachment to the familiar was unhealthy, and that by this shift in perspective, the system that he presents is restored to its health. From the point of view of the system, it mobilizes its antibodies (Tib. *gnyen-po*) in a so-called immune reaction. In the texts this is expressed by saying that all the acceptance-in-knowledge modes—four according to their distribution over the Four Truths, with special reference to the domain of desires—constitute the way on which there are no longer any obstacles (Tib. *bar-chad-med-pa'i lam*), because they have been made ineffective to the extent that they have been seen as what they are and in terms of what they are up to. The knowledge-(as-inalienable) modes—also four according to the same counting that listed four acceptance-in-knowledge modes—constitute the experiencer's existential freedom (Tib. *rnam-grol-gyi lam*) in the above-mentioned sense as freedom-in-operation. This antibodylike operation prevents the experiencer's existentiality from slipping into the pseudo-existentiality of his constructs.

The four follow-up acceptance-in-knowledge modes and the four knowledge-(as-inalienable) modes, as they pertain to the Four Truths in their application to the two "higher" domains of aesthetic forms and the as-yet-unformed (which are often counted as a single domain because of their common subtleness as constrasted with the grossness of the domain of desires), constitute a special and distinct way (Tib. *khyad-par-gyi lam*), which like an antibody, keeps the possibility of an intrusion of the familiar (analogous to an antigen) far away. Hence this sequence-in-simultaneity of the various acceptance-in-knowledge, knowledge-(as-inalienable), follow-up acceptance-in-knowledge, and follow-up knowledge-(as-inalienable) modes, which define the way of seeing, ensure the system's self-optimization with its growing immunity against infections (in the indigenous texts aptly termed "pollutants").

Here, in the context of the bodhisattva way, two major streams converged. One, which we shall call the older one, continues the ideas developed in the Hinayana with certain modifications. These modifications were prompted by the change from a mechanistic conception of the universe, in which material and mental substances collided with and impinged on each other, to a mentalistic conception—mentation being the sole criterion for what we call our experienced world. Common to both the Hinayana (specifically, the pratyekabuddha way) and the Mahayana (the bodhisattva way) is the distinction between five ideological and five emotional pollutants, as previously detailed. They relate to each of the Four Truths in the domain of our experiences dominated by desires (Kāmadhātu), thus amounting to forty pollutants. In the domains marked by experiences of aesthetic forms and colors (Rūpadhātu) and by experiences of the as-yet-unformed (Ārūpyadhātu), anger-belligerence is inoperative. Hence only nine make their presence felt with each Truth, thus amounting to thirty-six pollutants in each of these "higher" domains.[25]

The other major stream, a new and innovative movement that found its philosophical expression in the mentation-only (Skt. *cittamātra*) idea, conceived of the pollutants as pertaining to two levels of mentation, one being mentation's reflexive, thematizing aspect (Tib. *kun-tu brtags-pa*), the other its organismic, system-specific aspect (Tib. *lhan-cig skyes-pa*).

Both of these pollutants constitute a loss of the system's original lucency of experience. These pollutants, only to the extent that they pertained to the reflexive aspect of mentation (with its symmetry breaks, which were considered to be incidental, not essential), could be made inoperative by the way of seeing. To the extent that they pertained to the organismic aspect of mentation, they could only be made ineffective by the way of experimentation with creative imagination (Skt. *bhāvanāmārga*), which thus turns out to be a clean-up operation.

The first symmetry break to occur is the subject-object division, which in static terms describes the dynamic intentionality of a "grasping" (Ger. *begreifen,* Tib. *'dzin-pa,* Skt. *grāhaka*) act, identified with a subject; and a solicitation act of a "to-be-grasped" (Ger. *Begriff,* Tib. *gzung-ba,* Skt. *grāhya*), identified with an object. The implication of this intentionality is, as the Buddhists knew quite well, that subject and object are co-constituted—no subject without an object, no object without a subject. This specific symmetry break, like all other symmetry breaks, was considered a shrouding, an obscuration of the original unity, which itself was felt as a sheer lucency always present as a possibility. As an obscuration, it also presented an obstacle to tuning in to life's creativity. Since most cognitive processes involve this subject-object division, which brackets the experiencer as a mere subject, allows objects to exist so as to give the subject a chance to attend to them by controlling them, and leads him farther and farther away from coming to grips with existentiality. Hence this trend was an "obscuration-obstacle in the form of subject-object-specific cognitive processes" (Tib. *shes-[bya'i] sgrib,* Skt. *jñeyāvaraṇa*), which also reflected the reflexive and organismic aspects of mentation. There are thus two kinds of obscuration-obstacles. One is the obscuration-obstacle just specified, which prevents the experiencer from seeing the whole, because he becomes ever more engrossed in the abstract models of a world he has created from a specific ("subjective") point of view. The other obscuration-obstacle is the one presented by the pollutants (Tib. *nyon-sgrib,* Skt. *kleśāvaraṇa*). It prevents the experiencer from ever attaining the status of being free, because the pollutants lead him deeper and deeper into the morass of samsara.

The way of seeing has to cope with both kinds of obscuration-obstacles. Maitreya expresses this in the following words:

> There are two kinds of obscuration-obstacles:
> One by pollutants, one by the objectifiable.
> Here (on the way of seeing), all obscuration-obstacles are intended;
> Once they have been done away with, (the resulting state of affairs)
> is claimed to be one of freedom.[26]

Although obscuration-obstacles by pollutants continue to be given primary considerations, there is an innovation in their reclassification. All of them, of course, are marked by the system's stepped-down intelligence, which as such becomes a pollutant itself. All of them, also, each in its own way, infect the whole system in such a way that it remains involved in the limits set by its own dynamic. Maitreya discusses nine kinds of infection and in this connection regroups the traditional ten pollutants (five of an ideological variety and five of an emotional variety) into seven and adds two pollutants that had formerly been included in the set of the quasi pollutants. These nine kinds of infection are:

1. low-level intelligence
2. attachment in the form of desires
3. anger-belligerence
4. arrogance
5. indecision
6. reductionism, outrageousness, extremism, taken together as modulations of ideological pollution
7. dogmatism, ritualism, also taken together as modulations of ideological pollution in the sense of presenting over-evaluated ideas
8. jealousy
9. avarice[27]

We might ask why avarice is counted as a full-fledged pollutant, rather than as a quasi pollutant, and why Maitreya should mention it in his *Uttaratantra* in connection with his description of the split of experience as taking the form of two distinct notions that roughly correspond to our division into what we call the emotional and the intellectual side of a person.[28]

The solution of the problem lies in the following. The way of seeing, as will be remembered, constitutes a real breakthrough and marks the so-called first spiritual level, described as utter joy and also named "joyful one" (Tib. *rab-tu dga'-ba,* Skt. *pramuditā*). As everyone who has experienced such utter joy knows, this feeling of joy carries with it the desire to share it with others. To share means to give, and in the act of giving, a person transcends himself. The cultivation of self-transcendence (Tib. *pha-rol-tu phyin-pa,* Skt. *pāramitā*) passes, as we shall see, through many phases, but on this first level it expresses itself through "giving," which in Buddhism ranges from giving material goods, security, to an imparting of the feeling of being embedded in a dynamic connectedness of Man and universe. In his self-transcendence, Man reaches out beyond the boundaries in which his ego attempts to encapsulate itself, and in the act of giving he combats and eradicates his infection by avarice. This first level, however, is only the starting point for a process that grows in complexity and for this reason is dealt with as another phase of the way as a whole.

THE WAY OF CULTIVATING WHAT HAS BEEN SEEN

This way is one of experimentation with creative imagination that has both vertical (coherence in time) and horizontal (coherence in space) aspects. It emerges with the completion of what we may term the "holistic vision" that marked the way of seeing and continues up to the time when the system has become fully autonomous, as will be described in a subsequent section. In terms of spiritual levels, this way is claimed to comprise nine levels, beginning with the second and ending with the tenth. It is ironic that this way, the most dynamic one, has suffered most from reductionistic tendencies.

Apparently at an early stage in the development of Mahayana thought, which with its emphasis on process assigned a subordinate function to structure, it had become customary to speak of ten levels that evolved and proceeded one from the other, and in so doing, opened up new vistas and displayed an extraordinary intensification of the total process. This is made evident in the classification—a resurgence of the ever-present structure-oriented thought processes—of the nine levels that belong to this way of experimentation into sets of three, each set displaying an increased intensity (low, medium, high). Each of these sets has three members, which together display the same three intensity degrees as each of the three sets. This presentation may have been an attempt to point to the process character of what is "going on" by means of a language that is not geared to process thinking. Hence what was intended as a description of a process was quickly reduced to denoting an entity, the so-called "spiritual level" (the term "spiritual," not found in any indigenous texts, was probably added to camouflage gross reductionism.

I remember a few years ago when I addressed a group of psychologists in Berkeley, California, one psychologist asked me whether during my years in India as a professor I had met persons hailing from one of these "higher spiritual levels." My answer was that I had met all kinds of people, but not a single person who carried the tag "I'm an nth level guy." In this connection, it may not be out of place to point out that already, long ago, Rong-zom Chos-kyi bzang-po succinctly stated that the term "level"—the indigenous terms Tib. *sa* and Skt. *bhūmi* mean "soil," "earth"—was a metaphorical expression, not a denotatively given particular, and Klong-chen rab-'byams-pa described "level" as an autopoietic structuring.[29]

There are ten levels, and each level is connected with a specific operation by which the individual transcends himself. This transcending operation acts like an antibody against an antigen that it has recognized as endangering the system by its intrusion and against which it began mobilizing its specific powers. The complexity involved can be shown as in Table 3.

TABLE 3

LEVEL	ANTIGEN	ANTIBODY
The joyful one	avarice	giving
The stainless one	hypocrisy	self-discipline
The illumining one	anger-belligerence	patience
The flaming one	laziness	diligence
The one difficult to assail	restlessness	refinement (by way of concentration)
The one which has become a presence (pointing ahead of itself)	pseudo-intellectuality	critical acumen
The one that is going far	ineptness	expertise
The unshakable one	weakness	strength
The straightforward one	failure to live up to one's goal	resolve
The cloud of life's meaningfulness	the last remnants of being unaware	existential awareness

Traditionally only six transcending functions or operations were recognized, and the manner in which they were listed reveals that there is an internal logic to their sequence. They have been summarized by Maitreya, who states:

> Giving (*dāna*) without expecting anything in return or to gain a better existence hereafter by it,
> Self-discipline (*śīla*), patience (*kṣānti*) under all circumstances, diligence (*vīrya*) in promoting all that is positive,
> Concentration (*dhyāna*) that does not limit itself to the domain of aesthetic forms, and critical acumen (*prajñā*) that translates itself into expertise—
> These constitute the proper involvement of resolute persons in the six transcending operations.[30]

The discrepancy between ten spiritual levels, so intimately tied to the transcending functions, and only six transcending functions did not escape the notice of Buddhist thinkers, and attempts were made to harmonize this discrepancy. In the long run it seems that agreement evolved on the standard six transcending operations as basic and on an additional four as adjuncts. Thus Thogs-med bzang-po-dpal informs us, according to the teaching contained in the *Sandhinirmocanasūtra,* expertise (Skt. *upāya*) aids the first three transcending operations, while resolve (Skt. *praṇidhāna*), strength (Skt. *bala*), and existential awareness (Skt. *jñāna*) aid the remaining three transcending operations in this order. He adds that, according to the interpretation given to Maitreya's account in the commentary to his *Madhyāntavibhāga,* the six transcending operations are the "real" stuff, while the additional four have only a nominal existence and present offshoots of the sixth transcending operation, the person's critical acumen, which is indispensable for the emergence of his existential awareness.[31]

While the way of seeing effectively uproots and neutralizes the system's pollutants as far as they pertain to the reflexive aspect of mentation—this aspect presenting, as it were, a surface layer, the way of cultivating what one has seen and experimenting with it by creative imagination serves to wipe out the same pollutants, specifically as they pertain to the organismic, system-specific aspect of mentation. In it, the experiencer continues to be engaged in what is best described as a clean-up operation. As such, this deeper layer of mentation also has a dual nature in being both pollutant and thematic. Since the pollutants pose the greater danger to the system's integrity, they are dealt with in more specific terms. There are six pollutants. Their designations are general descriptions in which, in each case, nuances can be included. These six pollutants are specified according to their emotional and ideological manifestations as follows:

1. attachment in the form of desires
2. anger-belligerence
3. arrogance
4. low-level intelligence (in the sense that the system's inherent intelligence is not at its best; it is not the same as lack of intelligence or ignorance)
5. reductionism
6. extremism

In the domain in which desires hold sway and which is a mixture of the physical and the psychic, all six pollutants are operative, while in the domain of aesthetic form-and-color experiences as well as in the domain of experiences of what is as yet unformed, anger-belligerence is absent. Since these three domains constitute the individual's hierarchical organization, which is somehow "infected" by the pollutants, these present a total of sixteen pollutants (6+5+5), which, because of their resilience, need additional work on the part of the experiencer. Paradoxically, while the total number of these overt ideological and emotional pollutants is less than the number on the previous way of seeing (six compared with ten) their subliminal ramifications are many more.[32]

The Way of No More Learning

We have no difficulties in conceiving of the preceding phases or stages on the way as phases of a learning process that, once its problem has been solved, comes to an end. The designation of this last stage on the way as "no more learning" seems to support this assumption. However, this rash assumption fails to take into account that this last phase is itself a way that, by definition, goes on and on. It also fails to recognize the fact that there are no unambiguous answers and definitive solutions to the problem called "Man." Unfortunately, the thoroughly dynamic character of this last stage on the way has been described in terms that cannot conceal their pitifully narrow applicability, inasmuch as they attempt to establish a rational, mechanistic approach as an absolute. These terms are the familiar notions of "cause" and "effect." In the description of this phase, the term "cause" is used to indicate the fact that the individual has entirely gone through the four learning phases—the build-up phase, the probability-of-a-breakthrough phase, the way of seeing, and the way of cultivating what has been seen by experimenting with it through creative imagination. The term "effect" is used to indicate the fact that the individual (who in traveling the way grew and developed by way of an ongoing self-transcendence) now can act from a different level of reality, which, though remaining connected with the other levels of reality, cannot be reduced to them. In other words, while on the preceding levels there existed a feedback relation of the system (the human individual) with its environment, constituting the system's "cognitive domain" (as Maturana [1970] has called it in an attempt to overcome the primitive mechanistic association with the term feedback), on this level the system has become independent of its environment in the sense that it has become self-referential in a holistic way that no longer allows of any mechanistic and dualistic reductionism. This we shall call the system's autonomy in the dynamic sense of the active application of its complexity. This active application is, in the Tibetan texts, consistently referred to by the terms *phrin-las* (a noun) and *mdzad-pa* (a verb), which are clearly distinct from the corresponding lower-level activity designated by *las* (a noun) and *byed-pa* (a verb). The Sanskrit language unfortunately has only one term to cover both features—*karman,* which, irrespective of its popularization as "karma" in the English language, from the perspective of the system's autonomy, looks more like a blundering or learning by trial and error.

The four phases that constitute the way of learning—the build-up phase, which exposes the danger to the system by the pollutants; the probability-of-a-breakthrough phase, which deals the pollutants a stunning blow; the way of seeing, which uproots them; and the way of creative experimentation, which effects a general clean-up—describe in unmistakable terms what we nowadays would call the evolution of a dissipative structure. This is, as we have noted previously, precisely what the Tibetan term *sangs-rgyas* indicates—with the dissipation of outworn structures (*sangs*), a new structure emerges autopoietically (*rgyas*). As a paraphrase of the Sanskrit term *buddha* describing a state, the state of "having awakened," the Tibetan term retains the dynamic character of being a process and only secondarily assumes a static character when it is referred to as a level over and above the traditional ten levels.

As an experience, the evolution of a dissipative structure is shot through with intelligence and/or meaning. This is the system's cognitive nature as its existential, originary awareness. This indivisible unity of intelligence and meaning is the measure of the system's intensity and autonomy, which holistically takes on the form of a gestalt presenting the unity of quality and function. In it, the system's complexity is also reflected. Complexity increases with the opening up of new semantic levels. In this interplay between complexity and autonomy, we can easily recognize the principle of complementarity that underlies much of Buddhist Mahayana thought.

This complexity as the holistic knowledge of the system's own dynamics manifests itself in a sequence of different structures, each of which has its own intentionality and time-binding and space-binding characteristics, while all of these process structures form an intricate web of dynamic regimes. Three such dynamic structures have been listed, but this does not mean that they exhaust life's richness. They are named after the gestalt quality (Tib. *sku*) in which they are assessed by their cognitive dynamics (Tib. *ye-shes*) such that one is coextensive with the other in being both the expression and the expressed.

These three dynamic structures are given the Tibetan code names of *chos-sku, longs-sku,* and *sprul-sku,* their Sanskrit equivalent names being *dharmakāya, sambhogakāya,* and *nirmānakāya.*[33]

chos-sku (Dharmakāya)

The term *chos-sku* is a cover term for the deeply felt understanding of the nonduality of Being's open dimension and its originary (existential) awareness, dissociated from any and all stains that might mar its pure dynamics. As such, it is likened to the vast expanse of a cloudless sky. The indivisibility and coextensiveness of the act phase (the originary, existential awareness) and the object phase (the open dimension of Being) is indicated in a much quoted verse:

> In view of the fusion of the (multiple nuances of) originary
> (existential) awareness in an inseparable manner,
> With Being-in-its beingness, dissociated from the conceptual-
> propositional proliferations (that constitute the domain of) the
> knowable (in its entitative fragmentation)—
> Like water poured into water,
> Like oil blending with oil—
> This very fact is termed the genuine *chos-sku*
> Of all *sangs-rgyas.*[34]

This passage implies that *chos-sku* and *sangs-rgyas* are, broadly speaking, interchangeable, but there are subtle differences. As we have had occasion to note repeatedly, what is termed in Tibetan *sangs-rgyas* (Skt. *buddha*) develops like a dissipative structure, which in this case can be described as "wholeness-in-operation." Everything that limits or shrouds wholeness is on its way out (*sangs*), and wholeness-as-such structures itself holistically (*rgyas*) in a gestalt expressive of the meaningfulness of wholeness (*chos-sku*). This self-structuring of living systems we call experience, or to be more precise, experience-as-such (Tib. *sems-nyid*) in order to avoid confusing it with what we call "mind." By that term, we usually understand what the Buddhists called "mentation" (Tib. *sems*) and specified as objectifying representational operations that themselves present only one of two possible movements within experience-as-such (*sems-nyid*). Wholeness must not be confused with, or reduced to, a totality of granular, juxtaposed entities. Wholeness and experience-as-such turn out to be identical, so that the terms "wholeness" and "experience-as-such" can be used interchangeably. From the perspective of experience-as-such, wholeness expresses itself as meaning (*chos*), the essential feature of which is its gestalt quality (*sku*). Hence, in becoming the whole, Man-in-his-wholeness (*sangs-rgyas*) experiences wholeness in and through its gestalt quality (*chos-sku*). In other words, *sangs-rgyas* emphasizes the process, and *chos-sku* emphasizes the structure. The two cannot be separated.

A favorite simile for the dynamics involved here is the sun that spreads its light throughout the whole sky. Maitreya expressed this feeling of wholeness in a beautiful verse:

> Being the whole (*buddhatva*) is disclosed in and through (the rich array of its pure qualities), which are inseparable from it;
> Just like the sky (that is lit up by) the sun. Such is (the sheer lucency of its) originary awareness and (its self-)understanding through the dispersion (of whatever, cloudlike, temporarily obscures its luster).[35]

The principle of complementarity, which in the present context states that we cannot have a gestalt quality without a cognitive operation and vice versa, is well expressed by Maitreya:

> Being the whole (*buddhatva*) is such that it is uncontrived (in not being a construct of representational thought), just there spontaneously (and not something laboriously arrived at), and
> Incomprehensible by means other (than its own cognitive dynamics);
> It (also is such that it) is sensitive (to all and everything that is), responsive (to the frustration presented and caused by all that is), and vigorous (in dispelling all frustration).
> These (two sets of three features each) operate in the manner of (the principle of complementarity such that the first set constitutes its) "subject" pole, (the second set its) "object" pole.[36]

It is interesting to note that Maitreya's intention has been understood well by his Tibetan commentators Dol-po-pa Shes-rab rgyal-mtshan,

Rong-ston Smra-ba'i seng-ge, and Blo-gros mtshungs-med, a renowned contemporary of Rang-byung rdo-je (1284–1339) and Bu-ston Rin-chen-grub-pa (1290–1364). By contrast, the Indian Asanga missed the intention of his teacher's statement, and in his commentary, mechanically counted each indicator separately and arrived at a total of eight disconnected (3+3+2) features.[37]

longs-sku (Sambhogakāya)

The process of becoming increasingly self-reflexive is acted out at the level that is called in Tibetan *longs-sku,* short for *longs-spyod-rdzogs-pa'i sku.* As a gestalt (*sku*), it reverberates with Being's wholeness (*rdzogs*), which, in order to be experienced by Being (as "experiencer"), comes-to-presence as Being's autoprojection, as its geometrization (*longs*), with which the experiencer (who is none other than Being [the whole] itself) becomes fully engaged (*spyod*). As so often, the Tibetan hermeneutical interpretation makes explicit what is implicitly indicated by the Sanskrit term, here *sambhogakāya,* "the gestaltism (*kāya*) of mutual (*sam*) enjoyment (*bhoga*)." At the same time, it draws attention to the most profound problem a person has to face in growing up—his encounter with himself in his "real," not ideologically postulated, nature.

First of all, we have to be constantly aware of the fact that the idea of gestalts originated with the Yogācāra thinkers, and that none of the gestalts is a *terminus ad quem* of objectifying representational thought; rather, they are symbols of lived experience. The Yogācāra thinkers, as pointed out in a previous chapter, proposed that there is only mind/mentation (Skt. *cittamātra*). But the term "mind/mentation" (Skt. *citta,* Tib. *sems*) itself allows of different interpretations. One that gained the upper hand in philosophical discussions was to reduce it to the representational thinking mode in a very broad sense in such a way that, with emphasis on consciousness/perception (Skt. *vijñāna*), it ended up including all that we would call the preconscious and even unconscious. This interpretation may be said to be epistemology-oriented. Another interpretation that developed may be said to be experience-oriented. It came to the fore when, figuratively speaking, the way had been traveled to its end and the previous dualism, which had taken the subject-object dichotomy as normative, had been transcended. Or we could say, again speaking figuratively, that a change comes over the experiencing individual through rediscovering and regaining his wholeness (Skt. *buddhatva*). This change could be spoken of (not spoken *about* in the objectifying, thematizing sense) in terms of gestalts.

The problem is how can the whole cognize itself in view of the fact that every cognition, because of its inherent intentionality, is always cognition of an other? In other words, of what kind has this "other" to be so that it can be said to be the whole's "own"? Here, two possibilities present themselves. One is the whole's dynamics in its autoprojection, having all the earmarks of projective geometry.[38] The other possibility uses the image of a mirror. The whole holds up a mirror to itself that, because of the cognitive nature of the whole, is of its own making (referred to as a "mirrorlike originary awareness mode," Skt. *ādarśajñāna,* Tib. *me-long lta-bu'i ye-shes*) in which the image seen is precisely the whole and recognized as the whole's very own.[39]

Whichever line of interpretation we follow, it is always the whole (Being-in-its-beingness, in philosophical diction, pure experience, in experiential terminology) that comes-into-presence and makes its presence felt. Since Being-in-its-beingness (or, experientially speaking, one's being the whole, Skt. *buddhatva*) is not a thing (that can be said to come into existence and pass out of existence), it is, as far as words can express it, in the words of Maitreya:

> Unimaginable, everlasting, stable, tranquil, and eternal,
> Halcyon, all-encompassing, indivisible like the sky's (unbroken expanse),
> Unattached, unresisted, with all roughness gone,
> Invisible, inconceivable, pure, and flawless—such is (the experience of one's) being the whole.[40]

But such also is its presence—an "eternal" presence, though not an eternal "something." As a presence, its gestalt acts as the source that can fulfill all desires and expectations, like the mythical wish-fulfilling gem. Being nothing concrete, it is like the rainbow in the sky. In more dynamic terms, it is Being's self-picturing (autoprojective) dynamics that programs its own evolution. In the words of Maitreya:

> Through its gestalt, emitting rays of light (which carry) various messages of significance,
> It actively aids living beings to realize their existential value that is their freedom;
> This its program execution is (as effective as that of) the king amongst the jewels (the wish-fulfilling gem);
> (Although all this seems to be so many) various concrete things, they are nothing of this sort.[41]

The geometrization of the whole by the whole's dynamics presents itself as a pentasymmetric vector field in which each vector protects the others and, by implication, the whole. Taken separately each vector becomes meaningless, and the whole collapses into isolated bits and pieces. To make matters still more complex, each vector exhibits five "normative forecasts," as Erich Jantsch (1976, 240) calls these archetypal patterns that, as constant and continual features (Tib. *nges-pa lnga*), not only preorder a reality that is yet to unfold through the experiencer's participation in this process, but also are subjectively experienced as feedback relations whereby his feeling of being embedded in, as well as being an integral part of, a dynamic whole is enhanced.

The first forecast is specified as a "region" (Tib. *gnas*), which we may conceive of as "spiritual space," the near-infinite spectrum of what the world holds for us. Yet, this region is not of the kind of factor of which the triadic structure of the world—the domains of desire, aesthetic forms, and the formless or the as-yet-unformed—is made. Nor is this region of the stuff of which dreams are made and into which they resolve. Rather, it is, if we want to specify it, man's spiritual space, called in (Sanskrit) mythological language the Akaniṣṭha-Ghanavyūha realm.

The second forecast is referred to as the "audience" (Tib. *'khor*). This is described as being constituted by bodhisattvas on all ten spiritual levels. As noted before, the term "bodhisattva" itself refers to man's psychic receptivity and response to the world—his spiritual space—with which he interacts.

The third forecast is the "teaching" (Tib. *chos*). This, in particular, is the message of the Mahayana, which ultimately is the account of a human being's way to his humanity in all its complexity.[42]

The fourth forecast is the "teacher" (Tib. *ston-pa*), who as an illumining presence is termed Vairocana (Tib. *rNam-par snang-mdzad,* "the Illuminer"), but who may as well be called Akṣobhya (Tib. *Mi-bskyod-pa,* "the Unshakable"), or Ratnasambhava (Tib. *Rin-chen 'byung-ldan*, "the Source of Preciousness"), or Amitābha (Tib. *sNang-ba mtha'-yas,* "the One of Boundless Light"), or Amoghasiddhi (Tib. *Don-yod grub-pa,* "the One in Whom Life's Value Is Unfailingly Established"), according to which vector in the whole's geometrized field is in the ascendency.

The fifth forecast is "time" (Tib. *dus*), but this time cannot be measured in any way, nor be likened to clock time; nor can it be said to be lived time. Only very inadequately, one might say that this time is everlasting time, which already was and always is with us.

Although this term "everlasting" (Tib. *rtag-pa,* Skt. *nitya*) is introduced here (for the first time) in connection with the forecast called "time," it applies to the whole complex of the above mentioned forecasts that make up the *longs-sku*.

This specification of the *longs-sku* as everlasting does not contradict the insistence on the transitoriness of all that is. The *longs-sku* belongs to a superconscious dimension; only the "objective" and purely "subjective" array of entities, which remain separate from each other and only nominally enter into transient structures and form the contents of consciousness in its representational mode of thought, is subject to the ravages of time.

sprul-sku (Nirmāṇakaya)

The human individual, by virtue of his being, is both part of Being and the whole of it. And inasmuch as Being's dynamics are forever active in, and even engulf, the individual, they are felt to be the force that not only impels the individual to transcend the limitations set by the model he has created and calls the "world," but also makes him enter upon the path that will lead out of the turmoil of enworldedness to inner calm. This ensures his becoming mature and holds out the promise that he will be able to regain his lost freedom. As such a guiding forecast, this force manifests itself in various shapes and patterns suited to the perceptive capacity of the individual, and yet in all its variations it never parts from the gestalt through which Being's meaningfulness is experienced. This gestalt, which in its variations expresses Being's creativity, is the creative force in the human individual that makes him develop his cultural norms. The Tibetan technical term for it, which reflects the gestaltism that marks these norms in all their effusiveness, is *sprul-sku* (short for *sprul-pa'i sku,* Skt. *nirmāṇakāya*). The rich program it presents is expressed by Maitreya in the following words:

> That image that constitutes the momentum in setting out on the
> path to inner calm within the (various) world spheres and
> That ensures maturation and holds the promise (of success),
> Is also here (in us) everlastingly enshrined,
> Just as the domain of aesthetic forms lies embedded in space.[43]

Because of its inseparability from the gestalt through which Being's meaningfulness (Tib. *chos-sku*) is experienced, that which has been termed *sprul-sku* is, like the *chos-sku,* primarily pure potential. It is given concrete form in what we call culture by persons who are ready to respond to the challenge that is within and yet beyond them. It is impossible to predict at what time a person will be ready; all that one can say is, "when the time has come," and leave it at that. Thus Maitreya states:

> When the occasion (for Being's meaningfulness to light up in our
> lives) has arrived,
> For whomsoever and wherever and whenever
> It will be of benefit,
> In him it will light up.
>
> But just as a rotten seed will not sprout
> Even if (Indra), the ruler of the gods, pours down rain,
> Those who are unfortunate (because of their still lingering
> immaturity) will not experience the happiness (that goes with
> this lighting up)
> Even if the buddhas (as the embodiment of Being's meaningfulness)
> have appeared.[44]

As the driving force behind mankind's cultural endeavors and achievements, pointing to the fact that a vision has been given tangible form, the *sprul-sku,* specifically, expresses itself, according to Maitreya, as follows:

> By displaying (such qualities and events as) craftsmanship, birth,
> the awakening, and
> The passing away into nirvana,
> This manifestation of man's holistic beingness
> (*buddhanirmāṇakāya*)
> Is the great instrument in the (attainment of) freedom.[45]

Commentators have had considerable difficulties with this statement and have often been content to take it in the literal sense, against their better judgment, to mean that the moment of the awakening, the experience of pellucidity and consummation through which reality appears in a new light, is identical with the passing into nirvana as the fading out of old structures. So also they took "birth" in the traditional Indian sense as meaning the social status (caste) into which a person is born. There are, however, others who took the above statement as having cultural implications.[46] Klong-chen rab-'byams-pa "rewrites" the first two lines in Maitreya's above statement in the following way:

> Craftsmanship, and birth, and the great awakening
> Are the displays of supreme pellucidity and consummation.[47]

He then declares that craftsmanship involves literacy, proficiency in architecture, as well as in what we would call engineering (shipbuilding and construction of bridges), and above all, in the fine arts such as sculpture and painting. (He does not mention music, which is mentioned in the *dKon-mchog sgron-me.*) He goes on to say that "birth" refers to the solicitude people exert in the prevention of epidemics and famines; and that the "great awakening" implies all the events that took place in the Buddha's life, beginning with the intention to become a human being and ending after a long career as a human being with the passing into nirvana.

The probing of the depths of a living person's being is the leitmotiv of the bodhisattva way and leads the experiencer out of a static world view. However, the historical development related to this way ended on a dissonant note when its followers attempted to reinstate representational thinking in what was basically an ongoing and unending process. Stating it differently, in attempting a rational explanation, they imposed a limited kind of reason with its cornerstone of causality on that which goes far beyond the limits set by causality. Causality in Buddhism has never been exclusively linear but involved modifiers and was more or less of a circular nature. Here it was conceived of as operating in two ways. One idea was that the elimination of whatever shrouded the system's clarity, taking place with the help of outside agents such as teachers and friends who were instrumental up to the time the individual himself could bring his potential into full play, was the cause for attaining an already preconceived and predetermined goal.

The other notion of causality was conceived in terms of what had to be eliminated being the cause for the system's emergence as what it was. This involved a kind of transformation that was quite different and more radical than the transformations or changes the cognitive stuff or substance called *citta*—the Yogācāra thinkers never had any doubts about the concrete existence of this stuff (some of its modes existing *materialiter,* others *realiter*)—underwent (Tib. *rnam-'gyur,* Skt. *pariṇāma*) in becoming fully epistemology-oriented. This radical transformation (Tib. *gnas-'gyur,* Skt. *āśrayaparāvṛtti*) effected the very core of the personality. It certainly was not some temporary altered state of consciousness. Rather, it presented a level in Man's evolution to which few so far have advanced, the level of supermentality, which in spite of its mentalistic connotation, has its repercussions in the psychophysical dimension of the individual.

However grandiose this idea of a radical transformation may have seemed, it posed considerable difficulties, which were quickly pointed out and played a leading role in the rejection of this idea. To give only one example, if the core (Tib. *gnas*) can change (Tib. *'gyur*) in one direction (say, supermentality), there is no guarantee that it cannot, at any moment, change again in another direction (say, to the substandard mentality of a beast—according to Buddhist thinkers who do not share the hybris of Western man, animals also have a mind and, probably, morality also). Maybe the greatest fallacy in the idea of a radical transformation was that it reinstated a deterministic conception of Man and the universe, as if the way had come to an end. But in its dynamics, Being or the whole (or whichever term we may use to point to that which cannot be reduced to the triviality of one's everydayness), is and remains open-ended. Ilya Prigogine and Isabelle Stengers (1975) said: "We can no longer speak of the end of history, only of the end of stories." In this vein we can say that with the bodhisattva way, a chapter in the history of Buddhism ended, but some of the material for a new chapter was already present in it.

10 rDzogs-chen Supercompleteness I

Introductory Remarks

The closing sentence of the previous chapter must not be understood as implying that the rDzogs-chen teaching is a direct continuation of what went before. The history and origin of what is referred to by the Tibetan term *rdzogs-chen* is still very much unknown. The meaning of this term, best paraphrased in English by such terms as "ultimate completeness," "sublime wholeness," "impeccable entirety," or, in line with contemporary super-so-and-so diction, "supercompleteness," suggests that it contains much that may also be found elsewhere. Yet it would be a mistake to conclude from this that this teaching is eclectic. Rather, it presents a higher-order level of thought that includes the lower-order levels with which it interacts but to which it cannot be reduced.

What distinguishes rDzogs-chen thinking from all other modes of thought is that it is pure process thinking. This inevitably leads to a reinterpretation and redefinition of terms that are otherwise commonly used in the predominantly static context to which ordinary language, with its inherent poverty, is geared.

In any presentation of rDzogs-chen thought, three major difficulties a Westerner will encounter must be pointed out right at the beginning. The first difficulty is that our language is too deeply steeped in the Aristotelian categories of substance and quality. Furthermore, our language consists largely of nouns, and whatever is designated by them becomes a thing—in Aristotelian terms, a substance with properties—hence we believe the "world" to be made up of physical objects (Langer 1972, vol. 2, 320). Next, in our language any adjective ends up qualifying a noun. But in rDzogs-chen thought, what we would call adjectives are, as Alfred North Whitehead conceived of them according to the summary by Elizabeth M. Kraus (1979, 83),

> the subjective form of a relational activity: a vector feeling-tone not a bare passive quality, an adverb not an adjective. "Blue" cannot be abstracted from the eye's functioning in response to an environmental stimulus; it has *no* meaning apart from an eye. It is the eye's activity of grasping into itself the causality of a light wave objectified by an item in the wave's definiteness: its energy structure or frequency.

The second difficulty is that the rDzogs-chen ideas are not presented in syntactically constructed sentences, which, by the manner in which they relate the verbally designated key factors in the subject matter, enable the reader (listener) to comprehend what is so designated with practically no references to his imagination. rDzogs-chen texts arrange the linguistic symbols in the order in which they occur in the immediate experience of the thinker (speaker). This forces the listener to "listen to" and "think along" with the speaker and make the (necessary) connections between these items in experience by and for himself. This, of course, is not the same as imposing one's preconceived notions on what has been said without having listened or, putting it more bluntly, shooting off one's mouth before having thought at all. Klong-chen rab-'byams-pa, the foremost rDzogs-chen thinker, is very careful in beginning his presentations with the words: "Listen to my explication of how I have understood (the subject matter)." This modesty is in marked contrast with the Westerner's loudly trumpeted arrogance: "My opinion is the definitive and authentic meaning of what is under consideration." Unfortunately, his opinions are usually not worth a dime.

The third difficulty is that in view of the fact that process thinking does not know of any sharp separation between opposite aspects of reality and bases itself on the principle of complementarity, in which the opposites include each other, these opposites have to be thought *together,* not in the sense of a stale synthesis, but in a dynamic unity. This is, psychologically speaking, an extremely difficult operation; all our ingrained mental habits revolt against it; and the prevailing reductionism in objectifying representational thinking makes us continue acting in the manner so picturesquely described in the *Rin-chen spungs-pa:* "It is like (trying to) force a piece of cloth into the eye of a needle, which has no place for it and does not allow it to move."[1]

As a higher-order level of thought, rDzogs-chen is considered to be the peak of a person's endeavor to fathom the depth of his being, to gain an unobstructed view, and to order his life in a meaningful way. Its scope has been described in the *Rig-pa rang-shar* as follows:

> The peak-beyond-all-peaks of all the visions (man has ever developed)
> Is called the *ati-rdzogs-pa chen-po.*
> In view of the fact that it opens up (new) possibilities because of its vastness
> It should be known to be like the sky.
> In view of the fact that it is difficult to fathom its bottomless dimensions and size,
> It is similar to the depth of the ocean.
> In view of the fact that (all) luminous rays of light are concentrated in it,
> It should be known as the very disk of the sun.
> Because it is free from the limitations set by thematizing thought,

It is said to be the king implementing the language of
Being's mystery (compassion and critical acumen).[2]

This passage contains a new term, *ati-rdzogs-pa-chen-po,* which is an abbreviation for *atiyoga-rdzogs-pa-chen-po.* The Sanskrit term, *atiyoga,* prefixed to the Tibetan is not meant here to indicate another system. It may have been added to satisfy the censors in a political atmosphere that was hostile to anything indigenously Tibetan and that, following the example set by the Indian pandits, attempted to reduce living ideas to dead arguments in a debating society, with polemics thrown in for good measure. Anyhow, in adding this Sanskrit term, its original meaning of "superabundance" was retained. Thus the *Kun-byed rgyal-po* explicates this compound as follows:

As to *atiyoga rdzogs-chen*:
The meaning of the word *ati* is such that
a has the meaning of having no specifiable onset, resting in the internal logic of Being:
ti means effortlessness, spontaneous presence.
yoga means intensive application.
He who speaks of that which is complete and whole
As having cause and effect
Has no understanding of *rdzogs-chen.*
He who speaks of it in terms of the ultimately valid and the conventionally valid
Uses words of flattery and abuse.
He has no understanding of what nonduality means.[3]

The rather free floating application of the term *ati* is attested by the *Rig-pa rang-shar:*

The *ati-rdzogs-pa chen-po* is such that
(As) one it is perfect and complete; (as) two it is perfect and complete; and (as) everything it is perfect and complete.
In that which is the *rdzogs-chen ati*
All that is external, internal, and arcane is (present in a) perfect and complete (manner).[4]

This cryptic description of *rdzogs-chen* as that which is perfect and complete (by this double diction I attempt to bring out the subtle difference between *rdzogs* and *rdzogs-chen,* "supercompleteness" whether taken as one or two or everything), is elaborated in the *Kun-byed rgyal-po,* which, however, in its concise code language is hardly any less cryptic. The relevant passage runs as follows:[5]

There is nothing in it that is not perfect and complete.
Since it is perfect and complete (as) one, perfect and complete (as) two, and perfect and complete (as) the whole,

(It is the system's) optimal level (reverberating) in the hierarchical order of (the system's) complexities (informing) the stratum (from which the system deals with itself).
Perfect and complete (as) one means that it is perfect and complete as the intent toward pellucidity and consummation (or: one's mind suffused with the pellucidity and consummation of the whole, *byang-chub-sems*).[6]
Perfect and complete (as) two means that it is perfect and complete in and as what has been built by mentation (*sems*).
Perfect and complete (as) the everything means that it is perfect and complete in and as the hierarchical (triune) order of (Being's, the whole's) complexity (*phun-sum-tshogs*).[7]

Klong-chen rab-'byams-pa seems to have been the only person to offer an explication of the "elaborated codes" in the *Kun-byed rgyal-po*. His elucidation is too important to be dealt with by a passing reference, and it also provides an excellent intimation of what a student of rDzogs-chen will encounter and what is expected of him: to directly apprehend, experience (feel), and take time to think about (contemplate) that which is presented. In true rDzogs-chen fashion, Klong-chen rab-'byams-pa's presupposes, and consequently, incorporates, the whole of Buddhist thought. In his words:[8]

> *1*. "Perfect and complete as to what has been built up by mentation" means that the impure (Tib. *ma-dag,* the quantitative, discursive) that makes up samsara, (in other words), all that is summed up by what is termed the "psychophysical constituents" (Tib. *phung-po,* Skt. *skandha*), the system-potential (Tib. *khams,* Skt. *dhātu*), and the psychophysical domains of their operations (Tib. *skye-mched,* Skt. *āyatana*), which (in their totality) present themselves as the (physical) environment (Tib. *snod*) and living beings (Tib. *bcud,* as the psychic organization of it)—both features being the whole's coming-into-presence (Tib. *snang*) and being interpreted (Tib. *srid*)—as well as all that which is analytically presented as the starting-point, the way, and the goal of spiritual pursuits (as they are given expression in a person's) vision, creative imagination, and world-engagement, are a going-astray (Tib. *'khrul-pa,* prompted by) the ingrained tendencies in mentation, because (all this going-astray) has been effected, in a superficial manner, by the craftsman called "mentation."[9]
>
> Furthermore, since all this has presented itself as an (objective) presence of a going-astray and as a (subjective) belief in what is this going-astray, it seems to be true as far as truth goes, but actually it has nothing of truth about it because of the fact that it has never parted from the vibrant dimension of (Being's) originary awareness mode. It is for this reason that one speaks of perfect and complete (with reference to what has been built up by mentation).

2. "Perfect and complete in and as the hierarchical order of (Being's, the whole's) complexity" means that (Being's) self-existent originary awareness mode, in itself a sheer lucency, is in its facticity the gestalt in which Being's meaningfulness expresses itself (Tib. *chos-sku*); in its actuality or radiation/radiance, the gestalt in which Being (spatializes itself) as a world-spanning horizon of meaning (Tib. *longs-sku*); and in its resonance as an ec-static cognitive intensity, the gestalt in which Being expresses itself in images of cultural forecasts (Tib. *sprul-sku*). Since these three gestalts have been perfect and complete in their own right since (their beginningless) beginning, this is what is meant by saying "perfect and complete in the sense that they do not have to be searched for elsewhere and made up (as something metaphysical) elsewhere (but are right here within our spiritual being)." [10]

3. "Perfect and complete as the intent toward pellucidity and consummation" (or: "one's mind suffused with Being's pellucidity and consummation") means that to the extent that all that comes-into-presence as the pure (the qualitative-symbolic, see point 2.) and the impure (the quantitative-discursive, see point 1.), as which (Being's) lighting-up is interpreted, gathers in the vibrant dimension of Being's self-existent originary awareness, emerges from it, and remains in it, in the same manner as the various dream images of a person asleep gather in the vibrant dimension of the ec-static cognitive intensity, emerge from it, and remain in it in the manner of (the person's) being the founding (Tib. *rten*) and the (dream images) being the founded (Tib. *brten*). This is what is meant by speaking of the "perfect and complete in and as the intent toward pellucidity and consummation" (or: "one's mind suffused with pellucidity and consummation"), which is (otherwise termed) pure experience (*sems-nyid*).[11]

In this admittedly lengthy discussion of the idea of the "perfect and complete" by Klong-chen rab-'byams-pa, attentive readers will easily have recognized the connectedness with, and indebtedness to, the Yogācāra philosophers' three holonomic modes of experiencing as detailed in Figure 2.

The rDzogs-chen Program

For someone already somewhat familiar with rDzogs-chen ideas, the most lucid conspectus of the rDzogs-chen program is given by Klong-chen rab-'byams-pa in a six-line aphorism [12] that may—in spite of its conciseness and, for a Westerner, almost enigmatic diction—serve as the basis for our "unpacking" of the rDzogs-chen program. In the following translation, I have given the Tibetan key terms in parentheses and the most salient ones amongst them in boldface. In true rDzogs-chen style, I have avoided the use of verbs of which the "pure structural business . . . is to serve as a kind of 'logical glue,' literally a 'copula,' joining words into propositions" (Langer 1972, vol. 2, 320). Klong-chen rab-'byams-pa's aphorism then runs as follows:

The supercompleteness of the ground or reason or the whole or Being (***gzhi***)	establishing the primacy of pure experience (*sems-nyid*);
The supercompleteness of the way (*lam*)	scoring a hit with the vital charge of (Being's auto-) emancipation from perimeters (*mtha'-grol*)
The supercompleteness of the goal or climax (*'bras-bu*)	dispatching (itself) into the dimension where expectations and fears are over and done with (*zad-sa*)
The supercompleteness of the cognitive domain (*yul*)	(Being's) lighting-up (***snang-ba***) that (yet) fades away without subjective interference
The supercompleteness of mind/mentation (*sems*)	the emergence of dichotomic thoughts (*rnam-rtog*) as friend
The supercompleteness of (one's) existentiality (***don***)	a flickering (*'gyu-ba*) as a self-evanescent luminosity

Closer inspection reveals that this aphorism consists of two sections. In the first the key word is *gzhi,* which on the one hand has the double connotation of "ground/foundation" and "ground/reason for," and on the other hand, the connotation of Being as pure dynamics.[13] Being as pure dynamics, though irreducible to some ground or "thing," passes through phases termed starting point, way, and goal/climax that somehow are the correlates of the process of Being's experiencing. In the second part of Klong-chen rab-'byams-pa's aphorism, the key word is *snang-ba,* which means the "lighting up" of the whole, which in this lighting-up, spatializes itself, as it were, into a cognitive domain that implies a cognizing activity characterized by dichotomic processes (one's familiar subject-object division), all of which becomes centered in one's existentiality.

Being as pure dynamics is, with respect to this its dynamics, assessed in terms of symmetry transformations such that what is referred to as the facticity (Tib. *ngo-bo*) of Being is transformed into what is referred to as the actuality (Tib. *rang-bzhin*) of Being, and this combined transformation is again transformed into what is referred to as the resonance (Tib. *thugs-rje*) of Being. Although the transformation of facticity into actuality seems to imply a transition from a purely virtual state into an actual state, all that has been said or described so far is akin to what Werner Heisenberg (who was one of the few physicists attempting to describe the "world-in-itself") called *potentia,* a superposition of mere possibilities, "unrealized tendencies for action, awaiting the magic moment of measurement that will grant one of these tendencies a more concrete style of being which we humans experience as actuality" (Herbert 1987, 195). Each of the three facets of Being functions inseparably from and indivisibly with the two others. This functioning is described by what we call adjectives, but, as noted before, they actually are more like adverbs (Whitehead's vector feeling-tones). There are two sets used in connection with the facets of Being. One conveys the paradoxical idea of dynamic stasis, the other, functional dynamics. Figure 5, showing the Tibetan terms in parentheses, will make this clear:

FIGURE 5

diaphanous (*ka-dag*)	↔	spontaneous (*lhun-grub*)	↔	all-inclusive (*kun-khyab*)
facticity (*ngo-bo*)	↔	actuality (*rang-bzhin*)	↔	resonance (*thugs-rje*)
stong-pa	↔	radiant (*gsal-ba*)	↔	cognitively intensificatory (*rig-pa*)

In this diagram I have intentionally left the Tibetan word *stong-pa* untranslated, although in most cases I have rendered it by "open" or "openness/nothingness" in order to avoid the container-metaphor fallacy connected with the so-called standard translation of this word by "empty" or "void" on the basis of its Sanskrit equivalent *śūnya* (which is indeed an adjective). The Tibetan word is primarily a verb for which there is no corresponding word in any Indo-European language. Only secondarily can it be used as an adjective as we understand adjectives.

It is this triune inner dynamics of Being that eventually pushes it, figuratively speaking, over the instability threshold into its actuality so that the virtually operative actuality in Being now assumes a true actuality that may be called Being's "eigenstate" (Tib. *rang-bzhin*). (It is one of the shortcomings of language that there is only one word available for the virtual and the actual.) This process is termed *gzhi-snang* which, borrowing a term coined by David Bohm, I render as "holomovement," which in the rDzogs-chen context means that Being in its totality (*gzhi*) lights up (*snang*), and in this lighting-up makes its presence felt.[14] The implication is that, however paradoxical it may sound, Being is nowhere else than in the what-is, and with respect to our existentiality (*don*), this means that we are the whole and yet only part of it. Erich Jantsch (1975, 99) expresses this felt awareness in a more evocative manner by resorting to the image of the life stream: "We *are* the stream, source and flow, carrier and carried, the whole stream and yet only part of it—as a water molecule is the river and yet only part of it."

Again, a word of caution becomes necessary. We (as Westerners) are too steeped in a static dualistic mode of thought to be able readily to grasp the nuances of different modes of thinking. rDzogs-chen, like much of Buddhist thought, is dynamically triadic/triune; and, to make matters still more complicated, the holomovement (Tib. *gzhi-snang*) itself presents a double triune dynamics. "Internally," if we may say so, it is a process of symmetry transformations (facticity → actuality → resonance) that remains symmetric (invariant). "Externally," its actual lighting-up or coming-into-its-own (Tib. *rang-bzhin*) as its spontaneity (Tib. *lhun-grub,* see Figure 5) is halfway between pure possibility and actual presence. Not until the pervasively inherent intelligence (the ec-static cognitive intensity, Tib. *rig-pa,* functioning in discrete, yet intimately connected and mutually consistent, originary awareness modes, Tib. *ye-shes*) exercises its interpretation options, can we speak of the holomovement's possibilities having become actualities. In other words, even the possibilities in the holomovement are as yet not well defined. All we can do is to point to the dynamics of this movement that, through its ecstatic intensity, we feel working in us as our intent toward the whole's (Being's) pellucidity and consummation that is our mind to the extent that it is suffused with this pellucidity (Tib. *byang-chub-sems*).[15] These pointers very much reflect the presence of the experiencer in the unfolding drama, and each pointer gives testimony to its origin in lived experience. They are called "creativity" (Tib. *rtsal*), "play" (Tib. *rol-pa*), and "ornament" (Tib. *rgyan*), and their sequence (which is not a sequence in the strict sense of the word, but only appears to be a sequence due to the linearity of language) reflects the inner dynamics of the holomovement in aesthetically appealing images. A few examples may suffice. About the pellucidity-suffused mind's unique creativity and the fascinating play it enacts, Klong-chen rab-'byams-pa says:

> Although this intent toward pellucidity and consummation does not exist
> In or as that which lights up or does not light up, samsara or nirvana, the without or the within,
> It is through its coming-into-its-own, prompted by (inherent) creativity,
> That the manifold of what lights up in this way and is interpreted in terms of samsara and nirvana arises as a fascinating play.[16]

Commenting on this aphoristic verse in his autocommentary he says:

> Although a crystal's crystalness is nowhere else than in its flawless purity, it spontaneously glows in the five colors (of the rainbow) when it encounters a ray of the sun. Likewise, (Being's) ecstatic intensity is not found anywhere as anything, yet its openness/nothingness that is its lucency/radiation is there as the pure gestalt in which Being's meaningfulness (becomes experienced); it is through the

FIGURE 6

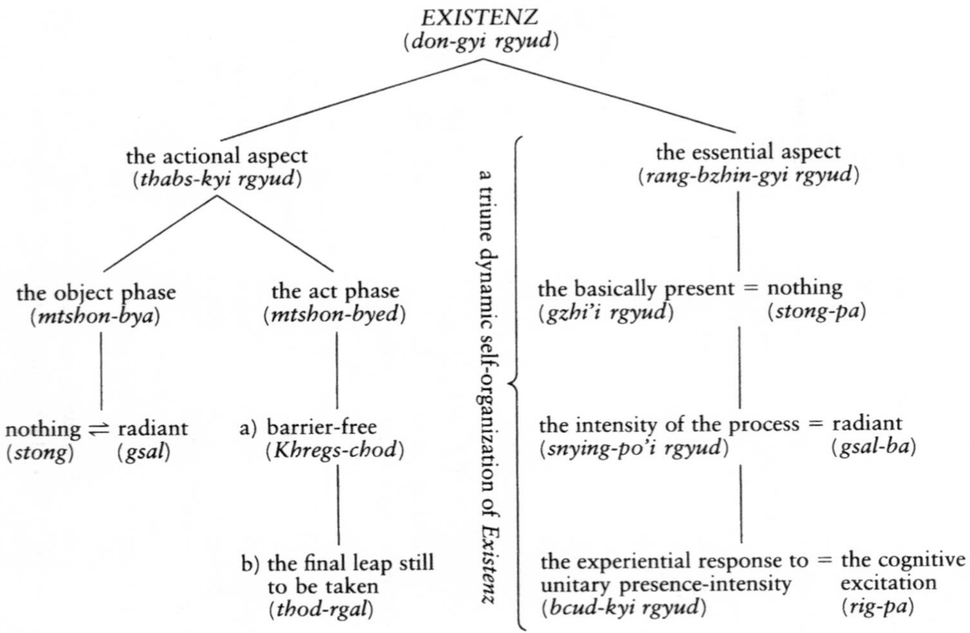

EXISTENZ
(don-gyi rgyud)
the actional aspect
(thabs-kyi rgyud)
the object phase
(mtshon-bya)
nothing ⇌ radiant
(stong) (gsal)
the act phase
(mtshon-byed)
a) barrier-free
(Khregs-chod)
b) the final leap still to be taken
(thod-rgal)
a triune dynamic self-organization of Existenz
the essential aspect
(rang-bzhin-gyi rgyud)
the basically present = nothing
(gzhi'i rgyud) (stong-pa)
the intensity of the process = radiant
(snying-po'i rgyud) (gsal-ba)
the experiential response to unitary presence-intensity = the cognitive excitation
(bcud-kyi rgyud) (rig-pa)

understanding or nonunderstanding of this that out of the creativity (presenting itself) as samsara and nirvana, it arises as the manifold of a fascinating play that is (Being's) lighting-up and interpretation.

It is characteristic of rDzogs-chen thinkers to present ideas in images of appealing beauty and suggestiveness. Thus Klong-chen rab-'byams-pa speaks of these three pointers in images the aesthetic quality of which impresses itself immediately on our sensibilities:

> Creativity is the liveliness of ecstatic intensity; its manifestation as either samsara or nirvana is like the working of a single ray of the sun that makes the lotus flower (Skt. *padma*) open and the lily (Skt. *kumuda*) close.
>
> Play is the effulgence of ecstatic intensity; it is like the shimmering of the flame in an oil lamp or the dancing of the sun's rays of light.
>
> Ornamentation is the display of this intensity's automanifestation that in its automanifesting process gives beauty to this intensity; it is like a rainbow in the sky or the latter's adornment by sun and moon and stars.[17]

It is in the upsurging of the holomovement, so picturesquely described in terms of creativity, play, and ornamentation, that there also occurs the crystallization into what is experienced as one's existentiality (Tib. *don*). This is by no means something monolithic, but a complex program that in being a program is technically known as *don-gyi rgyud*. This difficult term is best translated by the German word *Existenz* in the sense in which it was defined by Calvin O. Schrag (1969, 257) as "the common center in which organizing notions are rooted.") What we consider our existence is, according to rDzogs-chen thought, but the pseudoconcreteness of *Existenz*. It is important to keep this difference constantly in mind. The complexity of the program *Existenz* is diagramed in Figure 6.

Although this diagram is self-explanatory, a few words may be appropriate to elucidate the internal logic. The dynamic aspect of *Existenz* is indicated by the Tibetan term *thabs-kyi rgyud*, which indicates the autodisclosure of one's existentiality as the means to come to grips with its underlying dynamics, involving experiential techniques that base themselves either on the openness/nothingness aspect (Tib. *stong-pa*) and proceed in a barrier-free (Tib. *khregs-chod*) manner, or on the lucency/radiance aspect (Tib. *gsal-ba/snang-ba*) and proceed up to a level from which the final leap (Tib. *thod-rgal*) into one's original being-the-whole has still to be taken. The so-called "essential"—an admittedly unfortunate term, difficult to better because of the inability of our language to express the dynamics of the crystallization process of Being into *Existenz*—aspect of one's existentiality presents the triune dynamics of the whole, which for descriptive purposes can only be split up. This allows us to speak of one's existentiality (Tib. *don*) as presenting an (evolutionary) starting point (Tib. *gzhi* > *gzhi'i rgyud*), proceeding through an autopresencing/auto-disclosing phase (Tib. *rang-bzhin* > *snying-po'i rgyud*) to its climax, which actually triggers the whole process (Tib. *thugs-rje* > *bcud-kyi rgyud*). At the risk of oversimplification and of being misunderstood, the rDzogs-chen program is mankind's individuation process discussed in unprecedented details.

11 rDzogs-chen Supercompleteness II

The Homologous Evolution of Man and God/Teacher

The Evolution of the God/Teacher Idea

The triune complexity of Being's holomovement (Tib. *gzhi-snang*) prompted (not caused) by the dynamics of Being itself in what is called its actuality (Tib. *rang-bzhin*), itself already a virtual symmetry transformation of its facticity or nothingness (Tib. *ngo-bo*) into a brilliant radiance (that is indistinguishable from Being's nothingness), presents a paradoxically virtual-actual actuality (Tib. *rang-bzhin*) that is this holomovement's spontaneity (Tib. *lhun-grub*). It thus resembles what in quantum physics is known as a wavewise superposition of possibilities, or Heisenberg's world of *potentia,* the equally paradoxical nature of which is well summed up by Nick Herbert (1985, 195): "Until it's actually observed, a quantum entity must be considered 'less real' than the same entity observed. On the other hand, an unobserved quantum entity possesses 'more reality' than that available to ordinary objects because it can entertain *in potentia* a multitude of contradictory attributes which would be impossible for any fully actualized entity."

If we conceive of the possibilities as "waiting" to be made fully actual by the pervasive intelligence in this half-real universe of the holomovement, we get an inkling of what is meant by its "coming-into-presence in eight possibilities for actualization (Tib. *ltar-snang*)" [1] and its two modes. One mode is the holomovement's errancy into the phenomenon of Man (Tib. *sems-can 'khrul-tshul*), and the other is the holomovement's emancipatory mode summed up by the symbol Kun-tu bzang-po (*Kun-tu bzang-po'i grol-tshul*).[2] In the Buddhist context, the latter mode corresponds to the teacher idea, in the Western context, to the God idea.

The emancipatory mode is intimated by a frequently quoted verse from an as yet unspecified source, which states:

> In a single "moment" (*skad-gcig*) a differentiation has been effected;
> In a single "moment" (there is) a perfect and complete (*rdzogs*) dissipation (*sangs*)-unfoldment (*rgyas*).[3]

And the emancipatory mode itself is described in the following "packed" Tibetan passage:

> The movement a (symmetry) break occurs in Being (*gzhi*), the holomovement (*gzhi-snang*) sets in as an autopresencing (*rang-snang*) in

> eight (unfolding) possibilities (*sgo brgyad*) that are the spontaneity (*lhun-grub*) of this holomovement. Not conceiving (grasping) it is as something other (than an autopresencing), an astute mind will recognize it as (Being's) auto-effulgence and cut short this flickering right away.[4] By recognizing this occurrence at its very first moment as an autopresencing, an understanding (*rtogs*) is born, and (with it) a differentiation (in the original unity) is effected. In the second moment, the (possibility of the whole) gong astray has "gone away" (dissipated, *sangs*), and an originary awareness has unfolded (*rgyas*), whereby Being matures into what is its climax (goal, destiny, *'bras-bu*). (This is what is meant by the) statement that by understanding the facticity (of Being-in-its-holomovement) as a process of a primordial dissipation-unfolding (*ye sangs-rgyas*), there (comes with this understanding) a renewed dissipation-unfolding (*yang sangs-rgyas*). The teacher who (exemplifies this process of) dissipation-unfolding before (there was anything) holistically (*gzhi thog-tu*)[5] from the superdiaphaneity of Being (from which the autopresencing of Being as its holomovement has started and to which it returns) is called Kun-tu bzang-po.[6]

Special attention should be drawn to the phrase, "Being matures into what is its climax," by which Being's ec-static cognitive intensity is understood and which seems to give credit to Erich Jantsch's statement (1980, 231) that "evolution seems to facilitate . . . a four-dimensional experience to an ever higher degree. Not only the universe as a spatial structure is becoming increasingly self-reflexive, its evolutionary process itself is becoming self-referential." As Klong-chen rab'byams-pa elaborates: "The cognitive intensity (*rig-pa*) that breaks away from Being (*gzhi*) is like a seed as yet not well defined as to whether it will grow into the emancipatory mode or the errancy mode, and hence is called an "immature intensity" (*ma-smin-pa'i rig-pa*); that which makes it mature into the dissipation-unfolding (process, *sangs-rgyas*) is (one's) critical acumen that has become "understanding" (*rtogs-pa'i shes-rab*)."[7] This passage makes it unmistakably clear that the experiencer by virtue of his critical acumen, which also grows in this process, is an integral aspect of this evolutionary dynamics. Such understanding (Tib. *rtogs*), which is central to rDzogs-chen thinking, is more of an "innerstanding," as Klong-chen rab-'byams-pa has noted: "When without falling into the trap of discursive thought one understands (what occurs) as being one's very own being (*rang*) one is an astute person and, linking up with the fading away (of what has been Being's) spontaneity (into itself in its pure dynamics) one abides in inner lucency (*nang-gsal*)."[8]

The upshot of the matter is that what is indicated by the image of Kun-tu bzang-po is a self-structuring process that, on closer inspection, suggests the possibility of itself being something like a quantum effect. For certainly Kun-tu bzang-po is nothing static or absolute. He (short for male-female complementarity) is, as far as our language, ill-equipped to express the unity of contrary notions, can give a hint, a symbol for our being simultaneously the whole and yet only part of it. Or stating it differently, again using figurative language, Being (the whole) in its dynamics closes in on itself in what becomes its holomovement and thus sets up or turns itself into an inner (interiorized) dimensionality that is our finitude remaining open to the whole. Again, it is Klong-chen rab-'byams-pa, who has laconically described this process as it climaxes into this open-dimensional finitude:

> When in the first moment Being's resonance (*thugs-rje*) in its auto-effulgence that is its spontaneity has effected a differentiation, in the second moment it emancipates (itself from the danger of falling into the trap of discursiveness), and in the third moment it coils itself up as the climax (of the process that has started) in the precious envelope that is (Being's) spontaneity (in its infinite finitude, *lhun-grub rin-po-che'i shubs*).[9]

This precious envelope into which Being in its spontaneity transforms itself as being the site where it can take up its "residence" is described in terms that reveal the inseparability of Being's spontaneity from Being's superdiaphaneity. These seemingly contrary notions have to be thought together (not in the sense of some primitive synthesis, but as a unique unity), and it is this unique unity that again stresses the connectedness of the Kun-tu bzang-po evolutionary process with the dynamics of an all-encompassing universe:

> Pure, insubstantial, irreversible, invariant,
> Ceaseless, radiant throughout, the superforce of (Being's) originary awareness.[10]
> To give a summary indication of it, it is like a crystal.
> It is Being's holomovement as discussed before.
> This precious envelope is the gestalt in and through which Being's meaningfulness (*chos-sku*) becomes experienced.[11]

Although the qualification of Kun-tu bzang-po as presencing or being there as a gestalt (Tib. *sku*) evokes anthropomorphic associations, this gestalt (*sku*) has neither a face nor hands, its light (Tib. *'od*, Ger. *Lichthaftigkeit*) has no color, and its ec-static (cognitive) intensity (Tib. *rig-pa*) has nothing in common with the oscillations of consciousness.[12] And yet, when experienced as the Lord (Tib. *mgon-po*), Kun-tu bzang-po presences as the embodiment of the principle of complementarity in the image of man and woman in intimate embrace. He (Kun-tu bzang-po) is the lighting-up aspect (Tib. *snang-cha*) of what is the ec-static (cognitive) intensity of the whole in its palacelike dimensionality or spontaneity (Tib.

lhun-grub) of the whole's superdiaphaneity (Tib. *ka-dag*), in which as a superforce (Tib. *klong*) everything is embedded; and she (Kun-tu bzang-mo) is the openness/nothingness aspect (Tib. *stong-cha*) of the ec-static (cognitive) intensity expressive of Being's possibilizing dynamics (*chos-nyid*).[13] As the purest of the pure, Kun-tu bzang-po and Kun-tu bzang-mo are, in iconographic presentations, depicted as naked; no ornaments, no drapery can interfere with their pure dynamics.

From what has been presented so far, it should be clear that the Kun-tu bzang-po idea does not stand above and outside Being but is within the unfolding of Being to which we give the name of evolution. This is Being's self-organizing principle, through which the human and the divine are made to coincide.

To the pious, such a statement as the following one must have come, and still may come, as a shock:

> Kun-tu bzang-po, without having done anything good, through understanding the triune dynamics (of Being/Existenz, i.e., its facticity, actuality, and resonance) has become Buddha (*sangs-rgyas*), while the living beings in three (hierarchically organized) spheres of the world, without having done anything evil, through not understanding this triune dynamics, roam about in samsara. It is through (their) not understanding the facticity (of Being/Existenz) to be nothing (*stong*), its actuality (that is) nothing (*stong*), its actuality to be radiant (*gsal*), and its resonance to be a presencing (that is) nothing (*snang-stong*), that they roam about in samsara.[14]

When, as in rDzogs-chen thought, the subject at issue is the whole with its inherent dynamics, it is meaningless to talk about causation in the usual sense presupposing a universe of granular items. Klong-chen rab-'byams-pa's assessment of the problem is that of a process-oriented thinker—the whole by its dynamics "prompts" the whole to take its course. And so he says:

> If one investigates the statement that Kun-tu bzang-po has in a holistic manner become Buddha without having done anything good, (one will find that) since the recognition by the whole of itself as what it is, is the sea of the incorruptible and self-existent good, (which means that) the accumulation (of merits) in an ultimate sense is already perfectly and completely present in (Being's) primordiality (*yer,* as having a spatial character), and since the nondescript unknowing (concerning this good) has dissipated (and is gone), the veils (shrouding this good) have already torn in (Being's) primordiality (*ye'i,* as having a temporal character). Through knowing (the evolution of Kun-tu bzang-po to be an autopresencing process [*rang-snang*]), the ignorance (about it) dissipates, and with this dissipation all the pollutants (of which this ignorance is one) dissipate. That is to

> say, through the unfolding (the "becoming-manifest") of the latently present capabilities, (Kun-tu bzang-po's evolution in the) manner of a dissipative structure, (experienced in the unity) of a gestalt quality and its commensurate originary awareness, has come to pass.[15]

Within the whole history of Buddhist thought, rDzogs-chen thinking presents the only outlook according to which the concept of an event without a cause makes sense. In this respect, it is remarkably similar to quantum physics, as the latter is gradually led by its own momentum in the direction from which rDzogs-chen started—an inherently intelligent universe the dynamics of which we as human beings in one way or another present (not "represent"). To illustrate this rapprochement: Of late, quantum physicists and cosmologists have felt bound to deal with the problem of God and have come to state intellectually what formerly had been accessible only to mystic experience. Thus, probably independently developing a suggestion by Erich Jantsch (1980, 308), Paul Davies (1983, 210) states, "This would not be a God who created everything by supernatural means, but a directing, controlling, universal mind pervading the cosmos and operating the laws of nature to achieve some specific purpose. We would describe this state of affairs by saying that nature is a product of its own technology, and that the universe *is* a mind: a self-observing as well as self-organizing system." And Sir Fred Hoyle (1984) even speaks of an overall gestalt of intelligence or pure information.[16] And so it seems, we have come full circle. Kun-tu bzang-po is not a creator (with or without capital letter), he is the highest intensity of cognition, ecstasy in a dynamic perspective and not in a static sense; or, if a play of words be permitted, the "minding of mind" (Tib. *sems-nyid*); and his gestalt envisioned as Kun-tu bzang-po in intimate embrace with his consort Kun-tu bzang-mo reflects the inner tension as well as the harmony of intelligence-in-operation.

The Evolution of Man as the Holomovement's Errancy Mode

In the same manner in which the evolution of the Kun-tu bzang-po (teacher-God) idea as an expression of the full realization of potentialities and possibilities through an understanding (Tib. *rtogs*) of wholeness in ec-static intensity (Tib. *rig-pa*) started with the holomovement, so also the evolution of Man[17] begins with the holomovement, but in the opposite direction. In this case, Man is the end-phase of a process of embodiment, which in becoming ever more "concrete," misses out on the realization of what the holomovement in its spontaneity has to offer. This missing-out on realizing one's full potential is known as a going astray, an errancy mode (Tib. *'khrul-pa*), which in itself is a lack of understanding (Tib. *ma-rtogs*), a not-knowing-better or plain low-level (cognitive) intensity (Tib. *ma-rig-pa*). Highlighting the dynamics of the holomovement (as diagramed in Figure 5), the Tibetan text the *Mu-tig phreng-ba* states concisely:

> Although the ground and reason for going astray (*'khrul-gzhi*) is said to be of many varieties, (it boils down to)
> Spontaneity (*lhun-grub*) and resonance (*thugs-rje*).[18]

A more detailed account, significant in many respects, is found in another Tibetan text, the *rDo-rje-sems-dpa' snying-gi me-long*:

> All the sentient beings in the three world spheres have gone astray into all sorts of life forms out of a primal ground (*dang-po gzhi*)[19] that itself is not some life form. This ground is, with respect to its facticity (*ngo-bo*), a (dynamic) nothing (*stong-pa*); with respect to its actuality (*rang-bzhin*), radiation (*gsal-ba*); and with respect to its resonance (*thugs-rje*), the capacity to be felt as a presence (*snang-ba*) by sentient beings. From this (state of affairs) there originates, still within it, (but) out of a low-level intensity, a trend that makes the cognitive capacity to grasp (what is a mere presencing); from its subtle flickering the process of going astray sets in by this stupified cognitive capacity entertaining the idea of "have 'I here' come about from 'over there' or has the 'over there' come about from the 'I here.'" This low-level cognitive intensity does not exist (as some entity) in the ground, it exists in and as a vibration or a dream. From its presencing derives (the interdependence of) modifiers (of the evolutionary process, *rkyen*). From the ground's presence in the manner of a light dome (*'od-khyim*), there derives the "causal-momentum modifier" (*rgyu'i rkyen*), which is this very low-level cognitive intensity. When this turns into discursiveness, it is called the "dominance modifier" (*bdag-po'i rkyen*). By developing the ideas of an objective domain and an owner of the objective domain (*yul yul-can*), it is called the "epistemological-objectifiability modifier" (*dmigs-pa'i rkyen*). This is similar to a person seeing his face in a mirror. Since these three modifiers operate synchronously, this fact is called the "synchronous-connection modifier" (*mtshungs-pa de ma-thag-pa'i rkyen*). Thus by not recognizing themselves as being their own source, samsara as ranging over the three world spheres is established by a process of going astray. And once the pollutants ("emotions," *nyon-mongs*) have coarsened, the different shapes of sentient beings have come about.[20]

The last sentence in this passage is a cryptic reference to the rDzogs-chen conception of the low-level cognitive intensity as a pollutant, or loosely speaking, an "emotion." The far-reaching implication is that just as we do not *have* a body "in the sense that one exercises dominion over one's property" (Schrag 1969, 152), but *are* our body and nobody else's (as first pointed out by Gabriel Marcel), so also we do not *have* emotions as a possession, but *are* our emotions.

Particularly noteworthy in the above quoted passage is the Buddhist conception of causality, which, to be precise, continues the ideas already found in the *Abhidharmakośa*. The Buddhist conception presents a mode of thought quite different from the traditional Western one, which bases itself on a "billiard-ball" view of causality that is a linear chain of cause and effect, such that the prior impact of one thing is the sole cause of the motion of another. The Buddhist view of causality is reticular and hierarchically fluctuating. Reticularity is easily recognized in the dominance and epistemological-objectifiability modifiers. Dominance is, phenomenologically speaking, a process of singling out, which in the context of one's animate organism "gives to that organism its sense of being the embodiment of that consciousness whose organism it is" (Zaner 1964, 249), in other words, a "privileged" position that yet may be locally restricted. Thus, the eye as the center of the visual field has a privileged or 'dominance' position with respect to the visual objects it organizes around it as their center, this organizing being the epistemologically objectifying modification of 'what is in sight.'" The same analysis applies to the other senses, each of which may be dominant and epistemologically objectifying at any time. On whichever level this multiplicity of data and complexity of organization occurs, it occurs in a synchronous manner. Lastly, the hierarchical fluctuations are intimated and implied by the three world spheres (Kāmaloka, Rūpaloka, and Arūpyaloka), and in each, reticularity operates in a manner appropriate to that sphere.

Crucial for the going astray into the status of a sentient being (Tib. *sems-can*), particularly into the phenomenon called Man, is a drop in the intensity of the cognitive capacity pervasive of the holomovement. This, as a symmetry transformation of Being, is, strictly speaking, already a symmetry break, and in becoming the holomovement in this way, is best understood as the instability phase in the whole. According to the triune dynamics of Being and its holomovement, the drop in intensity, the ensuing low-level cognitive intensity state (Tib. *ma-rig-pa*), is threefold. In its triune operation, this low-level state is referred to as the prime causal-momentum (Tib. *dang-po'i rgyu*) in the errancy mode of the holomovement, and its three aspects are listed separately according to the function each facet in the triune dynamics performs. Thus, Klong-chen rab-'byams-pa states:

> By not recognizing (the holomovement's) conceptually undivided facticity for what it is, there (arises) the "absolute self" low-level cognitive state (*bdag-nyid gcig-pa'i ma-rig-pa*); by not recognizing (the holomovement's) actuality in its lustre of five hues as (the movement's) actuality, there (arises) the "coemergent-systemic" low-level cognitive state (*lhan-cig skyes-pa'i ma-rig-pa*); and by not recognizing (the holomovement's) resonance as an auto-excitatory intensity,

> there (arises) the "conceptual" low-level cognitive state (*kun-tu brtags-pa'i ma-rig-pa*),[21]

And:

> These three low-level cognitive states are named after the manner of their presence in the nonrecognition of what they are (in the holomovement's dynamics), such that the "absolute self" low-level cognitive state is still with the primordiality (of the whole, *ye-ldan*), the "coemergent-systemic" low-level cognitive state is synchronous (*dus-mnyam*), and the "conceptual" low-level cognitive state is a latecomer (*phyis 'byung*).[22]

In a manner typical of the process-oriented thinking of Klong-chen rab-'byams-pa, the holomovement is broken up into a series of symmetry breaks. This is important because, as we now know, symmetry breaks mark the various stages of evolution in the broadest sense of the word. In the narrower sense of the evolution of Man, further symmetry breaks, after the above initial breaks, introduce the break into the within and the without.

In this symmetry-breaking process, conceived of as a going astray into what is somehow felt as a kind of pseudoreality, each facet of the holomovement's triune dynamics plays a significant role according to the intensity of the cognitive excitation—"cognitive" because of the Buddhist presupposition that the universe is intelligent—operative in each facet. One of the earliest presentations of this symmetry-breaking is given in the *Thig-le kun-gsal:*

> The ground and reason for the going astray (into a pseudoreality) is threefold:
> The (holomovement's) possibilizing dynamics[23] is the ground and reason for the pseudoreality of a world of objects (*yul*);
> The (holomovement's) excitation is the ground and reason for the pseudoreality of a mind (*sems*); and
> The (holomovement's) five hues are the ground and reason for the pseudoreality of a body (*lus*).[24]

It need hardly be pointed out that, although not presented in the traditional order, the holomovement's possibilizing dynamics is its facticity (Tib. *ngo-bo*) and nothingness (Tib. *stong-pa*); the five hues are its actuality (Tib. *rang-bzhin*) and radiance (Tib. *gsal-ba*); and the excitation is its resonance (Tib. *thugs-rje*) or cognitive intensity (Tib. *rig-pa*). The text goes on to say:

> At first, the possibilizing dynamics is (both) unexcited and (just) nothing (*rig-med stong*);

Then there is the emergence of (an) originary awareness in five functions; and
Lastly, there comes the crudity of the tendencies for ego-centered apprehensions and notions.
This is a contaminated state of affairs that presences without there existing anything (of this sort).
Herewith the ground and reason for the pseudoreality of a world of objects has been pointed out.

The relationship between a world of objects (Tib. *yul*) and the unexcitedness (Tib. *rig-med*) and nothingness (Tib. *stong-pa*) of the holomovement's possibilizing dynamics is easily grasped when we remind ourselves that what we call "objects" are meanings (Tib. *chos*) in material concreteness that as such have nothing about them that might suggest that they themselves are in a cognitively excited or excitable state and that the nothingness of holomovement's facticity is not some abstracted and lifeless emptiness, but an utter fullness that, similar to the *pleroma* of the gnostic philosopher Valentinus, is vibrant with energy and hence a meaning-mobilizing potential (Tib. *nyid*). Taking up the two remaining topics, the text continues:

Now the ground and reason for the pseudoreality of a mind will be discussed:
At first, (the holomovement's) excitation is ceaselessly flickering;
Then the apprehension of its effulgence is born; and
Lastly, when the why and wherefore of the mind has emerged,
The many notions (such a mind) entertains have come-to-the-fore.
Herewith the ground and reason for the pseudoreality of a mind has been pointed out.

Now, the ground and reason for the pseudoreality of a body will be pointed out.
At first, it arises from the depth of the superforce that is (the holomovement's) excitation;
Then it arises from the depth of the superforce that is (the holomovement's) possibilizing dynamics; and
Lastly, through the (crudity of) inveterate tendencies,
It makes its presence felt as the material complex of color and shape.

The last line points to the hues in the actuality facet of the holomovement's dynamics; beyond this, the aphorism shows one's body to be both meaning in concrete form and a cognizing presence.

At this stage it may not be out of place to present in the form of a diagram the homologous development found in the Tibetan rDzogs-chen texts of the teacher/God idea and the idea of Man:

FIGURE 7

THE BUDDHA (TEACHER/GOD) LEVEL

The gestalt quality of Being (*sku*) as the gestalt of its lived meaningfulness (*chos-sku*)	↔	The "beaming" of the (existential) design by way of hues of light (*'od*) as Being's message (*gsung*), assuming the gestalt quality of an engagement in a world-horizon of meaning (*longs-sku*)	↔	The open-ended planning (*thugs*) operative as an originary awareness (*ye-shes*) of Being's meaning conveyed through guiding images (*sprul-sku*)

THE HOLOMOVEMENT'S TRIUNE DYNAMICS

facticity (*ngo-bo*)	↔	actuality (*rang-bzhin*)	↔	resonance (*thugs-rje*)
open (*stong*)	↔	radiant (*gsal*)	↔	excitatory (*rig-pa*)
superdiaphanous (*ka-dag*)	↔	spontaneously there (*lhun-grub*)	↔	all-encompasing (*kun-khyab*)

THE SENTIENT-BEING LEVEL

The cognitive domain (*yul*)	:	The physical body (*lus*)	:	mentation (*sems*)

The symbol ↔ indicates the unitary character of the process
The symbol : indicates its broken pieces

The holomovement with its symmetry transformations and seeming symmetry breaks—the facticity ↔ actuality ↔ resonance complexity, setting the scene for the evolution of the *kun-tu bzang-po* (teacher/God) idea as an approximate symmetry transformation with respect to Being/Being-in-its-beingness as the exact symmetry limit, and the evolution of Man as a displacement symmetry transformation (seemingly much more "interesting" since it concerns us directly in our deviation from exact symmetry)—displays an additional symmetry break in each of its symmetry-transformation facets. These were intimated in the passage quoted from the *Thig-le kun-gsal,* but not specifically elaborated. A detailed, "packed" account that links rDzogs-chen thought with Yogācāra ideas has been given by Klong-chen rab-'byams-pa:

> The (holomovement's) facticity (*ngo-bo*) as an innermost glowing-in-its-glowingness (*rang-mdangs*) (as yet) unexcited and (just) nothing—like the empty sky (one senses) "out there"—initiates the going astray into the pseudoreality of an object (-ified and objectifiable) domain (*yul*) that occasions all that may come to be to stand out in it. This same facticity, subtly excited but still nothing, sets up the pseudo-objects that serve, internally ("here within us"), as the operational site of the eight archetypal patterns of thought and per-

ception, (which make up) the continuum underlying them as a pattern of its own (*kun-gzhi*).

The (holomovement's) actuality (*rang-bzhin*) as the above innermost glowing-in-its-glowingness in its (breaking forth as an effulgent) brilliance (*gsal-mdangs*) with its tendency to make its presence felt as a dual (glowing) internally initiates the going astray into the pseudoreality of (one's) body (*lus*) with its ruddy complexion and distinct characteristics. The external replica of this glowing sets up the domain of the presencing of the four fundamental forces, each in its own dynamics.

The (holomovement's) resonance (*thugs-rje*), which makes its presence felt as the ceaseless creativity of (cognitive) excitation (and excitability, *rig-rtsal*), presents, in its subtle aspect, a sequence of mere flashes (indicative of its) readiness to receive impressions from the five sensory "objects"—like the surface of a bright mirror—as they arise from their (source), the cognitive capacity (that is latently operative) until the seven archetypal patterns of thought and perception[25] stir out of the continuum underlying them. Since there is as yet no concrete object presentation, there is no apprehension of what the object might be; rather, this cognitive "stuff" is like someone half-asleep (who well illustrates) this subtle pseudoreality of "apparent" objects not becoming "apprehended" objects. When, subsequently, affirmative or negative judgments are made in the framework of one's affectively toned thinking and one's ideas, entertaining in one way or another, and one's perceptions of colors, sounds, fragrances, tastes, and tactile sensations, one has moved into the coarse pseudoreality (of one's world), and the continuity of samsara through inveterate tendencies is guaranteed.[26]

Readers familiar with Buddhist epistemology will notice that the whole of its theory of perception, to which the Yogācāra philosophers paid special attention, has been presented here in a nutshell. More significant is that here the going astray into a pseudoreality is tied to a continuum underlying all cognitive and perceptual processes as an expression of the low-level energy state of the whole's "intelligence," about which more will be said in the following chapter.

12 rDzogs-chen Supercompleteness III

Ontological Difference and Coordinated Hierarchy

The Ontological Difference

Superficially seen, the reference to a continuum (Tib. *kun-gzhi*) underlying the archetypal patterns of thinking and perceiving in the last quotation in the previous chapter, seems to make rDzogs-chen thinking an aspect of the Yogācāra movement with its novel concept of an *ālaya-vijñāna,* a latently perceptual operation (Skt. *vijñāna*) that underlies (Skt. *ālaya*) all overt aspects of sentient life as a sort of reactivation of "stored" microstructures that have operational consequences in that they ensure the emergence of specific niches. There could be no greater misunderstanding of what rDzogs-chen thinking is about than this rash and superficial conclusion, which overlooks the fact that the rDzogs-chen idea of a continuum (*kun-gzhi*) in its own right is alien to Yogācāra thought and for this reason alone sets rDzogs-chen thinking apart from it.

As has been pointed out in an earlier chapter, the Yogācāra conception of the *ālayavijñāna* was epistemological (as was to be expected from the general mentalistic presupposition of Buddhist and other Indian thought forms reflecting the changing *Zeitgeist*). The lasting contribution by the Yogācāra thinkers to Buddhist thought was their realization that cognition (in the broadest sense of the word)[1] was a process, not a mechanistic collision of isolated entities having an "ontic" status, as had been the contention of the earlier schools of Buddhism with their objectivistic reductionism. Yet even with the Yogācāra thinkers there remained unresolved difficulties, partly because of their ties with the older predominantly rational and, by implication, representational mode of thinking. These difficulties were, among others, the problem of continuity—the *ālayavijñāna* goes on and on "like a river in spate"; and the problem of discontinuity—the *ālayavijñāna* has ceased doing so, as has its second transformation, in the case of an arhant who represented the old Hinayana ideal of an individual who had "gone his way." Worst of all, the emphasis on, if not to say restriction to, perceptual processes (*vijñāna*) merely accounts for the experiencing individual as being embedded in a thematized reality and leaves out an important "other" reality. Though this other reality was somehow glimpsed and pointed to as the gestaltism of Being's meaningfulness (Skt. *dharmakāya,* Tib. *chos-sku*), it was conceived of as change (Skt. *āśraya-parāvṛtti,* Tib. *gnas-'gyur*). But this very notion of change is problematic. Change can be understood in a dual manner, as an "upward" change and a "downward" change—in other words, back to mechanistic thinking with its intolerable reductionism. The fact that in speaking of change in the sense of a radical change, Vasubandhu replaced the term *ālaya,* with which he began his presentation of Yogācāra thought in his *Triṃsikā,* with the term *āśraya,* shows that he was aware of the fact that more than mere epistemology was involved, but failed to understand the ontological implication because of being preoccupied with rational-(reductionistic)-representational thinking.[2]

The rDzogs-chen conception of the continuum (Tib. *kun-gzhi*) as primarily a low-level intensity (Tib. *sems/ma-rig-pa*) and hence the errancy mode (Tib. *'khrul-pa*) of the holomovement (Tib. *gzhi-snang*) that secondarily initiates the protoperceptual operation known in Tibetan as the *kun-gzhi'i rnam-par shes-pa* or in Sanskrit as the *ālayavijñāna,* "the perceptual mode that reflects the experiencer's embeddedness in a particular niche" with which the Yogācāra epistemology-oriented thinkers started, is ontological. This ontological concern brought the rDzogs-chen thinkers face to face with the problem that in the Western world was recognized and formulated only in recent years by Martin Heidegger as the ontological difference. It relates to the difference between Being and beings, Being-in-its-beingness and the beingness of (any) being, with respect to which "there must be some final 'ground' which as *identity of difference* can be taken as the foundation of the difference" (Kockelmans 1984, 76). Or, as David Michael Levin (1985, 11) has elaborated it:

> A deep ontological understanding, then, in which our capacity for realizing this difference is deeply fulfilled, may accordingly be said to consist in a 'state' of continual presence, or continual openness: a lively, vigorous attentiveness which serenely rests in, or stays at, the primordial ground of awareness, *while at the very same time* it *moves* in a shifting succession of focusings from one being to the next. Thus, we may say that, regardless of 'content', regardless of the *beings* with which we are concerned, in the 'ontological attitude' we stay with, or dwell in, a ground of awareness—a ground which always opens limitlessly before, and around, any particular content, any particular being.

Although the ontological difference may be "both basic and simple, its articulation and understanding are matters of the greatest difficulty" (Levin 1985, 10) for the simple reason that "the difficulty derives from the fact that the typical, consensually validated understanding of Being, the shallow understanding which is characteristic of everyone-and-anyone, and which we all tend to in-habit without giving it deep and original thought, *reduces* Being to thinghood" (Levin 1985, 11f.). Within the context of rDzogs-chen thinking, our (Western) articulation of the ontological difference is made even more difficult because of the inseparability of the dynamics of Being-in-its-beingness (a superdiaphanous nothingness (Tib. *gzhi*) and Being-as-spontaneity (Being's luminous holomovement, Tib. *gzhi-snang*), which, in still being preconceptual and prereflective, is (and can be) both the foundation and identity of the (ontological) difference. The ambiguity that attaches to the idea of ground (reaching into us and being felt as) "reason-for," technically spoken of in Tibetan as *kun-gyi gzhi* (which may be literally translated as "the ground and reason for all that is") may be gleaned from the following passages: [3]

> With respect to the self-existent dynamics (of Being in its) invariance,
> (Whatever) is contrived by the intellect's (reductionistic postulations) is not the (real dynamic) ground (or Being itself).
> Therefore (Being itself) cannot be contrived by the vectorial complexity (of a thematizing experience, *rkyen*).
> (That which is) uncontrived and from (the perspective of its) primordiality (*ye-nas*) is the ground and reason for all that is (*kun-gyi gzhi*)—
> Self-existent (as the) gestaltism of (Being's pure) facticity (*ngo-bo-nyid-kyi sku*)—(is)
> The root, the ground and reason for everything existent,
> As has been declared by the buddhas (*sangs-rgyas*) throughout the three aspects of time.
> Hence, Being-(in-its-beingness) has nothing to do with displacement and change (*'pho-'gyur med*).[4]

But then also:

> Because (Being) is a self-existent spontaneity (*lhun-gyis grub-pa*) (and as)
> Sole buddahood (*sangs-rgyas nyag-gcig*) in its gestalt (expressive of Being's) meaningfulness (*chos-kyi sku*),
> It is the momentum (*rgyu*) underlying both samsara and nirvana.
> If one does not understand (this spontaneity), it becomes samsara;
> If one understands it, it becomes nirvana.
> But with respect to Being-in-its-beingness (and its spontaneity inseparable from it), there (exists neither (something called) "Buddha" nor (something called) "sentient being."
> Therefore, the nonexistence of both is a single vibrant dimension (and)
> Everything existent dwells in its dynamic facticity (*ngo-bo*).[5]

However difficult at first glance these two passages, typical for rDzogs-chen thinking, may appear to anyone who is steeped in rational thinking and cannot but posit and hypostatize Being as *a* being among other beings or things, they lucidly confirm David Michael Levin's assessment (1985, 23) of ontology and ontological thinking: "Ontology does not happen by itself. Ontology is a work of thought, and therefore it must be referred back to (or correlated with) the being who is thinking. As an undertaking of human beings, ontology manifests the character of the human being who is always already in relatedness-to-Being."

But what is it that matters in its relatedness-to-Being (as the whole) and that through our understanding opens up our human being to Being? Vimalamitra, one of the earliest rDzogs-chen thinkers, concentrates on three aspects of one's being a human being as something ontical, each aspect exhibiting its ontical foundation (Tib. *kun-gzhi*) in its own way.

The first of these is the "ontical foundation (provided by and shared by) mind" (Tib. *sems-kyi kun-gzhi*). Where "mind" serves as a cover term for wide-ranging egological thought processes. Vimalamitra gives the following account of it:

> The ontical foundation (provided and shared by) mind operates in such a manner that it gives rise to all the pollutants (*nyon-mongs,* that is, one's affectively toned responses),
> Because, in view of the fact that it has been set up by a wretched complex of cause-momentum and attendant modifiers,[6]
> It believes in and holds to something to be the case when it is not.
> It is the microstructure of samsara, which comprises the three worlds (of crude desires, aesthetic forms, and blurry formlessness).[7]

Elsewhere, Vimalamitra explains this state of affairs as a going astray into a dimension of one's being that, in effect, forecloses one's openness-to-Being by claiming its fictitious framework to be the truth:

> The real meaning of the mind's ontical foundation is that because with respect to that which lights up (in experience)
> Its various perceptual processes "think" (of what lights up) as objective "realities"
> And believe in what does not exist as absolute truth,
> It is like the mistaken notion of a rope being a snake.[8]

The second ontical aspect of our ontical being is the "ontical foundation (provided and shared by) the sedimentation of experiences as potentialities for again becoming involved in the different life forms of the experienced world" (Tib. *bag-chags kun-gzhi*). Vimalamitra says concisely:[9]

> This is the ontical foundation (provided and shared by) the sedimentation of experiences:
> Although it operates in the wake of previous (experiences), it
> Depends on certain modifier operations (for its activation) and is unable to start by itself.
> These modifiers, which activate (these sedimentations), are of four kinds.[10]

The third ontical foundation of our ontical being is the "ontical foundation (provided and shared by) the body as lived by the individual" (Tib. *lus-kyi kun-gzhi*). Long before modern phenomenology reinstated the body as an integral aspect of the human reality, rDzogs-chen thinkers knew that one's body "is the primal condition for the existence of the objective, physicocultural world (as Gabriel Marcel says, the "landmark" of all existence) in the sense that it is the "that by means of which there is a world and objects in the first place" (Zaner 1964, 250). Vimalamitra's account of the body brings out all the above points and much more. His words are:

> This ontical foundation (provided and shared by) the body as lived by an individual
> Engages concretely in matters of affection and aversion before
> Their result, frustration, comes about in
> The inconceivable manifold of birth, old age, disease, and death.
> Since this ontical foundation, which resides in and provides the onticalness of each and every sentient being,
> Is the beingness (*gzhi*) of samsara,
> It is not Being itself (*gzhi-nyid*) (which lights up in) the gestalt experience of Being's meaningfulness.
> Therefore, since this ontical foundation is a construct (of and by psychic life)
> It is samsara (kept going) through the power of the modifiers (forming the vectorial tissue of one's enworlded experience).
> Hemmed in by the confines of four rivers[11]
> There is no chance of emancipation as long as one is not set free from them.[12]

Vimalamitra is quite explicit that the above mentioned three ontical foundations are not to be understood as granular entities. They present levels of a self-organizing dynamics that find their coordination in the total person, summed up by the "body" with which he is familiar in a most intimate way. Thus Vimalamitra declares:

> Although (one's) ontical foundation is explicated as being of three varieties, (their interconnectedness is such that)
> The ontical foundation (provided and shared by) mind is an inner mapping;
> The ontical foundation (provided and shared by) the sedimentations of experience is an outer mapping;
> Where these unite, the ontical foundation (provided and shared by) the body as lived by the individual is given.[13]

This terse presentation of what amounts to a hierarchical order shows Man to be the existential center of "world" experience and it is by virtue of Man's being an embodied being that there also is a world, both physical and psychic, inhabited by him. Indeed, Man's body is where perception happens, where interests are occasioned, and where action takes place. As such, the lived body is inseparable from "mind," animating Man's body and mapping out the world to be experienced within the limits of its own finitude, a reduced excitability and yet embued with openness, somehow a prepredicative life world that is given concrete content by his desires, his expectations, and evaluations. It is these that map out the world in terms of what it can do to and for us and what we can do to and for it. It is as much part of ourselves as are our thoughts about it and our bodily existence in it.

In particular, it is the ontical foundation provided and shared by the mind (Tib. *sems-kyi kun-gzhi*), which in its dynamics initiates conceptual differentiations and diversifications. (Tib. *kun-gzhi'i rnam-par shes-pa*), that held the attention of the Yogācāra thinkers, whose approach to Being was, as noted previously, epistemological and analytically-reductive in character. The rDzogs-chen approach was determined, if this is the right term, by Being itself, and rDzogs-chen thinkers never tired of pointing out the limitations into which we as human beings are forced and which we perpetuate by clinging to dichotomic thinking that prevents us from experiencing wholeness. Vimalamitra is quite explicit on this theme when he declares that

> The root of samsara
> Is summed up in the duality of (perceived) objects (*yul*) and a
> (perceiving) mind (*sems*).
> Object, as the mistaken projection of one's mind, and
> Mind, as the sum total of the eight perceptual patterns as well as
> The fifty-one operators (*sems-las byung-ba*),
> Gather in what is their root, the very ontical foundation of ours
> (*kun-gzhi nyid*).[14]

He is also quite explicit when, in picturesque language, he describes the connectedness of the ontical foundation of ours with the rich spectrum of what the world holds for us by our mind-induced interaction with it:

> When a division is introduced by discarding (*spong-ba'i rtog-pa*),
> The fifty operators are like the lunar mansions;
> The eight perceptual patterns, rising and setting, are like the moon;
> and
> Their ontical foundation is like a clouded sky.
>
> When a division is introduced by espousing (*sdud-pa'i rtog-pa*),
> The (fifty) operators are like geese and ducks swimming on a lake;
> The eight perceptual patterns are like otters waiting for fish; and
> Their ontical foundation is like a vast lake.
>
> When a division is introduced by monopolizing (*zhen-pa'i rtog-pa*),
> The fifty operators are like a forest;

The eight perceptual patterns are like deer (roaming in it); and
Their ontical foundation with its residual potentialities is the abundance of grass.[15]

This beautiful passage, stimulating to one's imagination, is significant for another reason, too. It shows that Vimalamitra, like other rDzogs-chen thinkers, went beyond the mentalistic trend of Buddhist (Yogācāra) philosophy, presented here in a nutshell, by his assessment of the socio-cultural operators and the perceptual patterns as being related to an orientational point zero—in Husserl's (German) phenomenological diction, a *Boden* or *Urpunkt,* in Buddhist phenomenological-ontological terminology, one's ontical foundation (Tib. *kun-gzhi*). He thereby gained access to a deeper level of a human being's being that yet is ontologically different from a more "primordial foundation" (*ye-gzhi*),[16] which, however paradoxical it may sound, opens out and around and above it in nonlocal connectedness.

Another important contribution to the problem of the ontological difference is found in a small work attributed to the influential Śrīsiṃha (of unknown date, but probably belonging to the second or third century of our era), whose connection with China (whether he himself was Chinese or merely hailed from China) is always emphasized. In this work, we read:

In Being-in-its-beingness (*gzhi-nyid*), a diaphaneity since its beginningless beginning,
The duality of *sangs-rgyas* (Buddha) and *sems-can* (sentient being)
Does not exist as this duality.
"Buddha," which is the understanding of Being as Being-in-its-beingness (*nyid*),
Is Being's abidingness as (the inseparability of its) gestalt quality and (commensurate) originary awareness.
"Sentient being," which is the nonunderstanding of this,
Is Being's abidingness as (one's) lived body and its sedimented potentialities of experience.
This means that Buddha and sentient being
Are not different when it comes to an understanding of Being;
But they come-to-presence in distinctly different manifestations at the time of the path (*lam*).[17]

Śrīsiṃha's statement that the ontological difference is tied to Being's coming-to-presence (Tib. *snang-ba*) and the understanding of the (pre-conceptual and hence, nonmetaphysical) identity of Being and thinking (here termed "understanding") are strikingly similar to the idea of the identity of Being with thinking in the selfsame, as first pronounced by Parmenides in the Western world, and to Martin Heidegger's claim that the coming-to-presence of the difference stems from the coming-to-presence of the identity and the selfsame (Heidegger 1974, 18, 31). And what about the path? It is a movement in understanding and the motion of understanding.

Śrīsiṃha continues to elucidate the ontological difference through the simile of camphor, which, when properly administered, has healing properties, but when misapplied can kill a person; and through the simile of a conch, the aesthetic actuality of which may be misrepresented in the very act of seeing:

> Take camphor as an example:
> It is the best medicine if one knows it to be nothing (*stong*),
> But if one does not know it so, it is death to one's life.
> In the same way, if one understands the ontical foundation
> (*kun-gzhi*) as (Being's) "nothingness-turning-radiance"
> (*stong-gsal*),[18]
> It is the buddha state in the concrete.
> If one does not understand it so, it is the continuance of samsara.
> Although the very fact of (one's) existentiality has nothing to do
> with (one's) mistaken notions about it,
> These arise by the combination of the four vectorial modifiers (of
> representational thinking);
> It's like a conch in its aesthetic immediacy—
> Having nothing to do with such mistaken notions as yellowness
> and so on,
> The conch seems to be yellow for a person suffering from jaundice.

In speaking of *kun-gzhi* in terms of a "nothingness-turning-radiance" (Tib. *stong-gsal*), of the ontological difference as evolving with the path (*lam*) as the process of Being's becoming increasingly self-reflexive, and of the experiencer's existentiality as liable to be misrepresented in representational thought (which by its nature is oblivious to the immediacy of experience), Śrīsiṃha intimates that there are many levels of an ontological understanding. More significantly, he seems to have anticipated the Heideggerian distinction between *ontology* as the question concerning Being (Tib. *gzhi*) and *fundamental ontology* as the concern with a mode of Being (Tib. *gzhi-snang*) and the ensuing ontical foundation (Tib. *kun-gzhi*). But then, Being is nowhere else than in (its) mode(s). Thus, paradoxically, Being as a virtually active nothingness (*stong*) in its lighting-up or coming-to-presence (*snang-ba*) is an actual brilliance and radiance (*gsal*). The inseparability of this twofold (suggestive of Heisenberg's duplex quantum reality) is thus, from the perspective of Being, a simultaneous identity and difference, and from the perspective of the path, (their) complementarity. This is the main thrust of Śrīsiṃha's ontological thinking: the whole is wholly operative in its parts. His words are:

This superb triune dynamics of nothingness, radiance, and ec-static cognitive intensity (*stong-gsal-rig-pa*)
Is accessed by two ontical foundations:
The ontical foundation of our existentiality (that has been initiated by Being's) very primordiality (*ye-nyid don-gyi kun-gzhi*) and
The ontical foundation that is the set of modifiers through which we attempt to link up with wholeness (*sbyor-ba rkyen-gyi kun-gzhi*).
This latter ontical foundation is what is meant by (the phrase) each and every sentient being.
(Each one attempts to) link its equilibrium state to which it holds, (once it has been achieved, by)
Mixing, like earth with water,
The sedimentations of previous experiences in what is their latency and
The (affective) pollutants as the consequences (of the reactivation of these sedimentations) still in their pre-affective latency,
With (what it believes to be) the gestalt through which Being's meaningfulness is experienced (*chos-sku*).
But this is not (the real) gestalt through which Being's meaningfulness is experienced.
The ontical foundation of our existentiality (that has been initiated by Being's) very primordiality
Is like the limpid clearness of water with no mud in it.
This cognitive quality, which is not vitiated
By the sedimentations of (limited and limiting) experiences, by the dissociative tendencies of representational thought, and affective pollutants,
Is the (real) gestalt through which Being's meaningfulness is experienced, knowing of no subjective distortions and rising by itself.[19]

The discussion of the ontological difference as considered by Vimalamitra and Śrīsiṃha has shown that they were fully aware of the importance of formally investigating and articulating the individual's potential for becoming the whole and his primordial relatedness-to-Being-as-the-whole. Their efforts culminated in Klong-chen rab-'byams-pa's presentation of the modalities of the ontical foundation. His indebtedness to Śrīsiṃha is unmistakable.

He distinguishes between four modalities of the ontical foundation and is quite explicit that they do not represent four separate entities, but merely name dynamic nuances of a single reality.

1. *ye don-gyi kun-gzhi.* This is the ontical foundation in its modality of presenting one's existentiality (Tib. *don*) as the grounding for the organizing notions within experience. This, as it were, shares in two worlds. One is Being's primordiality (Tib. *ye*), which "antedates" any actuality; the other is Being's actuality, which is both open-to-Being and

ready to forsake its openness. In this its as yet not well-defined possibility, it functions as the basis and reason for any living being's going astray;[20] and in this going astray, the complementarity of samsara and nirvana as distinct possibilities presents itself.[21] As such, it is a coevolving low-level version (Tib. *ma-rig-pa*) of Being's optimal ec-static intensity (Tib. *rig-pa*) such that, figuratively speaking, from its incipience it has been "like gold and rust."[22]

2. *sbyor-ba don-gyi kun-gzhi*. This ontical foundation modality is the same as the previously detailed foundation, but in this case in its actively becoming engaged in a world, preeminently samsara, through actions the site of which is the lived body in such a way that thinking ("mind," Tib. *sems*) and body (Tib. *lus*) intermesh (Tib. *sbyor-ba*) and jointly encounter the joys and sorrows the world has to offer.[23] But it also links man to his self-transcendence, nirvana.[24]

3. *bag-chags sna-tshogs-pa'i kun-gzhi*. This ontical foundation modality presents the sum total of the sedimentations of experiences, which may be roused out of their dormancy whenever a suitable situation arises. When this happens, they lead to the polluting or poisoning of the whole system,[25] so that it repeats itself in its "downgraded" operations. The emphasis here is on repetition in terms of autocatalysis and autopoiesis. Generally speaking, it provides for the material system of an organism as well as for those mental processes that go on as irresistible drives, impulses, and emotional vagaries.

4. *bag-chags lus-kyi kun-gzhi*. This ontical foundation modality is any individual's lived body in the sense that it is the hardening of the system's propensities (Tib. *bag-chags*) on the physical level (Tib. *rags-pa'i lus*). We are most familiar with this level, because it lends itself to be turned into an impersonal "it" that can be assessed "objectively." But the physical level is not the only one on which the lived body manifests itself. It is also felt qualitatively as an iridescence that is vibrant with life (Tib. *'od-kyi lus*). Lastly, it is just a presencing that lights up in experience before it is represented, thematized as this or that body (Tib. *snang-ba'i lus*).[26]

To sum up, in assessing the ontological difference, the rDzogs-chen thinkers, of whom we have chosen the three most outstanding and influential ones, have been unanimous in maintaining that any experiencer's ontical foundation (Tib. *kun-gzhi*), though a more or less limited and self-limiting wholeness, yet retains a relatedness-to-Being that in its overarchingness gives meaning to the experiencer's quest for wholeness.

Coordinated Hierarchy

The idea of a hierarchical organization of the universe and of man evolving with it, rather than in it, is as old as Buddhism itself. We only have to think of the triadic world system of the Kāmaloka, Rūpaloka, and Arūpyaloka and the individual's corresponding levels of psychic awareness. In rDzogs-chen thinking, which is thoroughly evolutionary, this idea of a hierarchical organization is intimately intertwined with the principles of homology and complementarity. The most important aspect of this complexity is that a control hierarchy—information flowing upward and orders flowing downward, resulting in a stifling decrease of creative vibrations (that underlies each and every ideology of dictatorship)—is nowhere involved. The self-organizing dynamics of Being (Tib. gzhi) as it first manifests itself in its holomovement (Tib. *gzhi-snang*), itself already a kind of symmetry break initiating further symmetry breaks, presents two major potentialities for actualization—the errancy mode in the direction of Man (Tib. *'khrul-lugs*) and the emancipatory mode in the direction of teacher/God (Tib. *grol-lugs*). Each of these two crystallizes, as it were, into what is termed the individual experiencer's ontical foundation (Tib. *kun-gzhi*) and—here our objectifying-quantifying-representational-reductionistic thinking fails completely ever to come to grips with the endogenous dynamics of wholeness that has to be experienced directly within one's self—the gestaltism of Being's meaningfulness (*chos-sku*). Each of them constitutes a basis on and in which various cognitive processes are "spread out," in such a way that each is co-experienced simultaneously with the cognitive operation. In the words of Richard M. Zaner (1964, 257), "every sensuous perception, to speak at a higher level, necessarily involves a co-perception of the organism itself as that with which I perceive and that by means of which what is perceived is perceived." Analytically speaking, I can direct attention to either the basis on and in and through which cognitive processes occur or to the cognitive processes themselves. Yet both movements and their crystallizations, by virtue of having a common origin in Being's (the whole's) cognitive quality or intelligence (Tib. *shes-pa*),[27] without which the whole's self-organization would not be possible, are complementary to each other and remain coordinated, their hierarchy being determined by the intensity of the feeling in and with respect to the experience or understanding/innerstanding of them. This amounts to a recognition of the role fluctuations play in a system's (the human individual's or the whole of Being's) self-organization.

Thus Klong-chen rab-'byams-pa declares:

> With respect to (what is called) a sentient being's Beingness (*sems-can-gyi gzhi*) and a buddha's Beingness (*sangs-rgyas-kyi gzhi*), one has to know this to be the (operational presence of the whole's) pure fact of excitation/excitability (*rig-pa'i ngo-bo*), according to whether it is a flawless, superdiaphanous "state" or a flawed state, stained by a low-level excitation with its host of divisive concepts that has become the foundation for all the mistaken presences and the mistaken belief (in their reality), so that there is a dual aspect of an ontical foundation (*kun-gzhi*) and a meaning-rich gestaltism (*chos-sku*).[28]

He goes on to criticize the opinions of those who interpret general statements in the sutras and tantras without thinking about context and intention, as specific assertions about the identity of the *kun-gzhi* and the *chos-sku* in the abstract manner of an equation which is certainly not meant by the principle of identity. He is equally critical of the Yogācāra contention, accepted by some tantra teachings, that the *chos-sku* is a change in status (*gnas-'gyur*) of the *kun-gzhi*. This is thoroughly reductionistic and self-contradictory, because a change in status can operate either way. Obviously, at his time reductionism was as rampant as it is today at all levels of our Western society.

Although analogies as illustrative devices do not prove anything, they are useful in facilitating an understanding of a difficult problem. Klong-chen rab-'byams-pa takes up certain examples given in the *Rig-pa rang-shar*, a Tibetan work of unknown date that was suppressed at the time of its "translation" in the eighth century (p. 667). He elaborates on the necessary distinction between the *kun-gzhi* as similar to the ocean or falling asleep and the *chos-sku* as similar to a sailor or waking up, with special reference to the importance of waking up.

> The big difference between (the *chos-sku* and the *kun-gzhi*) is that one's flawless ec-static cognitive intensity which is (what the) *chos-sku* is made of is not something that is ever to be dismissed and exists (in us) as the ground and reason of one's emancipatory dynamics in an ultimate sense, while one has to (wake up and) move away from the *kun-gzhi* that is like sleep and the site for the emergence of all one's dreams in the wake of mistaken presences.[29]

He concludes his presentation of the difference between the *kun-gzhi* and the *chos-sku* with a lengthy discussion of what in modern terms we call a coordinated hierarchy and the principle of homology. Actually, his summary presentation is based on the *Rig-pa rang-shar*. A few examples (from a total of thirty-one), using picturesque language that is aesthetically appealing, may suffice to give the reader a glimpse of the depth of understanding of the rDzogs-chen thinkers:

> Since Being (*gzhi*) is one and the same with respect to its ec-static intensity (*rig-pa*), it is like the head since its understanding (*rtogs-pa*), the buddha-experience (*sangs-rgyas*), is an autoemancipatory movement involving the whole of Being (*gzhi-thog-tu rang-grol*); it is like the horns (on the head) since its lack of understanding (*ma-rtogs*), the (status of a) sentient being (*sems-can*), is a going.[30]

Or:

> Since Being's unitary field character (*dbyings*), when it is excited (*rig-dus*), dissolves into its legitimate dwelling (*rang-sa*), it is like a painting on water that dissolves with its medium; (Being's) low-level ex-

citation (*ma-rig-pa*) is like seeing water as fire, it sets up all the conditions for errancy.[31]

Or:

Although (in either case) there is no moving away from the unitary field character (*dbyings*) of Being, from the creativity of its excitation (*rig-pa*), which is like water, mind/mentation (*sems*), which is similar to water bubbles, may arise, its excitation (*rig-pa*) does not become subordinate to mind/mentation, since it is not the latter's effect.[32]

Or:

While the coming-to-presence of Being's errancy mode (*'khrul-snang*) and the coming-to-presence of Being (as its holomovement, *gzhi-snang*) are alike in being a coming-to-presence within the vibrant dimension of (the whole's) ec-static intensity, (the holomovement's) auto-effulgence (*rang-gdangs*) is like the day, its false glow (*log-gdangs*) is like night. It is the difference between brightness and darkness.[33]

In the above examples emphasis has been on hierarchy. In the following ones, emphasis is on homology—discussing similarities on the basis of their common origin—rather than on analogy,[34] which discusses similarities of functions not based on a common origin. We have to bear in mind that the interweaving of the complementarity of *kun-gzhi* and *chos-sku* as well as their coordinated hierarchy and their being the site for mind/mentation (Tib. *sems*) and ec-static intensity (Tib. *rig-pa*), respectively, is "rooted," as it were, in the holomovement (Tib. *gzhi-snang*). Here there is a resemblance to Heisenberg's duplex world of potentia and actuality and even a pointing toward a reality (*gzhi*) that is both in and beyond the holomovement. Thus, Klong-chen rab-'byams-pa, paraphrasing the rather evocative presentation in the *Kun-tu bzang-po klong drug-pa*, states:

Although mind/mentation in which dichotomic processes have been suspended (*sems rtog-med*) and the ec-static intensity in which no dichotomic processes exist (*rig-pa rtog-med*) are similar in not being divided by dichotomies, their difference is that the ec-static intensity is (something brightly) insubstantial (*zang-thal*) and mind/mentation is a shimmering puddle (*lhan-ne gnas-shing 'khyil-ba*).[35]

And:

The ec-static intensity, in whose glow, deep within, there is no surging (in the direction of some) object, and (the phenomenon of) mind/mentation as it stays shimmering at its detection threshold may be similar in their staying with themselves. The difference is that in the translucent ec-static intensity no (trend to get involved with an) ob-

> ject exists, while mind/mentation as the (presumed) owner of the objective situation (*yul-can*) is being fettered by its (subjective) grasping and holding to (the objective situation).[36]

And:

> That which comes-to-presence (to be envisioned by) the ec-static intensity in its auto-surging and that which surges in a manifold of mistaken presences may be similar in being some impure concreteness in this or that presence. The difference is that for the visionary (the yogi), this surging comes like the moon's reflection in water or like a dream image (which he sees and feels) as naturally unreal and is not fettered by it, while ordinary persons are fettered by it.[37]

rDzogs-chen thinkers are unanimous in envisioning the ontical foundation with its low-level cognitive intensity as a "state" of darkness, but differ in their choice of images to give expression to the brightness and luster and richness of Being's gestaltism. Vimalamitra, for instance, speaks of it as a jewel in an anacoluthic passage:

> In the depth of darkness, a lowered cognitive intensity, one's ontical foundation (*kun-gzhi*),
> Concerning one and the same reality a dual presentment has taken place:
> A contraption that moves up and down. (The downward movement of this contraption) is samsara (which is)
> Like mistaking a rope for a snake or a cairn for a human figure.
> In this lowered cognitive intensity eight errancy patterns[38] are active:
> Like blind persons, quite on their own,
> They unwittingly take the wrong turn and run around in samsara.[39]

After a rather involved discussion of nirvana, the upward movement of the contraption, he concludes with the words:

> Wretched people who do not understand Being
> In claiming this presencing to be Being
> Are like people who see a mirage as water and want to drink it.
> Samsara and nirvana are incidental defects;
> The abidingness of Being's facticity is the gestaltism of its meaningfulness (*chos-sku*).

But somehow Being's abidingness is in what is also darkness—our mind, which like clouds obscures the sun or like a usurper arrogates what is and cannot be his "property." Thus Vimalamitra declares:

> Through retrieving Being's meaning-rich gestalt experience from the depth of darkness, which is (Being's) low-level excitation as one's ontical foundation,

This darkness is gone (*sangs*).
When understanding has come to the fore, there occurs with the going (Darkness, *sangs*), the unfolding (of light and Being's richness, *rgyas*):
This is like recovering a jewel one had lost.[40]

Within the development of rDzogs-chen thought, which climaxes in Klong-chen rab-'byams-pa, who, as a matter of fact, *is* rDzogs-chen thinking, Vimalamitra plays an important role. He is the one who still uses the Tibetan term *kun-gyi gzhi* for what was referred to as *gzhi* at a later time, and marks it off from *kun-gzhi,* which he, like other rDzogs-chen thinkers, understands as pointing to one's ontical foundation. To us this way of speaking may seem confusing, but we should bear in mind that he faced the same problem we encounter when we attempt to think simultaneously of Being-in-its-beingness "before" (Tib. *ye*) or, as we also might say, "beyond" the world of potentia in its process of becoming an actuality through Being's holomovement (*gzhi-snang*), and of Being's spontaneity (*lhun-grub*) as the actual source of all-that-is-for-us as meanings in material concreteness.

It will be remembered that what is given the code names of *kun-gzhi* and *chos-sku,* respectively, evolved by homologous principles in such a way that both, as a symmetry break within Being as the exact symmetry limit, presented an approximate displacement symmetry (experientially "felt" as a going astray, Tib. *'khrul-lugs*) and an approximate symmetry (experientially felt as an emancipatory dissolving, Tib. *grol-lugs*), their relationship being expressed in a coordinated hierarchy. It will also be remembered that Vimalamitra spoke of three ontical foundations (Tib. *kun-gzhi*), specified as one's lived body (Tib. *lus*), mind (Tib. *sems,* a summary term for more or less overt perceptual processes), and the sedimentations of experiences as possibilities and potentialities for future experiences giving rise to affective fixations, Tib. *bag-chags*). There can be no doubt that in speaking of a triad of ontical foundations, Vimalamitra had in mind the complexity of a living being. He is unique in his presentation of the homology of the facets that go into this complex. Here are a few examples taken from the many scattered over a vast literary output.

If one comes face to face with one's mind as Being's meaning-rich gestalt (*chos-sku*),
(This will be realized as) having been radiating primordially with no separation into an earlier or later phase,
As one quarter among the ontic foundation(s) of one's being an embodied being (*kun-gzhi bzhi-cha*).
It is like the limpid clearness of water with no mud whatsoever in it.[41]

Elsewhere he states:

> An appropriate analogy for accessing Being's meaning-rich gestalt
> As one quarter among (one's) ontical foundation(s)
> Is that of a competent physician
> Who knows how to find out the properties of herbs and water.[42]

In still another place he incorporates the idea of the invariance of Being under any and all transformations:

> As to the meaning-rich gestalt as one quarter among (one's) ontical foundation(s),
> It remains invariable, in spite of the various (modes in which Being) comes-to-presence.[43]

Lastly, he declares:

> Although the self-existent meaning-rich gestalt may be present
> As one quarter (among) the ontical foundations of a sentient being,
> As such, it is shrouded over, because one simply has not been instructed about it.
> Therefore one should understand it as having been primordially (*ye*) present.[44]

Vimalamitra's unique attempt to represent the human personality as a quaternity, such that the *kun-gzhi* (his ontical foundations) forms a triune organization as a kind of diminished wholeness lacking a vital ingredient and the *chos-sku* (the meaning-rich gestalt) making up the "missing quarter" or vital ingredient in the whole, may at first glance seem rather startling. However, we should remind ourselves of the fact that, as the late psychologist C. G. Jung pointed out in his *Psychological Approach*

FIGURE 8

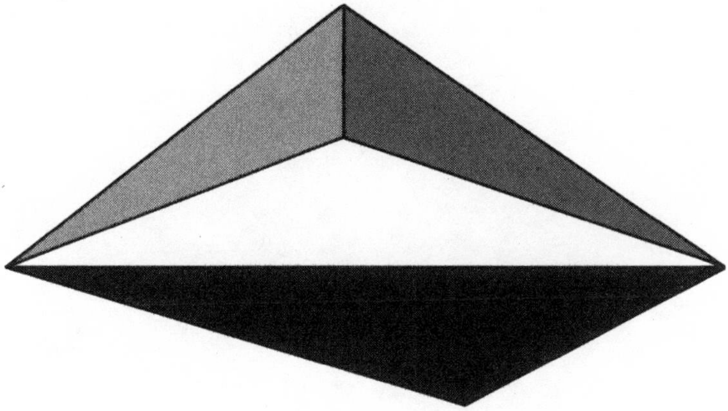

to the Dogma of the Trinity (1942, vol. 11, 167): "The quaternity is an archetype of almost universal occurrence" and "The ideal of completeness is the circle or sphere, but its natural minimal division is a quaternity." In order to gain a better understanding of what Vimalamitra had in mind, we, as modern men, can use the mathematical concept of homology to illustrate the existential structure of the human individual, as in Figure 8.

Here, the three modes of the *kun-gzhi* are represented by three shaded triangles (that could be of various sizes). They are shaded to indicate that they shroud or conceal the *chos-sku*. These shaded *kun-gzhi* triangles touch the *chos-sku* triangle only at one line in each case. In this way the *chos-sku,* though forming the center of the personality, is in no way affected by the shrouding of the *kun-gzhi* modes.

From all that has been said so far, it follows that rDzogs-chen is not something monolithic, but a rich tapestry of many ideas presented by authors whose presentation demands that one thinks along with them. It also follows that whatever had been said earlier within the Buddhist context was viewed with fresh eyes and reinterpreted accordingly. This will be the subject matter of the next chapter.

13 RDZOGS-CHEN *Supercompleteness IV*

THE ROLE OF FLUCTUATIONS IN AN INDIVIDUAL'S PSYCHIC EVOLUTION

The Homology of Mentation Pollutants and Originary-Awareness Modes

AS WE HAVE SEEN, the rDzogs-chen thinkers took as a basis the insight that the evolution of an ontical foundation (Tib. *kun-gzhi*) as the site on which one's psychic life (Tib. *sems*) is spread out,[1] presenting and being felt by the experiencer as a low-level cognitive intensity (Tib. *ma-rig-pa*) that has somehow gone astray (Tib. *'khrul-pa*), as well as the evolution of a high-intensity nonlocalized omnipresent singularity imaged, through one's particularly human filters, as a gestalt (Tib. *sku*) on and through which Being's originary awareness (Tib. *ye-shes*) in all its nuances expresses itself and is expressed,[2] arise from a common source, Being's holomovement (Tib. *gzhi-snang*) or spontaneity (Tib. *lhun-grub*). This insight made them conceive of the human individual or, more precisely, the human condition as a coordinated complexity rather than as a synthesis of basically disparate factors arrived at by postulation. They further realized that these two seemingly different movements owed their actualization to an internal fluctuation that, in view of the omnipresence of Being's "intelligence," its ec-static intensity (Tib. *rig-pa*) or pure experience (Tib. *sems-nyid*), was again, if we may say so, felt as the whole's (Being's) creativity (Tib. *rtsal*), which through its imaginative play (Tib. *rol-pa*) effected its own adornment (Tib. *rgyan*), which thus served to heighten the beauty of its background. The implication is that even the low-level cognitive intensity that characterizes a human being has nothing ugly about it. It is one of the many possible manifestations of an awe-inspiring mystery forever engaged in virtual and actual symmetry-breaking processes. As is stated in the *Rig-pa rang-shar*:

> In the coming-to-light of a superdiaphaneity (*ka-dag*), purer than pure, there is nothing (that could be called) low-level cognitive intensity, or mind, or subjectivity. It is from the creativity in the spontaneity (*lhun-grub-kyi rtsal*) that there comes about a low-level cognitive intensity (*ma-rig-pa*); from the latter's playfulness (*rol-pa*) there comes about a mind (*sems*); from the latter's adorning (*rgyan*) itself there comes about (one's) subjectivity (*yid*). From the latter's object-orientation there come about the five poisons (*dug*); from these the sixteen pollutants (*nyon-mongs*); from these the twenty-five; from these the fifty-one; and from these the eighty thousand.[3]

The rDzogs-chen thinkers' fresh look at the human condition also enabled them to resolve the problem of how what was generally considered to be the pollutants became operative in the contextuality of human experience ranging over multifaceted regions of concern. Certainly, the earlier Buddhist thinkers had noticed that there was something "preobjective" about the pollutants. The various ways of listing and relisting them indicated a growing awareness of the fluidity of their essences. Yet it was precisely this essentialistic structure-oriented thinking, most eager to give an "objective" account of the disturbing pollutants, that overlooked (and maybe was unable to grasp) the fact that the pollutants were not merely more like presuppositions of a concrete experience within a certain context, but also that in relating to and "tainting" the thematizing operations, they gave only a one-sided picture of the living system as a whole. Even the concession that there might be, or actually are, operations not subject to the impact of the pollutants and standing apart from them left the basic problem of the unity of the rational-cognitive and the affective-behavioral unresolved.

Inasmuch as the sequence of low-level cognitive intensity, mind, and subjectivity may be seen as a series of symmetry breaks, the emergence of the pollutants is just another symmetry break or series of such breaks. And all, as it were, conspire to break up the unity of the personality and to worsen the fragmentation interminably. Although there is an almost endless variety ("eighty thousand") to these pollutants, six were considered to be of primary importance. This "new" number was arrived at by the idea that the system in its low-level operation was itself a pollutant. thus, "the six pollutants are: low-level cognitive intensity (*ma-rig-pa*), passion-(addiction, *'dod-chags*), irritation-(aversion-hatred, *zhe-sdang*), delusion-(dullness, *gti-mug*), conceit-(arrogance, *nga-rgyal*), and jealousy-(envy-grudge, *phrag-dog*)."[4] It might be argued that delusion-dullness and low-level cognitive intensity are very similar in character. The answer given to this was that "low-level cognitive intensity comprises all five poisons of which delusion-dullness is one; hence low-level cognitive intensity is counted separately."[5] We can rephrase this by saying that every low-level cognitive intensity is a pollutant, but not every pollutant is low-level cognitive intensity.

Attention should be drawn to the fact that the rDzogs-chen listing of the pollutants differs from the traditional one by no longer making a distinction between pollutants and quasi pollutants. Basically, the latter are but variations of the major pollutants, themselves fragmentizing modes and "radical" symmetry breaks in the system's low-level intensity or excitability. It seems that the rDzogs-chen listing goes back to Vimalamitra and the *Nyi-zla kha-sbyor,* a Tibetan work of unknown date and authorship. In this work, quoted and commented upon by Klong-chen rab-

'byams-pa, it is clearly indicated that low-level cognitive intensity is meant to describe Being's holomovement in what is said to be its errancy mode, which is primarily a self-fragmentizing movement. The remaining five pollutants specify processes of wandering farther and farther away from that which existentially matters, of a continual being off course, and of straying deeper and deeper into obscurantism and self-deception. Thus

> Low-level cognitive intensity is the subjective appropriation of that split in Being that is its straying off course.
>
> Delusion-dullness, from the perspective of critical acumen (*shes-rab*), is a straying off course;
>
> Irritation-aversion, from the perspective of the symbolic re-creation of the world (*bskyed-pa'i rim*), is a straying off course.
>
> Conceit-arrogance, from the perspective of vision proper (*lta-ba*), is a straying off course;
>
> Passion-addiction, from the perspective of a coming-to-presence (of what will be interpreted as world, *snang-ba*), is a straying off course.
>
> Jealousy-envy, from the perspective of the nonunderstanding (of Being's self-organizing dynamics, *ma-rtogs*), is a straying off course.[6]

Klong-chen rab-'byams-pa, with his usual clarity, sums up the meaning of the straying off course by these pollutants as detailed in the above quotation, in the following words:

> These pollutants all take that which is nonexistent (*med-pa*) as some egological essence (*bdag*), which is like mistaking a mirage (which is nothing) for water (which is deemed to be something). In their concretion, they are similar to the belief that a rope is a snake. The world altogether with its living beings as well as the pollutants, is the manifestation of the paradox of (something) nonexistent (*med-pa*) being a luminous presence (*gsal-snang*).[7]

From this passage the experiential unity of the cognitive and the affective can easily be discerned: we may have the (cognitively) mistaken notion of a rope being a snake, and in this actual situation our (affective) response of fear is inseparably intertwined with this notion.

There is a close relationship between conceit-arrogance and jealousy-envy-grudge within the egological framework of the low-level cognitive intensity. Conceit-arrogance serves to confirm the individual in any one of his overevaluated ideas and makes him glory in his pseudovision of what is or could be. For a conceited, arrogant person there is, in his insensitivity to the finely woven web of qualities of the world with which he interacts, nothing that cannot be dismissed as trivial—"It's all the same and not worth bothering about." Similarly, jealousy-envy-grudge is any individual's intolerance of another person for having that which the first person regards as specifically his own. Both conceit and jealousy imply the much cherished oversimplification that goes with the pseudovision of reality as being reducible to the postulates of one's ego. Long, long ago Rong-zom Chos-kyi bzang-po boldly stated: "The root of all pollutants is the pseudovision of reductionism."[8]

One of the most innovative of the rDzogs-chen ideas was the recognition that what is referred to as the pollutants (Tib. *nyon-mongs*), which are modes of a low-level cognitive intensity (Tib. *ma-rig-pa*), on the one hand, and the originary awareness modes (Tib. *ye-shes*), which are functions of an ec-static cognitive intensity (Tib. *rig-pa*), on the other hand, were actualizations deriving from a common source, Being's holomovement. Its internal dynamics or pervasive creativity was precisely the "instability" of Being's intelligence, or dynamically ec-static intensity (*rig-pa*), which forced Being over the instability threshold into the holomovement, which thus became a giant fluctuation between high-intensity and low-intensity levels, which by virtue of their common origin, remain related to each other, though neither can be reduced to the other. The intensity of the fluctuation as it becomes experienced by the living individual within himself in any of its extreme levels is the theme of a presentation by Vimalamitra in powerful images that immediately appeal to one's imagination. The understanding of its deeper meaning will be facilitated if we bear in mind that low-level cognitive intensity and mind are synonymous and that the experiencer's ec-static cognitive intensity is inseparable from the cognitive intensity of the whole. Thus the experiencer is simultaneously the whole and yet only part of it. In the words of Vimalamitra:

> The difference between low-level cognitive intensity and originary awareness is as follows:
> Mind is like water, it gathers everything;
> Originary awareness is like the sun, it burns everything.
> Although water can gather rusty material
> It cannot burn it like fire can.
> Water, even if as huge as the ocean with the nine continents,
> Is consumed by the fire at the end of time and dries up.
> ....[9]
> By understanding originary awareness as a function of (one's) ec-static cognitive intensity (*rig-pa'i ye-shes*),
> The sedimentations of experiences resulting in the pollutants are consumed and do not again become operative.
> These sedimentations in the mind are the cause of samsara,
> For the mind muses over anything and everything and moves here and there.
> Whatever it calls up from its depth and holds as its present content makes it attached, averse to, or even more desirous of it.
> Originary awareness burns up the pollutants.

Therefore mind is a straying off course.
Listen, 'Dus-pa'i snying-po:
Originary awareness as a function of (one's) ec-static cognitive
intensity that does not stray off its course
So thoroughly annihilates the pollutants that nothing is left of them.
Water may gather chaff, but cannot burn it.
How can bees ever settle
On the tip of a flame?
Similarly, mind cannot become that state in which (all darkness)
has dissipated and (brilliant light) unfolded.
By understanding the originary awareness (that constitutes) Being
(*gzhi'i ye-shes*)
The pollutants and the sedimentation (of experience that are their
cause) can do no harm;
Being's possibilizing dynamics, dissociated from a before and a later,
Is what is termed originary awareness.[10]

As can be gleaned from another passage in the same text, the "before" refers to the sedimentations of experiences, and the "later" to the pollutants deriving from them. The pollutants thus set the atmosphere in which consciousness evolves in this circularity of pollutants, sedimentations, pollutants, sedimentations, etc., summed up in the single term samsara—"running around in circles."[11]

The abstract idea of the originary awareness consuming and annihilating the pollutants reflects the felt intensification of the experiencer's cognitive capacity. Thus this intensification may be understood as the actualization of the principle of "order through fluctuation" (Glansdorff and Prigogine, 1971) that has only recently been discovered in the field of nonequilibrium thermodynamics. Divested of its mechanistic implications and the mistaken notion of "order out of chaos" (Prigogine and Stengers, 1984)—wherever we look we find order, which we compulsively turn into chaos—this principle seems to be valid also in other domains such as the spiritual domain (where "spiritual" is meant to describe the emancipation from rigidity of structure and the reinstatement of the fluidity of process). The spiritual domain, however, is nowhere else than in an individual's body as experienced in the immediacy of its lived concreteness. The notion of the body as some dissectable thing has only limited applicability, for the body as lived by me is not an object among other objects but the center for the varied intentionalities of world experience, of vision, actions, and interests. In all these projects, one's cognitive capacity—consciousness, if one wants to call it so—is already at work, even if it is of the nature of a "three-tier opaqueness,"[12] which Klong-chen rab-'byams-pa explains as "the effulgence of (the whole's) ec-static intensity as it rides on its horse, (the organism's) breathing, galloping along the network of chreods between the heart and the brain, the (semi-material) facticity of which is a low-level ec-static intensity, the general "look" of which is mind, and the divisiveness (leading to further conceptual divisions) of which is subjectivity."[13]

About this reintensification of the total system's excitatory capacity (intelligence, for short), the *Seng-ge rtsal-rdzogs* has this to say:

> Within the live body of each and every sentient being,
> There abides the possibility for originary awareness to light up in its purity (*dag-pa'i snang-ba*)
> Even if under the given circumstances it cannot do so to its full extent.
> Just as a child still in the womb or a bird still in the egg
> Is not fully and immediately available, as it is still encased in the womb or the egg,
> But will emerge after its vitality has fully developed.
> So, with the dismissal of the body as it appears in thematizing thought,
> Originary awareness will encounter its autopresencing cognitive domain;
> (One's) ec-static cognitive intensity in its auto-excitation, which has been present (in one's self) since its primordiality,
> Is seen in its undivided (conceptless) facticity.
> With this originary awareness lighting up in its purity
> The validity of the buddha-experience (with its dissipation of spiritual darkness and unfolding of the whole's possibilities and potentialities) is seen.
> The facticity of originary awareness's lighting-up by itself
> Has nothing of the dividedness pertaining to ego-centered mentation about it.[14]

Originary awareness lighting up in its purity all by itself, the autopresencing of its cognitive domain, and the auto-excitation of the ec-static cognitive intensity are emphasized in order to point out that what is designated by these phrases is a simple and direct presentation of a possibility for renewal or revision of one's world and that its purity is precisely its independence of objectifying-representational thought. It also intimates that, before there could emerge something called samsara or something called nirvana, Being's dynamics is already present and activating functional relationships pertaining both to the experiencing act and to the environment in which it occurs. These relationships then become manifest in the living individual, who thus presents a multilevel reality that shares in the fluctuations centered in the system's "intelligence" (resonance). This intelligence can operate on a level that is felt to be an intensification of life (Tib. *rig-pa*) or on a level that is felt to be just the run of the mill, with nothing to get excited about (Tib. *ma-rig-pa*). Furthermore, from the inseparability of the excitatory capacity from its field and from the field's incessant lighting-up, it follows that this level of the system's ecstatic intensity is a far cry from the alleged void or emptiness that the reductionist yearns for. Rather, as far as language can describe its vast scope, it presents the paradox of a nothingness that in its dynamics is a sheer lucency and in the dynamics of this nothingness-lucency, an autopresencing. A quotation from the *Nyi-zla kha-sbyor* may suffice to illustrate this point: "Originary awareness as it abides as Being-in-its-beingness (*gzhi-gnas-kyi ye-shes*) is threefold: as (Being's) facticity, it is a superdiaphanous (*ka-dag*) originary awareness; as (Being's) actuality, it is a spontaneous (*lhun-grub*) originary awareness; and as resonance, it is an autopresencing (*rang-snang*) originary awareness."[15]

The consequences of the triune originary awareness character of Being-in-its-beingness are far-reaching. When the as yet virtual actuality is pushed over the instability threshold of Being-in-its-beingness and comes-to-presence as the holomovement in its primary dynamics—more-actual-and-less-virtual actuality and spontaneity, it presents itself as fivefold function-specific originary awareness (*mtshan-nyid 'dzin-pa'i ye-shes*) that forms a geometric structure, and as a bipartite *Lichthaftigkeit* (Tib. *'od*) that is colored and noncolored. The *Nyi-zla kha-sbyor* concisely states:

> The function-specific originary awareness is fivefold: Being's meaning-rich field originary awareness (*chos-kyi dbyings ye-shes*), the mirrorlike originary awareness (*me-long lta-bu'i ye-shes*), the compatibility originary awareness (*mnyam-pa-nyid-kyi ye-shes*), the specificity-initiating originary awareness (*so-sor rtog-pa'i ye-shes*), and the task-posed-and-accomplished originary awareness (*bya-ba grub-pa'i ye-shes*).
>
> The bipartite *Lichthaftigkeit* is a light that has autoluminous specific colors and a light that is beyond all colors, (since it is) the purity of the nonlocalized originary awareness modes in what is their legitimate dwelling.[16]

The "legitimate dwelling" of which the text speaks is Being's superdiaphaneity, a nothingness beyond any nothingness, and the light that is beyond all colors suggests a superluminal speed. In view of these intriguing statements in rDzogs-chen works, one is tempted to point to their similarity with Heisenberg's conception of the universe as founded on a wave of opportunity—Being's holomovement in Buddhist terms—and with Bell's theorem declaring that these fluctuating opportunities are linked together faster than light (Herbert 1987, 245).

Through a recombination of the originary awareness modes in this evolving geometrization that is like play (Tib. *rol-pa*) of the "psychic" that in its triune originary-awareness dynamics is pure creativity (*rtsal*), two complementary awareness modes evolve as the whole's adornment

(Tib. *rgyan*). These are the (1) "originary-awareness mode that is sensitive to everything as it is seen in the immediacy of its abiding thereness" (Tib. *ji-lta-ba mkhyen-pa'i ye-shes*), being the recombination of Being's meaning-rich field originary-awareness mode and the compatibility originary-awareness mode; and (2) the "originary-awareness mode that is sensitive to everything in its interrelatedness with everything" (Tib. *ji-snyed-pa mkhyen-pa'i ye-shes*), being the recombination of the mirrorlike originary-awareness mode, the specificity-initiating originary-awareness mode, and the task-posed-and-accomplished originary-awareness mode.[17] Together they are the so-called "omniscience" (*thams-cad mkhyen-pa*)[18] of what is popularly concretized into and consequently misunderstood as the *thing*-person named "The Buddha."

rDzogs-chen thinkers never made this mistake; they quite literally "saw" the evolution of the high-intensity level of what, for want of a better term, I have called the "buddha"-experience (Tib. *sangs-rgyas*), as a transformative process of Being's triune cognitiveness, the transformations of which—symmetry transformations, which in spite of being symmetry breaks, do not "break down" into disparate entities—are described in terms of creativity (Tib. *rtsal*), playfulness (Tib. *rol-pa*), and adornment (Tib. *rgyan*). They are also described in terms of their gestaltism. Thus the triune dynamics or creativity of Being presents the *chos-sku* (the gestalt experience of Being's meaningfulness); its playfulness or geometrization, the *longs-sku* (the gestalt of the coming-to-presence of Being's pure dynamics as possible regions of concern and world-engagement); and its adornment or recombination the *sprul-sku* (the gestalt of cultural forecasts). This complexity can be laid out as follows (Figure 9). The Tibetan terms, explained in the above presentation, have been retained for brevity's sake.

For the rDzogs-chen thinkers, the evolution of a human being as the expression of a low-level cognitive intensity (Tib. *ma-rig-pa*) operating through its fragmentation into mind/mentation (Tib. *sems*) and subjectivity (Tib. *yid*), and the evolution of a buddha as the expression of a high-level cognitive intensity (Tib. *rig-pa*) manifesting itself in coherent originary-awareness modes (Tib. *ye-shes*), started from a common source, the holomovement, and linked through homologous principles. This led them to the bold statement that "whatever pollutant has arisen is a concrete presence of an originary awareness."[19] And since there are five originary awareness modes that, so to speak, form the background of one's spiritual life, there also are five pollutants in one's concrete existence, which in its "materiality" has lost much of its "spirituality." Nonetheless, since both materiality and spirituality derive from a common source, in recapturing their lost unity, which in the last analysis is Being-in-its-beingness, even materiality, the pollutant and poisonous, can be put into the service of the individual's growth. As is stated by Vimalamitra:

FIGURE 9

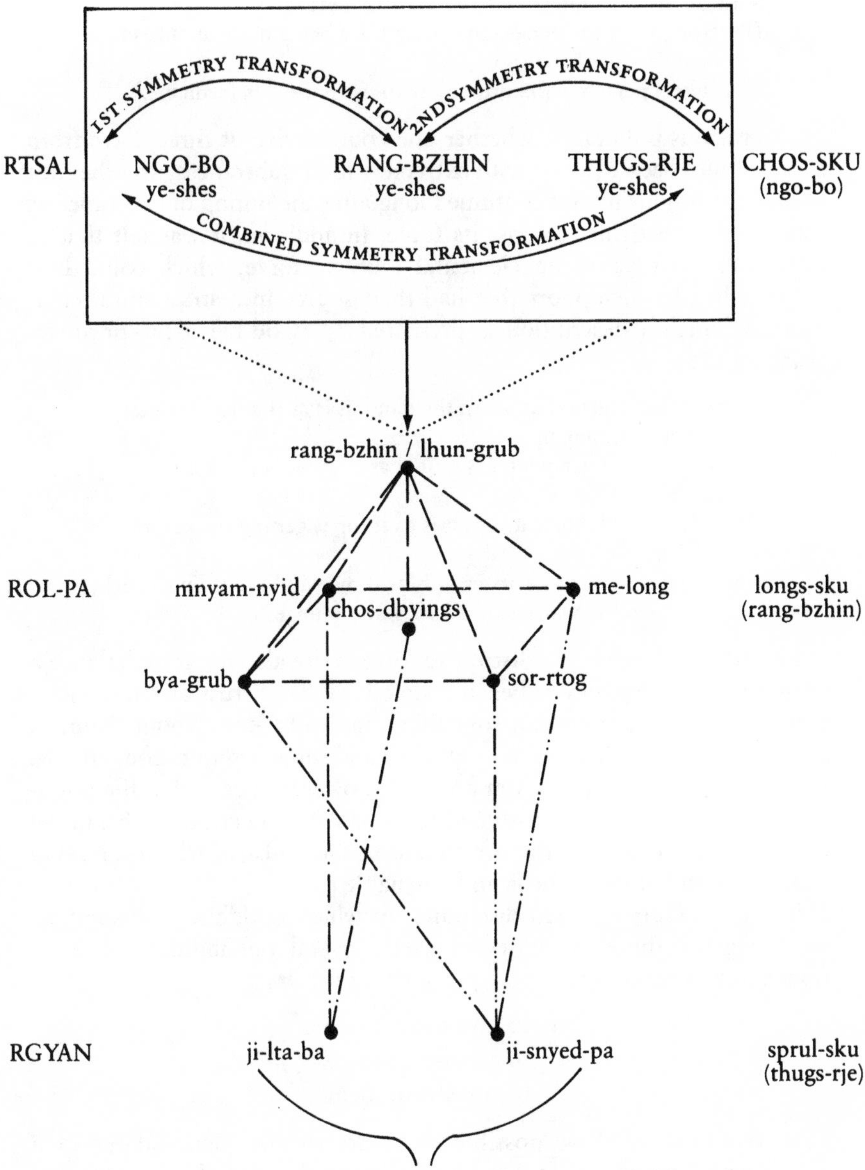
1ST SYMMETRY TRANSFORMATION
2NDSYMMETRY TRANSFORMATION
RTSAL
NGO-BO
ye-shes
RANG-BZHIN
ye-shes
THUGS-RJE
ye-shes
CHOS-SKU
(ngo-bo)
COMBINED SYMMETRY TRANSFORMATION
rang-bzhin / lhun-grub
ROL-PA
mnyam-nyid
chos-dbyings
me-long
longs-sku
(rang-bzhin)
bya-grub
sor-rtog
RGYAN
ji-lta-ba
ji-snyed-pa
sprul-sku
(thugs-rje)

When a yogi by his inner certitude
Knows that all that which lights up (as his phenomenal world)
Is a trap, he encounters Being-in-its-beingness.
Therefore, from the perspective of samsara being of the nature of Being's superdiaphaneity,
He is like a person who knows how to use poison as medicine.[20]

The various pollutants, whether one counted five or three, have from earliest times been equated with extremely toxic substances, and the idea of their poisonous nature continued long after the notion of substance as connected with them had lost its force. In addition, it was felt that in them there was active an elemental eruptive force, which could best be described by metaphors that had their source in man's natural environment. Such a description is presented by rGod-kyi ldem-'phru-can (1337–1386):

When hatred/aversion arises in the mind, it is as if a fierce winter storm is coming up;
When passion-attachment arises, it is as if water is cascading downhill;
When delusion/dullness arises, it is as if fog is getting thicker and thicker;
When conceit/arrogance arises, it is as if the wind is battling a rock;
When jealousy/envy arises, it is as if water plunges into a defile.[21]

Since these eruptive and disruptive forces were also felt to unbalance a person and to keep him or her in a vicious circle of frustration, the general consensus has been that something had to be done about them. In stronger terms, they had to be controlled and subjected to rational thinking, if not eradicated and given up. This, however, means that the pollutants (or emotions) were assumed to be isolatable entities (substances) that could be torn from the life stream in the midst of which a human being lives and of which he is an inalienable part.

In the structure-oriented disciplines in which Buddhist philosophical (essentialistic) thinking expressed itself, several possibilities are mentioned in this regard. The more prominent ones are:

to give them up
to cleanse them
to transform them

However, none of these possibilities is practicable, since all reflect a mechanistic approach that is not warranted in the case of living systems. First of all, the pollutants or emotions are not "things" that one can lay aside as I can a book I have been reading. A devastating critique of this naive notion that the pollutants or emotions are some concrete stuff has been given by Rong-zom Chos-kyi bzang-po. It relentlessly lays bare the fallacies and internal contradictions that characterize the objectivist's position.[22]

Secondly, in the framework of an essentialistic assessment, a pollutant or an emotion is what it is and hence there is no way to "sublimate" it, to use the psychoanalytical jargon. Two actually futile and counterproductive procedures were envisaged. The one was to get involved with the pollutant, to court and to palliate it. The futility of such an attempt is likened to wiping a bright crystal, which by this operation does not get any brighter. The other approach was to apply a counteragent. But this was noted to be counterproductive because it meant to stir up and, probably, worsen the whole situation created by the activity of the pollutant. It was likened to stirring up muddy water with a stick in the vain hope of getting clean water.

Thirdly, transformation was supposed to take place within a given setting, which was the thematic-representational mode of the mind; and this, as has been shown and is well known, allows only for quantification and measurement. Even if it were possible to transform the pollutants into originary awarenesses, as this procedure is described in the texts, this would only be an "upward" reductionism and involve the perpetuation of a static view of man and world. If anything is achieved by such a mechanistic approach, it is the substitution of a socially more acceptable "polluted" attitude for a less acceptable one; but nothing has been done for the individual's mental and spiritual growth.

Process-oriented thinking, as exemplified by the rDzogs-chen approach to man's problematic nature, does not know of any sharp separation between the opposite aspects this nature presents and does not favor the one over the other. The decisive point is to transcend both in understanding their complementarity. Klong-chen rab-'byams-pa expresses this non-meddling understanding as follows:

> The three poisons affecting the mind as it wavers between desire, distaste, and indifference
> Have come up as a playful flurry from Being's creativity (extending over) the three aspects of time.
> Having originated from Being's dynamic field, they have risen in the vibrant dimension of this field.
> Since there will be no cessation to their stirring as long as one does not understand them to be of the nature of the field,
> Do not try to crush them, or meddle with them, or transform them.
> Once you have recognized this very field for what it is and have settled in its dynamic dimension,
> The poisons subside by themselves, dissipate by themselves, and resume their freedom that is Being's freedom.[23]

In his autocommentary on this aphoristic verse, he dismisses any mechanistic attempt to deal with the pollutants (emotions). Here he says:

> Since both samsara and nirvana have never moved out of the vibrant dimension of Being's fieldlike character, they are but the form and shape that this openness/nothingness, which has no ground other than itself, has assumed. The pollutants, too, have never been experienced as existing as some (sort of) stuff; since they have no place to rest on and no root to grow from, they become free from their constraining encapsulation by a single act of letting-be. When the facticity of the ec-static cognitive intensity has been recognized as an utter insubstantiality, the pollutants, each in their own way, dissolve and are resolved in (what is their) legitimate dwelling (Being's superdiaphaneity), just like both strands in a huge knot become loose when the peg holding them is taken out. If one does not know so, one will never get rid of the pollutants, however much one may try, just as one cannot get rid of one's shadow.
>
> One will also not improve them by polishing them, however much effort one puts into it: a bright crystal is not made brighter by wiping it. There is, in this case, no difference between the improving action and that which is to be improved.
>
> One also will not be able to transform them, however much one may try: the color of a turquoise cannot be changed, neither can mind by mind.
>
> One also is unable to get the pollutants to come to rest by dismissing them into some state of quiescence, because the dismissing agent is not different from the divisive notion of dismissal.
>
> One also cannot get freedom from them by applying their counteragents; this is like making water more muddy by stirring muddy water with a stick in the desire for clear water, because the counteragent is on the same level as that which is to be countered.
>
> Lastly, the pollutants as such are not Being's possibilizing dynamics, and since (all) the (above) reductionistic and mechanistic notions are in no way different from how stupid people think, there is no possibility of getting out of samsara.[24]

Only in passing beyond any dualism can life's dynamic meaningfulness be lived on all levels of human existence. Of this passing beyond dualism, which is man's very self-transcendence, Klong-chen rab-'byams-pa says:

> While the pollutants, the actions that under their influence have certain consequences, as well as the sedimentations of experiences engendered by them
> Are but phantoms that have playfully arisen from Being's creativity,
> Their counteragents, good actions, and the way of being delivered from all that is negative
> Are also but phantoms that have playfully arisen from Being's creativity.
> Since both aspects of reality have playfully arisen from Being's creativity (in its) primordiality,
> The point is to recognize them as such and let them be as they

are in the vibrant dimension of Being without interfering with them.
Whether they rush with equal speed into the thematic mode of the mind or whether they fade with equal pace, they are alike (and compatible with each other) in having started from their source that is Being.
Since their movement does not go beyond the mechanistic notion of cause and effect, deriving from certain conditions favoring such a notion and being a thematic construction,
It is important to pass beyond this mechanistic notion of cause and effect by letting all this alone and by living on the basis of this letting-be.[25]

How, then, can we pass beyond the region poisoned by the pollutants, the manner in which one's "organismic mind" operates and spills over into one's "reflexive" and "self-reflexive mind," when nothing mechanistic works? The answer seems to lie in the statement that "by taking a "hard look" (lit.: looking undistractedly) at mind with its five poisons within ourselves, the five pollutants, without having to be discarded, will clear up by themselves in the vibrant dimension of originary awareness and dissolve (in the emancipatory dynamics of Being itself)."[26]

The Dynamics of Self-Organization: Obscuration and Clearing

The homologous evolution of (1) an ontical foundation (Tib. *kun-gzhi*) as an individual's low-level cognitive intensity (Tib. *ma-rig-pa*) upon which this individual's psychic life, his mind in the broadest sense of the word (Tib. *sems*), and his subjectivity (Tib. *yid*) in the narrower sense, is play-acting with the unruly and tempestuous pollutants (emotions, Tib. *nyon-mongs*); and (2) a gestaltism (Tib. *sku*) through which Being's ecstatic intensity (Tib. *rig-pa*) in multifaceted and multifunctional originary-awareness modes (*ye-shes*), glittering in subtle hues (Tib. *'od*), playfully weaves a geometrically laid out, world-spanning horizon of meaning from which, through its sensitivity to all that is going on, it reaches into the doldrums of life so that it does not end in utter stagnation—the homologous evolution of these two aspects has distinctly ontological connotations. But these ontological aspects are matched by the experiencer's assessment of them in terms of darkness, a feeling of being hemmed in, and light, a feeling of expansiveness and emancipatedness from all that prevents a person from living a full life. rDo-rje gling-pa (1346–1405) has summed up well the murkiness of one's private world with its self-created boundaries and self-inflicted limitations, beyond and out of which one is only too often reluctant to step:

That which is called the opaque and pollutant
Resides in a jungle town in (Being's) dynamic vastness
In a threefold layer of

Low-level cognitive intensity, mind, and subjectivity.
This dullness called "low-level cognitive intensity"
Obscures (Being's) energy in its being auto-excitatory (*rang-rig*);[27]
Mind obscures the very originary awareness that goes with (this) excitation; and
Subjectivity obscures the coming-to-presence (the lighting up) of excitation by dealing with it as something objective.[28]

Obscuration (Tib. *sgrib*), which is a diminishing of light and clarity as well as a concealment of that which existentially matters, while seeming to be the "normal" state of a person's being-in-his-world, has attracted considerable attention among Buddhist thinkers. It is usually coupled with what is described as "being at a crossroad," "going astray and taking the wrong turn" (Tib. *gol*). Here "wrong" means that this turn is somehow felt to prevent optimization and to hold the individual captive in his darkened state. A concise statement as to the nature of *sgrib* and *gol* is given in the *Thig-le kun-gsal:*

Taking the wrong turn and being in a darkened state are essentially the working of the low-level cognitive intensity.
The definition of these is as follows:
By not seeing the significance of "higher" levels, one finds oneself in a darkened state;
To engage in "lower" levels is to take the wrong turn.
For this reason, the two have been defined in this manner.
There are numerous differing modes of them,
But these can be summed up in four (major ones):
Vision, experimentation, engagement, and the end (of the road).
In each of these four major modes both obscuration and taking the wrong turn are operative.[29]
An illustration is the following:
Aiming for the north, a person goes to the south;
Having reached the south, he does not get what (only) the north has to offer.
Coveting higher levels he engages in lower ones;
The lower levels cannot see the higher ones.[30]

Reverberating in the notion of obscuration, which describes a darkening, obscuring, and veiling action, is also the notion of obstruction and hindrance, whereby a person is prevented from making any efforts to realize what existentially matters. In addition, obscuration covers two different, but closely related, modes. The one is characterized as involving the pollutants (Tib. *nyon-sgrib*). However, bearing in mind that we do not, as the Buddhists did, distinguish between pollutants and catalysts, but lump them together in the single notion of emotion, this mode describes the qualitative approach of how we feel about the world in which we live. This approach may assume the form of irresistible drives, impulses, and compulsive behavior and what once was called "being possessed" (which is the same, as the Swiss psychologist C. G. Jung has pointed out repeatedly, as what is nowadays called "neurosis"). But the omnipresence of the emotional is active in what we call the "rational," and whether we like to admit it or not, it always tends to turn any content in mind, any knowable, into an overevaluated idea, usually with disastrous consequences. There actually exists a kind of feedback loop between the predictability of a world reduced to regularities and the affective-emotional response to it, in that the one tends to reinforce the other. If we, quite irrationally, equate the knowable with the "objective" and the emotional with the "subjective," we can easily recognize the vicious circle that holds a man prisoner in his very private world. We see the world in a subjective way leading to ideologies (political, religious, and what-not), which in spite of their claim to reason are "the most outrageous unreason" (Böhler 1972), and this very unreason is made absolute as objective truth. In order to prove this point, people have happily cracked each others' skulls and still continue doing so.

The other obscuration is summed up in the predication of "that which can be known," "the knowable," and includes the whole of the thematic-representational (Tib. *shes-sgrib*). Epistemologically speaking, the knowable is the raw material for logic, and this in turn leads to a mechanistic conception of a static world that is presented in quantitative and structural terms and in which any change (the dynamic aspect of the world) is explained in terms of linearity and causality. Philosophically speaking, this mode constitutes a mentalistic reductionism.

Philosophical treatises are content with mentioning obscuration-obstruction by the knowable and obscuration-obstruction by pollutants without giving any further details. Rong-zom Chos-kyi bzang-po, however, familiar with this distinction but using a different terminology, gives an interpretation that shows that he was thinking of the concrete human individual who is afflicted by these modes, and also was thinking in terms of process rather than structure. He distinguishes between seven obscurations, of which three pertain to the knowable, three to pollutants, and one to the system in general. Obscuration-obstruction by the knowable refers to the manner in which the individual copes with his mistaken notions (Tib. *bslad-pas bsgrib-pa*) about the thrust toward pellucidity and consummation (Tib. *byang-chub-kyi sems*), which as an evolutionary dynamics (Tib. *snying-po*) underlies all activities in a person's growing up into his humanity.[31]

First, the individual may simply make a mental note to the effect that, since this thrust is nowhere else than in himself, he does not have to look for it—and in most cases also will not bother about it. Nonetheless, he may have difficulties in understanding what evolution means because it is no thing that can be pointed out among other things with which he is familiar.

Second, he may be aware of his plight, but not knowing that the remedy is within himself, he looks for outside help:

> Although he is this evolutionary thrust, he does not recognize this because of his mistaken notions about it; similarly, although medicine is by itself the cure for the disease, one yet (looks for) a physician as the medicine. So also, because of his mistaken notions being unaware of the fact that as a living being he is his freedom, he will have to give helpful friends a chance (to explain this) and to rely on them.[32]

Third, while the optimal functioning of the system as a whole cannot be zoned into territories nor classified into types, such apparent differentiation is but the play staged by the originary awareness of the whole system and constitutes its very beauty. In this play, the principle of complementarity is at work in simultaneously presenting itself as a possibility for the opaque and the transparent. As noted previously, the transparent may be considered as an approximation symmetry with reference to the whole of which it is a transformation, and the opaque as an approximate displacement symmetry. It is the attention to the opaque as if it were the sole reality that constitutes an obscuration-obstruction.

Rong-zom Chos-kyi bzang-po deals with the obscuration-obstruction by pollutants, which plays a significant role in the relationship between human beings as well as between them and their cultural paradigms (religious, ideological, etc.), to which individuals turn for help during many phases of their lives, even if only temporarily, only in passing. According to him, there is no point in elaborating on this, because one can easily find out what is genuine and what is merely a sham. As social beings we cannot but engage in various activities (worship, charity, etc.). But if these activities turn into ends in themselves, they are no longer a help but an unbearable fetter.

Apart from these obscurations and obstructions by the knowable and by pollutants, Rong-zom Chos-kyi bzang-po mentions another obscuration that seems to be specific to rDzogs-chen thinking and that can best be paraphrased as an interference with the system's self-organization, in his terminology "an obscuration-obstruction by positive and/or negative imputations on *lung*." The technical Tibetan term *lung* is usually used with reference to authentic statements or texts—authentic in the sense that they express and *communicate* a person's, specifically the "Buddha's," innermost experience. However, Rong-zom Chos-kyi bzang-po distinguishes between two kinds of *lung*. The kind just mentioned he defines as *tha-mal* "ordinary," "usual," with the implication that we take communication as it occurs between individuals for granted. The other he defines as *nges-pa* "certain," "definite," "real."[33] In this sense, "communication" corresponds to the interpretation that Maturana (1982) has given this concept. It does not involve any transfer of information from one system to another, but refers to the reorientation of indigenous processes within the system's cognitive domain, which coincides with the system as a whole. Any attempt to reduce it to the categories of representational thought and to a language system based on it constitutes an obscuration and by implication also an obstruction. As Rong-zom Chos-kyi bzang-po with his usual clarity of diction—he had studied Indian-Buddhist logic in the original Sanskrit language—elaborates:

> To deal concretely (with this process) means that all operations by the intellect oscillating between the categories of existence and non-existence, as well as all verbalized attempts to reach and (thereby) understand it, constitute a veritable obscuration and obstruction (to its free flow). (The outcome) is like a lake (otherwise calm) stirred up by a storm. Therefore, when this process is left to itself in what it is, it continues operating optimally; it certainly is not understood by thought constructions about it.
>
> For example, if one does not interfere with water and fire, they in themselves remain clear and bright, but to the extent that one meddles with them, they turn turbid and dark on their own. Similarly, if one understands that mind is nothing in itself, one does not have to meddle with it; (as a matter of fact,) one does not even find a basis for something that could be meddled with and for someone to meddle with it. But if one does not know so, one merely turns up a series of thought constructs in the vain attempt to come to grips (with the process itself). White and dark clouds both obscure the brightness of the sky.[34]

According to rDzogs-chen thought, the obscuration taking place is seen no longer in terms of a malfunctioning of perception, as was the case in the traditional Buddhist epistemology-oriented philosophical disciplines, but corresponds to a systemic function involving the totality of the processes. The obscuration takes effect in a concrete individual's "system potential" (Tib. *khams*), which is both physical and psychical at the same time. In the words of Klong-chen rab-'byams-pa:

> The system-potential becoming obscured is
> Like the sun (becoming obscured) by clouds.
> The body-as-lived (*lus*) obscures (Being's) actuality so that there is
> no lucency;
> The spoken word (*ngag*) obscures (Being's) resonance so that a
> dialogue is set up.[35]

Thematizing mind (*sems*) obscures (Being's openness-nothingness) factícity so that it gets bound up in bits and pieces.
Through the accumulation of propensities (extending over the) three realms of thematizing activities, (Being's) abidingness (in what it is) is obscured.
For ever (staying on) in samsara, one engages in the presentations offered by this going astray, (which is maintained by) the propensities (accumulated in this process).
Thus, whatever (is said to be) thematizing mind and whatever is present to it
Is declared to be that very obscuration that has to be dispelled.[36]

Clouds and sun are a favorite analogy for facilitating an understanding of how the system becomes overshadowed but also recovers its brightness. For Klong-chen rab-'byams-pa, this process is less an oscillation between two stable states than an interaction between processes. He develops the theme of the above quotation in four verses of singular beauty in which he mingles the individual with the cosmic.

In the first verse, he shows that Being's sheer lucency, similar to the luminaries of sun and moon in the sky, is within us, but is made invisible through the power of "nonunderstanding," which playfully conjures up the customary subject-object dichotomy, out of which one's environing world and the living beings in it with their interests in and concerns with it are constructed. All this is similar to a huge cloud passing over the sun:

Although sun and moon shine brightly in the sky,
When fully obscured by the power of the huge cloud "non-understanding"
They are not visible. (Such) is the manner in which (Being's) pellucidity and consummation exists in us.[37]

But nobody has ever put a cloud over the sun nor has anyone been able to remove it. Rather, clouds come and go by themselves. Thus, in the second verse which merges with his commentary on it (part of which will therefore be translated here), he says:

Just as a huge cloud, left to its domain (from which it was formed), will dissipate by itself,
So also, when without efforts and exertions, the sky has been cleared of the cloud (called the mechanistic) cause-and-effect (relationship)
The energy (leading to and stemming from Being's) pellucidity and consummation, which is (as vast) as the compass of the sky, will burst forth by itself.
Although different methods of removing this stain have been developed

In the different spiritual pursuits according to the intellectual
acumen of their followers,

here I will speak with reference to those who display an unusually high acumen. When a fierce storm, the force of which lies in its intensity, blows without effort and exertion (coming from elsewhere), sweeping away all the cloud masses (made up of) the (psychic) propensities of which the mistaken constituents of samsara with (their reduction to a mechanistic explanation by) cause and effect are an integral part, and returning them to the source (from which they had come) without dumping them somewhere, and when everything has become bright and clear by itself, then, just as the sun that had been covered by thick clouds and made invisible will brightly shine in the sky with no obscuration present the moment the clouds have dispersed, so also the experience of Being's meaningfulness pertaining to Being's spontaneity, which is no conceptual construct, will surge in the light of its experienced gestalt (*sku*) and experiencing originary awareness (*ye-shes*) the moment it has been divested of its incidental obscuration. This gestalt experience of Being's meaningfulness, possessing the double purity (of being diaphanous in itself and diaphanous with respect to the incidental stains having been removed),[38] by virtue of rising in its own luster (like) the sun that is not going to set, is said to be Being's self-existing spontaneity.[39]

In the third verse he describes how out of Being's creative dynamics, Being's obscuration proceeds in a playful manner:

(Being's) facticity, like the sun in the center of the sky, shines
throughout its meaning-rich field;
From its creative dynamics, like the sun's rays, the whole universe
comes into being with no segmentation.
When the heat (from the sun's rays) has engulfed land and sea,
From the mist and fog rising, the play of clouds develops and (in
this process)
(Being's) facticity as well as its creative dynamics become obscured;
likewise
By this play staged by the creative dynamics in (Being's) facticity
becoming ever more opaque,
The very nature of this energy becomes such that it obscures itself,
(and as a consequence)
The mistaken presences of (Being's auto-)presencing and presencing
and its interpretation as external and internal worlds are inconceivably manifold.[40]

In the fourth verse he states that the same dynamics that made the clouds rise and obscure the sun also dispels them by the wind it stirs up:

Just as clouds are dispersed by the wind stirred up by the creative
dynamics in the sun's rays,

So through understanding Being as what it is in itself, by (Being's) play the adornment (of Being by itself) comes about.
Since the going astray (into mistaken notions about itself) has been (returned to and) set free in what has been its legitimate dwelling (or) primordial freedom,
(Being's) mistaken presencing and the mistaken notions about it, without having been dumped somewhere, have become diaphanous in the source (from which they came).
In the bright sky where there are no sections to which one might go,
The sun of (Being's) spontaneity rises as (Being's) gestalt experienced through (its) originary awareness.
This has not come from somewhere else, but is Being's diaphanous auto-presencing.[41]

Obscuring and clearing as modes of Being's spontaneity (Tib. *lhun-grub*), another term for its holomovement (Tib. *gzhi-snang*) and its abidingness (Tib. *gnas-lugs*), call to mind Heidegger's ideas of concealment and revealment with respect to *Dasein,* with which the Buddhist terms have a certain affinity. But while with respect to Heidegger's conception of this admittedly difficult problem "we may therefore say that there is a certain priority of non-truth over truth, of concealment over revealment, and, consequently, that the mystery necessarily connected with concealment dominates man's *Dasein*" (Kockelmans 1984, 13), for the Buddhists no such priority exists. Concealment and revealment are the play Being stages through its creative dynamics, the phase in which pure possibility is about to become an actuality, thus pointing to still greater complexities beyond itself.

rDzogs-chen thinkers approaching the problem of Man from an evolutionary perspective were well aware of Man's basic orientation toward revealment and, by implication, toward freedom as pure dynamics, rather than as an end-state indistinguishable from utter stagnation. However, they also took cognizance of the fact that man is caught in, and also *is,* his errancy, which conceals, obscures, and obstructs. This concealment can be assessed in different ways without involving any contradiction. Two such assessments have been given, one from the *Bla-ma yang-tig,* the other from the *Chos-dbyings-mdzod,* both by the same author. Both texts agree that the phenomenon of Man as an embodied, speaking, and thinking being constitutes, by virtue of Man's finiteness, an obscuration of the infinite openness of Being's dynamics, but there is a marked difference between the two passages. The first, from the *Bla-ma yang-tig,* speaks of this obscuration in structural, ontic terms. Being has, seemingly, lost its integrity and coherence by having become fragmentized into the building blocks of body, speech, and mind. The second passage, from the *Chos-dbyings-mdzod,* speaks of this obscuration in terms of process, of how the lucency of Being grows dimmer and dimmer. But then it also speaks of how Man's orientation toward revealment reasserts itself in this play of obscuring and clearing. The upshot of the matter is the grandiose idea of rDzogs-chen thought that Being conceals and obscures itself by "immersing" itself in us as a kind of camouflage, but also reveals itself through us; and what is so revealed is Being itself that is our humanity.

Epilogue

THE METICULOUS ATTENTION to what constitutes the complexity of the way did not lead the Buddhist thinkers into the mistaken assumption that this was an end in itself. Rather, the idea of the way as merely a means to achieve a goal remained alive and was beautifully illustrated by the simile of a raft that one leaves behind once one has crossed the river. Nonetheless, the values of the future were stipulated in the present, and a naive teleology, inherent in any structure-oriented view, is detectable. This means that the whole movement summed up in the way was conceived of as a straight aiming at a recognized goal, variously specified as "awakening" (Pali, Skt. *bodha/bodhi*), "inner calm" (Pali *samatha*), a "crossing over" (Skt. *taraṇa*), and above all as "nirvana" (Pali *nibbāna*).[1] Metaphors used to describe more concretely the goal or state reached, preeminently involve images of localities. We read of "a place hard to see,"[2] "a foothold that does not slip,"[3] "a lovely level stretch of land,"[4] and of "an island"[5] in a stormy sea. But then, almost in the same breath, we are told that the goal is a "dimension that cannot be localized,"[6] which in the wake of the prevailing structure-oriented thinking of early Buddhism, was almost automatically reduced to an entity qualified as "nonlocalizable."

In contrast to this static, entitative reductionism, there is a conception of the goal as a process coming or having come to an end. The favorite image for it is a lamp or a flame becoming extinguished.[7] In either case, whether conceived of as a place at which one ultimately arrived or as a "becoming extinguished," both said to be the end of frustration and a release from the turmoil of samsara, the goal is an end state, if not a dead end.

Even if already at an early time Buddhist thought attempted to move away from crude reductionism that conceived of the whole as an assemblage of disparate entities (some "more" material than others), the stubborn quest for an ultimate entity persisted. Finally, such an entity was claimed to have been found in what was variously designated in Sanskrit as *vijñāna* (Pali *viññāṇa,* primarily sense-specific perception) or *citta* (primarily epistemologically oriented mentation). There is an intriguing passage in the *Dīghanikāya* (I, p. 223), which unless it is a later interpolation, foreshadows the Yogācāra conception of a "radiant *citta*" (Skt. *citta prabhāsvara*). The passage runs as follows:

> An attributeless *viññāṇa,* thematically illimitable, throughout
> lustrous:

> Here the fundamental forces of "water," "earth," "fire," and "wind" have no access;
> Here such attributes as long, short, subtle, gross, bright, and dark, as well as
> Such operations as name-giving and form-perception have entirely been obliterated;
> With the cessation of *viññāṇa,* it itself becomes obliterated here.

According to the commentary, the *Papañcasūdanī* I, p. 413), by Buddhaghosa,[8] the term *viññāṇa* in the first line of the quotation from the *Dīghanikāya* refers to nirvana, the same term in the last line to the psychic processes that link a person to specific samsaric situations.

The old idea of a goal gained renewed significance with the Yogācāra thinkers. Although they had accepted the structural model of the mind proposed by the Vaibhāṣikas (discussed earlier), they modified this static model by conceiving of mentation/mind (Skt. *citta*), which for them was the sole reality (Skt. *cittamātra*), as a process structure, constantly engaged in "phenomenal transformations" (Skt. *pariṇāma*), to use an expression coined by Michael Polanyi (1975). They also noted that, as we would say, living systems tend to optimize themselves, and thus introduced the idea of an "optimization thrust."[9] Superficially, this thrust looks as if it involves some kind of teleology; however, in contrast to the outmoded determinism of a materialistic, mechanistic view, it is more of the nature of a self-organizing principle. Nonetheless, the Yogācāra thinkers were hampered by their insistence mentation/mind as an ultimate entity or "thing." Thus, while the ongoing phenomenal transformations (Skt. *pariṇāma,* Tib. *rnam-'gyur*) were active in setting up and perpetuating the individual's samsaric situation, the goal, described in terms of an originary awareness (Skt. *jñāna,* Tib. *ye-shes*) and its gestaltism (Skt. *kāya,* Tib. *sku*), was conceived of as a radical transformation (Skt. *āśrayasya parāvṛtti,* Tib. *gnas-'gyur*) of an entity called either "pure information" (Skt. *vijñaptimātra*) or "pure mentation/mind" (Skt. *vijñānamātra*).[10] The question of how one and the same entity or thing could undergo a phenomenal or "surface" (Tib. *rnam-pa*) transformation resulting in the vicious circle of samsara and/or a radical status (Tib. *gnas*) transformation, becoming the goal or end state without losing its character of being an entity, remained unanswered. Furthermore, the Yogācāra thinkers' assumption of an ultimate (static) entity turned out to be incompatible with their claim of transformation. There is no indication that such an entity exists and, if it did, in view of its protean character, the possibility of what is considered to be a radical status transformation reverting to an ordinary phenomenal or "surface" transformation or such a transformation being itself a radical status transformation, cannot be excluded. The implication is that the much vaunted "freedom" would become the much decried "bondage" again, and an "ordinary person" would be a "buddha," since each could be reduced to the other. There is no cogent reason to accept either the earlier Hinayana or the later Yogācāra notions of an end state, however evocatively it may be presented.

The assumption that somehow the road must come to an end is the direct outcome of structure-oriented thinking, with its emphasis on a predetermined end state. Such a notion makes people succumb to the "lure of completeness" of which Sir Hermann Bondi has spoken (1977, 5–8), which stops them from asking further questions and from going on. rDzogs-chen thinkers who took over and even built on much of what had been said before and therefore could boldly state that what they had to offer tallied with everything (Buddhist) and yet was totally different, were less concerned with states than with processes and, in particular, with the dynamic quality in the structuration of the individual's life that transcends a mere feedback relationship between a within and a without. Consequently also, their focus of attention was not on a "way" in the traditional sense—actually, for them the "way" was Being's holomovement experienced in and through its dynamics by the person "in tune" with it. Rather, their focus of attention was on freedom (Tib. *grol*), which the Yogācāra thinkers had spoken of as having a gestalt (Skt. *muktikāya*)[11] and which the rDzogs-chen thinkers thought of as an unfolding process, a vector feeling-tone complementary to and inseparable from Being's resonance (Tib. *thugs-rje*) with itself as the whole and with all its manifestations. In the human context, this means that my concern for others (Tib. *gzhan-don*) affects me with a feeling of my own (Tib. *rang-don*) ability to be concerned; but this ability, in order to become effective, must be "free," though not in the sense of some passive quality modifying an equally passive substance (an object-*thing* or a subject-*thing*, depending on whether one is an objectivist or a subjectivist), but as a self-organizing process—"like a snake uncoiling," as the text so poignantly portrays this process.[12] This dynamic freedom does not suggest any indifference to the world, toward living beings. On the contrary, it engages with them as compassion or concern—"like a mahout's hook"[13]—guiding them out of their predicament. In particular, this dynamic freedom as a self-organizing process, by distancing itself, emancipating itself, and by implication us, from the restrictiveness of our organismic being with its propensities, inclinations, and tendencies—which, specifically, on our mental-spiritual level with its idiosyncracies, set up invisible barriers—opens up dimensions of reality other than the one with which we are familiar. In these dimensions, information and the pure energy of thought reign supreme and, from beyond the quantum reality, as it were, "direct" the individual to evolve into these wider and "higher" dimensions that do not deny but encompass the "lower" dimensions of our being. All this demands an entirely new understanding that switches from an examination of the parts of reality to reality itself as an undivided and indivisible whole, from being or beings to Being as it unfolds in its totality or spontaneity.[14] Such understanding needs new concepts, as the rDzogs-chen thinkers realized. Their writings abound in concepts not found elsewhere, and the difficulty which we encounter in understanding them does not so much lie in their obscurity, but in the fact that they pertain to a dimension or domain with which we are as yet unfamiliar. Here no facile reductionism to what is already known is of any avail. In other words, rDzogs-chen demands that we start learning to think. While all the grandiose Buddhist systems of thought have, quite literally, come to an end, rDzogs-chen thought remains a challenge, directing our attention to the *thinking* of thinking, not in a vacuum, but in the context of the whole.

Notes

Frequently Used Abbreviations

WORKS IN PALI AND SANSKRIT

AK = *Abhidharmakośa*
AN = *Anguttaranikāya*
ASA = *Abhisamayālaṅkāra*
Aṭṭh = *Aṭṭhasālinī*
DN = *Dīghanikāya*
MN = *Majjhimanikāya*
MSA = *Mahāyānasūtrālaṅkāra*
MV = *Madhyāntavibhāga*
SN = *Saṃyuttanikāya*
TV = *Triṃśikāvijñapti*
TVB = *Triṃśikāvijñaptibhāṣya*
UT = *Uttaratantra*
Vism = *Visuddhimagga*

WORKS IN TIBETAN

Ati = *rNying-ma'i rgyud bcu-bdun*
rNying-rgyud = *rNying-ma'i rgyud-'bum*

Chapter 1. Abhidharma

1. *Aṭṭh* I 2.
2. *MSA* XI 3.
3. *AK* I 2ab.
4. *Aṭṭh* II 10.
5. *Vism* VIII 246.
6. *gSung thor-bu*, pp. 28f.; also *gSang-snying 'grel-pa*, fol. 67b.
7. *Yon-tan mdzod-'grel* I, p. 12.
8. *Aṭṭh* I 27.
9. *Aṭṭh* I 44.
10. *Aṭṭh* I 73; VI 2.
11. *Aṭṭh* III 29; *AK* VI 24b. See also *AK* VIII 39ab, and *Vism* II 397f. Ati I, p. 812.
12. *AN* I 164.
13. *rNying-rgyud*, vol. 7, pp. 70, 291, 380; 8, p. 49.
14. *Theg-mchog* I 427f.; *rNying-rgyud*, vol. 5, p. 177. The three Tibetan terms *yon-tan, sku,* and *ye-shes* are of particular importance and difficult to render by a single term in English. Although rendered as "endowments," which may be understood in a material as well as a mental sense, *yon-tan*

comprises all that which we would call "capabilities," "capacities"—mental/spiritual ability as well as the unfolding of this (inner) richness. Both *sku* and *ye-shes* belong to the level of nonobjectifying thought; they are related to each other in such a manner that *sku* is the gestalt (perceived and felt as) quality in which *ye-shes,* the system's originary awareness, expresses itself. In other words, *sku* is both the expression and the expressed of *ye-shes* and as such reflects back on the qualitative character of the cognitive operation. The neologism "originary" (*ye*) derives from the French *originaire,* coined by French-speaking phenomenological philosophers in an attempt to capture the meaning of the German *ursprünglich,* which has dynamic connotations and does not refer to some static primordiality.

CHAPTER 2. THE OPERATIONAL SYSTEM "MIND"

1. *Dhammasangaṇi,* p. 21. It is important to note the use of the term *ñāṇa* (Skt. *jñāna*) here. My translation of this term by "intellectual-spiritual acumen" attempts to capture the connotation of spirituality, which under the impact of a growing analytical-representational trend, was more or less lost sight of, and as can be seen from a parallel passage, was replaced by *paññā* (Skt. *prajñā*), which is thoroughly "intellectual-analytical." See below note 17.
2. *Aṭṭh* III 26; *Bhāṣya* ad *AK* III 3. The three levels of existence are the realm of desires (Skt. Kāmadhātu/*kāmāvacara*), the realm of aesthetic forms (Skt. Rūpādhatu/*rūpāvacara*), and the realm of the unformed (Skt. Arūpadhātu or Arūpyadhātu/*arūpāvacara*).
3. *Aṭṭh* II 10; similar are III 29 and Yaśomitra's *Vyākhyā* ad *AK* I 30; where *prajñā* is used instead of *ñāṇa* (Skt. *jñāna*).
4. *Aṭṭh* III 29.
5. *Aṭṭh* III 29.
6. *TVB,* p. 38. Strictly speaking, the Sanskrit term *karma* covers two cognate notions. The one is that of an operative principle according to which a living being acts; the other is that of specific actions that define the individual as "agent" in the sense that he/she *is* his/her actions, the sequences of which constitute the continuum of life on a certain level. From the Buddhist perspective, we might nowadays identify this level with the one that in the triune hierarchical organization of an individual's somatopsychic life is largely dominated by the reptilian brain, one of the three "drivers" in the "neural chassis," as detailed by the American neurophysiologist Paul D. MacLean (1973). As Erich Jantsch (1980, 166) aptly remarks, "it does not have good learning capability." It is for this reason that I have added the adjective "headlong," which may as well be read "ill-considered." It is one of the shortcomings of language that the intimate connectedness, if not to say identity, of headlong actions (*karma*) and affective processes (pollutants, Skt. *kleśa*) can only be presented in such a way as to trap us in an unwarranted dualism. Because of their importance, the pollutants will be the subject-matter of a separate chapter (Chapter 4).
7. *Aṭṭh* III 33.
8. *Bhāṣya* ad *AK* II 34a.
9. *Aṭṭh* III 23.
10. *rNying-rgyud,* vol. 5, pp. 220, 253.
11. *rNying-rgyud,* vol. 5, p. 219.

12. *rNying-rgyud,* vol. 4, pp. 589f., 592.
13. *Aṭṭh* III 44. On *paññā*, see chapter 1, n. 1.
14. *Bhāṣya* ad *AK* I 2. In *Bhāṣya* ad *AK* II 23, Yaśomitra pertinently remarks: "An attitude (*citta*) does not arise without its co-operators (*caitta*), nor do the co-operators arise without an attitude. However, not every attitude arises necessarily with all co-operators; nor do all co-operators necessarily arise with every attitude."
15. *Aṭṭh* III 177. The fact that all authors assign *sparśa/phassa* the first place is ample evidence that they knew that a living being is installed in, and in constant interchange with, its environment.
16. *TV* 3cd. See also *AK* II 24.
17. *Aṭṭh* III 177.
18. *Aṭṭh* III 179.
19. *Aṭṭh* III 180.
20. *Aṭṭh* III 179. Thus he says in *Aṭṭh* III 180: "Even if there is a nonsensuous situation it (*phassa*) proceeds in the manner of touching." The metaphorical and dynamic character of *sparśa* is also emphasized by Yaśomitra in his *Vyākhyā* ad *AK* II 24.
21. *Vyākhyā* ad *AK* II 24.
22. *Aṭṭh* III 183.
23. *TVB*, p. 20.
24. *Aṭṭh* III 184, 188.
25. *Aṭṭh* III 188.
26. *Aṭṭh* III 189.
27. *Aṭṭh* III 189.
28. *AK* II 24.
29. *TVB*, p. 21 ad *TV* 3cd.
30. *Aṭṭh* III 191, 192.
31. See also above, p. 25.
32. *Aṭṭh* III 194, 195.
33. *Vyākhyā* ad *AK* II 24.
34. *AK* II 34.
35. *TVB*, p. 20 ad *TV* 3cd.
36. *TV* 10bc.
37. *TVB*, p. 25.
38. *Bhāṣya* ad *AK* II 24.
39. *TVB*, p. 25.
40. *Aṭṭh* III 220–222.
41. *TVB*, p. 26.
42. *TVB*, p. 26.
43. *TV* 4d.
44. *TVB*, p. 22 ad *TV* 4d.
45. *TV* 2c–4d.
46. *TV* 5b–7d.
47. It may not be without interest to point out that in Buddhist thought the

senses are triadically structured: First, there are the physical organs, such as the eye (Skt. *cakṣus*) and the remaining four classical senses (to which the Buddhist added "mind" [Skt. *manas*]). Second, there is a controlling power (Skt. *indriya*) corresponding to each of the organs and ensuring its functioning. Third, corresponding to each organ and power, there is a cognitive capacity or "consciousness" (Skt. *vijñāna*). The Buddhist conception certainly reflects the "modern" idea of the senses forming "a field of tension created in the encounter between material processes and psychic receptivity" (Jantsch 1975, 86).

48. *TV* 8d–9d.

CHAPTER 3. THE CONTEXTUALIZED SYSTEM "MIND"

1. *AK* II 23cd.
2. See above, p. 25.
3. *AK* II 25.
4. *Bhāṣya* ad *AK* II 25.
5. *Aṭṭh* III 213.
6. *TVB*, p. 26.
7. *Man-ngag*, p. 17.
8. *Aṭṭh* III 239.
9. *Aṭṭh* III 239. A similar account is given in *TVB*, pp. 26f.
10. *Vism* 142.
11. *AN* I 51.
12. *Aṭṭh* III 293; *Vism* XVII 70.
13. The points mentioned are detailed in *Aṭṭh* III 117, 242, 244, 245. See also *TVB*, p. 27.
14. For details, see *Aṭṭh* III 241–245.
15. For details, see *Aṭṭh* III 242, 243, 245; *TVB*, p. 27.
16. *Aṭṭh* III 217, 218.
17. *Aṭṭh* III 283; *TVB*, p. 27.
18. *Aṭṭh* III 248, 295.
19. *TVB*, p. 26.
20. *Aṭṭh* III 249–250; *TVB*, p. 27.
21. *Bhāṣya* ad *AK* II 25; *TVB*, pp. 27–28.
22. *TVB*, pp. 27–28.
23. *bKa'-'bum*, pp. 259, 261f.
24. *TVB*, p. 28.
25. See in particular his *Shifting Worlds, Changing Minds* (1987; the subtitle is "Where the Sciences and Buddhism Meet"). The strongest critic of behaviorism among scientists is Erich Jantsch (*Design for Evolution;* 1975). Another critic is Paul Davies (*The Cosmic Blueprint;* 1987). Among philosophers, there is Susanne Langer (*Mind: An Essay on Human Feeling*); and among psychologists who try to salvage some aspects of the reductionistic vagueness that has come over psychology, there are J. Z. Young (*Programs of the Brain;* 1978) and John H. Crook (*The Evolution of Human Consciousness;* 1980).

26. See in particular his *Women, Fire, and Dangerous Things* (1987; subtitle: "What Categories Reveal about the Mind").

CHAPTER 4. POLLUTANTS AND QUASI POLLUTANTS

1. On the term *autopoiesis,* coined by the Chilean biologists Humberto R. Maturana and Francisco Varela, see Introduction.
2. *AK* II 26. Since the pollutants are also sociocultural operators, though of an undesirable nature, the relationship of *moha, āśraddhya,* and *kausīdya* as "negative" forces with *amoha, śraddhā,* and *vīrya* as "positive" forces is easily detectable.
3. In commenting on Vasubandhu's presentation, Yaśomitra illustrates *uddhava* as that which provides the basis for the levity and gaiety that go hand in hand with dancing and singing, lovemaking, and wearing fashionable clothes and ornaments.
4. *TV* 11cd–12a; *TVB,* p. 28.
5. *TVB,* p. 28.
6. *AK* II 26.
7. *TVB,* p. 28.
8. The five psychophysical constituents (Skt. *pañcaskandha*) are: (1) the complexities of the ("objective" and "subjective" perceptible) domain of colorform (Skt. *rūpa*), (2) the feeling system (Skt. *vedanā*), (3) the sign and symbol system (Skt. *saṃjñā*), (4) the model-building activities and the models of one's reality so built (Skt. *saṃskārāḥ*), and (5) the perceptual operations (Skt. *vijñāna*) by the five senses (geared to the perception of the physical world) and by "thought" (Skt. *manas*) (which deals with ideas [Skt. *dharma*] and thus assumes the role of the "psychic" in the otherwise "physical" nature of the senses).
9. *TVB,* p. 28. This Sanskrit text continues:

   According to the intensity of the boost given to the mind, conceit can be classified as sevenfold:

   > 1. If someone says: "I am better by family standing, intelligence, and wealth" than another who is less so, or says: "I am his equal in these matters," this uptrend of the mind is plain conceit (*māna*).
   >
   > 2. If someone says: "I am superior in generosity, quality of character, and manliness" than the other who is equal to the speaker by virtue of family standing, intelligence, and wealth; or if he says: "I am his equal" although the other is superior in these matters, this uptrend of the mind is overconceitedness (*atimāna*).
   >
   > 3. If someone says: "I am superior by virtue of family standing, intelligence, and wealth" than the other who actually is so in these matters, this uptrend of the mind is super-overconceitedness (*mānātimāna*).
   >
   > 4. If someone identifies himself with (any one of the) five psychophysical constituents as being his self and property, although no such status can be claimed for any of them, this uptrend of the mind is the "I-am" conceit (*asmimāna*).
   >
   > 5. If someone claims that he has reached higher levels in his development when he has not, this uptrend of the mind is pompous conceit (*abhimāna*).

6. If someone who is superior by virtue of family standing, intelligence, and wealth declares that he is inferior in these matters (to others), this uptrend of the mind is self-debasing conceit (*ūnamāna*).

7. If someone who has no moral qualities claims to have them, this uptrend of the mind is pretentious conceit (*mithyāmāna*). Lack of moral qualities means to have a nasty character and other moral defects. He in whom these are present is said to be a person lacking in moral qualities. Therefore, if someone says: "I have moral qualities," but is lacking in generosity, positive character traits, and so on, he is merely giving himself airs and, since there is nothing to it, this is called pretentious conceit.

See also *AK* II 33b; V 10a.

10. *TVB*, p. 29. Because of the ambivalence of the Sanskrit technical term *dṛṣṭi*, the context decides whether it is intended to mean "vision-proper" or a mere pseudovision. The text continues to specify the pseudovisions as follows:

1. Reductionism (of reality to a disjunctive aggregate of atomic sensa) is the view of the five psychophysical constituents (see above, n. 8) in their organization as an individual as constituting a Self that owns them.

2. Extremism is the view of the above in terms of an eternalism *a parte ante* and an eternalism *a parte post*.

3. Outrageousness is the view that denies (the validity of) cause, effect, and action, or even destroys the existing order. Since it is the worst possible view it is termed outrageousness.

4. Dogmatism is the view (that overevaluates) the five psychophysical constituents in their organization as an individual such that (any one) is regarded as foremost, special, best or ultimate.

5. Ritualism is the view (that overevaluates) the five psychophysical constituents in their organization as an individual such that (any one) is regarded as a matter of purity, freedom, and deliverance.

11. *TVB*, p. 29.

12. Common to both the *Abhidharmakośa* (II 27) and the *Triṃśikā* (12cd–13a), though not in the same order, are the following quasi pollutants:

{*krodha, upanāha, mrakṣa, pradāśa, īrṣyā, mātsarya, māyā, śāṭhya, mada, vihiṃsā*}

{anger, resentment, slyness, spite, jealousy, avarice, deceit, dishonesty, arrogance, malice}

In the *Triṃśikā,* five pollutants proper, with the exception of *moha,* are added:

{*kausīdya, uddhava, āśrāddhya, styāna, pramāda*}

{lethargy, frivolity, disbelief, laziness, unconcern}

Inasmuch as the pollutants and quasi pollutants pose a threat to concentrative-contemplative practices and had to be dealt with, in order to be as comprehensive as possible, five other pollutants (that had been mentioned by the followers of the Abhidharma tradition who took as their basic text some work other than the *Vibhāṣā,* critically summarized by Vasubandhu in his *Abhidharmakosá*) were added:

{*āhrīkya, anapatrapa, muṣitasmṛti, vikṣepa, ayoniśomanaskāra*}

{shamelessness, effrontery, forgetfulness, distraction, inattention}

13. *TVB*, p. 32.
14. *TVB*, p. 32.
15. *Aṭṭh* III 198.
16. *TVB*, p. 32.
17. *TVB*, p. 33.
18. *TVB*, p. 32.
19. *TVB*, p. 33.
20. *Aṭṭh* III 200. Other similes he adduces here and in *Aṭṭh* III 201 are a bird flapping its wings in order to get up into the air and its subsequent calm moving of the wings while flying; a bee alighting in front of a lotus flower and its moving over the flower on which it has alighted. In connection with the simile of the bird, he quotes the lost *Aṭṭhakathā* in which *vitakka* had been compared with the movement of a bird in the sky, taking the wind with both wings and keeping them steadily in a line as it advances bent on a single definite object, while *vicāra* is the flapping of the wings in order to take the wind.

    Buddhaghosa concludes his lengthy discussion of the inseparability of *vitakka* and *vicāra* by offering three more similes. *Vitakka* is compared with a hand taking firm hold of a dirty copper bowl, while *vicāra* corresponds to the other hand vigorously scrubbing the bowl; or *vitakka* is like the hand of a potter pressing down clay, while *vicāra* is the hand turning the clay to and fro; and, finally, *vitakka* is compared with the point of a drawing compass fixed in the middle of the paper and *vicāra* with the revolving point.

CHAPTER 5. CONCENTRATION, CONTEMPLATION, MEDITATION

1. Tib. *dngos-po*. This technical term has two distinct applications. In conjunction with *mtshan-ma* (not to be confused with *mtshan-nyid*, "function"—the Sanskrit equivalent *lakṣaṇa* stands for both *mtshan-ma* and *mtshan-nyid*), it corresponds to our notion of substance in its categorical distinction from accidents. Alone it is used in a metaphysical sense of "an existent thing which requires nothing other than itself to exist" (Descartes, *Principles of Philosophy*, I.15), or, as stated by Alfred North Whitehead (*Process and Reality*, p. 79), "just its individual self with no necessary relevance to any other particular." This metaphysical notion, entertained by all schools of Buddhism, including the followers of the mentalistic reinterpretation of Buddhism in terms of "mind-only" (Skt. *cittamātra*, Tib. *sems-tsam*), was severely criticized by those disciplines that emphasized pure experience (Tib. *sems-nyid*) over and against mere speculation (Tib. *sems*).
2. *SN* I 39 and passim.
3. *Vism* III 75–77.
4. Saraha, *Dohakoṣa*, 27.
5. Organismic mind, interchangeably used with organismic mentation, are terms coined and elucidated by Erich Jantsch (Jantsch 1980, 169).
6. Reflexive mind, like reflexive mentation, are terms coined and explicated by Erich Jantsch (Jantsch 1980, 163, 171). Aspects of what Jantsch calls self-reflexive mind and self-reflexive mentation belong, from the Buddhist perspective, to reflexive mind/mentation.

7. *Aṭṭh* III 326.
8. The synonymity of *samādhi* and *ekāgratā* is well attested by *TVB*, p. 26. The subsequent definition of *ekāgratā* as *ekálambanatā* "having a single objective reference" shows that the Cittamātra followers, in spite of their insistence on experience, could not rid themselves of their preoccupation with representational thinking and succumbed to the "objectivist's fallacy." An excellent experiential account of *dhyāna, samādhi,* and *ekāgratā* (Pali *ekaggatā*) in the Pali tradition has been given by Jacques Maquet (1986, 53, 163).
9. The basic idea of the Sanskrit term *dhyāna* as a stabilizing and by implication, objectifying process is well brought out by its Tibetan translation, *bsam-gtan,* which literally means "basis of objectifying thought."
10. *DN* I 37.
11. On *vitarka* and *vicāra,* see pp. 59–60.
12. *AK* III 3; VIII 3c; *Aṭṭh* III 427.
13. *Ati,* vol. 1, p. 410.
14. Quoted in *Chos-dbyings,* p. 290.
15. *bKa'-'bum,* p. 306.
16. *bKa'-'bum,* p. 306.
17. See Chapter 1, n. 14.
18. *bKa'-'bum,* p. 307.
19. *bKa'-'bum,* p. 309.
20. *bKa'-'bum,* p. 310.
21. *bKa'-'bum,* p. 311.
22. *bKa'-'bum,* pp. 311f.
23. *bKa'-'bum,* pp. 256f.
24. In this context it is interesting to note that in Yogācāra (Cittamātra), the older idea of concentrating *on* something already predetermined plays hardly any role, and hence the term *dhyāna* is used very rarely. Emphasis is on tuning in (*yoga*) to the life stream, which only too often, due to the lingering on of objectifying thought, was turned into a something.
25. *bKa'-'bum,* p. 317.
26. *bKa'-'bum,* p. 324.
27. For further details see my *The Creative Vision* (Guenther 1988, 112). The predication "lower" is taken over from indigenous texts that by this term lump the Kriyā-, Caryā-, and Yoga-tantras together.
28. See also *Ati,* vol. 2, p. 449.
29. *bKa'-'bum,* p. 328.
30. On this term and its translation, see Chapter 1, n. 14.
31. *bKa'-'bum,* p. 330.
32. *Ati,* vol. 2, p. 141.
33. In older Western works on Buddhism as well as in newer ones that base themselves on the older ones, these holonomic modes of experiencing are, with reference to their Sanskrit name *trisvabhāva,* spoken of as the three natures. This "translation" reflects the mechanistic approach to language of the nineteenth century. As is well known, Newton's mechanics provided a successful

description of force and motion without ever making reference to the origin of the forces that accelerate matter. Impressed by Newton's paradigm, philologists (whose discipline originated in this mechanistic climate) transferred it to language with no reference to the speaker. Consequently, they could not make anything of the statement that these "natures" had nothing about them of what might be called their "nature" (*niḥsvabhāva*). Unfortunately, this mechanistic creed is still widely held by academics steeped in their objectivistic fallacies. And obviously they are oblivious to the fact summed up in the aphorism, "Everything said is said by someone" devised by Humberto R. Maturana and Francisco J. Varela (Maturana and Varela 1987, 26).

34. For a detailed study of the term *bodhisattva,* see my "Bodhisattva—the Ethical Phase in Evolution," in Leslie S. Kawamura (ed.), *The Bodhisattva Doctrine in Buddhism,* 111ff.

35. This practice was often done in solitary places where it was not always easy to get food and clothing. It was in this context that the technique of "living on air" originated.

36. *Ati,* vol. 1, p. 410.

37. *Theg-mchog* II, p. 163.

38. *Theg-mchog* II, p. 163.

39. *Theg-mchog* II, p. 163. On the developing phase (*bskyed-rim*) and the fulfilling phase (*rdzogs-rim*), see my *The Creative Vision* (Guenther 1988).

40. *grol-lam.* This term must not be confused with *thar-pa'i lam,* which indicates a way to an end-state. *grol-lam* refers to the way the emancipatory action takes by itself.

41. *bKa'-'bum,* p. 306.

42. *Chos-dbyings,* p. 67.

43. *bKa'-'bum,* pp. 305, 312–316.

44. Other terms used in Western literature and pointing to this superthought are "supermentality" and "supermind." In her book bearing the significant title *Supermind: The Ultimate Energy,* Barbara B. Brown says on p. 167: "The essential part of the evolutionary process that seems to have escaped the speculation about man's future is the determining role of his mental apparatus for his own mental growth. There can be no question but that the next phase of man's evolution, a phase in progress, can be the evolution of supermentality."

45. Concerning the details of the German term *Gelassenheit* (Tib. *cog-gzhag*) in the rDzogs-chen context, see *Theg-mchog* II, pp. 274f.; *Bla-yang* II, pp. 104ff.; *Chos-dbyings,* p. 196.

46. *Tshig-don,* p. 387.

47. Concerning the difference between the visionary gaze and ordinary perception, Levin's remarks on p. 234 are highly relevant in the present context. There he says: "Normal perception, the ontical perception of anyone-and-everyone, is inveterately grasping, as the very word itself should remind us. It is an anxiety-driven, restless intentionality: a grasping *of* light and a grasping *in* the light. But such perception cannot see the whole of things, because wholeness, unlike totality, is not something that can be grasped."

48. *gSang-snying 'grel-pa,* fol. 40a.

49. "Triune character of Being" is a free rendering of the technical terms *sku, gsung, thugs* in the original Tibetan. Each term defies any simple (reductionistic) rendering. Here a short paraphrase may suffice:

thugs (cognitive dynamics) manifests itself in a gestalt of intentionalities and is as such already a structure of meaning that henceforward infuses the whole texture of experience and gives it the character of situatedness.

gsung (speech, language) discloses and articulates the meaning of a situation and as such is a project (externalization) of "thought" in the sense that speech is the presence of thought or thought-in-action in the situatedness that now is the world.

sku (gestalt, embodiment) is both the expression and the expressed as manifested in the individual's bodily bearing, his gestures, his posturing. As such it is a continuously ongoing act of embodying and in this sense "my" body functions as a sort of implicit knowledge of the world. In other words, the body-proper, in the terminology of M. Merleau-Ponty, "expresses" the individual's total existence and his total existence is "expressed" in his body-proper.

50. *gSang-snying gsal-byed me-long,* fol. 17a:

> *de-bzhin gshegs-pa* means "to move into Being-in-its-beingness." Here *de* is a term for "rushing toward." Toward what is one rushing? (Toward) the abidingness of Being as the source and ground of the knowable, in its beingness. What is Being? As a ground without origination, it is an uncontrived beingness; as a ceaseless effulgence, it is an unerring beingness; as an indivisible dimension, it is a nondual beingness; and as lying beyond the reach of thematizing thought, it is spontaneous beingness. Having reached its ultimacy and having become this very dynamic ultimacy is what is meant by *gshegs-pa.*

51. *Ati,* vol. 3, p. 201. "Warmth" has a metaphorical sense, as when we say "someone warms up as he gets into his subject." How this warmth affects the total person is detailed in *Yid-bzhin mdzod,* pp. 71f.; *Yid-bzhin mdzod-kyi don-khrid zab-don rdo-rje snying-po,* fol. 7b.; *Bla-ma dgongs-'dus,* vol. 5, p. 802.

52. *Tshig-don,* p. 331.

53. *rang-bzhin babs.* This term occurs again in *Chos-dbyings,* p. 299.

54. *rtsa, rlung, thig-le.* These terms pertain to dynamic patterns in the body-image. Contrary to widely held beliefs, the indigenous texts make it abundantly clear that they have nothing to do with the physical aspect of one's body except by some misplaced concreteness. The body-image sums up the embodying process: the information input (*thig-le*) organizes (*bkod-pa*) the organism's evolution and in this sense moves (*rlung*) along the development lines (*rtsa*) of its own making.

55. *'khor-lo.* These are dynamic regimes that evolve within an individual's ontogenesis.

56. This statement refers to the purely epistemological approach to the problem of Being, as dealt with in the so-called "gradual" moving up in meditation. As I have pointed out in "'Meditation' Trends in Early Tibet" (in *Early Ch'an in China and Tibet,* 356), what is implied is the use of what in mathematics is known as the empty set. "Thus, if we let U denote the 'thematic set', that is,

the set of those things (*chos thams-cad*) to which we are naively accustomed, and if we denote the empty set by ϕ, then closer (epistemological) investigation reveals that $U = \phi$."

57. *ting-nge-'dzin gsum*. These "three in-depth appraisals" have been detailed in *Matrix of Mystery* (Guenther 1984, 75ff.) and *The Creative Vision* (Guenther 1988, 138, n. 56). Fallico speaks repeatedly of original or first utterance, "which asserts nothing and demonstrates nothing, but which nonetheless initiates everything by making it possible for us to speak at all" (p. 64); and "first utterance is not something which translates the unsaid, or what cannot be said, into speech: it is *its* very word or speech" (p. 103). To this add the remarks by Huberto R. Maturana and Francisco J. Varela (1987, 234): "Moreover, since we exist in language, the domains of discourse that we generate become part of our domain of existence and constitute part of the environment in which we conserve identity and adaptation."
58. *Ati*, vol. 1, p. 184.
59. More serious works that suffer from insufficient information concerning the tremendous difference between Buddhist and Hinduist ideas are Ronald Fischer, *Transformation of Consciousness: A Cartography*, in two parts, and John H. Crook, *The Evolution of Human Consciousness* (1980).
60. Susanne K. Langer, *Mind: An Essay on Human Feeling*, vol. 1, p. 32:

> It can be intellectually exploited, it has more illuminating implications than any other within my ken. Not only does it make feeling conceivable as a natural phenomenon, and some valuable subordinate notions (like "subjective" and "objective") derivable, but it permits one to construe the more impressive forms of mentation—symbolic expression, imagination, propositional thought, religious conception, mathematical abstraction, moral insight—as functions of that most active and complex of all organs, the human brain, with intense and prolonged physical phases.

CHAPTER 6. THE WAY: THE EARLIER VIEW I

1. *Udāna* VIII 3.
2. *Madhyamakavṛtti*, p. 525.
3. *AK* II 55d–56b.
4. *Aṭṭh* III 468.
5. *Vism* VIII 247. See also XVI 67f.
6. *Madhyamakavṛtti*, Chapter XXV 19–20.
7. An excellent assessment of Nāgārjuna is offered by Nolan Pliny Jacobson (1988, 61–80).
8. *Madhyamakavṛtti*, p. 524.
9. *Madhyamakavṛtti*, p. 359.
10. *Dohākoṣa-upadeśa-gīti* (in the *bsTan-'gyur* (Derge ed.), rgyud, vol. zhi, fol. 20a.
11. *bKa'-'bum*, p. 171.
12. Aṭṭh III 24. See also *Aṭṭh* III 508 for the term *gotrabhū*. Also *Vism* IV 74; XVII 8; XXII 5–13; XXIII 7.

13. *Aṭṭh* II 24.
14. *Aṭṭh* III 466.
15. *AK* VI 51. *Aṭṭh* III 468.
16. *Aṭṭh* III 475.
17. *Aṭṭh* III 475. *AK* VI 66–71.
18. *Aṭṭh* III 377f.
19. *AK* VII 25.
20. *AK* VII 25.
21. *Aṭṭh* III 884.
22. *Aṭṭh* III 486.
23. *Aṭṭh* III 487.
24. See above pp. 43–45.
25. *Aṭṭh* III 488.
26. *Aṭṭh* 490. Actually there is a progression from the one to the others, and only to the extent that the one or the other becomes the sole content of perception and the "going" does it specify the character of the way such that being impermanent corresponds and gives rise to the imageless aspect (*ānimitta*) of the way, being frustrating corresponds and gives rise to the nonleaning aspect (*appaṇihita*) of the way, and being without self-identity corresponds and gives rise to the (*suñña*) aspect of the way.
27. *gSung thor-bu,* p. 333.
28. *Aṭṭh* III 525, 526. Buddhaghosa describes him in the following words:

    > In a once-returner the pollutants do not turn up as often as in the case of the majority of people who follow the cycle of birth and death; they turn up only occasionally, and if they do so, they turn up sporadically like shoots in a sparsely sown field. Moreover, if they turn up, they do not do so as in the case of the majority of people who follow the cycle of birth and death, in a crushing, spreading, covering, and darkness-producing manner. Rather they turn up very slowly, because their power has been exhausted through these two ways (of seeing and cultivation), and also in a very scanty and flimsy manner, like a film of cloud or like a fly's wing.

    Buddhaghosa then gives some interesting insights into the sociocultural conditions of the earliest phases of Buddhism by citing the view of some Elders, who claimed that in persons who follow the route of the once-returner, the pollutants may turn up once in a while and then are as strong as ever, because one sees "that they have sons and daughters." Buddhaghosa rejects this view by maintaining that having children is, as we would say, a physiological aspect of one's biological nature, "a rubbing together of two epidermises" that does not contradict the generally weakened state of what is referred to as the pollutants, on this level.
29. *Aṭṭh* III 527.
30. *Aṭṭh* III 528.
31. *Aṭṭh* II 55.
32. *Aṭṭh* III 530.
33. *Aṭṭh* III 533.

CHAPTER 7. THE WAY: THE EARLIER VIEW II

1. *AK* IV 14a.
2. *AK* IV 14a.
3. *AK* IV 14d–15d.
4. As will be remembered, the term *vijñapti* became a crucial concept for Yogācāra thinkers. *Vijñaptimātra,* "information only," is synonymous with *cittamātra,* "mind/mentation only." Could it be that the "old" Buddhist thinkers intuitively anticipated the "modern" notion of "information"? Rudy Rucker (1987) even goes so far as to give the name "Everything is Information" to the last chapter in his book.
5. *AK* IV 16ab.
6. As noted previously, man *is* his karma and in this sense he is an ongoing process of embodying what, for want of a better term that would avoid the implicit but existentially unwarranted dualism, is called his psychic life.
7. *Bhāṣya* ad *AK* IV 16ab.
8. It is interesting to note that in conceiving of shame as "information," the Buddhist thinkers were close to modern phenomenological writers like Max Scheler. Richard M. Zaner (1964, 196) succinctly states:

   > As Scheler has shown, I do not experience another's anger or joy, boredom or sadness, as a "psychic state" hidden behind the gestures of these, which would be only the external accompaniments of these states and accidental to them: "It is *in* the blush that we perceive shame, *in* the laughter joy." (Max Scheler, *The Nature of Sympathy,* p. 10). There is no "inferring" (in the strict sense) by me from something presented (crinkled lines on an object in my visual field) to something not presented (joy of my friend); rather the other himself is there or me, his body is already an animate organism, embodying his psychical life.

9. *AK* VI 5.
10. *AK* VI 65b–d, 49ab.
11. *AK* VI 29ab, 31c.
12. *Bhāṣya* ad *AK* VI 63d.
13. *UT* IV 52.
14. *AK* VI 70.
15. *AK* VI 9d.
16. *Grub-mtha',* p. 214.
17. *Bhāṣya* ad *AK* VI 15.
18. Skt. *pañcaskandha.* The five are color-form (Skt. *rūpa*), feeling (Skt. *vedanā*), notion-sensation (Skt. *saṃjñā*), reality-construction (Skt. *saṃskārāḥ*), and perceptual operations (Skt. *vijñāna*). The group referred to by color-form is related to the physical side, and the remaining groups to the psychic side of one's concrete existence. However, the Buddhists did not share the implied dualism of matter and mind that since the time of Descartes has haunted Western philosophical thinking. A colored form, or let us say, a colored patch, is the objective constituent of a perceptual situation that imperceptibly fuses with a cognitive situation that states that this colored patch is, say, a

tree, which is the epistemological object of this situation. To this is added the belief that there is a corresponding ontological object "out there."

19. *AK* VI 14. When we say that we as human beings consist of the same "material" the whole universe is made of, namely, that we are the cosmic forces organized in an organism, we actually continue an old idea, albeit in a refined form. It is these elemental or fundamental forces (Skt. *mahābhūta*) that are an organism's "essential" characteristics; the "accompanying" characteristics are interpretations of the organization of the elemental forces into an organism in such a way that the body is "impure," feelings are "unpleasant," mind is "impermanent," and the building blocks that go into the construction of one's reality have "nothing about them that would allow us to call them a self."

20. *AK* VI 17.

21. *Bhāṣya* ad *AK* VI 69.

22. *AK* VI 18.

23. *AK* VI 19.

24. *Vyākhyā* ad *AK* VI 18. It will have to be remembered that the Four Truths encompass the whole world as experienced in terms of the realm of desires (Kāmdhātu), the realm of pure forms (Rūpadhātu), and the realm of formlessness (Ārūpyadhātu), so that, as the Vaibhāṣikas calculated, by lumping the realms of pure forms and formlessness together into one realm, there are thirty-two properties to be taken into account (four to each truth accounting for sixteen in one realm, and sixteen in the other realm). If these are related to the six sublevels of warmth and its peak value (three sublevels to each of them) and the lowest sublevel of acceptance, making up a total of seven, one arrives at a total of two hundred and twenty-four (7 × 32) properties. This amount certainly provides a variety of possibilities to choose from and to experiment with. But to leave them merely with operational planning is not enough. The operational targets have to be linked to strategic goals that may be viewed as a function to be performed in a context. It is here that selection begins to play an important role. In the Śrāvaka context, the goal is to understand the Four Truths, of which the first one, frustration, is of primary importance, because it draws attention to the human situation in general. Accordingly, the properties selected for goal realization reflect the individual's disposition. If he/she is dominated by strong feelings of attachment, suitable properties to concentrate on, experiment with, and cultivate are the impermanence and unpleasantness of the given. A person dominated by certain perspectives, which because of their lack of critical acumen are more of the nature of opinions, should concentrate on the properties of the given as not being something as such and not having anything about them that is of the nature of a self.

25. *AK* VI 28cd. Seeing "with fresh eyes" is particularly important in visualization techniques, which play such an important role in the existential (tantra) approach, as contrasted with the epistemological (sutra) approach, to the problem that is Man. On visualization techniques on a broad scale, see Mike and Nancy Samuels, *Seeing with the Mind's Eye* (1975).

26. *AK* VI 28ab.

27. The temporality involved in this process is that with respect to the Four Truths, there is first an awareness of the meaning of each truth as it ranges over the world of desires and the realms of gestalt and no-gestalt experiences,

taken as a unit, and then a follow-up awareness of the meaning of each truth, all together amounting to sixteen moments.

28. *AK* V 1.

29. *AK* V 4. Vasubandhu introduces this aspect of the way of seeing (always understood in the sense of perceiving meanings (Skt. *jñāna*) not in the sense of picking out things (Skt. *prajñā*) and being content with a lifeless world) with the words:

> There are ten, seven, seven, eight (pollutants)
> By subtracting three or two ideological (pollutants from the total of ten).

This numerical assessment of what is eliminated by perceiving meaning must not be dismissed as idle speculation. It is the nature of representational thought to be concerned with what can be objectified and in some sense quantified. The mathematical and empirical sciences are a prime example of the operation of representational thinking (Indians have been and still are excellent mathematicians). Since the main objective of the Buddhist "way" is to get rid of the pollutants that prevent us from getting at the "meaning" of the Four Truths, particularly in their latent and subliminal dynamics, it is first of all important to pinpoint them. Here the analytical acumen (*prajñā*) played an important role in distinguishing between ideological and emotional pollutants (see Table 1). All together there are, as intimated by Vasubandhu's aphorism, thirty-two (10+7+7+8) subliminally operative pollutants to be discarded by seeing what the Four Truths "mean."

Thus, in this our world of desires (Kāmadhātu), by seeing the meaning of the truth of frustration, both the five ideological and the five emotional pollutants are, generally speaking, eliminated. By seeing the "meaning" of the truth that frustration has an origin and by seeing the meaning of the truth that frustration also has an end, in each case seven pollutants, barring reductionism, extremism, and ritualism, are eliminated. By seeing the meaning of the way leading to the end of frustration, eight pollutants, barring reductionism and extremism, are eliminated. Thoughtful readers will easily detect the inner logic of this assessment.

Since in the realms of gestalt experiences (Rūpadhātu) and no-gestalt experiences (Ārūpyadhātu), anger-belligerence does not obtain, there are here with reference to the Four Truths, which apply to these realms as well, only twenty-eight pollutants operative in each realm. Adding up all the pollutants subliminally operative in this triadic world system of ours (32+28+28), the total amount is eighty-eight pollutants that are to be eliminated by seeing the "meaning" of the Four Truths. Such was the account given by the Vaibhāṣikas.

The Sautrāntikas claimed that, within the realm of desires, all ten pollutants concerning the First Truth were eliminated by seeing its meaning; concerning the three remaining truths, all the pollutants, barring reductionism and extremism, were eliminated by seeing the meaning of these truths. They thus arrived at a total of thirty-four (10+8+8+8) pollutants.

Since in the realms of gestalt experiences and no-gestalt experiences, anger-belligerence is inoperative with respect to the Four Truths, as was also claimed by the Vaibhāṣikas, there were in each of these realms thirty pollutants to be discarded. In the Sautrāntikas' assessment, there were, accordingly, ninety-four (34+30+30) latently operative pollutants to be eliminated by seeing meaning.

If we want to pass judgment, we may say that this reductionism is as silly as the view of the extreme reductionists among scientists. As Paul Davies succinctly states: "Complete reductionism is nothing more than a vague promise founded on the outdated and now discredited concept of determinism" (1987, 140).

30. *AK* V 5. Specifically, these four latently operative pollutants are attachment (in the form of) desires, anger-belligerence, arrogance, and low-level intelligence. As such, they can be said to present genotypal behavioral patterns. They are distributed over the hierarchically organized universe experience as follows. In the realm of desires, all four are operative, while in the realms of gestalt and no-gestalt experiences, only three are operative, since anger-belligerence is missing. Thus, there is a total of ten (4+3+3). Another numerical account results in a total of twenty-eight (4+12+12) due to the fact that, on the level presented by the realm of desires, all four are operative and that, on the level presented by the four phases of the concentrative process and the level presented by the four phases of no-gestalt experience, only three in each phase are operative. Finally, by relating the nine levels of the hierarchically organized universe of experience (the realm of desires and the fourfold realm of gestalt experiences and the fourfold realm of no-gestalt experiences) to the nine intensities of the way of cultivation itself as it discards the latently operative pollutants of attachment (in the form of) desires, arrogance, and low-level intelligence, each of them presenting eighty-one facets due to their ranging over all the nine levels of the universe of experience, and by adding the nine facets of anger-belligerence, which is operative solely in the realm of desires, a total of 252 pollutants (81+81+81+9) to be eliminated by the way of cultivation was accounted for. In spite of this obvious reductionism, it was never forgotten that the "way" was a dynamic concept, indicative of a person's growth and development. In this respect Buddhist reductionism differs from Western reductionism.
31. *AK* VI 77.
32. *AK* VI 67ab.
33. *AK* VII 7.
34. *AK* VI 65 and Louis de la Vallée Poussin (1925, vol. 5, 276, n. 1).
35. On these catalysts see Guenther (1975–76, vol. 1, 106–122).
36. *AK* III 94.
37. *Madhyamakakārikā* XVIII 12.
38. *Madhyamakavṛtti*, p. 378.
39. See above, n. 19.
40. *Grub-mtha'*, pp. 227f.
41. *Saddharmapauṇḍarīkasūtra* III 98.

CHAPTER 8. THE WAY: THE LATER VIEW I

1. On this term see also Chapter 1, n. 14. The term already occurred in the context of the śrāvaka way pertaining to the way proper and had been translated as "meaning-awareness," because the *terminus ad quem* of this cognitive process was each of the Four Truths. In the present context, the term is used in an open-ended manner due to the change in perspective: epistemology has given way to ontology and what this awareness intuits is no longer something ontic.
2. *bKa'-thang*, p. 740.
3. This is one of the three constituents of the *prakṛti* from which the psycho-

physical universe evolves according to the ancient Indian Sāṃkhya system of philosophy.

4. Literally, "someone who has a mind (in the sense of an opinion)," "someone who engages in representational thought processes."
5. *gSung thor-bu,* pp. 42f.
6. See Zaner (1964, 24, 183).
7. *bKa'-'bum,* pp. 176ff.
8. *bKa'-'bum,* p. 175.
9. *Grub-mtha',* p. 229; Rong-ston, pp. 30, 33; Dol-po-pa, p. 24. The decision to retain the (rather unfamiliar) Tibetan terms instead of using the (more familiar) Sanskrit terms is based on the fact that the Sanskrit terms are inadequate to express the subtle nuances involved in what is basically a process and not a static entity. Also the Sanskrit terms have suffered the assault by the linguistic reductionism prevalent in the past century, when Buddhist texts became known, to such a degree that their philosophical and psychological significance has been irrevocably lost.
10. *MSA* III 4.
11. *UT* I 154.
12. *UT* I 25.
13. *UT* I 155.
14. *UT* I 51.
15. See Chapter 2.
16. Collected Writings, vol. 2, p. 47.
17. The Tibetan translation of this term by *sangs-rgyas-khams* shows again that the Tibetans *thought* about what they translated. The Tibetan language distinguishes between *khams,* one's psychophysical potential, and *dbyings,* the field character of Being-in-its-beingness. The Sanskrit language has only one word, *dhātu.* This may be considered as a certain poverty on the part of the Sanskrit language. Thus, in the two verses, *Uttaratantra* I 40 and V 1, the Sanskrit term *buddhadhātu* has been rendered by *sangs-rgyas-khams,* not by *dbyings* (which Dol-po-pa Shes-rab rgyal-mtshan [1292–1361] offers by way of paraphrase in his commentary on *Uttaratantra* I 40). The reason for choosing the term *khams* in preference to *dbyings* was that the tenor of the *Uttaratantra* was primarily the explication of a person's being "programed" for developing in the direction of his transcendence.
18. *Grub-mtha',* p. 235.
19. *UT* I 27.
20. See his commentary on the *Uttaratantra,* p. 34; also his defence of the use of the term *sems-can-gyi snying-po* by him as synonymous with *sems-can-gyi khams,* on p. 54.
21. See Figure 2 for these points in the context of holonomic modes of experiencing.
22. *UT* I 156.
23. *UT* I 157.
24. *UT* I 166–167.
25. Klong-chen rab-'byams-pa says in his *Yid-bzhin,* p. 659:

> By raising mentation (to the level of existential awareness), its
> (concomitant) operators are automatically raised to this level.
> Mentation is by its own power cognitive of the object (before it),

> The operators are by their own power cognitive of the object's specific qualities.

By way of commentary he elaborates:

> While mentation is by its own power cognitive of the object before it, let us say, a pillar, its concomitant operators are by their own power cognitive of the object's qualities, such as the pillar's length and thickness. As is stated in the *Madhyāntavibhāga* (I 8):
>
> To see an object is a (pure act of) perception;
> (The perception of its) qualities is the act of the operators.
>
> Moreover, just like the sun and its rays, mentation and its concomitant operators are on the same level, hence by raising mentation (to the level of existential awareness), the operators are also raised to this level. The point is that after mentation has been raised to the level of existential awareness, there is no necessity to start with raising its operators to this level.

26. *Yid-bzhin,* p. 659.
27. *ASA* I 18.
28. *Bodhicaryāvatāra* I 15–16.
29. *MSA* IV 2.
30. See Thogs-med bzang-po-dpal's commentary on the *MSA* (1979, 76). This writer lived from 1295 to 1369.
31. *Yid-bzhin,* p. 659. In this connection, he cites Maitreya's aphorism (p. 139) and adds:

> Just as a single river acquires a specific sparkling and name according to the region through which it flows, so also this single activation of a shift involving intent and engagement, presents a level that has been engendered by devotion when it passes through the preliminary (build-up) and linking (probability-of-a-breakthrough) phases; a refined level due to an out-of-the-ordinary intent when it moves from the first spiritual level to the seventh spiritual level; a mature level when it passes through the three remaining levels; and a still higher level on which all obscurations are wiped away when it operates on the *sangs-rgyas* level.

32. See *ASA* I 19–20; *MSA* IV 15–20. Thogs-med bzang-po-dpal, p. 81; Mi-pham 'Jam-dbyangs rnam-rgyal rgya-mtsho, *Collected Writings,* vol. 3, pp. 29f.

It follows from the barriers that the symbols are liable to set up that the literalist (reductionist) will take them as denoting so and so many entities, and in view of the fact that Śāntideva had declared *bodhicitta* to be twofold—"the intent as an inclination toward *bodhi,* and the actual engagement in this (*bodhi*) realization"—will divide them up to make them conform to Śāntideva's two aspects. Thus, Asanga and his brother Vasubandhu considered the "worldly way," that is, all the phases up to the breakthrough moment, as intent, and only that which began with "seeing reality with fresh eyes," and which followed this vision, as engagement. Abhayakara and others considered only the preparatory phase as intent and the nineteen facets beginning with the linkage to the way of seeing as engagement. Other scholars had still other opinions. It is Klong-chen rab-'byams-pa who sees the unitary character of this activation of the shift from representational thinking to an existential awareness and declares (*Grub-mtha'*, p. 254 [See also *Yid-bzhin*, p. 658]): "In this (my presentation of the bodhisattva way), the desire to realize pellucidity and consummation for the sake of (helping) others is the intent; to be absorbed in sedulousness that is cointensive with the intent is engagement. Both are (merely) different aspects of one and the same process." This statement is a clear rejection of Śāntideva's sequential interpretation of the shift.

33. *MSA* IV 7.
34. *MSA* IV 22 and *Collected Writings*, vol. 2, pp. 76f.
35. *Bodhicaryāvatāra* I 10.
36. The source for these is the *sDom-pa nyi-shu-pa*, a Tibetan text covering twenty vows. The text is no longer available in its original Sanskrit version.
37. *Grub-mtha'*, p. 256.
38. The source for this list of the norms, though not the arrangement of them, is said to be Śāntideva's *Śikṣāsamuccaya*, p. 41, which quotes as its source the *Gaganagañja(paripṛcchā)sūtra*. Klong-chen rab-'byams-pa mentions as their source the *Śikṣāsamuccaya* and the *Ākāśagarbhasūtra*.
39. *Bodhicaryāvatāra* V 23. The Sanskrit version has *sarvayatnena*, which the standard Tibetan translation renders by *thams-cad 'bad-pas* "with an overall effort." Klong-chen rab-'byams-pa replaces this phrase by the stronger expression *srog-la bab kyang*, "even at the risk of their lives."
40. *Kāśyaparivartasūtra*, pp. 6 and 8, respectively.
41. *Sems-nyid*, p. 623. See also my *Kindly Bent to Ease Us* (Guenther 1975–76 vol. 1, 134).
42. *Sems-nyid*, pp. 624f. See also my *Kindly Bent to Ease Us* (Guenther 1975–76 vol. 1, 134).
43. *Sems-nyid*, pp. 624f.

CHAPTER 9. The Way: The Later View II

1. Thogs-med bzang-po-dpal, p. 421.
2. *Grub-mtha'*, p. 260.
3. *Grub-mtha'*, p. 260. The following lines have been combined: *MSA* XIV 3abc, 17c, XVII 22c, and XIV 3d.
4. *Grub-mtha'*, p. 261; Thogs-med bzang-po-dpal, pp. 294f.
5. Quoted in *Grub-mtha'*, p. 261, and Thogs-med bzang-po-dpal, p. 295.
6. Thogs-med bzang-po-dpal (p. 98) gives a very detailed account of this symbolic re-creation on the basis of a once famous sutra, the *Gocaraparisuddhi-sūtra*, which no longer exists in either its Tibetan or Chinese translation, and which is quoted by name only by Asanga and Śāntideva.

   It may not be out of place to point out that the term "buddha-son" (Skt. *jinātmaja, buddhātmaja*, Tib. *rgyal-ba'i sras, sangs-rgyas-ki sras*) is symbolic (mythological) language for a climactic process in which four "operators" participate. There is, according to Thogs-med bzang-po-dpal (p. 60), the "seed" of devotion to the Mahayana—"seed" here being synonymous with the "genetic" information coming from the father's side; then there is the transcending operation by critical acumen that creatively develops the theme of Being's openness, acting as the mother. The womb in which the child grows is the bliss that derives from a state of concentration in which inner calm and wider perspective form a unity. Lastly there is compassion as the nurse who brings up the child. Thus, the initially undifferentiated potential appreciatively developed by critical acumen as the organizing principle within the framework of a complementarity and nourished by the embeddedness in a social context is the deeper meaning of the term "buddha-son" who, figuratively speaking, embodies the complementarity of the within and the without.

7. *MSA* V 9.
8. *MV* IV 1.
9. Thogs-med bzang-po-dpal, pp. 425f.
10. Thogs-med bzang-po-dpal, p. 425.
11. Thogs-med bzang-po-dpal, pp. 206f.
12. *AK* VI 68cd–69ab.
13. *MV* IV 7cd.
14. *MV* IV 6.
15. *MSA* XVIII 56cd.
16. *ASA* I 33.
17. *MSA* XIV 23.
18. *MSA* XIV 24.
19. *MSA* XIV 24.
20. *MSA* XIV 26.
21. MSA XX 32.
22. *ASA* III 11. Rather than viewing time only in its flow from a past into a present, Klaus Müller and Georg Picht (1974) have proposed that time be also viewed in a kind of "fine-structure," which it has in every moment. As Erich Jantsch (1980, 232) elaborates, "This fine-structure may again be represented by assigning to each moment aspects of the past (*P*), the present (*N* for "now"), and the future (*F*). The present of a dynamic system not only has a present (*NN*) which consists of the immediate experiences of the moment, but also a past (*PN*) which includes the vertical evolution process which has led to the present structure of the system, and a future (*FN*) which corresponds to the options in further evolution."
23. *Collected Writings*, vol. 3, p. 157.
24. *Grub-mtha'*, p. 269. See also Mi-pham, *Collected Writings*, vol. 3, p. 130.
25. Inasmuch as the bodhisattva way in a certain sense continues the śrāvaka way, the assessment of the pollutants as they prevent a proper vision of the Four Truths is similar to that by the śrāvakas. In spite of this continuity, the bodhisattva way is marked by greater complexity, which is expressed numerically. Thus, counting all the pollutants as they are distributed over the three levels of the experienced world (Kāmadhātu, Rūpadhātu, Ārūpyadhātu), there are one hundred and twelve (40+36+36) pollutants to be uprooted and swept away by the way of seeing. See also above Chapter 7, nn. 29, 30.
26. *MV* II 17.
27. Mi-pham 'Jam-dbyangs rnam-rgyal rgya-mtsho (*Collected Writings*, vol. 3,

pp. 682f.) elaborates on the infections by these pollutants and the effects they have on the system as follows:

> An infection by attachment in the form of desires obscures and hinders the development of a feeling of disgust for samsara, because it makes a mind attached to the ephemeral, which it takes to be the real stuff, unable to see the drawbacks of samsara.
>
> Similarly, anger-belligerence prevents mentation from calming down in what is (termed) a dynamic balance. The same holds good for the remaining seven (pollutants), which, in a general way, prevent and obscure a vision of Being-in-its-beingness.
>
> Specifically, arrogance obscures the fallacies of (any) reductionism, because it takes its overevaluated idea of an ego to be of ultimate validity.
>
> Low-level intelligence, which is at the bottom of (any) reductionism, prevents and obscures the recognition of the real state of the five psychosomatic constituents in their organization as an organism and makes a deep understanding of their true nature impossible.
>
> Opinionatedness [which covers the viewpoints of reductionism, extremism, and outrageousness] prevents the emergence of realization of the truth of cessation such that, under the impact of reductionism, the experiencer who holds the view that there is an (abiding) ego gets frightened of the fact that, in the presence of the cessation (of all that is ego-related), there will no longer be an ego, and therefore he will not involve himself with (that which constitutes his) emancipation; while extremism (will make him assume that) cessation is unattainable and outrageousness (will make him categorically) deny the very existence of a state (described as) cessation. Thus (opinionatedness in each of its three varieties) blocks the attainment of (the felt state of) emancipation.
>
> Dogmatism prevents (a person) from initiating the way within himself, and ritualism fools a person with the wrong views to which it subscribes and the perverse observances that it overevaluates, though they are irrelevant as to emancipation. Thus he does not set out on the real way (to emancipation). Indecision obscures the recognition of the potential that lies in the Three Jewels by making the mind be in a dilemma and by not letting it be certain.
>
> Jealousy obscures the comprehension of the pitfalls of gain and honor. As long as there is jealousy that is concerned with and attached to gain and honor for oneself and that cannot bear the idea that others may have them, it is impossible to think in proper terms about the pitfalls of gain and honor.
>
> Avarice obscures the comprehension of the (value of being content with) few of the necessities of life, because it makes a person in his insatiability, regardless of how much of them he has piled up, believe that more is better.
>
> Thus, as long as these nine infections have not been eradicated, a person will remain fettered in the world of his own making, and emancipation from it will not be attained.

28. *UT* V 14.

The notion (that becomes patent as) avarice and other such contaminating agents (specifically hypocrisy, anger-belligerence, laziness, and restlessness)
Is considered to be an obscuration-obstacle (initiated by and exemplifying a) pollutant;
The notion (that manifests as) a triadic pattern in a (given) situation [analyzed as consisting of the giver, the gift, and the act of giving]
Is considered to be an obscuration-obstacle (initiated by and exemplifying) thematization.

29. *Grub-mtha'*, p. 274. See also *gSung thor-bu*, p. 67.

30. *MSA* XIX 28–29.

31. Thogs-med bzang-po-dpal, p. 248.

32. Another way of looking at this state of affairs was to count the four phases through which concentration-(meditation) passed in the domain of aesthetic form-and-color experiences, as well as the four modes of feelings of infiniteness in the domain of the experiences of the as-yet-unformed, separately, so that one arrived at a total of forty-six pollutants $(6+(4\times5)+(4\times5))$. Lastly, claiming that each of the six pollutants had nine degrees of intensity (low-low, low-medium, low-high, medium-low, medium-medium, medium-high, high-low, high-medium, and high-high), one arrived at a total of 411 pollutants. Thus on the nine levels of the individual's hierarchical organization, five of these pollutants operative on the "higher" levels yielded a total of 405 pollutants $(5\times(9\times9))$, to which one then added the nine intensity degrees of anger-belligerence operating solely in the domain of desires.

    As noted previously, the danger in giving a numerical account is that one might get bogged down in the numbers game and become a numberskull. This type, as Rudy Rucker (1987, 76) declares "falls into the illusion that his talk about millions is puissant enough to effect real-world changes. This is a false and dangerous dream."

33. Unfortunately the Sanskrit terms have suffered both from philological (linguistic) reductionism, which grew out of the mechanistic-rationalistic approach of a past age (the inadequacy of which in matters of live processes is now well known), and mystification by occultists who are notorious for their aversion to knowledge. Consequently, the Sanskrit terms are, because of the many, often hilarious, associations they evoke, rather useless in a serious discussion of what is intended by these code names.

34. *Grub-mtha'*, p. 277. Here as the source the *sBrid-yig bdud-rtsi thig-le* is given. This work remains as yet unidentified.

35. *UT* II 4. See also Dol-po-pa Shes-rab rgyal-mtshan, p. 131; Rong-ston smra-ba'i seng-ge, p. 103; Blo-gros mtshungs-med, p. 419; Mi-pham, *Collected Writings*, vol. 3, pp. 442f.

36. *UT* I 5. See also Dol-po-pa Shes-rab-rgyal-mtshan, p. 10; Rong-ston smra-ba'i seng-ge, pp. 12f; Blo-gros mtshungs-med, pp. 76f; Mi-pham, *Collected Writings*, vol. 3, p. 360.

37. Mi-pham, *Collected Writings*, vol. 3, p. 360.

38. In the Western context the idea of geometrization goes back to Anaxagoras (ca. 500–428 B.C.), who was one of the most profound thinkers of early Greek philosophy. According to Democritus of Abdera (ca. 460–370 B.C.),

Anaxagoras developed his ideas on the basis of still earlier thinkers of whom nothing has come down to us. One of Anaxagoras' statements is strikingly similar to the Buddhist notion of unorigination (Tib. *ma-skyes-pa,* Skt. *anutpāda*), which means that the process of evolution does not involve the production of something new, but is the manifestation of what is eternally available (Tib. *rtag-pa,* Skt. *nitya*). The idea of geometrization has come to the fore again in recent times in the book *Geometrodynamics* by J. A. Wheeler (1970), which also contains the article *Classical Physics as Geometry* by Ch. W. Misner and J. A. Wheeler. Apart from an overview of the problem of geometrization in various disciplines V. V. Nalimov, *Space, Time, and Life* (1985), the following two richly illustrated works may be profitably consulted: Olive Whicher, *Projective Geometry: Creative Polarities in Space and Time* (1971) and A. T. Winfree, *The Geometry of Biological Time* (1980).

Projective geometry is instrumental in the creation of mandalas. After all, the *longs-sku* is a gigantic, world-spanning mandala.

39. The only reference to this problem in Western philosophy I have been able to find is in Paul Häberlin, *Philosophia Perennis* (1962).
40. *UT* II 29.
41. *UT* II 40. See also Dol-po-pa Shes-rab rgyal-mtshan, p. 132; Rong-ston smra-ba'i seng-ge, p. 46; Blo-gros mtshungs-med, p. 455; Mi-pham, *Collected Writings,* vol. 3, p. 458.
42. On the richness of the Mahayana, see Thogs-med bzang-po-dpal, p. 484.
43. *UT* II 41.
44. *ASA* VIII 9–10.
45. *MSA* IX 64.
46. Their interpretation is based on the *dKon-mchog sgron-me,* a work now lost and also not included in the two great (though biased) collections of Buddhist texts in Tibet, the *bKa'-'gyur* and *bsTan-'gyur,* but must have been available to Thogs-me bzang-po-dpal, who quotes it approvingly on p. 181 of his commentary on *MSA.*
47. *Grub-mtha',* p. 284; *Yid-bzhin,* p. 695.

CHAPTER 10. RDZOGS-CHEN: SUPERCOMPLETENESS I

1. *Ati,* vol. 3, p. 112.
2. *Ati,* vol. 1, p. 773.
3. *rNying-rgyud,* vol. 1, p. 90.
4. *Ati,* vol. 1, p. 544.
5. *rNying-rgyud,* vol. 1, p. 25.
6. See also above p. 82ff. and, in particular, Guenther 1981 (112–117) and 1983 (228 n. 55, 237 n. 22, 257 n. 37, 267 n. 100) on the rich, if not to say, almost inexhaustible meaning content, which much to the chagrin of the objectivist-reductionist defies any one-to-one correspondence translation.
7. Klong-chen rab-'byams-pa quotes this passage in his autocommentary to his *gNas-lugs rin-po-che'i mdzod* as it occurs in the *Kun-byed rgyal-po;* but in his *Grub-mtha' rin-po-che'i mdzod,* he assigns "what has been built by mentation" to the perfect and complete (as) one, "the hierarchical order of (the system's) complexities" to the perfect and complete (as) two, and "the mind evolving into limpid clearness and consummate perspicacity" to the perfect

and complete (as) the whole. This may have been due to the fact that, as was so often the case, he quoted from memory, although as an independent thinker he often "reworked" old passages. But in his *Chos-dbyings rin-po-che'i mdzod,* where he twice takes up this idea, he is in agreement with the statement in the *Kun-byed rgyal-po*. Thus, to give only one example, in his auto-commentary on the aphoristic verse in his *Chos-dbyings* VI 11 (p. 131)—

> Perfect and complete (as) one, perfect and complete (as) the whole,
> (this) superforce in which the whole of reality has gathered,
> Is settled (in itself) since its beginningless beginning (and) gathered
> in an autoluminescent superspontaneity (*lhun-grub chen-po*)

—he says:

> Each and everything is (an expression of) the perfection and completeness of the mind suffused by (Being's) pellucidity and consummation (which also is the mind's intent toward it such that in being perfect and complete (as) one, it is perfect and complete in the vibrant dimension of (the total system's) ecstatic (cognitive) intensity; in being perfect and complete (as) two, it is perfect and complete in and as what has been built up by mentation; and in being perfect and complete (as) the whole, it is perfect and complete in and as the hierarchical order (of the total system's) complexity in whichever way this whole may come-into-presence (and make its presence felt).

The various interpretations the often quoted aphorism from the *Kun-byed rgyal-po* has received are ample proof of the fact that rDzogs-chen thinking is an *ongoing* process of thinking, not some ready-made hypothetical model that can be filed and, deservedly, be forgotten.

8. *Grub-mtha'*, p. 351.
9. This listing of all that is considered to be the substance of Buddhism, particularly the inclusion of what is generally referred to as meditation, as impure, opaque (Tib. *ma-dag-pa*) must come as a shock to many people. Without going into details, this summary is also the strongest repudiation of any kind of creationism, a travesty of scientific ("knowledge-oriented") thought mixed with a theology the nature of which the creationists do not understand and which Voltaire already ridiculed as a discipline that makes us talk about what we do not understand and confused about what we do understand.
10. This is technically known in Tibetan as *dag-pa*, "pure," "transparent," "symbolic." Usually this term refers to the (various) gestalts (Tib. *sku*) that are envisioned and understood (Tib. *ye-shes*) at the end of a long road. rDzogs-chen thinking makes it abundantly clear that they are not the "last word." This assessment was already foreshadowed by the three holonomic modes of experiencing (see Figure 2), though not worked out in detail by the Yogācāra thinkers.
11. *rten* and *brten-(pa),* the founding and the founded, are terms used in connection with a systematic phenomenology of the complex phenomenon described in terms of *sku,* "gestalt," and *ye-shes,* "originary awareness." On a lower level, as the problem of an animate organism, this was, in the Western context, first tackled by Edmund Husserl (1859–1938). The phenomenological approach does not consist in a mere enumeration of characteristics, but in the determination of the relations among the components of this complex phenomenon. That is, it is necessary to establish "which of these components

is more fundamental (founding) and which are higher level components (founded) (Zaner 1964, 250). According to rDzogs-chen thought, the founding (*rten*) is *sku* and the founded (*brten*) is *ye-shes*. There exists a rich, hitherto uninvestigated, literature concerning this problem in Tibetan.

12. *Man-ngag*, p. 47.

13. The meaning of Being (Tib. *gzhi* "ground/reason," "the whole") in rDzogs-chen is similar to Martin Heidegger's conception of Being. An excellent summary of Heidegger's conception has been presented by Joseph K. Kockelmans (1984, 47ff.). Because of its relevancy to an understanding of the rDzogs-chen idea, Kockelmans's words may be quoted at length:

> Being in some sense is the ground in which all significations of Being are to be grounded and from which all understanding of Being must nourish itself. On the other hand, the meaning of Being cannot be understood in terms of an eternal standard of Being (Plato's Ideas, Aristotle's First Mover, the Christian God, the God of the philosophers, etc.). Rather, it itself must be conceived of as an abysmal ground. For *the fact* that an understanding of Being emerges in the way we actually find it, no one can indicate a ground, because each process of grounding already presupposes the meaning of Being. When the meaning of Being lets a determinate signification of Being become the standard signification for a certain epoch, it "groundlessly" bars all other significations and even itself *as* the ground of the manifold possible other significations.

14. Although in common parlance the Tibetan verb/noun *snang-ba* roughly corresponds to our "to appear," "appearance," I have intentionally rejected this rendering and gone back to the original meaning of a "lighting up." That which "lights up" and "appears" as what we call a phenomenon (a Latinization of Greek *phainomenon*) is the whole and not an appearance *of* something, which latter understanding has given rise to phenomenalism, first presented by Kant. It claims that we cognize things only in the manner in which they *appear*, not as they really are. This claim makes real knowledge impossible and holds us prisoner in pseudoknowledge.

15. This reminds us of a statement by an unknown medieval German mystic, quoted by Johann Wolfgang von Goethe in the introduction to his *Farbenlehre* (*Theory of Colors*):

> Wär' nicht das Auge sonnenhaft,
> Die Sonne könnt' es nicht erkennen.
> (If the eye were not of the nature of the sun,
> It would not be able to know the sun.)

16. *Chos-dbyings* III 12, pp. 85f.

17. *gNas-lugs*, pp. 36f.

CHAPTER 11. RDZOGS-CHEN: SUPERCOMPLETENESS II

1. Tib. *ltar shar-ba, ltar 'char-ba*. There are, strictly speaking, only six such possibilities for actualization that give a specific poignancy to the experiencer's experience of his humanness in a cosmos that is not fundamentally different from this experience as its source. This, of course, does not mean—as the reductionist rashly assumes—that the universe has "human characteristics." The very choice of the word *ltar* "like," "as if," should make it abundantly

clear that these possibilities for actualization are "inclinations," "leanings," "propensities," "dispositions" as yet not well defined as intimated by Werner Heisenberg and John A. Wheeler. The presentation of these six possibilities for actualization is, with minor details, consistent throughout, wherever they are mentioned. Hence a single passage from the *mKha'-yang* II, p. 102 will suffice:

> In emerging as if (this presencing) were (the whole's) resonance (with itself as everything, *thugs-rje ltar*), compassion (*snying-rje*) for living beings is made possible;
> In emerging as if (this presencing) were (some diaphanous, colorless) light (*'od ltar*), the world spheres seem to be bathed in its rays;
> In emerging as if (this presencing) were (a multitude of) gestalts (*sku ltar*), all that lights up (to become one's phenomenal world) comes-to-presence as clusters of five protopatterns of experience;
> In emerging as if (this presencing) were originary awareness modes (*ye-shes ltar*), the pure buddha-realms are sensuously experienced in immediacy;
> In emerging as if (this presencing) were a nonduality (*gnyis-med ltar*), a staying in a conceptually undivided in-depth appraisal is made possible; and
> In emerging as if (this presencing) were (a process in which all) limitations dissolve (*mtha'-grol ltar*), a momentary staying in (Being's) possibilizing dynamics is made possible.

To these six possibilities for actualization, "two gates" are added, thus accounting for the number eight. One gate leads into samsara, the other into nirvana.

2. The rendering of the Tibetan *grol-tshul* by "emancipatory mode" is makeshift. There is, as in the case of the verbal *stong-pa,* no word in any Western language to convey the verbal character of *grol,* which cannot be reduced to the categories of transitive or intransitive without destroying its aliveness. Conceiving of *grol* as a vector feeling tone in the Whitehead sense, Western words like "free" and/or "freedom" reveal their inadequacy because they are static concepts. Actually, to convey the verbal character of *grol* in any Western language is to demand the impossible. According to our language system, we should say that in the compound *grol-tshul, grol* is an adjective qualifying the noun *tshul,* while actually it is used adverbially (which we cannot emulate because adverbs cannot be used with nouns). In the compound *mtha'-grol* (see n. 1), it is a verb with *mtha'* as its subject. This latter compound is used in connection with Being (*gzhi*) as (pure) experience (*sems-nyid*) in its "way" aspect (see "The rDzogs-chen Program," Chapter 10). In an attempt to bring our notion of "freedom" into the picture by saying that "experience divests itself of limitations," we would introduce mechanistic considerations into what is pure process.
3. *Theg-mchog* I, p. 311, II, p. 340; *Bla-yang* I, p. 296, II, p. 27; and elsewhere in Klong-chen rab-'byams-pa's writings.
4. *'gyu-ba.* This term refers to some slight movement where there should actually be none. A comparison with Brownian movement in statistical mechanics may not be out of place, which is not to say that *'gyu-ba* and Brownian movement are identical. Certainly, *'gyu-ba* is related to what is or is becoming our existentiality (Tib. *don*). See above p. 189.

5. *gzhi thog-tu*. A more correct rendering of this technical term would be the unusual "Beingwise" (*seinsmässig*).
6. This is taken from the *sGra-thal-'gyur-ba* in *Ati*, vol. 1, p. 107.
7. *Tshig-don*, p. 184.
8. *ibid.*
9. *Zab-yang* II, p. 233.
11. *rNying-rgyud*, vol. 5, p. 245.
10. In *Zab-yang* II, p. 445, where this passage is quoted at length, the reading is *ye-shes sku* instead of *ye-shes klong*. While *klong*, "superforce," has a wider connotation than *sku*, "gestalt," and while *ye-shes sku*, according to *Chos-dbyings*, p. 337, refers to the *longs-sku* rather than to the *chos-sku*, we should remind ourselves again of the fact that in process thinking there is no sharp separation between opposite aspects of reality. The *longs-sku* is both identical with and different from the *chos-sku*.
12. *Zab-yang* I, p. 294.
13. *Theg-mchog* I, p. 313.
14. *mKha'-snying* I, pp. 348, 416, 486; *dGongs-pa zang-thal*, vol. 4, p. 253. For the first part of this sentence, see also *Theg-mchog* I, p. 311.
15. *Theg-mchog* I, p. 311.
16. A critical valuation of Hoyle's often controversial ideas has been given by Michael Talbot (1988, 194ff.).
17. I use the word Man with a capital letter to avoid its maybe unavoidable association with a male member of the human species. Sexist extremists in the feminist movement might have difficulties in getting rid of the obnoxious "male" in fe*male* and the equally obnoxious "man" in wo*man* and in hu*man*.
18. See *Ati*, vol. 2, p. 535.
19. *dang-po'i gzhi* is not the same as *thog-ma'i gzhi* or *ye-gzhi*, which are used with reference to Being itself, while *dang-po'i gzhi* refers to the holomovement that for us somehow is the "beginning."
20. See *Ati*, vol. 1, pp. 232f.
21. *Bla-yang* I, pp. 455f.
22. *Bla-yang* II, p. 17.
23. In rDzogs-chen writings, the Tibetan term *chos-nyid* is understood as a compound of *chos*, "meaning in material concreteness," and *nyid*, "meaning-mobilizing potential." The former is all that "lights up" and makes its presence felt (*snang-ba*), the latter is the all-encompassing dynamic nothingness (*stong-pa*).
24. See *Ati*, vol. 5, pp. 148f.
25. The seven "archetypal" perceptual patterns are those of seeing, hearing, smelling, tasting, and touching, together with those of the thinking of thoughts and the evaluative thinking that in the grip of the emotions (pollutants) makes positive or negative judgments in such a way that we accept and approve what we like and reject and frown upon what we do not like.
26. *mKa'-yang* II, pp. 87f. The statement that the innermost glowing-in-its-glowingness in its breaking forth as an effulgent brilliance sets up the four fundamental forces (named after their effects: earth, water, fire, wind) as an external replica of its internal dynamics reminds one of the aphoristic dictum by Novalis (Friedrich von Hardenberg):

Das Äussre ist ein in ein Geheimnis erhobenes Innre.
(The outer is the inner raised into a state of mystery.)

CHAPTER 12. RDZOGS-CHEN: SUPERCOMPLETENESS III

1. It is worth quoting the definition of the term "cognition" in Arthur S. Reber, *The Penguin Dictionary of Psychology* (1985, 129):

> A broad (almost unspecifiably so) term which has been traditionally used to refer to such activities as thinking, conceiving, reasoning, etc. Most psychologists have used it to refer to any class of mental "behaviors" (using that term very loosely) where the underlying characteristics are of an abstract nature and involve symbolizing, insight, expectancy, complex rule use, imagery, belief, intentionality, problem-solving, and so forth.

Equally worth quoting is his definition of the term "cognitive science" (p. 130):

> A newly coined name for the cluster of disciplines that studies the human mind. The term refers to an amalgamation: it is an umbrella term which includes a host of once disparate approaches such as cognitive psychology, epistemology, linguistics, computer sciences, artificial intelligence, mathematics and neuropsychology.

2. The Sanskrit terms *ālaya* and *āśraya* are practically synonymous: *ālaya* is formed from the verbal root *lī*, "to lie or rest on, stay or dwell in," with the preposition *ā;* and *āśraya* is formed from the verbal root *śri*, "to cling to, to depend on, to dwell in," with the preposition *ā*. Both the *ālaya* as *vijñāna* and the *āśraya* undergo transformations or "changes." The change the *ālaya* undergoes is termed in Sanskrit *pariṇāma* (Tib. *rnam-'gyur*) and indicates that it "looks" (*rnam-*) different every time. The change the *āśraya* undergoes is termed in Sanskrit *parāvṛtti* (Tib. *gnas-'gyur*) and indicates a kind of volte-face or change in status (*gnas-*). In either case, change is expressed in the static terms that mark any rational approach. This approach has been elucidated by Erich Jantsch (1975, 84) as follows: "The *rational approach* assumes separation between the observer and the observed, and focuses on an impersonal "it" which is supposed to be assessed objectively and without involvement by an outsider observer; the basic organizing principle here is *logic*, the results are expressed in *quantitative* or *structural* terms, and the dynamic aspects are perceived as *change*." There is no need to point out that in Yogācāra thought, *citta* is such an impersonal "it" and the Yogācāra thinkers' abiding interest, like that of their negativistic Mādhyamika opponents, was logic.
3. *rNying-rgyud,* vol. 7, p. 45, identical with vol. 8, p. 302.
4. This frequently used phrase *'pho-'gyur med-pa,* literally translated "there is no stepping out of itself into something other than itself nor some changing into something other than itself" is a critique of the Brahmanical *ātman* idea. In the early Upanishads, it was claimed that the *ātman* either moved from one place (existence) to another, thus giving rise to the idea of transmigration, or underwent transformation or changes that altered its character.
5. *rNying-rgyud,* vol. 7, p. 45, identical with vol. 8, p. 302.
6. *rgyu-rkyen.* This compound sums up the Buddhist conception of causality, which is reticular and hierarchically fluctuating, not singly catenarian and

particulate. If any succession was recognized, it remained subordinate to the basic idea of interdependence.

7. *rNying-rgyud,* vol. 7, p. 149.
8. *rNying-rgyud,* vol. 8, p. 9; see also p. 144.
9. *rNying-rgyud,* vol. 7, p. 149.
10. Tib. *rkyen-bzhi.* They are the "momentum" (Tib. *rgyu*) as an integral aspect of the network or reticular continuum of what is called causality; the "dominant modifier" (Tib. *bdag-po'i rkyen*), which may be any sense-specific operator taking the lead in a given situation; the "reference modifier" (Tib. *dmigs-pa'i rkyen*), which is a sense-specific, visual, auditory, olfactory, gustatory, or tactile field; and the "synchronous modifier" (*mtshungs-pa de-ma-thag-pa'i rkyen*), which ensures the synchronous operation of all modifiers on whatever level in the hierarchical organization of an organism they may function.
12. *rNying-rgyud,* vol. 7, p. 149; see also p. 399.
11. Vimalamitra does not explain the "four rivers," but they were known since the time of early Buddhism as the rivers of desire, world interpretation, (reductionistic) views, and the low-level intensity of the whole's cognitiveness.
13. *rNying-rgyud,* vol. 8, p. 14.
14. *rNying-rgyud,* vol. 8, p. 167.
15. *rNying-rgyud,* vol. 7, p. 211 = vol. 8, p. 160.
16. *Tshig-don,* p. 178.
17. *rNying-rgyud,* vol. 4, p. 162.
18. This rendering for *stong-gsal* attempts to convey the idea of a symmetry transformation that is very characteristic of rDzogs-chen process-oriented thinking. The term implies that Being's nothingness (*stong*) *is* its radiance (*gsal*) and vice versa. A further difficulty with this compound is that both components have a verbal connotation. Our language and our way of thinking simply cannot express or do justice to the dynamic (verbal, not adjectival) notion of *stong-pa* or *stong-pa-nyid,* which has nothing to do with our container metaphors of emptiness and emptying or a void (preferably and evocatively written with a capital letter) and a voiding.
19. *rNying-rgyud,* vol. 8, p. 109.
20. *Theg-mchog* II, p. 35.
21. *Zab-yang* II, p. 207.
22. *Tshig-don,* p. 235. Although the text uses the words for gold and rust, what the author has in mind is bronze and patina.
23. *Theg-mchog* II, p. 35; *Tshig-don,* p. 235.
24. *Zab-yang* II, p. 208.
25. *Theg-mchog* II, p. 35; *Tshig-don,* p. 235; *Zab-yang* II, p. 208.
26. *Tshig-don,* p. 235.
27. This term is descriptive of the cognitive quality of Being in a general way. When its optimal and ec-static intensity is emphasized, the term *rig-pa* is used. It is unfortunate that to this very day no semantic studies of terms relating to cognition in the Tibetan language have been made.
28. *Theg-mchog* II, p. 32.
29. *Theg-mchog* II, p. 35.
30. *Theg-mchog* II, p. 100; *Ati,* vol. 1, p. 667.

31. *Ibid.* The term *rang-sa,* which I have translated as "its legitimate dwelling," is clearly differentiated in Klong-chen rab-'byams-pa's writing from *grol-sa.* This latter term refers to the holomovement as the site on which the emancipatory (*grol*) process takes place and ultimately dissolves (*grol*) in its "legitimate dwelling," the superdiagsphaneity (*ka-dag*) of Being itself.
32. *Theg-mchog* II, p. 101; *Ati,* vol. 1, p. 668.
33. *Theg-mchog* II, p. 101.
34. The 19th century British biologist Sir Richard Owen defined both homology and analogy in precise terms. Yet confusion between the two still prevails and is a major source of error. The idea of homology has proved useful in understanding biological, sociobiological, and sociocultural evolution, and as Erich Jantsch (1980, 8) succinctly states: "This should not come as a surprise since the whole universe evolved from the same origin."
    On the role of homology in projective geometry, see the richly illustrated work by Olive Whicher, *Projective Geometry* (1971, 167ff., 181).
35. *Theg-mchog* II, p. 102.
36. *Ibid.*
37. *Ibid.*
38. These are the well-known perceptual patterns as developed by the Yogācāra thinkers.
39. *rNying-rgyud,* vol. 7, p. 113.
40. *rNying-rgyud,* vol. 8, p. 250.
41. *rNying-rgyud,* vol. 7, p. 402.
42. *rNying-rgyud,* vol. 8, p. 76; see also pp. 44 and 241.
43. *rNying-rgyud,* vol. 8, pp. 80, 300.
44. *rNying-rgyud,* vol. 7, p. 347.

CHAPTER 13. RDZOGS-CHEN: SUPERCOMPLETENESS IV

1. In *rNying-rgyud,* vol. 8, p. 167, we read:

    Mind (*sems*) which is the ensemble of the eight perceptual patterns (together with)
    The fifty-one operators (*sems-las byung-ba*)
    Gathered in what is their root, the very ontical foundation (*kun-gzhi nyid*).

    This passage summarily refers to fifty-one operators, others mention only fifty. This difference is partly due to a method of counting. Indians were fond of numbers, but this very fondness also prevented them from becoming numberskulls of the fundamentalist type. If one likes, one can always look for still more (*ye-va-panaka,* as we so often read in the old Pali literature, for instance, the *Aṭṭhasālinī*). The above text goes on to say:

    Since the eight perceptual patterns make their presence felt as mind and
    Since (in its wake) the propensities for samsara gain in strength,
    They are not the (Being's vitalizing) energy in the strict sense (of the word, *nges-don snying-po*).

2. This subtle distinction between a *chos-ku thig-le nyag-gcig,* also referred to as *sangs-rgyas nyag-gcig* (*Chos-dbyings,* pp. 220, 221) as pure potential and

chos-sku as this very potential in the process of becoming an actual experience, seems to go back to the *Byang-chub-sems-kyi man-ngag rin-chen phreng-ba* (bearing the subtitle *Bang-mdzod 'phrul-gyi lde-mig*) in *rNying-rgyud,* vol. 2, 201, where the former is said to be *dri-med* "flawless," the latter *dri-bcas* "flawed." See also *Chos-dbyings,* p. 332; *Zab-yang* I, p. 224.

3. *Ati,* vol. 1, pp. 679. See also *ibid.*, p. 335; *Theg-mchog* II, p. 54; *Tshig-don,* p. 245.
4. *Tshig-don,* p. 188.
5. *Tshig-don,* p. 188; *Theg-mchog* II, p. 49.
6. *Ati,* vol. 3, pp. 181f.
7. *Theg-mchog* I, p. 61.
8. *gSung-thor-bu,* p. 200; see also *ibid.*, pp. 46ff.
9. The two verse lines which have been left out here, seem to have been a gloss by the copyist. They do not anything to the content except that depth-experiences are involved. They may even have been taken from a different (unidentified) text.
10. *rNying-rgyud,* vol. 7, pp. 444f.
11. *rNying-rgyud,* vol. 7, p. 455.
12. *Ati,* vol. 1, p. 528.
13. *Tshig-don,* p. 245.
14. *Ati,* vol. 2, p. 308.
15. *Ati,* vol. 3, p. 190.
16. Ibid.
17. *Yid-bzhin,* p. 698.
18. This term, which has nothing to do with cumulative knowledge, as which it is popularly misunderstood, has been discussed in relation to the cognate term *rnam-pa thams-cad mkhyen-pa* in detail in *Theg-mchog* I, p. 313, and *Bla-yang* I, p. 11. All these terms are used exclusively with *sangs-rgyas,* the buddha-experience.
19. *mKha'-snying,* vol. 2, p. 54. See also *Bla-yang* II, p. 242.
20. *rNying-rgyud,* vol. 7, pp. 458f.
21. *dGongs-pa zang-thal,* vol. 4, p. 117.
22. *bKa'-'bum,* pp. 42–82.
23. *Chos-dbyings,* XI 8, p. 244.
24. *Chos-dbyings,* pp. 244f.
25. *Chos-dbyings,* XI 9, pp. 246f.
26. *mKha'-snying,* vol. 2, p. 263.
27. This term *rang-rig,* literally and mechanically translated as "self-knowledge," has aroused as much controversy in the Indian context as in the Western world. For the Yogācāra philosophers, it meant "introspection." The validity of this was disclaimed by the Madhyamaka logicians. In rDzogs-chen thought it denotes the "auto-(Tib. *rang*) excitation (Tib. *rig-pa*) of Being or Being-in-its-beingness.
28. *rNying-rgyud,* vol. 4, p. 266.
29. This text reflects a subtle rejection of the traditional "way" of Buddhism, which begins with a vision (Tib. *lta-ba,* primarily and quite objectivistically

of the so-called Four Truths), followed by the cultivation of what has been seen (Tib. *sgom-pa,* usually termed "meditation"), and the implementation of it in one's life style (Tib. *spyod-pa*), resulting in what was considered the goal of one's life (Tib. *'bras-bu*).

Rong-zom Chos-kyi bzang-po, one of the first great process thinkers, introduces an important distinction in the application of the two closely related trends of "obscuration" (Tib. *sgrib*) and "taking the wrong turn and ending up in a blind alley" (Tib. *gol, gol-sa*). He restricts the use of the term "obscuration" as applicable to those who cling to objectivistic models of reality. These, whether Buddhists—he specifically mentions the followers of the Hinayana—or non-Buddhists (probably referring to the many Brahmanical systems and their adherents), promulgated a naive kind of fundamentalistic (objectivistic) reductionism, according to which man and his world are made up of entitative, atomistic building blocks.

"Taking the wrong turn and ending up in a blind alley" he understands as having a general and a specific descriptive character. The general descriptive character of this phrase applies to the various philosophical and religious belief systems that developed with the Mahayana Yogācāra thinkers. They were, as we have noted previously, the first to glimpse the fact that "mind" (Tib. *sems*) was not an entity among other entities, as had been claimed by their Hinayana predecessors, but a process organizing itself. However, they were unable to rid themselves of their language-specific reductionistic tendencies—"mind" is a noun, and nouns stand for things; hence mind, too, must be some thing, maybe of a very high order. Even when emphasis was laid more and more on the images in which the mind's dynamics made itself felt and initiated specific life styles, an all-powerful concretism ensnared the practitioners in a world of mythological figures.

As a fresh approach to the problem of man's predicament and as an attempt to release man from the tyranny of the concrete and impersonal, the Mahayana contributed greatly to an assessment of the quality of life as manifested in the manifold relationships between human and other human and nonhuman beings and forces. These relationships are marked by strong subjective feelings toward whatever a person encounters. Thus, for instance, in the so-called Kri-ya (Skt. *kriyāyoga*), emphasis may be placed on ritual purity or on the visualized forces operative within the human system, the intensity of which is termed "god" or "goddess." Relating himself to these powerful and attractive images, the practitioner feels himself as their servant. Or, in the so-called U-ba (U-pa, Skt. *ubhayayoga*)—which is similar to the Kri-ya as far as ritual purity is concerned and similar to the perspective provided by Yoga proper—the personal relationship of the subject to his visualized forces is that of brother and sister or that of a friend. In any case, the subject remains at a distance and does not really "tune in" to the life processes and their evolving order. Corollary to this activity is the development of a welter of cults, incorporating social habits and taboos, all of which are defended by dogmatism, intimidation, force and other forms of fanaticism.

The specific descriptive character of "taking the wrong turn and ending up in a blind alley" applies to the various techniques developed in connection with the attempt at "tuning in" to the life processes. These attempts, specifically, marked a shift from the attention to the "external," such as ritual acts and other forms of social behavior, to the attention to the "internal" processes as they express themselves in multifaceted symbols. Although symbols are connected with the physical world, they clearly transcend the framework of the physical and serve as aids in the re-creation of the world. This world becomes increasingly emancipated from the material, such that, as we might say, matter and mind are complementary aspects of the play staged by Being's self-organization dynamics. However, the moment a certain phase in what is pure process is taken as an end in itself, one finds oneself in a blind alley.

The tendency to take a mere phase as an end in itself was clearly recognized by the Buddhists, who did not hesitate to label the various techniques, when made ends in themselves, as blind alleys. Such phases were the so-called Maha(yoga), the aim of which was to effect a transformative vision through the so-called Developing Stage. In this, one attempted to see oneself and other individuals as "gods" and "goddesses" and the environing world as a "divine" mansion. It certainly was an attempt to restore quality to what had become, and was felt to be, suffocatingly quantitative. In this attempt, a feedback link between the observer and the observed was established. Thus the whole situation, including the participants in this "play," changed. Here, the individual was and felt himself as an active participant in staging (Tib. *thabs*) the magnificent play (Tib. *rol-pa*) written by Being's originary awareness (Tib. *ye-shes*) in terms of the indivisibility and complementarity of the two realities—that which is commonly accepted (the quantitative) and that which really matters (the qualitative) (Tib. *bden-pa dbyer-med*). Still, it was felt by the rDzogs-chen thinkers that attention was too easily riveted on the symbols thus activated and that this constituted an impediment to the process itself. The next step or phase, therefore, was to become emancipated from the tie to the symbols by feeling and becoming more and more sensitive to their meanings. This phase was known as Anu(yoga), in which emphasis was on the so-called Fulfillment Stage. In this phase, through a heightened sensitivity and perceptivity (Tib. *shes-rab*), the nonduality of Being's field character and its pervasive originary awareness (Tib. *dbyings dang ye-shes gnyis-su med-pa*) was relished without thematic proliferations and their restrictive limitations. This phase marks a further step in the direction of "pure" process.

The principle of complementarity, which was realized in the Developing Stage, asserts that in describing reality we have to invoke complementary concepts (that which is commonly accepted and that which really matters) that exclude each other and yet depend on each other for their definition. Nonduality, realized in the Fulfillment Stage, is a dynamic concept and must not be confused with monism, which is a reductionistic term. In this connection, it may not be out of place to point out that in the Sanskrit texts that have survived, the Buddhists were careful to use the term *advaya* (not-two) to emphasize their process-oriented thinking, while the Brahmanical thinkers used the term *advaita* (one-without-a-second) and thus gave evidence of the fact that they were unable to cope with the dynamic aspects of reality. These they merely saw as change, but not as a self-organizing process, and hence could not but resort to an oversimplified reductionism.

For further details see my *The Creative Vision* (1988).

30. *rNying-rgyud*, vol. 5, p. 216.

31. *bKa'-'bum*, p. 254. See also *Chos-dbyings*, p. 294.

32. *bKa'-'bum*, p. 248.

33. Rong-zom Chos-ky bzang-po's words are: "Communication as such (*lung de-nyid*) is the intent toward pellucidity and consummation (*byang-chub-kyi*

sems), the total system's energy (*snying-po*), pellucidity and consummation as (Being's) actuality (*byang-chub-kyi rang-bzhin*), (a process) as such (*de-nyid*), the most sublime support ground (*rten-gzhi*)."

34. *bKa'-bum*, pp. 251f.
35. Intimated is the difference between language that has something to say and talk that hardly ever has anything to say.
36. *Bla-yang* I, pp. 323f.
37. *Chos-dbyings* XIII 2, p. 318.
38. This is an allusion to *Uttaratantra* I 155. This twofold purity is frequently mentioned in rDzogs-chen texts. See for instance *Theg-mchog* II, p. 342; *Tshig-don*, pp. 497–499.
39. *Chos-dbyings* XIII 3, p. 318.
40. *Chos-dbyings* XIII 4, p. 319.
41. *Chos-dbyings* XIII 5, p. 320.

EPILOGUE

1. *DN* III, p. 54 = *MN* I, p. 253.
2. *MN* I, p. 167; *SN* I, p. 136.
3. *SN* III, p. 143.
4. *SN* III, p. 109.
5. *Suttanipāta* 1093–1094.
6. *Udāna* 80.
7. *Suttanipāta* 235; *AN* I, p. 236.
8. There is sufficient evidence in Buddhaghosa's writings to prove that he was favorably inclined toward the Yogacara philosophy that was in the ascendency at his time (fifth century).
9. The Indian (Sanskrit) term *tathāgatagarbha* (the "translation" of which into English by Sanskritists is too hilarious, if not nonsensical, and hence deserves no mention) has been rendered by the Tibetans according to the context in which it occurs. In works of a more abstract philosophical nature, it is rendered as *de-bzhin gshegs-pa'i snying-po*, "the dynamics in the moving into the Beingness-of-being," and in works emphasizing its experiential character, as *bde-bar gshegs-pa'i snying-po*, "the dynamics in the moving into bliss supreme," which I paraphrase as "optimization thrust."
10. *TV* 26–29.
11. *TV* 29. Technically speaking, this term is synonymous with *dharmakāya*, the gestalt that Being's meaningfulness assumes in the experiencer's awareness of it. Objectivistic accounts of these key terms have turned them into patent nonsense, because for the objectivist, understanding is allegedly "subjective" and hence taboo for him. Certainly, the Buddha (on whichever semantic level this word may be used) does not have a "body" (*kāya*) called *dharma* (a term consistently left untranslated to allow the person who uses it, to indulge in—o horror!—private fancies and hallucinations) or *mukti*, which he can put on or lay aside like a pair of shoes, but he *is* meaning, *is* freedom.
12. *Theg-mchog* II, p. 296; *Zab-yang* II, p. 480.
13. *Zab-yang* II, pp. 481.

14. In this connection we may quote V. V. Nalimov (1985, 96f.), who introduces into science the novel concept of a probabilistic ontology. This, as he himself admits, owes much to pre-Socratic thinking and Eastern philosophy. In his *Space, Time, and Life,* he says about spontaneity:

> Spontaneity is the Incomprehensible.
> Spontaneity is what acts through Measure, not through Law.
> Spontaneity is Freedom of the World.
> Spontaneity is Love.
> Spontaneity is Gnosis, revelation of meanings, their extraction from Non-existence.
> Spontaneity is Man himself.
> Spontaneity is Entity.
> Spontaneity is the Potentiality of the World.

References

WORKS IN WESTERN LANGUAGES

Böhler, Eugen. 1972. "Psychological Prerequisites of Forecasting and Planning." *In:* Technological Forecasting and Social Change, vol. 4, no. 2.

Bohm, David. 1980. Wholeness and the implicate order. London: Routledge and Kegan Paul.

Bondi, Sir Hermann. 1977. "The Lure of Completeness." In Ronald Duncan and Miranda Weston-Smith, eds. 1977. The Encyclopaedia of Ignorance. New York: Wallaby Pocket Books.

Broad, C. D. 1925; 6th ed. 1951. The Mind and Its Place in Nature. London: Routledge & Kegan Paul.

Brown, Barbara B. 1980. Supermind: The Ultimate Energy. New York: Harper & Row.

Casey, Edward C. 1976. Imagining. Bloomington: Indiana University Press.

Crook, John H. 1980. The Evolution of Human Consciousness. Oxford: Clarendon Press.

Davies, Paul. 1987. The Cosmic Blueprint. London: Heinemann.

Fallico, Arturo B. 1962. Art & Existentialism. Englewood Cliffs: Prentice-Hall.

Feyerabend, Paul. 1975. Against Method: Outline of an Anarchistic Theory of Knowledge. London: New Left Books.

Fischer, Roland. 1975/76. "Transformations of consciousness. A cartography," in two parts: I. "The perception-hallucination continuum," *Confinia Psychiatrica,* 18 (1975), 221–244. II. "The perception-meditation continuum," *Confinia Psychiatrica,* 19 (1976), 1–23.

Gadamer, Hans-Georg. 1977. Philosophical Hermeneutics. Translated and edited by David E. Linge. Berkeley: University of California Press.

Glansdorff, P., and Ilya Prigogine. 1971. Thermodynamic Theory of Structure, Stability, and Fluctuations. New York: Wiley-Interscience.

Goethe, Johann Wolfgang von. Faust I & II. Edited and Translated by Stuart Atkins. Boston: Suhrkamp/Insel.

Gosztonyi, Alexander. 1972. Grundlagen der Erkenntnis. Munich: C. H. Beck.

Guenther, Herbert V. 1975–76. Kindly Bent to Ease Us. 3 vols. Emeryville, CA: Dharma Publishing.

Guenther, Herbert V. 1978. "Bodhisattva—The Ethical Phase in Evolution." In Leslie S. Kawamura, ed. 1978. The Bodhisattva Doctrine in Buddhism. Waterloo, Ont.: Wilfrid Laurier University Press.

Guenther, Herbert V. 1983. "'Meditation' Trends in Early Tibet." In Whalen Lai and Lewis R. Lancaster (1983), Early Ch'an in China and Tibet. Berkeley Buddhist Studies Series 5. Berkeley: Asian Humanities Press.

Guenther, Herbert V. 1984. Matrix of Mystery. Boulder, CO: Shambhala Publications.

Guenther, Herbert. 1988. The Creative Vision. Novato, CA: Lotsawa.

Häberlin, Paul 1952. Philosophia Perennis. Berlin: Springer-Verlag.

Hayward, Jeremy W. 1987. Shifting Worlds, Changing Minds. Boston: Shambhala Publications.

Heidegger, Martin 1962. Being and Time. Translated by John Macquarrie & Edward Robinson. New York: Harper & Row.

Heidegger, Martin. 1962. Kant and the Problem of Metaphysics. Translated by James S. Churchill. Bloomington: Indiana University Press.

Heidegger, Martin. 1972. On Time and Being. Translated by Joan Stambaugh. New York: Harper & Row.

Heidegger, Martin. 1974. Identity and Difference. Translated and with an Introduction by Joan Stambaugh. New York: Harper Torchbooks.

Heidegger, Martin. 1975, 1984. Early Greek Thinking: The Dawn of Western Philosophy. Translated by David Farrell Kroll and Frank A. Capuzzi. San Francisco: Harper & Row.

Herbert, Nick. 1987. Quantum Reality. Garden City, NY: Anchor Books.

Hoyle, Sir Fred. 1984. The Intelligent Universe. New York: Holt, Rinehart and Winston.

Jacobson, Nolan Pliny. 1988. The Heart of Buddhist Philosophy. Carbondale: Southern Illinois University Press.

Jantsch, Erich. 1975. Design for Evolution. New York: George Braziller.

Jantsch, Erich. 1980. The Self-organizing Universe. Oxford: Pergamon Press.

Jantsch, Erich and Conrad C. Waddington. 1976. Evolution and Consciousness. London: Addison-Wesley Publishing Company.

Jung, Carl Gustav. 1942/48. "A Psychological Approach to the Dogma of the Trinity," in Psychology and Religion: West and East. 1958, 2nd ed. 1969. Princeton: Princeton University Press. (Collected Works 2).

Jung, Carl Gustav. 1971, rev. 1976. Psychological Types. Princeton: Princeton University Press. Collected Works 6.

Kockelmans, Joseph J. 1984. On the Truth of Being. Bloomington: Indiana University Press.

Kraus, Elizabeth M. 1979. The Metaphysics of Experience. New York: Fordham University Press.

Kuhn, Thomas S. 1970. The Structure of Scientific Revolutions. Chicago: University of Chicago Press; 2nd enlarged ed., 1970.

Kuhn, Thomas S. 1977. The Essential Tension: Selected Studies in Scientific Tradition and Change. Chicago: University of Chicago Press.

Lakoff, George. 1987. Women, Fire, and Dangerous Things. Chicago: The University of Chicago Press.

Lakoff, George and Mark Johnson. 1980. Metaphors We Live By. Chicago: Chicago University Press.

Langer, Susanne K. 1967, 1972, 1982. Mind: An Essay on Human Feeling. 3 vols. Baltimore: Johns Hopkins University Press. Vol. 1: 1967, 1985 fourth paperback printing; Vol. 2: 1972, 1983 third paperback printing; Vol. 3: 1982, 1984 paperback printing.

Levin, David Michael. 1985. The Body's Recollection of Being. London: Routledge & Kegan Paul.

Levin, David Michael. 1988. The Opening of Vision. London: Routledge & Kegan Paul.

MacLean, Paul D. 1973. "A Triune Concept of the Brain and Behavior." In T. Boag and D. Campbell, eds., The Hincks Memorial Lectures. Toronto: University of Toronto Press.

Maquet, Jacques. 1986. The Aesthetic Experience: An Anthropologist Looks at the Visual Arts. New Haven: Yale University Press.

Marcel, Gabriel. 1952. The Metaphysical Journal. Translated by Bernard Wall. London: Rockliff.

Maturana, Humberto R. and Francisco Varela. 1980. Autopoiesis and Cognition. Dordrecht, Holland: D. Reidel Publishing Company.

Maturana, Humberto R. 1982. Erkennen: Die Organisation und Verkörperung von Wirklichkeit. Braunschweig, West Germany: Friedr. Vieweg & Sohn.

Maturana, Humberto R. and Francisco Varela. 1987. The Tree of Knowledge. Boston: Shambhala Publications, Inc.

Merleau-Ponty, Maurice. 1962. Phenomenology of Perception. Translated by Colin Smith. London: Routledge & Kegan Paul.

Merleau-Ponty, Maurice. 1964. Signs. Translated, with an Introduction by Richard C. McCleary. Evanston: Northwestern University Press.

Müller, A. M. Klaus. 1974. "Naturgesetz, Wirklichkeit, Zeitlichkeit." *In:* Offere Systeme. *See* Weizsacker 1974.

Nalimov, V. V. 1985. Space, Time, and Life. Philadelphia: ISI Press.

Polanyi, Michael. 1964. Personal Knowledge. New York: Harper and Row.

Prigogine, Ilya, and Isabella Stengers. 1975. "Nature et Créativité." Revue de l'Aupele, 13, no. 2.

Prigogine, Ilya, and Isabella Stengers. 1984. Order Out of Chaos. Toronto: Bantam Books.

Reber, Arthur S. 1985. The Penguin Dictionary of Psychology. Harmondsworth, Middlesex: Penguin Books.

Rucker, Rudy. 1987. Mind Tools. Boston: Houghton Mifflin Company.

Samuels, Mike and Nancy Samuels. 1975. Seeing with the Mind's Eye. New York: Random House.

Scheler, Max. 1954. The Nature of Sympathy. Translated by Peter Heath. London: Routledge & Kegan Paul.

Schrag, Calvin O. 1969. Experience and Being. Evanston: Northwestern University Press.

Talbot, Michael. 1988. Beyond the Quantum. New York: Bantam Books.

Vickers, Sir Geoffrey. 1968. Value Systems and Social Process. Tavistock, NY: Basic Books.

Vickers, Sir Geoffrey. 1970. Freedom in a Rocky Boat: Changing Values in an Unstable Society. London: The Penguin Press.

Vickers, Sir Geoffrey. 1973. "Motivation Theory—a Cybernetic Contribution." Behavioral Science, vol. 18, no. 4.

Weizsäcker, Ernst von, ed. 1974. Offene Systeme I: Beiträge zur Zeitstruktur von Information, Entropie und Evolution. Stuttgart, West Germany: Klett.

Wheeler, John A. 1962. Geometrodynamics. New York: Academic Press.

Whicher, Olive. 1971. Projective Geometry: Creative Polarities in Space and Time. London: Rudolf Steiner Press.

Whitehead, Alfred North. 1960. Process and Reality. New York: Harper Torchbooks.

Winfree, A. 1980. The Geometry of Biological Time, Berlin: Springer Verlag.

Zaner, Richard M. 1964. The Problem of Embodiment. The Hague: Martinus Nijhoff.

WORKS IN PALI, SANSKRIT, AND TIBETAN

PALI

Canonical:

Dīghanikāya. Edited by T. W. Rhys Davids and J. E. Carpenter. London: Pali Text Society, 1890–1911.

Majjhimanikāya. Edited by V. Trenckner and R. Chalmers. London: Pali Text Society, 1888–1902.

Saṃyuttanikāya. Edited by Leon Feer. London: Pali Text Society, 1884–1898.

Aṅguttaranikāya. Edited by R. Morris and E. Hardy. London: Pali Text Society, 1885–1900.

Udāna. Edited by P. Steinthal. London: Pali Text Society, 1885.

Suttanipāta. Edited by Dines Andersen and Helmer Smith. London: Pali Text Society, 1913.

Noncanonical:

Dhammasangani. Edited by E. Muller, London: Pali Text Society, 1885.

Aṭṭhasālinī. Edited by P. V. Bapat and R. D. Vadekar. Poona: Bhandarkar Oriental Series. No. 3, 1942.

Visuddhimagga. Edited by Dharmananda Kosambi. Bombay: Bharatiya Vidya Bhavan, 1940.

SANSKRIT

Abhidharmakośa. With Vasubandhu's Bhāṣya and Yaśomitra's Vyākhyā. Edited by Swami Dwarikadas Shastri. 4 vols. Varanasi: Bauddha Bharati, 1970–73.

Abhisamayālaṅkāra. Edited by Th. Stcherbatsky and E. Obermiller. Leningrad: Bibliotheca Buddhica, 1929.

Bhāṣya. *See* Abhidharmakośa.

Bodhicaryāvatāra. By Śāntideva with the commentary Pañjikā by Prajñākaramati. Edited by P. L. Vaidya. Darbhanga: Mithila Institute, 1960.

Dohākoṣa-upadeśa-gīti. Lost in the original Sanskrit or Prakrit but preserved in the Tibetan Tanjur (bsTan-'gyur), rGyud-'grel section, under the title Mi-zad-pa'i gter-mdzod man-ngag-gi glu.

Kāśyapaparivartasūtra. Edited by Baron A. van Stael-Holstein. Shanghai: Commercial Press, 1926.

Madhyamakavṛtti. *In* Mūlamadhyamakakārikā de Nāgārjuna avec la Prasannapadā commentaire de Candrakīrti. Published by Louis de la Vallée Poussin. St. Petersbourg: Bibliotheca Buddhica, 1913 *et seq.*

Madhyāntavibhanga (Madhyantavibhāga-Bhāṣya). Edited by Gadjin M. Nagao. Tokyo: Suzuki Research Foundation, 1964.

Mahāyānasūtrālaṅkāra. Edited and translated by Sylvain Lévi. 2 vols. Paris: Librairie Honoré Champion, 1907.

Saddharmapuṇḍarīkasūtra. Revised edition by Nalinaksha Dutt. Calcutta: Asiatic Society, 1953.

Trimśikāvijñapti. Edited by Sylvain Lévi. Paris: Librairie Honoré Champion, 1932.

Trimśikāvijñaptibhāṣya. Edited by Sylvain Lévi. Paris: Librairie Honoré Champion, 1932.

Uttaratantra. Edited by E. H. Johnston. Patna: Bihar Research Society, 1950.

Vyākhyā. Vyākhyāyukti: lost in the original Sanskrit but preserved in the Tibetan Tanjur (bsTan-'gyur), mDo-'grel (Sems-tsam) section, under the title rNam-par bshad-pa'i rigs-pa. *See* Abhidharmakośa

TIBETAN

Collections

Ati = rNying-ma'i rgyud bcu-bdun. New Delhi, 1973–77.

dGongs-pa zang-thal. Leh, 1973.

rNying-rgyud = rNying-ma'i rgyud-'bum. Thimbu, 1973.

sNying-thig ya-bzhi. Author: Klong-chen rab-'byams-pa. New Delhi, 1970.

Bla-dgongs = Bla-ma dgongs-'dus. Gangtok, 1972.

Works by Known Authors

Klong-chen rab-'byams-pa. Yid-bzhin = Theg-pa chen-po'i man-ngag-gi bstan-bcos yid-bzhin rin-po-che'i mdzod. Delhi, 1983.

Chos-dbyings = Chos-dbyings rin-po-che'i mdzod, together with Chos-dbyings rin-po-che'i mdzod-kyi 'grel-pa lung-gi gter-mdzod. Delhi, 1983.

Theg-mchog = Theg-pa'i mchog rin-po-che'i mdzod. Delhi, 1983.

gNas-lugs = gNas-lugs rin-po-che'i mdzod, together with sDe-gsum snying-po'i don 'grel gNas-lugs rin-po-che'i mdzod ces-bya-ba'i 'grel-pa. Delhi, 1983.

Tshig-don = gSang-ba bla-na-med-pa 'od-gsal-rdo-rje-snying-po'i gnas-gsum gsal-bar byed-pa'i tshig-don rin-po-che'i mdzod. Delhi, 1983.

Man-ngag = Man-ngag rin-po-che'i mdzod. Delhi, 1983.

Grub-mtha' = Theg-pa mtha'-dag-gi don gsal-bar byed-pa grub-pa'i mtha' rin-po-che'i mdzod. Delhi, 1983.

Sems-nyid = rDzogs-pa-chen-po sems-nyid ngal-gso, together with rDzogs-pa-chen-po sems-nyid ngal-gso'i 'grel-pa shing-rta chen-po. Gangtok, 1974.

mKha'-snying = mKha'-'gro snying-tig. In: sNying-thig ya-bzhi, vols. 2–3.

mKha'-yang = mKha'-'gro yang-tig. In: sNying-thig ya-bzhi, vols. 4–6.

Bla-yang = Bla-ma yang-tig. In: sNying-thig ya-bzhi, vol. 1.

Zab-yang = Zab-mo yang-tig. In: sNying-thig ya-bzhi, vols. 10–11.

Mi-pham 'Jam-dbangs rnam-rgyal rgya-mtsho 'Jam-mgon 'Ju Mi-pham rgya-mtsho. Collected Writings. Gangtok, 1976.

Thogs-med bzang-po dpal. Theg-pa-chen-po mDo-sde'i rgyan-gyi 'grel-pa rin-po-che'i phreng-ba. Gangtok, 1979.

Dol-po-pa Shes-rab rgyal-mtshan. Theg-pa-chen-po rGyud-bla-ma'i bstan-bcos legs-bshad nyi-ma'i 'od-zer. Bhutan, 1977.

Blo-gros mtshungs-med. Theg-pa-chen-po rGyud-bla-ma'i bstan-bcos-kyi nges-don gsal-bar byed-pa'i rin-po-che'i sgron-me. Tibetan Nyingmapa Monastery, Tezu, Dist. Lohit, Arunachal Pradesh, 1974.

Yon-tan rgya-mtsho. Yon-tan mdzod 'grel = Yon-tan rin-po-che'i mdzod-kyi 'grel-pa nyi-zla'i sgron-me. Gangtok, 1969–71.

g.Yung-ston rdo-rje dpal bzang-po. gSang-snying gsal-byed me-long = dPal gsang-ba snying-po'i rgyud-don gsal-byed me-long. n.p., n.d.

Rong-ston Shes-bya kun-rig (smra-ba'i seng-ge). Theg-pa-chen-po rGyud-bla-ma'i bstan-bcos legs-par bshad-pa. Gangtok, 1979.

Rong-zom Chos-kyi bzang-po. bKa'-'bum. n.p., n.d.

gSang-snying 'grel-pa = rGyud-rgyal gsang-ba snying-po'i 'grel-pa dkon-cos 'grel. n.p., n.d.

gSung thor-bu (Selected Writings). Leh, 1974.

Vairocana. rGyud-'bum. Leh, 1971.

Index of Technical Terms

SANSKRIT

vimuktimārga, 109, 116
vimokṣamukha, 101
viśeṣamārga, 109
viṣa, 18
vihiṃsā, 254n.12
vīra, 49
vīrya, 42, 43, 49, 100, 160, 173
vedanā, 25, 27, 28, 124
vyāpāda, 103

śamatha, 69
śāṭhya, 214n.12
śānta, 95
śikṣamānā, 107
śīla, 108, 138, 154, 173
śūnya, 101, 114, 190
śūnyatā, 70, 147
śūnyatāvimokṣa, 102
śraddhā, 42, 43, 44, 45, 102, 121
śraddhānusārin, 110
śraddhādhimukta, 110
śramaṇera, 107, 108
śrāmaṇerikā, 107
śrāmaṇya, 99

ṣaḍ-āyatana, 124

saṃvara, 106, 108
saṃsāra, 11, 19, 37, 49, 69, 71
saṃskārāh, 123
saṃskṛta, 85
sakṛdāgāmin, 98, 103
saṃjñā, 25, 28, 32, 37
sattva, 82
sattvadhātu, 134
samatā, 158
samayavimukta, 110
samādhi, 32, 67, 92, 100, 102, 138, 160, 256n.8
samāhita, 157
saṃbhāra, 151
saṃbhāramārga, 111, 151
saṃbhogakāya, 176, 178
samyakkarmānta, 100
samyakpradhāna, 113, 160
samyakprahāṇa, 113, 160
samyaksambuddha, 13
samyagājīva, 100
samyagdṛṣṭi, 104
samyagvāc, 100
sarvatraga, 40
sarvayatnena, 267n.39
sucarita, 108
skandha, 187
styāna, 54, 254n.12
sparśa, 26, 27, 37, 124, 251nn.15,20
smṛti, 31, 32, 100
smṛtyupasthāna, 111, 112, 157
srota-āpatti, 98
svabhāvaśūnya, 158
svalakṣaṇa, 11
svasaṃvitti, 8

hetu, 16, 124, 125
hetu-pratyaya, 125
hrī, 42, 43, 45

Pali

akusala, 17
anattā, 102
anicca, 102
araha, 98
avijjā, 104

ujukatā, 50
uddhacca, 104
uddhaṃbhāgīya, 104
upekkhā, 100

oraṃbhāgīya, 102

kammaññatā, 56
kilesa, 18
kusa, 17
kusala, 17

khaṇa, 16

ñāṇa, 16, 18, 250n.1

taṇhā, 53

dassana, 98
dukkha, 102
dosa, 53, 99

dhammavicaya, 100
dhammā ti sabhāvā, 11

nibbāna, 245

paguññatā, 50
paññā, 23, 100, 250n.1, 251n.18

TIBETAN

Index of Persons and Subjects